ISSUES IN RACE
AND ETHNIC RELATIONS

CONTRIBUTORS

BOGGS, JAMES

BOLNER, JAMES

CARMICHAEL, STOKELY

COHEN, DAVID K.

EATON, JOSEPH W.

FLOREZ, JOHN

GALBRAITH, JOHN K.

GILBERT, NEIL

GOERING, JOHN M.

GRANT, WILLIAM R.

HAMILTON, CHARLES V.

HIMES, JOSEPH S.

KIRK, JEROME

KUH, EDWIN

LEVINE, IRVING M.

LEWIS, RALPH

MARX, GARY T.

PALMORE, ERDMAN

PINARD, MAURICE

RUSTIN, BAYARD

SPECHT, HARRY

ST. JOHN, NANCY

THUROW, LESTER C.

TUMIN, MELVIN M.

TYLER, GUS

USEEM, MICHAEL

VON ESCHEN, DONALD

WHITTINGTON, FRANK

Issues in Race and Ethnic Relations

Theory, Research and Action

Jack Rothman
THE UNIVERSITY OF MICHIGAN

 F. E. PEACOCK PUBLISHERS, INC.

CONTENTS

ACKNOWLEDGEMENTS

This book was composed with the stimulus and support of Dr. John Slawson, through the John Slawson Fund for Research, Training and Education. Dr. Slawson, Executive Vice-President Emeritus of the American Jewish Committee, has been a respected leader in the race and ethnic relations field for almost half a century, and has been instrumental in multiple ways in fostering professional developments in the field. It was through him that the monumental *Studies in Prejudice* series was commissioned and executed, bringing substantive social science perspectives to bear on group relations practice. This volume is an outgrowth of that long standing commitment, having the purpose of providing basic background and training materials regarding race and ethnic relations for students interested in the area and for professionals already practicing in pertinent agencies.

The book is a sequel to a previous one, *Promoting Social Justice in the Multigroup Society,* which I also edited with the encouragement of Dr. Slawson. The earlier volume consisted of a series of realistic case studies illustrating programs and actions in the group relations field. The present work supplements the earlier effort by providing theory and research related to several of the key issue areas that had been treated. Through the interest and good offices of Dr. Slawson, I have been afforded time and needed resources required for the preparation of these professionally oriented documents.

Another significant person in this endeavor has been Ms. Vivian Roeder, my secretary and administrative aide. She has carried through, in a highly competent and painstaking way, all the technical details essential for the production of a publication of this type. I am both grateful for her contribution and admiring of her perspicacity in completing a series of demanding tasks.

Ted Peacock has personally backed the venture from the start, and as publisher made numerous professionally sound while practically necessary suggestions along the way. Although the vagaries of the publishing industry necessitated a delay in going into production, Ted's loyalty to the project and commitment to his stated intentions saw it through.

Chapter 1

ANALYZING ISSUES IN
RACE AND ETHNIC RELATIONS:
A CONCEPTUAL FRAMEWORK

Purpose and structure of the book

The 1960s and 1970s have been years of turbulence and uncertainty for America and the world. Technological and social changes have been vast and endemic; conflicting values, political claims, and lifestyles have become normal features of the social terrain. In contrast to an earlier, more stable normative environment, the climate of the seventies presents the individual with the need to make significant choices among alternative goals, means, and values. Long-held assumptions are being brought into question—including those concerned with the nature of government, the meaning of social justice, the validity of traditional morality, and the viability of established modes of achieving reform. For those in the social professions as well as for citizens committed to advancements in social welfare and human rights, such dilemmas are emerging in sharp relief.

This book will deal with the subject of race and ethnic relations, which also (or even particularly) has been caught up in contemporary unrest and confusion. For this reason we will not be proffering principles or prescriptions; rather, we will approach the subject in terms of *issues,* conceding that there are genuine differences of viewpoint and that "truth," to some degree, will emerge only out of a process of trial which involves pluralistic experimentation and struggle.

One purpose of this book is to bring the alternative positions on the issues into coherent focus, so that they can be analyzed and weighed with a reasonable measure of clarity and intelligence. This should be an aid to decision making about the issues in a situation which is marked by uncertainty. We will take on the task of giving a realistic, objective presentation of alternative positions, to provide a basis for reflective consideration and an approach to responsible problem solving. We will not be proposing solutions or advocating our own rhetorical predisposition. This formulation is meant explicitly to open up fruitful lines of inquiry, not to engender an authoritative closure to discourse or a "solution" for the problems. In part the approach has the overriding objective of stimulating a rational, knowledge-based consideration of racial and ethnic problems; in part it reflects our own unresolved state of mind with regard to the perplexing issues which are considered.

It has been customary for the thinkers and actors in the race and ethnic arena to operate in isolation from one another. Theoreticians and philosophers dwell in one realm, researchers and hard-data social scientists often in another, activists and reformers in a third. The literature of each school of thought is segmented, communicated in distinctly different media, and directed at and read by different audiences. The perspectives, information, and experiences of the different groups, while germane to one another, generally are not shared. Varying languages, varying emphases on analysis or policy, and varying levels of scholarly treatment have fostered and sustained the apartness.

Such a diversity of intellectual contributions is useful and even necessary, however, in a field as complex and multifaceted as group relations. Specialized, competent inputs—including theoretical-philosophical considerations, factual-informational data, and policy-action strategies—provide the basis for analytic comprehension of the issues in race and ethnic relations. Properly orchestrated, these inputs make it possible to design legitimate programs of correction.

The structure of this book, then, takes two considerations into account. First, we will make an effort to articulate, honestly and cogently, alternative positions on a number of selected issues in race and ethnic relations. Second, in the presentation we will draw from different literatures so that the words and conclusions of social theorists, researchers, and social activists will all be heard and brought to bear on the same issues. Theory, research, and practice will be consolidated, rather than fragmented as is so often the case. The reader will therefore have available a diversified set of intellectual resources as an aid in defining problems and assessing the consequences of the various policy options.

The issues to be discussed have been selected from another work of ours which consists of a series of case studies in race and ethnic affairs.[1] In keeping with the proposed framework, these issues are posed in an either/or, contentious formulation. This is not meant to preclude the formulation of blended or "compromise" views and solutions by readers. The issues, in the order of their appearance in the book, are as follows:

1. Equality of Opportunity versus Preferential Treatment
2. Integration versus Local Community Control in Education
3. Coalitions versus Independent Action as a Minority Strategy
4. The White Ethnic: Oppressor or Victim?
5. Conflict versus Consensus as an Intergroup Relations Strategy

These issues were considered to be relatively significant and interesting among those that might be dealt with. Others were passed over because of reasons of space limitations and manageability within a single

---

[1] Jack Rothman, *Promoting Social Justice in the Multi Group Society: A Casebook for Group Relations Practitioners* (New York: Association Press, in cooperation with the Council on Social Work Education, 1971).

volume (e.g., "black capitalism" vs. collective minority economic development; changing the minority individual vs. changing society; changing majority attitudes vs. changing majority institutions). Once our mode of inquiry is evident, teachers or individual readers can proceed along similar lines in investigating other issue areas.

For each of the issues considered, the reader will find an introduction and four pieces selected from the works of authors who have treated the subject with discernment. Under the heading "Theoretical and Philosophical Considerations," the first two articles will offer a theoretical or philosophical base by setting forth the major dimensions of viewpoints expounded by proponents on opposing sides of the matter. This will be followed by the heading "Factual and Research Considerations," which will introduce a research article presenting systematically acquired factual data on an aspect of the issue. These data presentations embody different methods of obtaining information and varying results of empirical investigation. The reader should be prepared to examine these studies carefully in order to judge their respective limitations or biases, as well as what they do to illuminate the points at issue. The final section, "Policy and Practice Considerations," deals with strategies, policies, and programs that have been conceived of to deal with the issue. The articles in this section include sets of recommendations, examples of programs, and descriptions of practical experiences and approaches. These avenues of action can be analyzed and critiqued in their own terms (i.e., how might recommendations have been presented more persuasively, or practice interventions implemented more effectively?) or in terms of their consequences relative to the theoretical or factual background provided in the earlier readings in the chapter.

The four selections yield only a core informational foundation for each issue. The reader is encouraged to search out additional sources of the three types (theory, research, and practice), using the kinds of journals from which the selections are taken, references cited within the selections, and other available methods of library research. We have left the selected articles basically in their original form, with only minor editorial changes when necessary, in order to convey realistically the character and even the flaws of the different streams of literature in the race and ethnic field.

In the balance of this chapter we will articulate a broad frame of reference concerning race and ethnic affairs, to permit the reader to explore the issues from a comprehensive, eclectic perspective. The components of this frame of reference include alternative theories or models of race and ethnic relations (defining the problems), and alternative strategies and policies for resolving race and ethnic relations problems (defining the solutions). We will draw heavily on available theory and research in developing this analytic frame.

Defining the problems: Theories of race and ethnic relations

Recently there has been an avalanche of books and articles dealing with race and ethnic problems. The analysis and opinion presented in these works reflect considerable divergencies, and the obstacles to any attempt to summarize or consolidate the multiplicity of approaches is formidable. Nevertheless, theoretical perspectives in the field can be divided roughly into two clusters of thought: one which deals with the attitudinal and psychological dimensions of prejudice (promulgated largely by psychologists and social psychologists), and another which deals with the sociostructural dimensions of inequality (put forth by some sociologists, economists, and political scientists). The social-psychological literature concerns itself with the mental processes related to prejudice, including benefits such as enhanced status; the other literature deals with structural factors related to group domination and oppression, including benefits such as monetary gains from economic exploitation.

The juxtaposition of the two positions was expressed pointedly by Peter Rose in this passage:

> Followers of Marx and other economic determinists view prejudice as the result of the strained relationship between the exploited and the exploiter. . . . Oliver Cox and others have hypothesized that the whole system of race relations and segregated patterns, especially in the United States, is directly related to the maintenance of a cheap labor supply. While all social scientists do not agree that economic interests play the most important role in bringing about and maintaining prejudice and discrimination, many have found that intergroup conflict continues in large part because of the gains—both material and psychological—that are realized by assuming an attitude of superiority and enforcing social distance between one's own group and others. Early studies . . . suggested that the principal basis for differential ranking of ethnic groups is the desire to maintain or enhance one's social position by associating with groups considered to be of high status and by disassociating from those low in the prestige hierarchy.[2]

Some of the main concepts that are commonly associated with the attitudinal and sociostructural schools as defined above are set forth in the sections that follow immediately.

[2] Peter Rose, *They and We: Racial and Ethnic Relations in the United States* (New York: Random House, 1964), p. 87.

ATTITUDINAL APPROACHES

The attitudinal approach concentrates on intrapsychic phenomena which lead individuals to delineate among various groups, to set one off from the other, and to allocate differential status or values among them. Leonard Bloom states that "when the protagonist of race differences insists upon the differences between races he is seeking to justify the exclusion of one race from humanity: he seeks to create strangers. If there are no biological differences between the groups, he will invent them . . . . if there are differences, he will exaggerate them. . . ."[3]

It has been suggested that there are three components of attitude which contribute to prejudicial differentiation among groups.[4] These are as follows:

Cognitive Components. The cognitive components of attitude have to do with what an individual believes to be true with regard to the characteristics of different groups. In studies of this aspect subjects may be given a list of traits (such as intelligent, lazy, artistic) and asked to indicate which are most typical for members of various racial and ethnic groups. These components are concerned with the *knowledge* the individual claims to have about the behavior and attributes of different groups.

Affective Components. The affective components deal not with knowledge about different groups but with *generalized feelings* of favorability-unfavorability or friendliness-hostility toward them. The individual experiences this type of attitude emotionally and directly, rather than through a cognitive medium.

Conative Components. The conative components pertain to *feelings regarding interaction and relationship* with members of various groups—willingness to have close social contact, aggression vs. nonaggression in associations, withdrawal vs. nonwithdrawal in relationships, as well as the acceptance of status equality vs. status differentials in the pattern of association.

It is not clear whether these attitudinal components form a unified configuration in the prejudiced individual or they tend to stand independently. In any case, the list above suggests some of the complexities involved in dealing with a presumedly unitary concept in group relations, such as attitude.

---

[3] Leonard Bloom, *The Social Psychology of Race Relations* (Cambridge, Mass.: Schenkman Publishing Co., 1972), p. 15.

[4] John Harding et al., "Prejudice and Ethnic Relations," in Gardner Lindzey and Elliot Aronson, *The Handbook of Social Psychology,* vol. 5 (Reading, Mass.: Addison-Wesley Publishing Co., 1969), pp. 1–76.

Leaving aside the analytic substructure of prejudicial attitudes, we can confront the question of how people get that way: What are the influences that cause such predispositions? There is a rather rich literature on this which can only be touched upon in a cursory way here.

James Vander Zanden, a respected student of minority problems, has suggested some of the salient origins of intergroup hostility.[5] They are:

Contact.   One cause of intergroup hostility is contact, or associations among different peoples and cultures brought about as a result of migrations of various kinds. In circumstances of proximity, existing racial and cultural differences do not ipso facto create hostilities, but the social definitions which accompany them may provide a convenient peg upon which to hang invidious social distinctions.

Social Visibility.   When distinguishing marks are attached to various groups, they can become a vehicle for subordination. Such group "signs" may be racial—skin color, hair texture, facial expression—or cultural—names, dress, accent, and so on.

Competition.   In social life, resources are always finite, and jockeying takes place among various groups for economic advantage, power, and status. When such competition has as its referent racial and ethnic interests and identities, hostile intergroup attitudes may erupt.

Ethnocentrism.   The way of viewing the world whereby one's own group is seen as being at the "center of everything," and its standards of judgment are seen as the criteria for appraising and rating all others, is called ethnocentrism. Outgroups are seen as inferior in their ways; indeed, their acts are defined as deviant. Ironically, ingroup virtues are seen as outgroup vices. When Lincoln worked into the night he was being industrious, resolute, and diligent, but Japanese people who exhibit such zeal are seen as ruthless, competitive, and crafty.

Ethnocentricity, viewed as ingroup socialization, may be taken rather neutrally. All individuals need a focal social reference, and group identity is generally accepted as a positive mental health influence. For ethnocentrism to be transformed into prejudice requires the introduction of other variables. Robin Williams suggests two in particular as critical.[6] They are:

Social Distance.   Group members who are unwilling to accept or approve some level of intimacy in their interaction with other group members are said to exhibit a high degree of social distance. (This is the

---

[5] James W. Vander Zanden, *American Minority Relations,* 3rd ed. (New York: Ronald Press, 1972).
[6] Robin M. Williams, Jr., *Strangers Next Door: Ethnic Relations in American Communities* (Englewood Cliffs, N.J.: Prentice-Hall, 1964).

conative component in attitudes.) Feelings of social distance which include aloofness or rejection constitute an attitudinal configuration which is predisposed to prejudice.

Stereotypes.   Labels or identities, "pictures in the mind," which are attributed to different groups of human beings so that the entire group is pigeonholed as falling within a given category, are called stereotypes. They are often culturally disseminated and are inculcated through socialization processes. Stereotyping is considered to be pervasive in that almost all groups are subject to generalized classification. However, the practice is particularly pernicious when directed at groups who are already suffering social disadvantages.

A prominent psychological explanation of prejudice which utilizes frustration-aggression as a key concept has been hypothesized by Gordon Allport. This formulation focuses on the displacement of hostility in the form of scapegoating.[7] The rationale of this practice is as follows:

Scapegoating.   Individuals experience frustrations or deprivations from diverse sources in the society. The source of these deprivations may be difficult to locate, or they may originate with individuals or groups possessing substantial power. The perpetrators may even have strong bonds of affectional relationship with the individuals on the receiving end. The hostilities that are aroused under these circumstances are blocked from direct expression, which leads to free-floating frustration. These frustrations are displaced by projecting them on substitute objects who are both highly visible and vulnerable and lack the capacity to retaliate. Minority groups may be choice targets for such displacement.

In concluding this brief synopsis of the hypothetical causes of prejudice, it is necessary to introduce the rather broad variable of personality, and in particular the "authoritarian personality." This concept can be described as follows:

Personality.   Some researchers have proposed that negative attitudes toward ethnic groups are part of the larger organization of an individual's personality. The major work along these lines was conducted by T. W. Adorno and his associates in the late forties, culminating in the influential book *The Authoritarian Personality.*[8] In this study, subjects were exposed to a series of tests (A Scale—Anti-Semitism; F Scale—Fascism; E Scale—Ethnocentrism), as well as to an intensive clinical

[7] Gordon W. Allport, *The Nature of Prejudice* (Boston: Beacon Press, 1954).

[8] T. W. Adorno et al., *The Authoritarian Personality* (New York: Harper, 1950).

interview. The authors concluded that the more prejudiced individuals had a definite personality configuration comprised of rigidity, conventional values, the rejection of socially deviant impulses within themselves, the externalization of such impulses by projecting them onto others, and a propensity toward a power and status orientation in their relations with others. These tendencies were hypothesized to be an outgrowth of early childhood experiences characterized by harsh parental discipline, coupled with conditional parental love. The conflict between fear and dependency on the one hand and hatred and suspicion on the other is seen as shaping a personality structure which expresses basic repressed hostility in the direction of vulnerable outgroups. The work of Adorno and his colleagues received extraordinary attention and stimulated a spate of studies aimed at examining personality variables. It also generated much controversy, including criticism of the methodology employed.[9] Personality study as a dominant theme has subsided in more recent years.

Social psychologists have introduced several other concepts related to intergroup relations, such as relative deprivation,[10] status threat,[11] and racial roles.[12] Thomas Pettigrew, for example, suggests that the racial "game" works only if whites and blacks are willing to play the roles of superior and subordinate. When the players demur, the entire superstructure of established intergroup relationships may face a crisis.

In his monograph on prejudice and racism, James M. Jones summarizes a historical pattern wherein work by earlier social scientists concentrated on attitudes and personality factors, whereas a more recent emphasis has been on sociostructural elements, particularly those that are economic. His historical perspective is as follows:

. . . . through the first four decades of this century . . . a social scientific analysis of racial problems dealt particularly with the concept of attitudes and correspondent methodological and statistical approaches necessary to their measurement. These early developments in social psychology tended primarily to orient the analysis of race relations toward the concept of racial attitude. A major interest developed around the study of stereotyping and various other attitudinal indications of racial bias. This focus on attitudes tended to guide theorists away from racial behaviors, ... Research on [personality factors], the authori-

[9] Richard Christe and Marie Jahoda, eds., *Studies in the Scope and Method of "The Authoritarian Personality"* (New York: Free Press of Glencoe, 1954).

[10] Carl F. Grindstaft, "The Negro, Urbanization and Relative Deprivation in the Deep South," *Social Problems,* vol. 15 (Winter 1968), pp. 342–52.

[11] John Teacher, "Status Threat and the White Backlash," *Journal of Human Relations,* vol. 18, no. 2 (1964), pp. 939–45.

[12] Thomas R. Pettigrew, "Complexity and Change in American Racial Patterns: A Social Psychological View," *Daedalus,* Fall 1965, pp. 974–1008.

tarian personality and on frustration and aggression, or the scapegoat theory of prejudice, was given greater attention in the 1940's.[13]

In the more recent period, according to Jones, there has been concern over the location of minorities in "marginal economic situations" and "basic problems of discrimination at every level of economic activity in this country." It may be assumed that this shift was brought about by the realization that attitudinal factors alone are not sufficient to explain the persistence of prejudice, nor are programs based on that analysis powerful enough to impact racist patterns. It is to the economic factors that we turn our attention in the next section.

SOCIOSTRUCTURAL APPROACHES

Sociostructural approaches assume that collective, institutional components of the society operate (in social system terms) so as to impose objectively different statuses and positions on members. Such differentials, it is reasoned, allow the superordinate group to exploit subordinate groups to its own advantage, particularly with regard to material benefits in the economic sphere. Such patterns of exploitation may take various institutional forms and be directed at different types of minorities. Charles Marden and Gladys Meyer, for example, describe the following varieties of domination: the slavery pattern, the annexation pattern, the colonial pattern, and the voluntary immigrant pattern.[14] Those subscribing to this school of thought are generally influenced to a greater or lesser degree by aspects of Marxist thinking which view exploitative relationships as an inherent feature of a free enterprise or capitalist socioeconomic order. O. E. Cox states the proposition starkly in the following passage:

> Our hypothesis is that racial exploitation and racial prejudice developed among Europeans with the rise of capitalism and nationalism, and that because of the worldwide ramifications of capitalism, all racial antagonisms can be traced to the policies and attitudes of the leading capitalist people, the white people of Europe and North America.[15]

There has been a growing trend among respected social scientists of various disciplines, including Herbert Gans in sociology,[16] Christopher

---

[13] James M. Jones, *Prejudice and Racism* (Menlo Park, Cal.: Addison-Wesley Publishing Co., 1972), p. 170.

[14] Charles F. Marden and Gladys Meyer, *Minorities in American Society,* 3rd ed. (New York: Van Nostrand Reinhold Company, 1968).

[15] O. E. Cox, *Caste, Class and Race* in Bloom, *Social Psychology of Race Relations.*

[16] Herbert Gans, *More Equality* (New York: Pantheon Books, Random House, 1973).

Jencks in education,[17] and Robert Lekachman in economics,[18] to analyze group relations problems in the light of sociostructural processes of inequality. John Rawls's writings reflect the same tendency in the field of philosophy.[19]

There have been two distinct but interrelated basic modes of analysis associated with this economically oriented sociostructural approach: the
√ neocolonialism notion and the marginal–working class concept. William Tabb has provided a lucid portrayal of these two "race relations models,"[20] and we shall borrow from his treatise in this presentation.

The neocolonialism concept

√ According to Tabb, colonialism analysis conceives of the ghetto as a separate social entity which has been subjected to a definite pattern of economic control and political subjugation. The sheer geographic segregation of the ghetto is secondary in significance to its manipulation through outside political and economic domination by white society. Tabb contrasts the traditional colonialism and neocolonialism concepts in the following statements:

> The vast majority of colonies were established by Western powers over technologically less advanced peoples of Asia, Africa and Latin America. Military supremacy, combined with judicious bribing of local leaders and a generous sprinkling of Christian missionaries, enabled an outside power to dominate an area spatially separate from the ruling state. . . .
>
> The black experience in America was somewhat different. Here the colonized were brought to the "mother" country to be enslaved and exploited. Internal colonialism thus involves the conquest and subjugation of a people and their physical removal to the ruling state. The command of the resources of the captive people (their labor power) followed. . . . [In the ghetto,] local businesses are owned, in large numbers, by nonresidents many of whom are white. Marginal, low-profit businesses are more likely to be owned by blacks; larger, more profitable ones are owned by whites. Important jobs in the local public economy (teachers, policemen and postmen) are held by white outsiders. . . . Welfare payments and other governmental transfers are needed to help pay for the ghetto's requirements. Welfare, however, only reinforces the dependency relationship, reinforces the psychology of inferiority. . . .[21]

---

[17] Christopher Jencks, *Inequality: A Reassessment of the Effects of Family and Schooling in America* (New York: Harper & Row, 1973).

[18] Robert Lekachman, "The Economics of Inequality" in Alan Gartner et al., *What Nixon Is Doing to Us* (New York: Harper & Row, 1973).

[19] John Rawls, *A Theory of Justice* (Cambridge, Mass.: Belknap Press of Harvard University Press, 1971).

[20] William K. Tabb, "Race Relations Models and Social Change," *Social Problems,* vol. 18 (Spring 1971), pp. 431–44.

[21] Ibid., pp. 433–35.

Common elements of both types of colonialism include such factors as low per capita income, high birth rate, a small middle class, and low rates of increase in capital formation and domestic savings. Both are heavily dependent on external markets, and this is coupled with the "demonstration effect"—the desire to consume products that are generally available only on the outside.[22] Robert Blauner, who can be credited with providing important intellectual underpinnings for the neocolonialism theory, adds also that in both internal and external colonialism, the culture and social organization of the oppressed group is systematically weakened or destroyed—thereby accenting further the dependency relationship.[23]

It should also be noted that while neocolonialism writings have centered on black minorities, the same analysis has been applied to other racial and ethnic groups. Joan Moore discusses internal colonialism with regard to the Chicano community, pointing out that the concept is both broader and more complex than it is often portrayed.[24] She demonstrates that different forms of internal colonialism may unfold, based on the immediate social context and the nature of power relationships between majority and minority groups. For example, "classic colonialism" developed in New Mexico, where conquest was bloodless, the indigenous elite retained much of its standing, and the structure of the annexed society remained largely intact. Texas had a markedly different historical experience; there great upheaval and violence accompanied a revolution against the Mexican government by settlers in Texas. This "conflict colonialism" was characterized by the destruction of political participation by the Mexican elite and suppression of the village masses through instrumentalities such as the Texas Rangers. While in New Mexico Chicanos were the numerical majority, in Texas they were considerably outnumbered by Anglos. "Economic colonialism" in California was midway between the conflict and the smooth-transition varieties. The small Mexican population was swamped by Anglo immigrants following the Gold Rush. The original Mexican settlements and economy had been built around large land holdings rather than villages and hence lacked a strong social organization. This resulted in a low level of political participation, inadequate to counteract the economic manipulation possible with an available labor pool for agricultural and extractive enterprises.

The neocolonialism concept has been criticized from a number of

---

[22] Ibid.

[23] Robert Blauner, "Internal Colonialism and Ghetto Revolts," *Social Problems,* vol. 16 (Spring 1969), pp. 393–408.

[24] Joan W. Moore, "Colonialism: The Case of the Mexican Americans," *Social Problems,* vol. 17 (Spring 1970), pp. 463–72.

different points of view. For example, Raymond Franklin and Solomon Resnik, who generally support the sociostructural approach, raise several objections to the colonial analogy.[25] For one thing, minorities in this country are somewhat dispersed, rather than fundamentally separated. This mitigates against the rise of a cohesive political movement capable of autonomous control of the resources and destiny of a subordinate group. A minority within a larger majority society has inherent limits on the independent power it can mobilize and exercise. Further, since minorities are not *culturally distinct and isolated,* it is not possible to eliminate the "demonstration effect" by which they internalize the consumer desires and styles of the dominant group. The lack of physical separation makes for greater economic drains from the subordinate to the superordinate group, particularly since countermechanisms such as protective tariffs and import controls are not feasible. Fiscal and monetary autonomy is also not available in the form of taxation powers, control over an internal money supply, and so on. These considerations, argue Franklin and Resnik, place limitations on the colonialism theory in terms of defining minority problems, as well as designing solutions. In addition, analyses such as those by Ben Wattenberg and Richard Scammon indicate a sharply rising economic position for blacks, which argues against a colonialist perspective.[26]

The marginal–working class concept

The marginal–working class interpretation takes cognizance of existing distinctions among workers; some derive adequate levels of economic well-being from their work, and others, the marginal group, realize a lower degree of status and economic advantage. While managers and other elites benefit from the contributions of both groups, the existence of marginality permits the operation of privilege within lower levels of society and forces a cleavage in the ranks among those near the bottom. Tabb describes this as follows:

> The extent to which the capitalist class is able to isolate segments of the working class from each other strengthens its position. By creating a marginal working class of blacks and giving white workers a relatively more privileged position, it strengthens its control. If one group of workers are able to command higher pay, to exclude others from work, and if the other group or groups of workers are limited in their employment opportunities to the worst jobs and lowest pay, then a marginal working class has been created which benefits the labor aristocracy and

[25] Raymond S. Franklin and Solomon Resnik, *The Political Economy of Racism* (New York: Holt, Rinehart & Winston, 1973).

[26] Ben J. Wattenberg and Richard M. Scammon, "Black Progress and Liberal Rhetoric," *Commentary,* vol. 55 (April 1973), pp. 35–44.

to an even greater extent the capitalist class. The marginal working class produces goods which are generally available below the cost which would have been obtained if they had received wages closer to those paid to the labor aristocracy which had used its bargaining position to its own advantage.[27]

The marginal working class is depicted as holding comparatively less desirable jobs (doing the "dirty work"), receiving lower wages, and having a less stable job tenure. It is viewed as inherent in the free enterprise economic system that some individuals must play this role; immigrant groups have traditionally been so assigned, but racial minorities in particular suffer from the arrangement, whereby, says Tabb, "a special kind of poverty and a special kind of labor reserve is maintained."

A more comprehensive dissection of the forces at play in this process has been offered by economists such as Michael Jo Piore and Daniel Fusfeld.[28] We will be guided in our discussion, in particular, by Fusfeld's graphic analysis. Fusfeld posits the presence of two major labor forces in metropolitan areas: one attached to "export industries" and another to "service industries." The export industries are the backbone of the regional economy. They aim at nationwide and international markets, as for example the auto industry in Detroit or steel manufacture in Pittsburgh, and they attract monetary resources from these external sources. A complementary set of industries provides direct inputs into the export industries or uses their products for further processing. These two primary industrial groups typically are composed of large firms that pay high wages to unionized workers engaged in modern technological operations. The service industries may be defined as supporting the internal maintenance needs of the local economy, including food, shelter, recreation, municipal services, hospital care, and education. These "low-wage industries" form the sector which employs large numbers of ghetto residents. Such industries are characterized as follows: small firms with little capital investment, labor-intensive undeveloped technology, low profits and labor productivity, little research or product development, high incidence of unemployment and labor turnover rates, and "unprotected" features, including the absence of unionization and of minimum wages.

A symbiotic and exploitative relationship is established between the two industrial groupings. Because of their low-wage economic struc-

[27] Tabb, "Race Relations Models and Social Change," p. 438.
[28] Michael J. Piore, "Public and Private Responsibility for On-the-Job Training of Disadvantaged Workers," Department of Economics Working Paper No. 23, M.I.T.. Cambridge, Mass., 1968; and Daniel R. Fusfeld, *The Basic Economics of the Urban Racial Crisis* (New York: Holt, Rinehart & Winston, 1973).

ture, the service industries have imposed on them the burden of holding down living costs in the metropolitan region. Costs of production in the export industries are constrained and in a sense subsidized by the service industries. That is to say, if the services rendered by restaurant workers, hospital orderlies, domestic helpers, and the like were higher, salaries in the export industries would need to be higher in order to provide employees with a given standard of living. Fusfeld describes the structurally binding nature of these dynamic relationships as follows:

> The economic relationship makes it difficult for any local government to take strong action to eliminate ghettos and the poverty found there. If one area made a serious effort along these lines, there would be an increase in the cost base of the area's export industries and their complements. Services would cost more, the cost of distribution would be higher, and governmental expenses would rise. Higher living costs would require higher wages in the export and complementary industries in order to attract and keep necessary amounts of properly skilled labor. These higher costs (relative to other metropolitan areas) would result in slower economic growth and perhaps even retrogression if the cost effects were great enough. Low wages in service industries are as important to a city's export industries as are low taxes. . . . The basically exploitative nature of the urban ghetto is readily evident. It is easy to understand why there are strong economic and political barriers to its elimination. The structure of power is allied with those economic interests that have a vested interest in continued poverty.[29]

In a political rather than economic analysis of the urban racial situation, Frances Fox Piven suggests that not only are marginal and other working classes played off one against the other, but both are played off against the middle class, with economic elites maintaining their dominance and advantage in the interaction.[30] Attempts at equalization of economic resources (whether through equality of opportunity, preferential treatment, governmental service or other programs) ordinarily are designed in such a way as to redistribute benefits among middle-class, working-class, and lower-class elements, rather than between the upper classes and the others. Piven notes:

> In the United States in the 1960's it was the urban blacks who made the trouble, and it was the organized producer groups in the cities who made the greatest gains. Those of the working and middle classes who were not among the organized producers got little enough themselves, and were made to pay with their tax monies for gains granted to others.

---

[29] Fusfeld, *Basic Economics of Urban Racial Crisis,* p. 33.
[30] Frances Fox Piven, "Cutting up the City Pie: Who Gets What," *New Republic,* February 5, 1972, pp. 17–22.

Their resentments grew; now to appease them, the small gains that blacks did make in the course of the disturbances are being whittled away.[31]

Other methods of sociostructural analysis

There are, of course, other formulations that can be related to structural variables. Some authors examine various patterns of social discrimination—political, legal, economic—and attribute them to normative cultural patterns (systems of belief leading to established behavior modalities) or to prejudicial attitudes of individuals within the society. Society, because it is misinformed, evil, immature, or defective in some other way, singles out certain visible racial or ethnic groups and mistreats them. The *function* of such discrimination for the social system or its relevant subparts is not brought out with any precision. In contrast to the Fusfeld analysis, consider this more usual sociological posture toward economic discrimination:

> We may define economic discrimination as any activity or lack of activity that prevents a member of a minority group from earning a living or getting other material benefits from society because of his membership in a minority group and not because of any defects in his training or ability.[32]

The analytic blandness of this approach is evident. In addition, there are different action implications that can be derived from each approach. The colonialism model suggests separatist political and economic development within minority ghettos, barrios, and reservations. The marginal–working class model implies the formation of political alliances along class lines across racial divisions. The more general sociological approaches suggest changing attitudes, modifying particular social or institutional practices through civil rights action, or, in the words of the Kerner Commission report on civil disorders, "rearranging priorities."

OTHER APPROACHES TO DEFINING THE PROBLEMS

The attitudinal and sociostructural approaches we have described may be viewed as constituting the extremes of individualistic vs. structural orientations—orientations which view prejudice as simply misguided or materially instrumental. Elaboration of these extreme positions has helped us set the parameters within which race and ethnic theories can be considered. However, there are other models, particularly cultural conceptions, which fall between these poles. Only a few

[31] Ibid., p. 22.
[32] Arnold M. Rose, *Race Prejudice and Discrimination* (New York: Alfred A. Knopf, 1951), p. 114.

will be mentioned here. These additional approaches are not considered of less importance than the others in terms of either analysis or implications for policy and action. Indeed, they might well claim a right to equal time; the major obstacle is the lack of space.

One commonly held view takes a "cultural pluralism" point of departure, depicting racial and ethnic entities as distinct, valid subcultural units of American society which interact to generate the general culture. The concern is not with beleaguered minorities or exploited populations per se, but rather with a pattern of complex social relations in a pluralistic, multigroup society. Shifting configurations of group accommodation and adjustment, on the one hand, or conflict and rearrangement of power and status relationships, on the other, are involved. The focus is on group aspiration, identity, status, conflict, and accommodation.

Spokesmen for the pluralist perspective include theorists such as Andrew M. Greeley and Nathan Glazer, and professional group relations practitioners such as Irving M. Levine.[33] Levine spelled out some of the main tenets of the pluralist position in his 1973 address to the American Immigration and Citizenship Conference. He maintains that an individual's basic identity is an amalgam of personal and cultural elements. In keeping with Eric Erikson, Levine brings forth the view that identity derives not only from the core of the individual but also simultaneously from the core of a communal culture. In keeping with Kurt Lewin, he holds that ethnic identity provides the individual with a solid "social ground" on which to stand in a complex and shifting social terrain. Group identity, therefore, is a natural and necessary aspect of life for all individuals and should not be ignored or played down. Levine makes his point as follows:

> While men and women have yearned since the beginning of time for the kinds of humanistic social environments where people would be accepted as individuals, not on the basis of the ethnic group or class they were born into, there has always been an equally intense desire to create community, based around family, clan, and physical proximity.
>
> Whether group identity is "good" or "bad" defies resolution. It is, at any rate, "beside the point," since it is a fact of life. Anyone who might hope that Blacks, Chicanos, Puerto Ricans, American Indians, Jews, diverse white ethnics, feminists, homosexuals and others would simply

---

[33] Andrew M. Greeley, *Why Can't They Be Like Us?* (New York: Institute of Human Relations Press, American Jewish Committee, 1969); Daniel P. Moynihan and Nathan Glazer, *Beyond the Melting Pot* (Cambridge, Mass.: M.I.T. Press, 1963); Irving M. Levine, "Social Policy and Multi-Ethnicity in the 1970's," address to The Annual Seminar of The Committee on Integration of the American Immigration and Citizenship Conference, New York City, 1973. Published by The National Project on Ethnic America (Mimeo, 20 pp.).

dissolve into the common culture, fails to understand that it is all of these groups and their interactions which in fact comprise the common culture in America.[34]

In its manifestations, Levine continues, cultural pluralism entails interaction and competition among groups, symbolized in the exercise of power—including abuses and complications associated with the uses of power.

> When we talk about ethnic consciousness, the upsurge in ethnic identity, and shifting alliances between ethnic groups and other interest groups, we are really talking about power—about who has it and who doesn't, and for whose benefit it is being used.
>
> As the dimensions of ethnic group relations and group power continue to grow beyond the bounds of our cities, we have reached a stage of urban-suburban trade-offs. A crucial question now emerges: How can the cities, with their relatively powerless minority and ethnic groups, relate to suburbs in a manner in which power can be equitably shared? To put it another way, how can we insure compassion for those who really need aid, without demanding unrealistic sacrifices from those whose suburban existence is far from problem-free?[35]

Two pluralist solutions to this power dilemma are offered by Levine, one dealing with governmental programs and policies, and the other with coalitional politics among different groups. With regard to governmental initiatives, it is suggested such programs take into account and nurture subcultural and ethnic affiliations:

> We need the kind of governmentally-supported policy which offers a series of options for people, based on a diversity of lifestyles and preferred forms of aid. . . . In an age where the forces of technology and industry have operated solely to protect and expand their own self-interests, viable communities have gradually been destroyed, and individuals have increasingly been robbed of the capacity to function communally. What the "limits-of-social-policy" advocates do not appreciate is that it will take untold financial resources to rescue what is still alive of the "old communalism," to stimulate new forms of neighborhood development, and to create an environment where people can realistically return to the "naturalness" of self-help.[36]

The counterpart to governmental activity is voluntary association among cultural and ethnic groups. Such activities, while enhancing and strengthening group life, should also pay heed to matters of overarching general welfare.

---

[34] Levine, "Social Policy and Multi-Ethnicity," p. 13.
[35] Ibid., pp. 14–15.
[36] Ibid., pp. 16–17.

Multi-ethnic coalitions, diverse by their very nature yet cemented by concrete common concerns, can be extremely effective mechanisms for social and economic progress. That cannot be said, however, without some words of caution. . . . I see the role of organizers and of leaders in ethnic communities as one of sanctioning bridge-building forms of organization, and avoiding like the plague the kind of demagogic appeals that lead to fragmentation, separatism, ethnocentrism and a host of other "isms" which polarize.[37]

Levine specifically takes issue with those who believe that basic advances will come about only through class-related action which submerges subgroup and other "divisive" elements.

People will continue to organize along class lines, a form that many "progressives" believe predisposes toward social activism, but they will also continue to organize along ethnic and religious lines as well. And contrary to the notions of some, there are as many examples throughout history of ethnic and religious institutions serving as vigorous advocates of social progress, as there are examples of their resistance to change.[38]

The main task of group relations and other agencies in the period ahead, according to the pluralists, is group development across the wide spectrum of ethnic and cultural expression, together with intergroup activity which binds groups together in a coherent whole. Levine says: "Coalition-building across ethnic lines should be the job of mainstream institutions in America. To do it well, they will have to overcome decades of failure to relate to particularism and group identity needs."[39]

Still another prevalent way of describing group relations problems may be referred to as a "cultural deprivation" or "social pathology" concept. Again a cultural dimension is involved; however, it is the culture of the minority group that is the object of analysis. As a consequence of past discrimination, historical happenstance, or whatever, the cultural composition of minorities is hypothetically downgraded and damaged, and the result is predispositions toward high crime rates, poor family cohesion, inadequate educational motivation, apathy, and so on. While the minority group may have been blameless originally, the existing intragroup level of cultural deprivation—which has sometimes been conceived as the "culture of poverty"—is seen as operating as an autonomous perpetrator and generator of minority problems. Daniel Moynihan's discussion of black family breakdown[40] and Lee Rainwater's

---

[37] Ibid., pp. 18–19.
[38] Ibid., p. 18.
[39] Ibid., p. 20.
[40] Daniel P. Moynihan, *The Negro Family: The Case for National Action* (Washington, D.C.: Office of Policy Planning and Research, U.S. Department of Labor, 1965).

description of lower-class social relations in the Pruitt-Igoe public housing project are well-known exemplars.[41] This posture leads to the use of such terms as "the Negro problem" and to the formulation of solutions that are directed at changing the attitudes or behavior of the minority community. Many human service organizations gear their programs in a way which suggests implicit acceptance of this perspective.

It is useful to contrast this approach with the cultural nationalism orientations which have been gaining prominence in the past several years within minority communities. Here the emphasis is on the uniqueness and vitality within minority cultures, their viability and beauty in the face of majority-group denial and oppression. The Afro-American[42] and the Chicano "La Raza"[43] movements typify this stance. Existing minority cultural features are viewed not as debits to be eliminated or modified but as assets to be enhanced. The source of difficulty is located in the majority society, where the "white problem" of suppression, racism, and inhumanity is found to be prevalent.

Significantly, within the cultural nationalism movement a different interpretation is made of minority family structure and life which emphasizes the strengths rather than the pathology in the situation.[44] This revisionist trend shifts attention to the "system" and away from the individual in analyzing cultural phenomena, particularly family structure.[45]

The cultural deprivation and cultural nationalism approaches may be seen as opposites, involving diametrically different assumptions concerning causes and cures in the race and ethnic relations field. It is on the cures—programmatic and strategic avenues of action—that we will next focus our attention.

---

[41] Lee Rainwater, *Behind Ghetto Walls: Black Family Life in a Federal Slum* (Chicago: Aldine Publishing Co., 1970).

[42] See, for example, LeRoi Jones, *Blues People* (New York: William Morrow, 1963). The emerging program of CORE pertains also.

[43] Armando B. Rendon, *Chicano Manifesto* (New York: Collier Books, 1971).

[44] Andrew Billingsley, *Black Families in White America* (Englewood Cliffs, New Jersey: Prentice-Hall, 1968); Robert B. Hill, *The Strengths of Black Families* (New York: Emerson Hall Publishers, 1972).

[45] William Ryan, *Blaming the Victim* (New York: Pantheon Books, 1970).

Defining the solutions: Strategies of action in race and ethnic relations and evaluation of their impact

OVERVIEW OF STRATEGIES

While there is a large number of different theories and interpretations concerning causes of race and ethnic relations problems, when one examines programs geared to eliminating or solving these problems the number of variations expands astronomically. An example is the list compiled by Goodwin Watson, after surveying the activities of typical human relations–civil rights organizations.[46] Watson's list of problem-solving methods follows:

Education
    Spreading knowledge
    Emotional reeducation
Participation
    Getting acquainted across group lines
    Working together on common problems
    Living together as friends and neighbors
Revelation (disclosing problems that had not been recognized or acknowledged)
    "Telling it like it is"
Exhortation (sermonizing for brotherhood)
Negotiation (mediating disputes and conflicts)
Contention
    Equalizing opportunities
    Removing segregation
    Fighting political bias
    Defending differences
Prevention
    Diagnosing areas of potential conflict
    Introducing prophylactic measures
    Training public officials toward better human relations practices
    Self-discipline (self-improvement measures for minorities)
    Removing general sources of frustration

Such a compilation is helpful in suggesting a range of alternative actions from which to choose. However, it stops short of providing the diagnostic tools that could connect a given course of action with a par-

---

[46] Goodwin Watson, *Action for Unity* (New York: Harper & Bros., 1947).

ticular analysis of a problem situation—that is, it does not articulate the strategic dimensions of the choice. If efforts in the race and ethnic relations field, an emotionally charged and ideologically saturated area, are to exhibit greater rationality and professionalism, not to mention a higher level of impact and effectiveness, there must be some provision for systematic, strategic planning.

In discussing the reduction of discrimination, J. Milton Yinger focuses on this point:

> Our task now is to investigate problems of strategy; how can we best move toward greater equality goals? Ought major attention be devoted to changing attitudes of prejudiced persons? What is the place of legal and judicial action? Do sit-ins, freedom rides, protest marches and picket lines change the situation?[47]

If the change agent seeking to reduce discrimination is concerned in particular about prejudice and the educational approaches to it, for example, even within this more delimited sphere there are questions of strategy options. Prejudices, Yinger points out, may originate from a number of different sources: informational deficits, conformity to stereotypic norms, status striving, or emotionally derived feelings of hostility. There are distinctly different action alternatives for each of these problem assessments. Such relationships are demonstrated by Yinger in the table below:

Dimension of prejudice	Approach likely to be effective
1. Lack of information, stereotyped view	1. Education, contact
2. Need to conform	2. Clear specification of legal and other standards of nondiscrimination
3. Desire for status, insecurity of status	3. Creating more secure life, more opportunity for all
4. Emotional need feelings of hatred and hostility	4. Reduction of the frustrations of prejudiced persons

It has been noted that in the sociostructural interpretation, there are different action implications, depending upon whether a neocolonialism or a marginal–working class posture is assumed. The former suggests separatist minority-group community development endeavors, while the latter leads to coalition building on a class basis among different racial and ethnic groups. The section to follow provides an overarching framework for considering various strategy options across a wide

---

[47] J. Milton Yinger, *A Minority Group in American Society* (New York: McGraw-Hill Book Co., 1965), p. 96.

range of problem definitions, including whether individual or social causation is assumed.[48]

A framework for considering policy options

Our orientation to strategy, as in the Watson study cited above, starts by examining what group relations agencies and organizations actually do in their ongoing operations.[49] However, the programmatic modalities are conceptualized at a higher level of abstraction, so there are only four basic categories: group rights, group solidarity and power, intergroup attitudes and relationships, and group welfare. These categories then are related to a set of key variables, such as assumptions concerning causation, targets of change, and value preferences.

Group Rights. Programs in the group-rights category are geared to securing civil rights for members of disadvantaged or oppressed groups and eliminating discrimination in areas such as employment, housing, and education. Much of this work has a legal and judicial character involving the enforcement of laws and administrative directives, and it is often carried out by federal or state antidiscrimination agencies such as the Equal Employment Opportunity Commission, the Department of Health, Education, and Welfare (HEW), and the Federal Civil Rights Commission. More generally, voluntary pressure groups such as the National Association for the Advancement of Colored People (NAACP), the Southern Christian Leadership Conference (SCLC), and the civil rights movement also make their major contributions with this type of strategy. Included are mass political and social action, advocacy, litigation, and legislative campaigns.

Group Solidarity and Power. Programs in this category are most frequently conducted by locally based racial and ethnic groups. The approach involves an accumulation of resources and influence which raises the status and position of the group in society through increasing its political or economic power or its role in national or community decision making. Fostering ingroup identity through building a sense of a common history, culture, and destiny may be a part of this work. Self-help and cooperative ventures, such as black capitalism programs, also pertain. The contemporary Black, Brown, and Red Power movements, feminist groups, and gay liberation activities in this country embody this approach.

---

[48] This discussion essentially follows Jack Rothman and Richard A. English, "The Group Relations Field: A Conceptual Overview," in Jack Rothman, ed., *Promoting Social Justice in the Multi Group Society* (New York: Association Press with CSWE, 1971), pp. 12–28.

[49] Unlike Watson's work, the conceptualization is more impressionistic and does not emerge from a specific empirical investigation.

Intergroup Attitudes and Relationships.   This is the area that in the past has often been at the heart of group relations or human relations work. One dimension of it has to do with improving the attitudes of some groups (majority groups) toward other groups (minority groups). A wide variety of techniques has been employed toward this end—human relations workshops, encounter groups, mass media educational campaigns, personal contact activities, and the like. Another dimension pertains to conflict management through such programs as riot prevention and rumor control centers. The National Conference of Christians and Jews has historically symbolized the "brotherhood" aspects of this approach. Some other representative human relations agencies include the American Jewish Committee, American Friends Service Committee, and the Anti-Defamation League. Municipal human relations agencies also utilize these strategies in some aspects of their programming, particularly tension control.

Group Welfare.   Assuming that citizens who experience disadvantage or injustice sometimes suffer personal damage and require individualized support, some organizations provide a variety of services aimed at personal upgrading or advancement. These include vocational guidance, job training, scholarships, dissemination of information about community resources, and the provision of casework or group-work services. In the past, the National Urban League has been identified with a variety of such programs.

These four categories are not viewed as mutually exclusive; they overlap and interact with one another. Some agencies devote their full resources exclusively to one of these functions, while others pursue several of them simultaneously.

Note that we are talking about emphasis by certain agencies or programs, rather than dealing with rigid constructs. The scheme is necessarily arbitrary, but it has the advantage of being convenient for analytical purposes. By abstracting from the world of practice it attempts to reduce a highly complex, dynamic phenomenon to a level that makes it manageable for analysis.

We will next examine these four categories in terms of a number of factors related to intervention. For this purpose the following variables have been singled out as potentially useful:

1. Problem area focus.
2. Assumptions concerning causes of problems.
3. Modal strategies of change.
4. Targets of change effort.
5. Value stance.
6. Goals of change effort.
7. Typical programs.

Table 1 lists dimensions of group relations work for each of the four categories, according to these factors of intervention. Space does not allow discussion of details or explication of this table in terms of particular situations or goals. The reader can readily make such applied elaborations on the basis of the types of information provided, however. Since this material is in highly concentrated form, time should be taken to absorb and reflect on it before proceeding.

EVALUATION OF PROGRAMS

Over the years a body of literature has evolved which deals with evaluations of programs in this field, and it is useful to discuss this material briefly as a concomitant of strategy. This can best be done in terms of attitudinal (or individualistic) approaches, which generally include the categories of intergroup attitudes and relationships and group welfare, and sociostructural approaches, which are related to the categories of group rights and group solidarity and power.

Evaluations of attitude-change programs

Attitude-change programs have been subjected to more numerous, more systematic studies than have the broader structural strategies, perhaps because the research task is more delimited and manageable in this area. Various initiatives in these types of programs are listed below, and evidence is given indicating the general direction of outcomes.

Mass Media–Propaganda Programs. Mass media programs are easy enough to develop. Among specific devices that have been used are pamphlets, bulletins, fact sheets, billboards, street posters, TV programs, films, and filmstrips. Results are variable. Some studies have indicated success in the modification of attitudes through, for example, the use of films.[50] Other studies have found the converse (an actual increase in prejudice).[51]

It has been pointed out that biased individuals have an array of devices available to them to thwart the impact of antiprejudice messages, including derailing or misunderstanding the message, invalidating the message through constructing exceptions or assuming a lack of generalization of the messages, changing the frame of reference from the one intended, or finding the message too complex to deal with.[52] All-

---

[50] Russell Middleton, "Ethnic Prejudice and Susceptibility to Persuasion," *American Sociological Review,* vol. 25 (1968), pp. 679–86.

[51] Ruth C. Peterson and L. L. Thurstone, *Motion Pictures and Social Attitudes of Children* (New York: Macmillan Co., 1933).

[52] Eunice Cooper and Marie Jahoda, "The Evasion of Propaganda: How Prejudiced People Respond to Anti-Prejudice Propaganda," *The Journal of Psychology,* vol. 23 (1947), 15–25.

port's summation of evidence is cryptic: "There are grounds for doubting the effectiveness of mass propaganda as a device for controlling prejudice."[53] Those who need the message do not ordinarily go out of their way to receive it. If exposed, they can easily apply the techniques of propaganda blindness and deafness that have been trained into all of us as a way of coping with the commercial onslaught of Madison Avenue. Impressionistically, a medium such as TV can have an immense impact on the public mind. Research thus far, however, has failed to discern specific effects in turning people toward positive intergroup attitudes on the one hand or toward delinquency or violence on the other. Mass media techniques are probably most effective in reinforcing those who already have a particular disposition.

Personal Contact Programs. The personal-contact notion embodies the simple logic that when people from different groups come to know each other better they will also understand and like each other more. Again, different studies have produced differing results, in favor of the concept[54] and counter to it.[55] In surveying a wide range of literature, Vander Zanden was able to draw up a set of specific conditions under which intergroup contact is likely to foster more favorable attitudes:

1. The contact is between status or social class equals.
2. The contact situation is based on some common task, interest, or goal which is the focus of the interaction.
3. The contact is sufficiently sustained in duration and intimacy to challenge stereotypes seriously.
4. The individuals involved are reasonably secure personally and have low aggressive needs.
5. Outside reference groups provide positive support.[56]

Thus contact seems to be a feasible method when certain facilitating conditions can be optimized. On the other hand, it is not likely to work for everybody, and it assumes that some particular, already favorable tendencies exist in the situation.

Education. There is a pervasive belief abroad that increased education brings about more humane, unbiased attitudes: "Give people the facts and it will make them free"—of prejudice. One set of researchers indeed has found a negative correlation between level of education and

---

[53] Allport, *Nature of Prejudice*, p. 493.

[54] Morton Deutsch and Mary Evans Collins, *Interracial Housing* (Minneapolis: University of Minnesota Press, 1951).

[55] John Harding and Russell Hogrefe, "Attitudes of White Department Store Employees toward Negro Co-Workers," *Journal of Social Issues,* vol. 8 (1952), pp. 18–28.

[56] Vander Zanden, *American Minority Relations,* pp. 468–69.

TABLE 1

	Group rights	Group solidarity and power	Intergroup attitudes and relationships	Group welfare
Problem focus	Legal inequities Public discrimination in social institutions	Low self-esteem in minority group Low organization and psychological cohesion in minority group Low minority-group power in control of or representation in political and social institutions	Inimical attitudes in majority (prejudice, religious defamation) Intergroup tensions and hostile relations Violence—riots, extremism	Limitations in skills, resources, or cultural forms (family structure) in minority-group members Limited opportunities resulting in social, economic, educational disadvantage
Assumptions on causes of problems	Discrimination and injustice by majority group, causing legal inequities and limited opportunities	Lack of group identity, solidarity, or power within minority group Political and economic weakness Majority-group exploitation	Inappropriate, distorted majority-group attitudes Minority-group overreaction	Inadequate training or socialization in minority-group membership Limited opportunities given by majority group
Strategies of change	Conflict, contest strategies Legislative action, administrative compliance machinery, litigation, conventional legal and political activism Nonviolent pressure tactics	Mass grass-roots organizing Use of conflict (protest, militant confrontation, violence) Establishing minority institutions Training for local community leadership roles	Consensus (persuasion, mediation, educational impacts) using small groups and mass media Mediation and intergroup contact Use of workshops, conferences, institutes, mass media, written word Conjoint community problem-solving structure	Consensual approaches stressing services and expanded opportunities Education and training of minority members Persuasive interaction with target systems (industries, schools, etc.) Development of technical and social skills
Targets of change effort	Majority social institutions, legal structure in particular	Minority-group individuals, institutions and communities Overall community system and its distribution of power and status	Majority-group members majority institutions Minority-group individuals and organizations	Minority group members Some majority institutions

Value stance	Social institutions are flexible and responsive to democratic public pressure	Social structures and institutions are rigid; Institutionalized racism will only respond to extreme pressure and new power alignments	Individuals and society can change if provided with appropriate information and values on racial and ethnic matters	Individuals need aid to change so they can be more acceptable to majority or at least cope better in an unfavorable milieu
Goals of change effort	System change, middle-range change or social reform in institutions	Redistribution of power and status in society; Restructuring of institutions; Elimination of institutionalized racism	Create positive image of minority-group members; Quell disturbances and avert hostilities; Social integration	Changed minority-group persons; New policies and opportunities in majority institutions
Typical programs	Enacting fair housing ordinances, antidiscrimination laws; Compliance programs re above; School desegregation policies and programs; Voter registration programs	Establishing local mass minority-group organization, usually issue oriented—local control of schools, welfare; Training for local control; School board membership, voter registration and political participation campaigns; Formation of local business, coops, other institutions; Ethnic identity and cultural expression programs; Dealing with local utilities, banks, businesses to make them more responsive to local people	Human relations workshops and other programs—sensitivity training; Work with whites in suburbs, with blue-collar ethnic groups, with extremist groups (Birch Society, etc.); Minority ethnic coalitions, Jewish-black relations, black anti-Semitism, social mediator and negotiator roles in extreme conflict situations; Interreligious programs; Violence prevention, control, management in ghettos, high schools, colleges; Police-community relations programs; Dealing with black militant groups at colleges, high schools, communities	Employment counseling and educational guidance programs; Education of the disadvantaged child; Training programs for foremen, teachers, social workers to give better services and treatment; Work with employers in rehiring, training, promotion

prejudice;[57] others find that such results are basically related to the educated person's more subtle and sophisticated expression of prejudice, which leads to concealment.[58] The Marden and Meyer summary of the evidence is probably consistent with the opinion of most contemporary knowledgeable investigations. They conclude that the educational approach "has relatively little value in reducing discrimination or prejudice. Furthermore, recent research has tended to question the previous belief that educated people are less prejudiced than the less educated."[59]

Williams and his colleagues, in their studies, determined the prejudice of the more educated to be "harder, colder, more polite, and more thoroughly buttressed by rationalizations, but it is less likely to be global, diffuse and all or none in character."[60] The well educated may be differently prejudiced, rather than less so, as well as better armed to defend their views in intellectual terms. Education as a human relations panacea is called in question by hard scrutiny of the empirical findings.

Individual Therapy.   Assuming that prejudice is, as some observers assert, an expression of a sick mind or of deep-seated psychological needs, perhaps intensive psychotherapy measures are needed to get at the roots of the problem. Not a great deal of evidence is available on the subject. One report indicates that short-term treatment contributed little to prejudice reduction,[61] and we have scanty knowledge concerning the impact of long-term treatment. In any case, psychotherapy cannot be considered a serious means in this connection. Because of its heavy cost in time and money and the relatively small pool of trained therapists, only a small proportion of the population can be reached this way. In addition, the very people who are most prejudiced may be presumed to be among those who are the least receptive to the philosophy and methods of psychotherapy.

Group Methods.   Group methods for dealing with prejudice have come increasingly into vogue, perhaps because they include some of the purposes of individual therapy but can cover larger numbers of people. The popularity of encounter groups, Gestalt therapy, and the sensitivity training movement have spilled over into the race and ethnic field. The general effectiveness of these techniques has come under serious ques-

---

[57] Gertrude J. Selznick and Stephen Steinbert, *The Tenacity of Prejudice* (New York: Harper & Row, 1969).

[58] Charles H. Stember, *Education and Attitude Change* (New York: Institute of Human Relations Press, 1961).

[59] Marden and Meyer, *Minorities in American Society,* p. 465.

[60] Williams, *Strangers Next Door,* p. 375.

[61] David Pearl, "Psychotherapy and Ethnocentrism," *Journal of Abnormal and Social Psychology,* vol. 50 (1955), pp. 227–29.

tion in the few systematic studies made of such groups,[62] and the impact of group therapy specifically on reducing prejudicial attitudes was found in one instance to be negligible.[63] Other investigators report discernible attitude improvement following group therapy.[64] The evidence does not provide clear guidelines concerning optimum conditions for the use of this approach, and it suggests that we reserve judgement here—with a skeptical eye—until further findings have been offered.

Again, the limits of space preclude a more thorough treatment of the subject of attitude-change programs. Enough has been said and demonstrated on some salient matters in this area, however, to suggest further lines of inquiry to you.

Evaluation of sociostructural approaches

The research material in the area of sociostructural approaches to programs is in less consolidated form. Unlike social psychologists— sociologists, economists, anthropologists and those in similar disciplines have done little to codify or evaluate sociostructural strategies in a broad race and ethnic relations framework. Nevertheless, a few areas can be commented on. This may provide a useful organizing framework for considering studies which have dealt with legal and administrative methods for creating structural change on the one hand, and to studies of social movements geared to this purpose on the other.

Legal Action. Programs concerned with legal action approach the topic from two points of view: the enactment of law or policy and its later enforcement. A similar thread runs through a series of studies which has been conducted on the establishment of desegregation policies in American cities. R. J. Dwyer concluded desegregation is positively related to a clear, definite, firm administrative position.[65] Uncertain administrators seem to have brought about increased community opposition and fewer intergroup contacts within schools. Robin Williams and Margaret Ryan also found the determination of school board officials to be vital: Delay based on broad community discussion mobilized the

[62] Alan L. Mintz, "Encounter Groups and Other Panaceas," *Commentary,* vol. 56 (July 1973), pp. 42–49; Morton A. Lieberman, Irwin D. Yalom, and Mathew B. Miles, *Encounter Groups: First Facts* (New York: Basic Books, 1973).

[63] Morris L. Haimowitz and Natalie Reader Haimowitz, "Reducing Ethnic Hospitality through Psychotherapy," *Journal of Social Psychology,* vol. 31 (1950), pp. 231–41.

[64] Irwin M. Rubin, "Increased Self-Acceptance: A Means of Reducing Prejudice," *Journal of Personality and Social Psychology,* vol. 5 (1967), pp. 233–38.

[65] R. J. Dwyer, "A Report on Patterns of Interaction in Desegregated Schools," *Journal of Educational Sociology,* vol. 31 (1958), pp. 253–56.

opposition and impeded desegregation.[66] An influential paper by Kenneth Clark, reviewing available evidence, indicated that positive action is associated with decisive, unequivocal leadership which refuses to tolerate subterfuges.[67] The general implication of these findings is that in certain legal and policy areas successful adoption is associated more with the resolve and commitment of community elites than with engendering broad public awareness and participation.

The enactment of a law or policy is only a step toward objective change in given social conditions. John Slawson, a long-time observer and change agent in the human relations field, says: "A rich body of practical experience warrants the generalization that the administrative agency which would enforce a change in intergroup relations must be firm and show strength. Vacillation, uncertainty, hesitation—any appearance of weakness—not only encourages resistance, but may actually provoke it."[68] At the same time, Slawson expresses the realization that for laws to be effectively implemented they must acquire a measure of community acceptance. Hence, the enforcing agency, while demonstrating determination, should also exhibit sensitivity and utilize "social engineering in order to generate willingness to abide by the law." John Harding et al.'s review of the research data led them to concur with this conclusion: in addition to the skill and energy of the enforcing body, they note, implementation is affected by the extent of key groups such as employers or landlords, as well as by the degree of support expressed by favorable groups.[69] These suggest additional variables to be dealt with by those interested in promoting effective enforcement.

Social Movements.   Programs designed around social movements deal with collective grass-roots organizational efforts aimed at promoting greater equality. There have been a number of studies pertaining to aspects of the effectiveness of grass-roots social action groups. Evaluations of these programs are based on specific studies rather than tendencies of numerous studies, and they are expressed in terms of social movement leadership and participation by members.

The pattern of community leadership across an action system can affect social movement outcomes. One thought-provoking study is based

---

[66] Robin M. Williams, Jr., and Margaret W. Ryan, eds., *Schools in Transition: Community Experiences in Desegregation* (Chapel Hill: University of North Carolina Press, 1954).

[67] Kenneth B. Clark, "Desegregation: An Appraisal of the Evidence," *Journal of Social Issues,* vol. 9, no. 4 (1953), pp. 2–76.

[68] John Slawson, "Intergroup Relations in Social Work Education," in *Education for Social Work,* Proceedings of the Sixth Annual Program Meeting (New York: Council on Social Work Education, 1958), p. 110.

[69] Harding et al., "Prejudice and Ethnic Relations."

on a comparative investigation of civil rights leadership in 14 cities.[70] It had been previously suggested that competition among civil rights leaders tends to aid the black community's battle against segregation. Gerald McWhorter and Robert Crain found that organized competition among civil rights leaders led to intense activity but inadequate outcomes. Individual competition resulted in more sustained civil rights activities, but cities with no leadership competition seemed most capable of maintaining a disciplined drive for specific goals. Thus when a practitioner has specific social action objectives in mind he or she might work to minimize competition among relevant action groups and their leaders. Such competition presumably can be reduced through various mechanisms that enhance communication, bargaining, or coordination. When the objective is to increase the general level of activity rather than to attain specific action outcomes, then the practitioner could maintain or elevate the level of competition among groups.

Another study, by Michael Lipsky, examined the leadership of Jesse Gray in the 1963–1964 rent strikes in Harlem.[71] It concluded that in part the strike failed because competing demands for different types of leadership were placed on one man. Lipsky suggests that the requirements of key constituent groups in a social movement system frustrate such efforts. Therefore the practitioner could try to build into such movements multiple leadership capacities which are relevant to different implicated groups. The considerations he or she would take into account include the following:

1. *Organizational members.* If members of a group are deprived members of society who lack the gratifications customarily derived from joining groups, such as improved status or more money, the leader may have to adopt a militant style and promise rewards that will satisfy the members' needs for retaliation and emotional release. In the absence of immediate tangible rewards for participation, the leader will have to supply intangible incentives.

2. *Mass media appeal.* Leaders should be able to plan organizational events and public tactics with an eye to what is news to the mass media. Some of their tactics, therefore, should be dramatic, with perhaps a hint of conflict—demonstrations, sit-ins, sensational statements. In addition, leaders must cultivate relationships with reporters assigned to the or-

---

[70] Gerald A. McWhorter and Robert L. Crain, "Subcommunity Gladiatorial Competition: Civil Rights Leadership as a Competitive Process," *Social Forces,* vol. 46 (September 1967), pp. 8–21.

[71] Michael Lipsky, "Protest as a Political Resource," *American Political Science Review,* vol. 62 (December 1968), pp. 1144–58.

ganization or to the area of civil rights or social problems and attempt to meet the reporters' special needs for news.

3. *Third-party aid*. Appeals to third parties are likely to be directed to established social welfare organizations or the more conservative civil rights organizations. These appeals must consider the possible long-term relationships and interdependencies the agency or movement is likely to have with these organizations, their modes of operating (which are likely to be less sensational than those of the agency), and their penchant for careful organization and administrative details. Appeals to these groups may require the protest group or agency to adopt a more moderate leadership style (perhaps a different leader can be trained for these skills), to present less dramatic appeals, and to pay careful attention to the administrative matters that these organizations respect.

4. *The target decision-making agency*. A combination of leadership styles may be necessary to move the target decision agency the movement is seeking to influence. For example, dramatic protests involving the use of the mass media (in order to embarrass the target decision agency and provide negative publicity to which it is sensitive) could be combined with a less militant, negotiation-oriented and organizationally conscious style. The goal of such efforts is to gain the long-term rewards of admission to decision-making bodies and the continuing support of third parties.

Social movements require some degree of mass participation to sustain them and to make an impact on adversaries and governmental officials. Circumstances surrounding the various strategic approaches may affect this participation. For example, a study of the desegregation controversy in New Rochelle, New York, found that more lower-class than middle-class parents became involved in transferring their children to integrated schools.[72] Other studies had indicated that middle-class parents were more apt to aid desegregation programs. The authors of this study believe the difference is explained by the prolonged and intense controversy in New Rochelle which served to educate and mobilize the lower-class group. This period of conflict "awakened discontent of the lower stratum and set it in motion." The implication is that an atmosphere of controversy is a predisposing condition that lays the groundwork for lower-class participation in social movements.

Differential participation may be relevant in terms of various objectives and situations. A study of desegregation of public transportation in the South singled out individuals who are more likely to participate

---

[72] Elmer Lutchterhand and Leonard Weller, "Social Class and the Desegregation Movement: A Study of Parents' Decisions in a Negro Ghetto," *Social Problems,* vol. 13 (Summer 1965), pp. 83–88.

in civil rights activities in that region.[73] Persons who violated precedents by breaking patterns of segregation were to a greater degree young people (especially among the blacks), and males if white and females if black. It seems easier and less stressful in the South (at least in the past) for white males and black females to engage in activities that break castelike norms.

These studies suggest possible directions for program evaluation in the sociostructural area. They do not constitute a summary of a body of systematic evaluation literature, however.

REFINEMENTS OF STRATEGIES OF ACTION

In drawing the discussion of strategy to a conclusion, we will comment on three areas: the notion of multiple intervention, the partialing out of various types of goals, and the concept of flexibility in executing a particular strategy.

Multiple interventions

As we have indicated, the field of race and ethnic relations is extremely complex and encompasses various levels of social interaction, involving culture, personality, and structural features of the social system. Group relations problems are composed of a multifaceted and interconnected set of variables. Thus, "The student of minority-majority relations. . . . discovers that he is led, step by step, to the study of a complicated system of interlocking and mutually reinforcing patterns."[74]

It is necessary, therefore, to take a multiple-causation view of group relations issues, which leads to the conclusion that a multiple-intervention approach should be considered in planning strategy. In their study of integrated housing, Morton Deutsch and Mary Evans Collins advised a five-pronged program of amelioration: (1) a change in the politico-economic circumstances of society, (2) a change in the objective socio-economic status of minorities, (3) the elimination of specific practices of discrimination, (4) the elimination of harmful prejudicial attitudes, and (5) the enhancement of the democratic ideology in society.[75] Thus the change agent should consider the viability of drawing a number of different options among the group rights, group solidarity and power, intergroup attitudes and relationships, and group welfare orientations discussed above. Yinger's imagery is pertinent:

---

[73] Morris Davis, Robert Seibert, and Warren Breed, "Interracial Seating Patterns on New Orleans Public Transit," *Social Problems,* vol. 13 (Winter 1966), pp. 298–306.

[74] Yinger, *Minority Group in American Society,* p. 185.

[75] Deutsch and Collins, *Interracial Housing,* pp. 144–45.

A one-variable approach is likely to be as ineffective as the quarterback who knows only one play. This analogy may suggest that the combination of plays most likely to be successful depends on the opposition, that is, upon the particular situation with which one is dealing. . . . Efforts that failed in one circumstance to improve intergroup relations by education may succeed in another situation where the developments in economics, community structure, or law give them support.[76]

Though we have made a case for multiple intervention, this does not vitiate the concept of strategic planning. We are not advocating a buckshot approach which directs the practitioner to "do everything you can think of, at once, all the time." There are considerations of economy of effort (or efficiency), as well as of impact (or effectiveness). Any change agent or organization has limited time, manpower, and resources available for the various objectives being pursued. Selective, judicious application within a range of possible alternative actions is always necessary, merely on the basis of conservation of energy. With regard to effectiveness, two or more different strategies are sometimes reinforcing, sometimes mutually interfering (such as using a conflict tactic with a group in tandem with an approach that requires mutual trust). Certain targets or constituencies or institutional areas may exhibit much receptivity to a particular strategy, while others will meet it with antagonism and resistance. Entering into the latter situation when it is hopeless may be inadvisable, even though it represents use of another prong of a multifaceted set of actions. The multiple-strategy concept does not advocate barking up a lot of wrong trees.

Types of goals

We will begin this discussion with a particular issue, by way of illustration. Despite a great number of years of sustained study of the question, social science has little definite to say concerning the relationship between attitude change and behavior change. Sometimes a change in attitudes results in a change of behavior, and sometimes it does not. Sometimes a change in behavior (when required by policy or law) leads to a change in attitude, and sometimes it does not. Certainly one cannot assume that any given ethnic seminar or workshop, in the first instance, is bound to change attitudes, or that, in the second instance, if attitudes are modified, behavior change is likely to follow.

This suggests the need to consider goal clarification. The question of short-range vs. long-range goals surfaces, as well as the question of instrumental and end-state goals. In a particular intervention situation, is the primary objective of the change agent to modify attitudes or to change behavior? Is one seen as a medium for later impact on the

---

[76] Yinger, *Minority Group in American Society*, p. 186.

other? For example, is education necessary in order to attain open-housing legislation, or should one aim directly at enactment of the legislation? On the other hand, open-housing conditions may be necessary in order to make certain kinds of intergroup education possible. Applying this type of question to another area, we can consider whether separatist minority action is an objective in its own right or a short-term goal, with minority ingroup solidarity forming the basis for more meaningful coalitions and a more distant objective of an integrated society. These kinds of clarifications are important to the promotion of effective effort.

Flexibility in strategy

Establishing a program or a course of action should, of course, be based on available information and careful inferences concerning cause-effect relationships. Therefore, a degree of confidence and drive in carrying out actions is both appropriate and useful. At the same time, it is important to avoid becoming frozen in attachment to a given course of action. New and better information may present itself, conditions may change, mistakes may be recognized. The willingness to redesign planned actions is as important in successful change agentry as meticulous planning at the outset.

It is useful to have the capability to move in a particular direction, say group rights or group welfare, and to shift from one to the other as circumstances warrant. It is difficult to predict with certainty the racial and ethnic shape of America in the period ahead. Because of the shifting contours of the social scene, one cannot precisely forecast avenues of forward movement and sources of resistance and repression. Whether a general strategy of integration or separatism would be most fruitful for various minorities and the society as a whole is a matter of conjecture. Therefore, it seems logical on this question, as well as others, to take a developmental approach and keep the strategic options fluid.

CONCLUDING NOTE

This concludes our discussion of the conceptual frame of reference we set out to develop as an aid to considering the issues that will be presented in this book. We have not provided a formula for this consideration or a single, simplistic point of view. The burden of reflection, evaluation, and choice rests with the reader, his or her fellow students and teachers. The importance of that process cannot be overestimated. In the realm of race and ethnic relations many fundamental questions have been raised concerning the extent of social injustice, oppression, and inhumaneness in American society. The stability, the safety, and the basic moral integrity of the nation may depend on how these are answered.

Chapter 2

EQUALITY OF OPPORTUNITY VERSUS PREFERENTIAL TREATMENT

A. Introduction

Equality of opportunity has been the hallmark of the civil rights movement over the years. The phrase conveys the idea of removing barriers to upward mobility by eliminating discriminatory practices and substituting a posture of color-blind, scrupulous impartiality. The call has been to let individual merit and achievement be the standard for advancement in society.

This meritocracy notion places overriding emphasis on individual worth and ability. It values achieved status (based on the individual's concrete performance level) as compared to ascribed status (based on the relative position of the groups into which an individual is born, such as class, race, sex, and nationality). The main thrust of civil libertarian effort in this country has been to eliminate group criteria for gaining status, because by such standards privilege has been conferred by tradition, rather than being achieved through mobility that comes from fair and open competition.

More recently, these philosophical assumptions have been brought under question. Equality of opportunity, it is argued, provides even access in a social context that is basically unequal. The game is played under rules whereby some individuals and groups start with a severe handicap, acquired as a result of the oppression and injustice to which they have been subjected historically. Consequently, it is asserted, they will not be able to catch up under prevailing circumstances if they are merely given improved chances. The accumulated disadvantages in economic resources, educational attainment, and political power conspire to freeze conditions of inequity. In this view, a fundamental level of equity restoration must precede the opening up of opportunities. The structural situation itself should be changed initially, to ensure that equality of opportunity will result in equality of outcome. In addition, the idea of commutative justice or indemnification has been proposed; this idea suggests that reparations should be used as a way of compensating exploited populations for the injuries suffered over the centuries and to make up for the unfair prerogatives that have been enjoyed by majority groups. The general rationale for this position is presented by James Bolner in the first article in this chapter, "Toward a Theory of Racial Reparations."

While basically in agreement with policies favorable to minorities, Neil Gilbert and Joseph Eaton, in "Favoritism as a Strategy in Race Relations," also acknowledge the difficulties that can be encountered in implementing compensatory programs. Some obvious issues quickly come to mind. Qualified majority persons who are bypassed by minority individuals may suffer a personal abuse of their own civil liberties. Such individuals may claim that an unjust burden has been imposed on them because they personally are forced to bear more than their proportional share for society's past failures. Backlash political reactions from members of the majority may be invoked, with detrimental results. It also may be an undesirable precedent to elevate ascribed status above achieved status as a standard of mobility, since in the long run this can easily be used as a weapon against vulnerable minorities, as it has been recurrently in the past. Further, in the short run productivity or efficiency in society may suffer if criteria of merit are set aside in implementing this approach.

It is also suggested that preferential treatment as an approach involves minor tinkering with the economic inequities of the system. Minorities at the bottom of the economic structure (blacks, Chicanos, Puerto Ricans) vie for a position with other minorities (Jews, Irish, Italians) who have only recently struggled up into the middle class. Meanwhile, comprehensive redistribution of wealth is sidetracked, and economic elites escape responsibility for helping to correct racial injustice, of which they are the major beneficiaries.

The rejoinder to this argument, as expressed by Bolner, asks the question: In the absence of immediate compensatory programs, how long will it take for racial and ethnic minorities to overcome the debilitating scars of accumulated disadvantage?

Three distinct points of departure for institutionalizing the concept of racial justice can be discerned. First is equality of opportunity, which postulates the removal of discriminatory barriers to individual mobility. The second, more aggressive approach of Bolner is referred to by Gilbert and Eaton as "discrimination in reverse." This approach attempts to provide compensation for disadvantaged minority groups through such group-oriented policies as racial quotas and reparations.

A third approach is Gilbert and Eaton's more moderate position, which can be designated "preferential treatment." In popular usage, it should be noted, quota arrangements frequently also are referred to in these terms. This middle position is close to equality of opportunity in that individual achievement is an important consideration, but group membership factors are part of a range of criteria rather than the overriding criterion. The middle position is an escalated form of equality of opportunity, an invigorated approach to affirmative action. It may entail such procedures as intensive recruiting in minority communities for qualified personnel, crash training and upgrading programs, and the allocation of given numbers of positions to be filled by qualified minority members when they can be recruited or trained. Like the quota arrangement, this approach entails favoritism, but standards of individual performance remain firm and prominent in balance with the criterion of group affiliation. It might be said that the Bolner approach represents a group solidarity and power strategy, while Gilbert and Eaton lean toward a group-rights strategy (see Chapter 1).

This issue of advancement for minorities has been considered in the past mainly in relation to hiring and admissions policies. Its counterpart in times of economic hardship concerns policies for dismissing people from jobs when retrenchment is required. Advocates of affirmative action take the view that minorities and women should be the last fired, even if the last hired. The position is that the gains achieved in recent minority hiring will be washed away if seniority rules are followed during retrenchment. It is argued that only recently have new laws and procedures enabled minorities to move advantageously into the employment stream. If traditional seniority rules are followed, these groups will be the most immediately and the most seriously affected. In this instance, affirmative action ideals which favor social justice for ethnic and racial minorities clash philosophically with values of fairness and orderliness reflected in seniority policies which have been developed by trade unions to protect the workingman.

Not only are complex philosophical differences invoked in this issue, but legal and administrative differences as well. While HEW presses universities and other institutions toward firmer and stronger policies of affirmative action,[1] a black law firm in Detroit defends a white against reverse discrimination by a black radio station, and in Connecticut the state Human Rights and Opportunities Commission orders that a white coach replace a black at a ghetto high school because the latter was unfairly favored in the hiring process.

Important crosscurrents of the controversy are revealed in the De Funis case, which was the first test of these matters before the Supreme Court. Marco De Funis, Jr., a *magna cum laude* and Phi Beta Kappa graduate of the University of Washington (with a 3.62 average on a 4-point scale), was denied admission to the law school of that institution in 1971. Of the 150 applicants who were admitted in the class, there was included a quota of 44 minority students. Six of this group had overall records better than that of De Funis, but the remaining 38 had records that were not as good.

The law school conceded it placed blacks and other racial minority applicants in a separate group from whites, evaluating their grades and test scores against one another rather than against the remaining appli-

---

[1] Paul Seabury, "HEW and the Universities," *Commentary,* vol. 35 (February 1972), pp. 38–44.

cants. This assured a basic minimum of minority admissions in any entering class. All the minority applicants were rated as "deprived," while no attempt was made to similarly evaluate the economic position of white applicants, according to De Funis.

De Funis filed suit in Washington Superior Court charging that he had been denied equal protection of the law, guaranteed by the 14th Amendment. The court ruled that indeed he had been discriminated against by the law school quota system, and it ordered the school to enroll him. The state Supreme Court, however, reversed the decision, maintaining that the school has the prerogative of determining whether the general quality of its program would be improved by the inclusion of a larger percentage of minority students. Weighing race as a factor in admissions, according to this reasoning, is responsive to educational questions rather than constituting an arbitrary or capricious consideration.

It is interesting to note that in early 1974 a coalition group of Jews, Italians, and Poles filed a brief *amici curiae* in support of De Funis, claiming that the university's action violated the equal protection clause and indicating that the approach was unsound from a more general social policy standpoint. The brief held that young people from minority groups should be helped and encouraged to prepare for professional careers, but they should be expected to meet the academic standards demanded of other applicants. Assistance to minorities, according to the coalition, should consist of affirmative action programs which include such features as recruitment, remedial services, open enrollment for high school graduates, and summer institutes.

When the United States Supreme Court issued a judgment in April of 1974, its decision was on narrow, technical points of law rather than in terms of the substantive issues involved in the case. De Funis was no longer an applicant to a law school, said the Court, but a person who had made suitable arrangements to complete his law training; therefore the case was moot. Thus the basic questions remain unresolved from a legal standpoint. It can be sensed that the Court, recognizing this to be a highly charged social controversy dividing the nation, preferred to put off a legal solution until the matter had achieved a greater degree of resolution through normal political and social processes of accommodation.

A philosophical predisposition toward the alternatives could be predicated, in part, on an assessment of current trends in the economic and social sphere, together with a judgment concerning the extent to which equality of opportunity as a policy can alone bring about desired outcomes—and within what time frame. These are empirical matters which involve analysis of factual data and a projection of trends. A representative study is presented here which provides entree into such an assessment: "Differential Trends toward Equality between Whites and Non-whites," by Erdman Palmore and Frank J. Whittington, which deals with long-range economic factors. Their conclusions seem to lie in the middle range among forecasters; they see considerable equality coming about, perhaps in one generation (30–40 years), but with unevenness among the different spheres. For example, equality in educational levels may take almost a century to achieve. A similar type of study by Stanley Lieberson and Glen Fuguitt envisions a longer time frame, in the order of several generations, as necessary before racial parity in the labor force can be reached.[2] A considerably more optimistic appraisal than either of these, recounting dramatic gains *already* made by minorities, has been offered in a widely circulated and much debated statement by Ben Wattenberg and Richard Scammon.[3]

From a programmatic standpoint, one practical action recommendation is for a rigorous public policy approach through legislative processes to improve the employment situation of minorities. J. K. Galbraith, Edwin Kuh, and Lester G. Thurow suggest such a Minorities Advancement Plan in "Toward Greater Minority Employment." (Reproduced here.) A different type of action is represented by the voluntary programs and procedures that can be instituted in private industry, as summarized in an article by Fred Johnson.[4]

Consideration of specific employment practices in industry may be important in the light of findings that to some degree discriminatory practices in industrial and commercial enterprises are unintentional, and lower-level personnel have often misinterpreted and misapplied management antidiscrimination policies. Americans seem to accept integration in the area of employment to a greater degree than in other social spheres, such as the neighborhood, and this makes it a more likely area for immediate gains.

These types of programs can be assessed in relation to the background materials presented in the first parts of the chapter. What philosophical assumptions do affirmative action programs reflect? Are they responsive to the research data? Is the action affirmative *enough?* What strategies and specific action steps might need to be developed to have programs or policies adopted, or effectively implemented, nationally or in a given community or organization? Answers to these types of queries represent the cutting edge of at least short-run progress toward equality.

---

[2] Stanley Lieberson and Glen V. Fuguitt, "Negro White Occupational Differences in the Absence of Discrimination," *American Journal of Sociology,* vol. 73 (September 1967), pp. 188–200.

[3] Ben J. Wattenberg and Richard M. Scammon, "Black Progress and Liberal Rhetoric," *Commentary,* vol. 55 (April 1973), pp. 35–44.

[4] Fred Johnson, "Recruiting, Retaining and Advancing Minority Employees," *Training and Development Journal,* January 1972, pp. 28–31.

B. Theoretical and philosophical considerations

JAMES BOLNER

Toward a theory of racial reparations

One of the chief concerns of contemporary public law in the United States is also one of the most ancient—the treatment of nonwhite minorities, especially the Negro minority. During the major portion of the post-slavery period the "liberal" ideal in treatment of Negroes has been "nondiscrimination."[1] There are few, if any, indications that this policy is proving successful in assimilating Negroes into the social order. The successor to nondiscrimination is benign racial treatment, and it is this policy which this paper explores. Specifically, the essay examines certain aspects of the attempt to render legitimate and orderly the assimilation of Negroes through benign racial treatment of them. A sketch of a theory of racial reparations and the major criticisms of the approach are examined and, finally, the prospects for racial reparations programs are surveyed.

TWO JUSTIFICATIONS OF RACIAL REPARATIONS

Reparations in the sense used here denotes benefits extended in various forms to those injured by racial discrimination practiced by, or with the acquiescence of, the government of a representative democracy. Reparations are not to be understood as an indiscriminate bonus for nonwhites, but merely as payment of damages to those nonwhites who have been injured by racial discrimination.[2] Claims advanced by a nonwhite resident of a jurisdiction which has observed a policy of nondiscrimination should be viewed in a different light from claims pressed

---

Source: *Phylon,* vol. 29 (1968), pp. 41–47. Phylon, Atlanta University, Atlanta, Georgia.

[1] In support of this proposition see Vern Countryman (ed.), *Discrimination and the Law* (Chicago, 1965) and Robert J. Harris, *The Quest for Equality* (Baton Rouge, 1960).

[2] One may consider the government extending reparations to be upholding the conditions of the "social compact" by compensating parties whose terms of agreement have been violated. For an elaboration of this aspect of social compact theory see Joseph Tussman, *Obligation and the Body Politic* (New York, 1960), especially Chap. 1.

by a resident, say, of Alabama. It would seem untenable to assume that a nonwhite, regardless of how successful he seems to be in life, has not been injured by discrimination. Neither are we suggesting a sophisticated retaliation against living white persons for the misdeeds of their ancestors.

A quite different approach—one which perhaps is more persuasive —must now be considered: reparations extended to minority groups humiliated or injured in the past is a simple way out of a nasty problem. Justice in this connection is a bonus. The interest in civil order, public tranquility and public peace is considered so great that it is permissible to single out individuals on the basis of their race where social malaise is demonstrably associated with that group. Assuming that social and economic disorder is chronically associated with a particular racial group, one may argue that the community may employ race as a criterion in breaking the vicious cycle. On this rationale, integration, or the deliberate bringing together of individuals because of their race, is considered good since it contributes to the general welfare in the broadest sense. The use of racial criteria to separate individuals and groups, the argument continues, is sometimes bad and sometimes good, depending on the circumstances. What proportion of the racial mix to prescribe would depend on the circumstances.[3] There will be those, of course, who will recommend benign racial treatment of minority group members precisely because it seems to buy racial peace at the same time that it gives nonwhites their due. A federal district judge approximated this position when he noted:

> It is neither just nor sensible to proscribe segregation having its basis in affirmative state action while at the same time failing to provide a remedy for segregation which grows out of discrimination in housing, or other economic or social factors.[4]

A CRITIQUE OF THE THEORY

At the outset two objections can be anticipated. The first concerns constitutional color blindness; if the first Mr. Justice Harlan's felicitous phrase, "Our constitution is color blind,"[5] were taken to bar any and all

---

[3] See Owen M. Fiss, "Racial Imbalance in the Public Schools: The Constitutional Concepts," *Harvard Law Review,* LXXVIII (January, 1965), 571; Robert F. Drinan, "Racially Balanced Schools: Psychological and Legal Aspects," *Catholic Lawyer,* II (Winter, 1965), 16; Robert L. Carter, "De Facto School Segregation. An Examination of the Legal and Constitutional Questions Presented," *Western Reserve Law Review,* XVI (May, 1965), 502; and *Morean* v. *Board of Education,* 210 A. 2d 97 (1964).

[4] *Barksdale* v. *Springfield School Committee,* 237 F. Supp. 543, 546 (1965).

[5] *Plessy* v. *Ferguson,* 163 U.S. 537, 559 (1896).

treatment on the basis of race, then the country would be deftly laced into a constitutional straitjacket and prevented from dealing with a major social problem. The remarks which follow assume that the Constitution permits racial treatment save where such treatment is oppressive. The second objection is that any reparations program is by definition a show of preference to nonwhites. In one sense, benign treatment on racial grounds does not mean adverse treatment for certain individuals (in the present case these are whites) with whom they compete; when persons compete for housing, jobs, or school assignments, there will be winners and losers. But rigging the process so as to make whites the automatic losers can best be explained by saying that whites here are being called upon to assist the community in meeting its obligation. That the disappointed white applicants may never have inflicted racial injury is not a relevant consideration. It is not a case of "an eye for an eye," but a case of doing one's duty in setting aright a community wrong. It is difficult to see how an approach which would treat whites as having been deprived of their rights can provide a satisfactory and realistic point of departure.

Now let us assume that a political regime embarks on a thoroughgoing racial program based on either the reparations or the buying peace foundations. What happens to the keystone principle of the humanitarian credo: treat each individual on his intrinsic merits and not on the basis of the accident of color? While it might be more conducive to the public order, is racial integration less violative of public morality than racial segregation? If barring nonwhites from "private" public places and housing and "private" employment is offensive to good morals because it rests on an accidental factor such as color, and if the essence of the wrong is the refusal to treat them like everyone else, is it permissible to base a decision on the same accidental factor in granting them benefits? It would seem that in discriminating in favor of the individual the individual may be gleeful during the entire operation, but moral injury would be perpetrated just the same. (One may also suggest that benign racial treatment of nonwhites is a substitution of a community paternalism for the paternalism of a former "master"; on this basis benign racial treatment ought to be as offensive as the post-slavery dependency of Negroes upon their former masters, since it implies a judgment of racial inferiority.)

Treatment on the basis of race, as an attempt will be made to show below, is not per se indefensible; the worthiness of the objective is a salient consideration. Nevertheless, it is not a pretty business, for there remains the implication of inherent racial inferiority of the minority group members; nonwhites' "special characteristics and circumstances" (analogous to those of physically handicapped or neurotic persons) are found to be occasioned by racial differences parallel to "physiological, psychological or sociological variances from the norm occasioned by other factors."[6]

A most forceful judicial statement critical of benign racial treatment was set forth by Judge Van Voorhis in his dissenting opinion in a recent New York case upholding the principle.[7] Said the judge:

> Where is the line to be drawn between allocating persons by law to schools or other institutions or facilities according to color to promote integration, and doing the same thing in order to promote segregation? Is the underlying principle not the same in either instance? Both depend on racism. If one is legally justifiable, then so is the other. . . .[8]

The argument that benign racial treatment would "force governmental authorities to re-enter the field of racial classification,"[9] cannot be lightly dismissed. Today the governmental attitude might be sympathetic only to benign racial laws, but tomorrow the result might well be different. Consider the best known example of a justifiable use of race by government: the *Japanese Exclusion Cases*[10] decided during World War II. There the Court sanctioned military orders employing race as a criterion for segregating Japanese-Americans from allegedly "more loyal" citizens. In attacking the majority's deference to military expediency, Justice Murphy declared that "racial discrimination" in any form and in any degree had no justifiable part whatever in our democratic way of life."[11] In even stronger language Justice Jackson accused the majority of sanctioning "the principle of racial discrimination . . . and of transplanting American citizens." That principle, he argued:

> . . . then lies about like a loaded weapon ready for the hand of an urgent need. Every repetition imbeds that principle more deeply in our

---

[6] See *Springfield School Committee* v. *Barksdale,* 348 F. 2d 261, 266 (1965).

[7] *Allen* v. *Hummel,* 258 N.Y.S. 2d 77 (1965).

[8] Ibid., p. 82. Continued Van Voorhis: "There is an important difference between obliterating the color line by admitting a boy or girl or man or woman to school, to employment, to a residential location or to a place of public accommodation without regard to color, and allocating people to locations, employments or facilities because of their color . . . It is one thing to insist that a person should not be excluded by law from a vocation, school, theatre, hotel, restaurant or public conveyance because of race; it is quite another matter and, as it seems to me, doing the reverse, to allocate these advantages according to racial quotas or on some other proportional basis."

[9] John Kaplan, "Segregation Litigation and the Schools—*Part II:* The General Northern Problem," *Northwestern University Law Review,* LIII (May–June, 1963), 188. See also the dissenting opinion by Moore, Circuit Judge, in *Taylor* v. *Board of Education,* 294 F. 2d 36, 40.

[10] *Hirabayshi* v. *United States,* 320 U.S. 81 (1943) and *Korematsu* v. *United States,* 323 U.S. 214 (1944). See Eugene V. Rostow, "The Japanese-American Cases—a Disaster," *Yale Law Journal,* LIV (June, 1945), 489.

[11] *Korematsu* v. *United States,* 323 U.S. 214, 242 (1944).

law and thinking and expands it to new purposes. All who observe the work of courts are familiar with what Judge Cardozo described as the tendency of a principle to expand itself to the limit of its logic.[12]

Even in the 1955 decree in *Brown* v. *Board of Education*[13] the Supreme Court spoke of "public schools [administered on a racially nondiscriminatory basis]"[14] as the goal toward which it was striving. In the companion case of *Bolling* v. *Sharpe*[15] in which the *Brown* was applied to the District of Columbia, the Court specifically said: "Classifications based solely upon race must be scrutinized with particular care, since they are contrary to our traditions and hence constitutionally suspect."[16] Indeed, it would seem that the Supreme Court and federal courts generally were unaware that benign racial programs would be needed or forthcoming. In any event, it is clear that it is as easy to extract support for such programs from the school desegregation litigation as it is to find, in the same place, absolute condemnations of the use of race as a criterion by public authority.

It would seem that if an ethnic minority's reparations claims can never be met on the basis of ethnic differences, then the damage would go unrepaired. If the wrong consists in using race as a criterion, it would seem curious to repair the damage with more of the same. Yet, the injured individuals are identifiable solely by their ethnic traits. A way out has been suggested above. In order for the community to make reparations to injured members of a racial minority, it must use factors other than race. The community must be attributed a duty to extend reparations to all injured by governmental action or inaction before reparations for racial injuries may be justified. ("Community" injury to American Indians and the poor, and the victims of crime come to mind.) Proponents of benign racial treatment may contend that their claim deserves high priority because of the gravity of the community's offense. The approach is appealing, since individuals are not being compensated because they are members of a racial minority, but simply because they were injured and the community considers itself responsible. The relevant questions then become: what constitutes racial injury and how may persons so injured be afforded benign racial treatment.

It is only possible here to suggest how such questions may be answered. The definition of *racial injury* could be prescribed by statute,

---

[12] Ibid., 246, citing Benjamin Cardozo, *The Nature of the Judicial Process* (New Haven, 1921), p. 51.

[13] 349 U.S. 294 (1955).

[14] Ibid., 301.

[15] 347 U.S. 497 (1954).

[16] Ibid., p. 499. The Court cited as authority the *Korematsu* and *Hirabayshi* cases (see note 10 above).

or left to emerge from the body of rules created by the adjudicating agency, subject, of course, to modification by statute. Very probably a case by case approach would be necessary. The form benign racial treatment would take would pose certain problems. Where simple racial discrimination is involved it is possible to redress grievances by declaring discriminatory acts amenable to the judicial process; where racial identification is to be followed by treatment on a racial basis, the problem is different.[17] Once minority group members can no longer claim that they are being denied access to education, public accommodation, employment, the political process, and housing because of their race their claims become blurred. It cannot be argued, at least not convincingly, that nonwhites should be given a handicap in the courtroom by barring witnesses from appearing for their adversaries, or that nonwhites should be given two votes while majority group members have only one. Indeed, if direct cash payments or tax benefits are ruled out, the areas in which compensation for racial injury are plausible are limited to those in which such programs are physically practicable. The chief areas are housing, education and employment; these are the very areas which seem to loom large in the mind of the policy planner as he searches for racial peace.

THE FUTURE OF RACIAL REPARATIONS

The prospects for full-fledged racial reparations programs brighten with the increase in the incidence of racial disturbances and with the increase of the political strength of nonwhites. To proponents of such programs, the passage of the 1964 Civil Rights Act[18] and the 1965 Voting Rights Act[19] seems a logical step to the enactment of reparations programs. The thrust of the 1964 and 1965 legislation, however, was largely directed against the values of Southern whites; the support of the non-Southern public for the housing provisions of the proposed Civil Rights Act of 1966[20] was less than overwhelming. If the federal executive and legislative branches decide on a policy of racial reparations, however, there are indications that the judiciary would erect no obstacles in their path.[21]

---

[17] This is the course followed in Titles II and VII of the Civil Rights Act of 1964, 78 Stat., 241, and in Title IV (Housing) of the proposed Civil Rights Act of 1966 (see H.R. 14765 and S. 3296, 89th Cong. 2nd Sess). The technique of the 1965 Voting Rights Act, 79 Stat. 437, whereby Negroes disfranchised arbitrarily in the past may be summarily placed on the voting rolls is somewhat different.

[18] 78 Stat. 247.

[19] 79 Stat. 437.

[20] See H.R. 14766 and S. 3296, 89th Cong. 2d sess.

[21] For some insights as to why state and local antidiscrimination laws are ineffective see Duane Lockard, "The Politics of Antidiscrimination Legislation,"

The national commerce power seems to be an inexhaustible source of federal authority. The federal government has effectively preempted regulation of labor relations. Where dwellings are constructed with materials and by persons obviously involved in activities affecting interstate commerce, can there be any doubt that legislation barring the creation of nonwhite concentrations would be upheld?[22] The constitutional rationale for reparations legislation has already been suggested by the Supreme Court in its 1964 opinions in the *Civil Rights Cases*.[23]

Moreover, it is significant that the Supreme Court has sanctioned the use of race in administering public programs so long as the use was for a "good" purpose. While the Court has relied on its 1954 *Brown* v. *Board*[24] precedent in overturning racial segregation in a variety of public endeavors,[25] in 1961 the Court let stand (by denying *certiorari*) a lower federal court ruling compelling local authorities to take corrective steps to balance the schools' nonwhite and white populations.[26] In 1964 the Court let stand another ruling asserting that no one has a constitutional right to attend a racially balanced school.[27] Apparently the Justices were satisfied that Gary, Indiana, public schools were operated

---

Harvard Journal on Legislation, III (December, 1965), 3; Michael I. Sovern, *Legal Restraints on Racial Discrimination in Employment* (New York, 1966), Chap. 2; and Herbert Hill, "Racial Inequality in Employment: The Patterns of Discrimination," *The Annals,* 1957 (January, 1965), 30. Testifying before the House Judiciary Committee in support of H.R. 14765, the Attorney General of the United States noted that "some seventeen states, the District of Columbia, Puerto Rico, the Virgin Islands, and a large number of municipalities" had enacted fair housing laws. The work of volunteer groups, judicial and executive action, and the "patchwork of state and local laws" were found inadequate. Department of Justice, "Statement by Attorney General Nicholas de B. Katzenbach," May 4, 1966.

[22] For an enlightening treatment of this point see Boris I. Bittker, "The Case of the Checker-Board Ordinance: An Experiment in Race Relations," *Yale Law Journal,* LXXI (July, 1962), 1387. *Mulkey* v. *Reitman,* 50 Cal. Rptr. 881, 413 P. 2d 825 (1966), gives a summary of the open housing controversy in California; for a survey of the open housing controversy in Michigan see Normal C. Thomas, *Rule 9: Politics, Administration, and Civil Rights* (New York, 1966).

[23] *Heart of Atlanta Motel* v. *United States,* 397 U.S. 241 (1964); *Katzenbach* v. *McClung,* 397 U.S. 274 (1964).

[24] 347 U.S. 483 (1954).

[25] *Baltimore* v. *Dawson,* 220 F. 2d 386, *aff'd.* 350 U.S. 877 (1955), (public beaches and bathhouses); *Holmes* v. *Atlanta,* 233 F. 2d 93, *aff'd.* 350 U.S. 879 (1955) (golf course); *Gayle* v. *Browder,* 142 F. Supp. 707, *aff'd.* 352 U.S. 903 (1956) (city buses); *New Orleans Park Improvement Assn.* v. *Detiege,* 252 F. 2d 122, *aff'd.* 358 U.S. 54 (1958) (public park facilities). See also the cases cited by Clark, J., in *Goss* v. *Board of Education,* 373 U.S. 683, 687–688 (1963).

[26] *Taylor* v. *Board of Education,* 191 F. Supp. 181, *aff'd.* 294 F, 2d 36, *cert.* denied, 368 U.S. 940 (1961).

[27] *Bell* v. *School City of Gary,* 213 F. Supp. 819, *aff'd.* 324 F. 2d 209 (1963), *cert.* denied, 377 U.S. 924 (1964). See John Kaplan, "Segregation Litigation and the Schools—Part II: The Gary Litigation," *Northwestern University Law Review,* LIX (May–June, 1964), 121.

on a "neighborhood school plan, honestly and conscientiously con-structed and with no intention or purpose to segregate the races."[28] Later in 1964 the Court refused to review a New York state court decision upholding the authority of state officials to take steps to correct racial imbalance by rearranging school attendance zones.[29] In March, 1965, the *Gary* principle was reaffirmed as the Court concurred in a lower federal court's approval of "honest" neighborhood schools in Kansas City, Kansas, despite the resulting racial imbalance.[30] At the opening of its 1965 Term the Court once again endorsed New York's deliberate use of race as a factor in administering its schools; the Court declined to review a state court ruling that state officials were not acting "arbitrarily or illegally" in taking steps to correct racial imbalance in public schools.[31] In none of these cases has the Supreme Court written an opinion, but the constitutional rule seems to be as follows: while members of racial minorities have no constitutional right to attend racially balanced (or even integrated) schools, state authorities may use race as a criterion in administering the educational system (presumably to achieve racial balance or integration, but not to achieve segregation).

If public authority may use race as a criterion in providing quality, integrated education, it would seem that parallel steps in the housing and employment areas would be permissible. Laws guaranteeing integrated neighborhoods by limiting nonwhite concentrations to certain quotas and providing incentives to attract whites into nonwhite neighborhoods would seem beyond constitutional reproach. To require employers to hire a certain percentage of nonwhites (say, corresponding to the local or national nonwhite percentage of the labor force) would seem equally defensible.

SUMMARY AND CONCLUSIONS

Members of racial minorities have a justifiable claim to reparations from the community which has either participated, directly or indirectly, or acquiesced in racial discrimination. If one accepts the principle that individuals should be treated on their merits and not on the basis of color, then racial treatment, whether benign or adverse, is inconsistent

---

[28] 313 F. Supp. 819, 823 (1963).

[29] *Balabin* v. *Rubin*, 248 N.Y.S. 2d 574, *aff'd.* 250 N.Y.S. 2d 281, 199 N. E. 2d 375, *cert.* denied, 379 U.S. 881 (1964).

[30] *Downs* v. *Board of Education*, 336 F. 2d 988 (1964). Justice Douglas was of the opinion that *certiorari* should have been granted.

[31] *Vetere* v. *Mitchell*, 251 N.Y.S. 2d 480 (1965), *aff'd.* in *Allen* v. *Hummel*, 258 N.Y.S. 2d 77 (1965), *cert.* denied in *Vetere* v. *Allen*, 86 S. Ct. 60 (1965); *Addabbo* v. *Donovan*, 256 N.Y.S. 2d 178, *cert.* denied, 86 S. Ct. 241 (1965).

with this principle. However, the community may proceed to extend reparations in the form of special treatment, in such areas as housing, employment, and education to individuals injured by racial discrimination. The implementation of reparations programs by the executive and legislative branches of the central government would probably not be blocked on constitutional grounds by the judiciary.

NEIL GILBERT and JOSEPH W. EATON

Favoritism as a strategy in race relations

Social policies of favoritism are among the strategies used to compensate people for socioeconomic disadvantages suffered due to racial discrimination. The range is from preferential treatment to discrimination-in-reverse. In the former the emphasis is on equity restoration; in the latter on indemnification. Preferential treatment and discrimination-in-reverse vary in their effect on potential beneficiaries, their technical qualifications, and their self-perception. Socially sanctioned favoritism is a relatively new approach in the area of race relations. The subject is inherently sensitive. Research data concerning the impact of these policies on individuals and the society are sparse. In the absence of such findings, a number of plausible propositions are presented to stimulate empirically tested comparisons between these two policies in terms of their possible social consequences as well as on the individuals who are affected.

The ideal of equal opportunity is gaining in universal acceptance, but not without competition from other persuasive ideals which give normative sanction to inequality. In-group loyalty, kinship, localism, the "school tie" spirit, and manifestations of responsibility for mutual aid which most persons acquire for those of "their kind" support many traditional and legal barriers to equality. In every country there are people who encounter limited opportunities because of their nationality, their religion, their occupation, or their lack of the proper "clan" antecedents, along with other of the numerous distinctions that men have created and magnified to differentiate among groups. Freud (1926:61) characterized such social caste phenomena as "narcissism of minor differences."

Invidious group distinctions based upon race are particularly difficult to counteract. Family names and religious practices can be changed or obscured with relative ease. Residence requirements can be met, given enough time. Accents and mannerisms, while harder to divest immediately, can be altered by the second generation. Racial discrimination is not so easily mitigated by social camouflage or the passage of time.

Note: This article is a follow-up of ideas first published by Joseph W. Eaton and Neil Gilbert in "Racial Discrimination and Diagnostic Differentiation," in *Race, Research, and Reason,* ed. Roger Miller (New York: National Association of Social Workers, 1967), pp. 79–88.

Source: *Social Problems,* vol. 18 (June 1970), pp. 38–52. By permission of The Society for the Study of Social Problems, and the authors.

Civil rights legislation in the mid 1950's brought about intensified public efforts to eliminate racial barriers to equal opportunity. These laws have been able to effectuate only limited gains in areas such as housing, education, and employment. In many instances, implementation of legal mandates has been sluggish. In addition, legal means, no matter how vigorously enforced, cannot undo overnight the accumulated disadvantages which have accrued due to past discrimination. There is evidence that many medical schools have indeed abolished racial quotas that were once imposed. But minority under-representation in medical school applications and acceptances will continue for at least a decade if there are barriers to good academic preparation of disadvantaged students in the lower grades. There are no instant solutions to many of the consequences of past discrimination. In light of this harsh reality, the enactment of non-impartial social policies to compensate those who have suffered the injustices and debilitating effects of outcast status is advocated.

Such compensatory policies are defended as necessary to bring about an equity restoration and as the quickest way to produce equality in the near future. The theory is that groups which have, for generations, been starved of education, skills, and self-respect cannot be expected to compete successfully with those who have consumed an ample supply of these commodities, simply by the introduction of an equal diet of social opportunity. According to this theory, equal opportunity will not produce equal results. Something more is needed. As Titmuss (1968: 159) explains:

> The problem, then, is not whether to differentiate in access, treatment, giving, and outcome but how to differentiate. What factors are or are not relevant? How in some respects can we treat equals unequally and in other respects unequals equally?

And how can this be accomplished without stigma? These questions provide a backdrop for examining the characteristics and consequences of two models of compensatory non-impartial social policies, preferential treatment and discrimination-in-reverse.

Preferential treatment: A social policy in compensation for past services, past or present injustices, or handicaps, whereby affiliation with a group of victims is included as one of the relevant criteria given positive weight in determining the allocation of services, opportunities, and resources.

Discrimination-in-reverse: A social policy in compensation for past services, past or present injustices, or handicaps, whereby the allocation of services, opportunities, and resources is based primarily upon group affiliation, to the exclusion or subordination of technically relevant criteria for determining such allocations.

Compensatory policies to counteract the effects of past discrimination vary in the respective weight assigned to the values of indemnification and equality. The range is from preferential treatment to discrimination-in-reverse. These ideal type concepts may be easily confused because both advocate favoritism.[1] They require that a designated low status person or group be given advantages as a matter of social policy in the competition for services, resources, and opportunities. In the abstract, such special attention may be deemed acceptable, particularly when advanced in the name of equity restoration. But when the facts of such policies are spelled out in detail public attitudes are likely to be more equivocal. This is illustrated in a survey conducted in 1967 of approximately 6,000 people in six major American cities (San Francisco, Boston, Pittsburgh, Cleveland, Dayton, and Akron), which showed a readiness to countenance some degree of favoritism among both majority and minority group members. Both favored policies for allocating more employment opportunities to previously discriminated black people. The respondents in both groups were similar in their rank order of a set of alternate proposals (see Table 1). Most highly favored was the policy of equal opportunity (Item 1). But there also was support in both groups for preferential treatment through compensatory training by private industry (Item 2). Third was preferential treatment through compensatory training by the government (Item 3). Preferential treatment through compensatory ratings was in fourth place, considerably below the other policies (Item 4); and fifth place, least favored, was discrimination-in-reverse (Item 5), where preference was to be absolute.

With the exception of the "equal opportunity" item, there was a considerable difference in the proportion of white and non-white persons favoring each of these policy alternatives. The discrepancy between minority and majority attitudes increased as the policies move towards a greater degree of compensatory emphasis. Thus, compared to white respondents, one and one-half times as many non-white respondents favored preferential treatment through compensatory training. Almost three times as many non-whites favored preferential treatment through compensatory ratings. Only 13 percent of the non-white respondents

---

[1] For example, in the *New York Times* (1967:47) Governor Harold Hughes of Iowa is quoted as advocating "reverse discrimination." But the article goes on to indicate that by this he means Negroes, Indians, and other minorities should be hired in preference to whites of *equal ability,* which would be preferential treatment rather than discrimination-in-reverse. Also see Danzig (1966:42).

TABLE 1

Question: "In view of the fact that until recently many jobs were not open to Negroes, how many of these things, if any, would you favor?"

	In favor	
	Nonwhite (N = 3,023)	White (N = 3,027)
1. Seeing to it that Negroes and whites are given equal job opportunities	70.8%	66.2%
2. On-the-job training by industry so Negroes not fully qualified can be hired	61.1	38.1
3. Special government training programs for Negroes	42.5	27.2
4. Giving Negroes a chance ahead of whites in promotions if they have the necessary ability	19.3	7.2
5. Giving Negroes a chance ahead of whites in hiring for jobs they have not had in the past	13.2	3.5
6. None of these	.2	5.1
7. Don't know/no answer	2.4	5.1

Note: The authors would like to thank the staff of the Lemberg Center for the Study of Violence, Brandeis University, for making these data available.

favored discrimination-in-reverse, but among them this outlook was nearly four times as prevalent as among the white respondents.

SELECTED STRATEGY ALTERNATIVES

Preferential treatment involves granting a relative advantage to some group in the competition for esteemed social roles or scarce resources. Veterans, for example, receive a ten to 15 point credit on civil service examinations. When this compensatory rating was originally awarded, veterans were a group of recipients generally perceived as having sacrificed career opportunities while doing esteemed national service. Veterans also were well-organized, often discontent, and trained in the use of firearms. Administrative preference through a point system of compensatory rating has also been extended to other groups. The Human Resources Administration of New York City gives up to 12 extra points on civil service tests to those who qualify as poor. Under this arrangement, having suffered past disservices is considered an "asset" rather than a deficit in estimating an individual's overall qualifications.

The overall qualifications of any two individuals competing for the same post can never be fully equated by purely objective external criteria. Is the person who scores 97 on a civil service exam really more qualified than one who scores 95 or even perhaps 89? Are two years as a Peace Corps Volunteer equal to two years of army service in Vietnam? Does a diploma from Slippery Rock State College mean the same as one from Yale University? What if otherwise similar students have different grade point averages? Is one year of experience as a carpenter a uniform measure of technical skill all over the USA? Differential estimates of individual qualifications are always being made.

Even when quantitative criteria are utilized, the assessment results are subjected to social and normative choices. Men are often preferred to women, local residents to recent arrivals, and friends to strangers. Compensatory ratings operate to counterweight these estimates in favor of previously disadvantaged candidates.

Preferential treatment is sometimes administered through compensatory training. Even when administrative policies for some degree of favoritism are sanctioned, members of a disadvantaged or previously oppressed minority are frequently unable to qualify or reach the minimum criteria required for access to a desired post. In Israel, where children from environmentally disadvantaged families are frequently given scholarship aid and admitted to an academic high school with somewhat lower test scores than are generally required, a significant proportion are still unable to complete the course and, therefore, cannot enter the university (Eaton, 1970). Compensatory ratings can open one door to opportunity; they do not, however, guarantee a successful passage to all those who cross the threshold. Compensatory training tries to facilitate this passage. It aims to give disadvantaged candidates an added chance to acquire the skills necessary to compete for subsequent social opportunities.

When preferential treatment is used, social status is still primarily influenced by achievement. The achievement orientation is the main ideological distinction between preferential treatment and discrimination-in-reverse. The latter accepts the concept of *absolute* advantage to some previously oppressed group in the competition for esteemed social roles.[2] Discrimination-in-reverse subordinates considerations of individual achievement to a desired social policy objective. In the U.S., for instance, it is now advocated by some that allocations of certain work or power roles be foremost determined by ethnicity. In place of a ten point preferential credit on civil service exams, nearly any minority group applicant would be given priority access to a job ahead of any majority person, regardless of their respective qualifications. This policy may be implemented by establishing "benign" quotas or by clearly substituting ethnicity for traditional entrance requirements.[3] An

---

[2] For a discussion of status by achievement and ascription see Linton (1936).

[3] Some thoughtful comments on the topic of benign quotas are given by Fleming and Pollack (1970).

important point here bears clarification. That is, there are jobs where ethnicity (as well as other forms of ascribed status, such as sex and religion) may in fact be considered a valid entrance requirement. This can apply for example to highly personalized social and psychological services where intimate knowledge of the in-group culture may be required to establish rapport and to engender trust, and to jobs where the objective is the transmission and reinforcement of an in-group culture, such as teaching in a private religious institution. Under these circumstances it is not ascribed status per se that qualifies an applicant, but his presumed knowledge and comprehension of shared social-psychic experiences—what Mannheim (1936:42–46) describes as "sympathetic understanding"—obtained by virtue of membership in a particular group. However, there are few clearcut cases wherein successful performance is clearly predicated upon such group membership. It is not necessarily the only means to achieve sympathetic understanding. In Israel, where there is a great shortage of manpower and some degree of ideological acceptance of sex equality in work roles, female Gadna instructors will teach pre-military subjects to young men—even in the field (Eaton, 1969). A seemingly plausible case can be made that black teachers are "better able" to teach black students because of the mutual understanding that arises from their common group affiliation. But a somewhat similar case has been used for a long time by white southerners with regard to teaching white students. This example may be debated from many points of view, depending upon how the role of a public school teacher is defined, the subject matter involved, and how well majority and minority groups are thought to understand each other.

The policy of discrimination-in-reverse is most clearly reflected in the occasional proposals that minority applicants be accepted by universities regardless of any evidence of aptitude or educational achievement. It is also seen in demands that benign quotas be established for employment of minority group members in different occupations, to be filled without concern for the availability of candidates with relevant skills or training potential.

There are two basic types of benign quotas: absolute and conditional. An absolute quota supports the value of equity restoration; it stipulates, for example, that X number of jobs be awarded to members of a specified minority. A conditional quota supports two values, equity restoration and maintenance of standards. The stipulation here is that X number of jobs be awarded to minority applicants deemed *qualified*.

Social status is influenced by ascription under the policy of discrimination-in-reverse. This ideological orientation is evident in some of the currently popular minority group slogans, such as "Black is Beautiful." Birth is the only relevant requirement for this cherished attribute.

Such reverse stereotyping by ascription for purposes of raising minority self-esteem has been employed throughout history. Moses led the Jewish slaves out of Egypt as the "chosen people." Mohandas Ghandi, in his efforts to improve the social conditions of the "untouchables," gave pre-eminence to their "special ancestry" when he renamed them "Harijans"—children of God.

The distinction between societies in which an achievement orientation or an ascriptive orientation predominates in the allocation of social status is important to bear in mind when reflecting upon the characteristics and potential implications of preferential treatment and discrimination-in-reverse. (See Table 2.)

TABLE 2

Characteristics of favoritism strategies

	Preferential treatment	Discrimination-in-reverse
Beneficiaries...............	*Selected* individuals in minority groups	Any member of a minority group who aspires to a post
Qualifications..............	Relevant skills and knowledge plus minority group affiliation	Minority group affiliation can be sufficient
Status disposition...........	By achievement	By ascription

DOES MINORITY GROUP FAVORITISM WORK?

What are the implications of preferential treatment and discrimination-in-reverse for minority group mobility? Minority demands for special treatment have made this a question of much contemporary concern to businessmen, government officials, and educators. The question is asked often, but there is a dearth of relevant research to help gauge the consequences of these policies. Both policies have been previously employed on a large scale for groups such as veterans and the blind. Only recently have they been strongly advocated as a way to accommodate disadvantaged racial minorities.

Up until 1967, the main thrust of minority group aspirations in the United States had been centered upon civil rights and equal opportunity. Towards the end of that year *Newsweek* (1967) magazine published a special report which, in part, stated:

Hence, even as steps are taken to promote dispersal of the ghettos, the government, in cooperation with the private sector, might someday have to set limits on the numbers of Negroes in given localities. This sort of "positive discrimination" would undoubtedly require legislation of a sort hitherto unthinkable, and the courts may have to depart radically from past Constitutional interpretations. Positive hiring quotas may also become necessary if Negroes are to be insured real equality of opportunity.

Less than two years later, racial quotas in college admissions were being vigorously advocated from City College of New York to the University of California at Berkeley; similar demands were being made for minority admissions to building and trade unions, where exclusory practices against minorities continue to be employed with relentless force, even against persons who have demonstrated technical experience.

In addition to the recency of these policies, research findings regarding their impact on individuals and the society are lacking because of the inherent sensitivity of the subject. In an achievement-oriented society where the ideal of "equal opportunity" is venerated, those who employ non-impartial policies are understandably hesitant to advertise it. These persons are in conflict over two deeply-rooted values: equal opportunity and equity restoration. The idea that because of past inequities society should "pay off debts" by creating new, but reversed, disparities in the opportunity structure, is not easily squared with the American dream of full equality. Moreover, the current atmosphere in race relations is not conducive to objective research on policies having economic, social, and psychological implications for minority groups. Note for instance, the remarkably hostile reception given the "Moynihan Report" (Rainwater and Yancey, 1967). These considerations may help to explain why up to now there is a lack of "hard" data to make precise comparisons between the consequences of preferential treatment and discrimination-in-reverse.

In the absence of such data, this essay presents a number of theoretical propositions and explores logical alternatives that could be used to guide future research or as assumptions to be considered in current policy formulations. In either case, the principal intent of the essay is to stimulate more empirically tested comparisons between these two policies of favoritism in terms of their probable social consequences.

EXPLORATIONS IN FAVORITISM

Both preferential treatment and discrimination-in-reverse are advocated as forms of favoritism to facilitate the upward mobility of disadvantaged minority groups. Preferential treatment would allow those most qualified to achieve quickly higher status. But we suspect that for the minority group as a whole, this would result in only a "moderate" rate of mobility. In contrast, discrimination-in-reverse, conferring advanced status by political action on almost all segments of a minority population, is advocated as a plausible means of providing rapid mobility for the entire group.

In addition to the general objective of social mobility, there are other benefits that may be derived in varying measures from policies of preferential treatment and discrimination-in-reverse. Two of these benefits—human resource development and social order—deserve special attention. These normative social goals address very fundamental concerns of the day. The resentment and frustrations of minority groups that came to a boil in the 1960's have made it abundantly clear that the gross disparities existing between ethnic groups in their access to the nation's social and material resources will no longer be tolerated with equanimity. A more equitable redistribution of these resources has been transformed from a moral precept to a prerequisite for the preservation of social order. The policy question has been defined—even in many parts of the formerly legally segregated sections of the country— as: "How and at what pace shall this redistribution take place?" One possibility is to accelerate the development of human resources and the economic integration of minorities through strong policies of favoritism. In different ways and to different degrees preferential treatment and discrimination-in-reverse are options for opening the minority group reservoir of human potential that is blocked by formal qualifications many have been unable to acquire due to inherited socioeconomic disadvantages and by discriminatory practices against those who do possess the qualifications. However, social policies always can have a range of potential consequences, the least pleasing of which are easily ignored in the formulation of strategy. It is with this thought in mind that the differential consequences of preferential treatment and discrimination-in-reverse need to be studied much more thoroughly than has been done in the past.

Discrimination-in-reverse no doubt opens up many otherwise closed opportunities. But we also need to investigate the possibility that when widely used, this strategy could begin to retard the upward mobility of minority groups, which it is intended to expedite. This notion is based on evidence of the existence of four social processes: *performance breakdown, occupational stigmatization, backlash,* and *erosion of credentialism.*

Performance breakdown

It is plausible to assume that a direct relationship exists between the probability of success in meeting formal (often educational) requirements of a technical role and the extent to which this role is performed with merit. According to this assumption, a policy for allocating technical roles which places a low priority on prior evidence of meeting the formal requirements assumes a very high risk that the beneficiaries of this policy deviation will ultimately fail merit tests of performance. Such anticipated performance breakdown, if it were actually to occur on a widespread scale, would lend credence to previously existing stereotypes of minority group incompetence. The most virulent prejudice could then be masked in the self-righteous postulates of what Gordon Allport (1958:85) describes as the "well-deserved reputation theory."

When formal entrance requirements are waived in the realm of higher education, the possibility of performance breakdown is suggested by data reported on the academic status of freshman admissions to the University of California, Berkeley from Fall 1966 through Fall 1968 (Committee on Admissions and Enrollment, 1970). Among others, two groups of disadvantaged minority students are examined: Those admitted by the University's regular standards and those who did not meet the regular entrance requirements, but were admitted by special action. The data indicate that only 45 percent of the disadvantaged minority students admitted by special action remained in academic "good standing"; i.e., were in attendance and not on probation. In comparison, 70 percent of the disadvantaged minority students that were admitted by regular standards remained in academic "good standing." Of the other students admitted by regular standards, primarily white and middle class, 79 percent remained in academic good standing. While these data suggest that the risk of performance breakdown increases when the regular academic entrance requirements are not satisfied, it is equally important to note that with adequate academic preparation, the retention rate for the disadvantaged minority students was almost the same as that of the more privileged majority students.

Occupational stigmatization

Such a development is least likely in visibly technical occupations such as engineering, surgery, and architecture. These demand relatively precise skills. Incompetence could be fatal. Discrimination-in-reverse can be practiced with less risk in occupations where skills and results are somewhat nebulous, such as social work, teaching, counselling, nursing, and the whole range of other "soft science" social roles. In many such jobs professionalization rests more on convention and assertion than hard evidence on the relationship of specific educational prerequisites and technical competence. The white collar services and not-quite-established professions can and always have accommodated to the employment of people possessing less than the minimum formal requirements. There is strong evidence that some such "unqualified" people perform their roles quite well (Mobilization for Youth, 1964; Kobrin, 1959; Reiff and Riessman, 1967; Pearl and Riessman, 1965). But unless such performances are accepted socially as "common," the admission of a high concentration of formerly underqualified persons could reduce the status of a relatively prestigious occupational role into a bailiwick for those unwilling or unable to compete on technical grounds. Such a development would further detract from the already uncertain status of social professions which have struggled hard to establish a recognized level of prestige for their members. Thus, the strategy of mobility through discrimination-in-reverse could result in a "treadmill effect"—stepping up to occupy a position of ostensibly higher status only to find that the status value of this position has depreciated.

A "treadmill" phenomenon is illustrated by India's educational system. Demands for higher education in that country have grown more rapidly than relevant secondary school preparation. University enrollment has increased eightfold in the last 20 years. The technical quality of this education, however, may have substantially diminished. One observer indicates that in many universities a passing grade on exams is only 35 percent—"and they are graded with a leniency that raises the question of why they were given" (Lelyveld, 1968). Increasing the number of graduates by lowering standards has done very little to raise the social and economic status of those possessing the B.A. degree. In India the B.A. degree hardly leads to a lowly clerkship. Upon graduation many students are disillusioned to find that secure and rewarding positions do not await them. Will this happen when Master's degrees in social work are increasingly awarded to nearly all who are allowed to enroll, even if they had no prior Bachelor degree? Or will such evasion of formerly "rigid" academic standards serve to document their possible irrelevancy and force a search for new more meaningful criteria for manpower selection?

Backlash

Another possible consequence of discrimination-in-reverse is a backlash response from the majority group members placed at a disadvantage by this policy, mainly those residing in the lower- and middle-echelons of the middle class, people characterized by Schrag (1969) as "Forgotten Americans." They earn between $5,000 and $10,000 a year, are up to their ears in debt, and occupy a brittle rung on the ladder of social mobility. Many of them, like the unionized ethnic white construction workers, have striven all their lives to accumulate the points, grades, and credits necessary to "negotiate the system." When urged to open their union widely to outgroup members, these people would be asked to discharge a part of the social debt of the total society that has accrued due to years of general minority group exploitation, through reducing their own chances for scarce well-paying jobs. As the data in Table 1 reveal, only a very small percent of majority group members are agreeable to settling past and present inequities by discrimination-in-reverse.[4] It appears that few of them will wish to accept the direct responsibility of payment for what some of their ancestors might have done in the past, for what bigoted members of their group are still trying to perpetuate.

Erosion of credentialism

In addition to these potential consequences, the policy of discrimination-in-reverse presents a formidable challenge to the legitimacy of traditional credentialing procedures. If minority group members can breach the wall of exclusion surrounding status-conferring occupations without having first to acquire the necessary formal qualifications (usually education and experience), it would also be likely that majority group members, particularly those at the bottom of the status hierarchy, will begin questioning the ascribed value of these credentialing "standards." The rapid demise of credentialism would follow.

There are some reasons to welcome this. Credentialism always has its limits, its irrelevancies, and its abuses. By exaggerating the education and skills prerequisite for performing tasks, it has often provided a convenient screening device to eliminate rebels, innovators, and disprivileged minority applicants.[5] There is as yet no evidence that professionally untrained nurses, social workers, and teachers cannot achieve a level of performance that will earn them much esteem by those whom they serve. Cogent arguments have been made for modifying the credentialing processes in these and other fields by making the primary credentialing institutions more flexible and allowing for alternate channels of mobility (Miller and Riessman, 1968). But discrimination-in-reverse falls outside these reform proposals. It advocates the subordination of *all* technical prerequisites for credentialism to technically irrelevant characteristics—such as the substitution of ethnicity for prior education.

In contrast, preferential treatment would have only a slight effect on traditional credentialism. Compensatory rating would make current

---

[4] These data also reveal that only a small percent of minority group members favor discrimination-in-reverse as a policy for allocating employment opportunities.

[5] The use of credentialism to exclude minorities from apprenticeship programs, where federal regulations demand that applicants be selected according to objective standards, is described by Marshall and Brigges (n.d.).

standards of occupational and educational admissions more flexible and more attainable by qualified minority applicants. Compensatory training could be offered to help minority applicants to meet the accepted formal standards.

THE CONSERVATIVE POTENTIAL OF PREFERENTIAL TREATMENT

Preferential treatment contains its own backlash potential. This policy would benefit primarily the most able and achievement-motivated of minority group members—the already partly-credentialed middle class and the aspiring lower-middle class. There is a strong tendency towards recruiting minority candidates for compensatory training who already have much of the needed experience and credentials.[6] These actually or nearly qualified people can be rapidly absorbed into the mainstream of social opportunities. As they are "creamed off," the status gap between minority group achievers and the still disadvantaged masses would increase. Or, as one minority group spokesman has commented: "Integration today means the man who 'makes it,' leaving his black brothers behind in the ghetto as fast as his new sports car will take him" (Carmichael, 1966).

As newly arrived achievers, those who rise on the basis of preferential treatment policies could easily be coopted by an otherwise inequitable system. Some have been accused of having become "Uncle Toms" with an oversized stake in maintaining the basic institutional structure from which their recently acquired prerogatives emanate. Thus, in providing selective mobility for the most talented, preferential treatment could in the long run be counter-productive for the minority group as a whole by inadvertently depriving it of the skills and leadership necessary to advocate for broader social reforms that would have impact upon the entire group.

However, there is another possibility. The proposition that upwardly mobile people tend to become politically conservative (Lipset and Bendix, 1959:66–75) bears further investigation in the case of minorities—where upward mobility accentuates status discrepancies between caste and occupation. The talented and successful black doctor who, despite occupational status, finds it difficult to hail a cab, get seated in a restaurant, cash a check, vacation where he pleases, and buy a suitable home, should not be counted too quickly as grist for the mill of political conservatism. Some studies suggest that status discrepancy accompanying minority group mobility may produce increased support

---

[6] The U.S. Department of Labor (1965) reports that programs for training the unemployed under the Manpower Development and Training Act were least successful in reaching the inexperienced and undereducated.

for fundamental change of the status quo (Lenski, 1954; Richard, 1969).

THE SOCIAL-PSYCHOLOGICAL DIMENSION

There are also social-psychological implications of preferential treatment and discrimination-in-reverse that bear investigation. For example, it is well known that a subtle and complex relationship generally exists between social mobility and mental illness (Hollingshead and Redlich, 1958; Leventman, 1968). In addition to the stresses and strains accompanying mobility there is also greater access to treatment and greater probability that mental illness will be diagnosed as neurosis—a fairly reliable indication of having finally achieved middle-class status. When dealing with racial minorities, the common strains of adjusting to upward mobility are compounded by enlarged discrepancies between racial and occupational status. Would there be an increasing ambivalence towards group identification, particularly if such mobility is achieved primarily by a select segment of the minority population, those who can advance by means of preferential treatment? The results of this policy could transform minority achievers into marginal men; persons standing on the boundary between their "natural" group, those who have suffered the same indignities and deprivations as they, and the middle-class majority. Residing in this social "no man's land," the marginal man has been characterized from a social-psychological perspective as oversensitive, emotionally unstable, and given to frequent shifts between extremes of contradictory behavior (Lewin, 1964:143–145). Riesman (1964:163) persuasively argues that these negative attributes can be countered by recognizing that marginality often serves to stimulate a heightened level of insight and creativity. He suggests: "The intellect is at its best, and its ethical insights are at their best, when one is in a marginal position that is not too overpowering."

Where the tipping point rests between heightened sensitivity and over-sensitivity is difficult to specify. Nevertheless, with the increasing emphasis upon ethnic solidarity, pride, and identification among minorities, upwardly mobile members of these groups may find themselves in marginal positions that are at least psychologically discomforting, if indeed not overpowering.[7]

The phenomenon of marginality is probably primarily associated with *selective* minority group mobility. Thus, if a higher status were to

---

[7] Newcomb (1950:539) suggests that marginality is more likely to persist from generation to generation when the earmarks of minority are anatomical rather than behavioral.

be conferred upon a larger segment of the minority population, as would be the case with discrimination-in-reverse, the relationship between marginality and mobility might diminish significantly. But the policy of discrimination-in-reverse is also not without its potentially strain-producing psychological consequences. Catapulting into a position for which one may not be even minimally qualified raises the self-searching question: how did I get here? It is probably much more ego-tolerable to attribute this rise to one's own initiative and some latent superior quality than to political accommodation or to the beneficence of majority group policy-makers.

The delusion of the "self-made man" could be maintained by responding with increased hostility towards the majority group; this type of reaction formation by minority group members benefiting from policies of discrimination-in-reverse would effectively deny that any political concessions were granted or that their new found status reflects power rather than merit. The beneficiaries of this policy would not, of course, enjoy a monopoly on the delusion of being "self-made." Unrealistic capabilities are attributed to themselves by many "self-made" majority group members who occupy positions for which they lack relevant qualifications. Many of Horatio Alger's heroes, after much poverty and struggling, achieved their quickest mobility by the act of marrying the boss's daughter.

CONCLUSION

Preferential treatment and discrimination-in-reverse are distinct policies with varied social, psychological, and political implications. Both policies of favoritism contain potential advantages and disadvantages for their beneficiaries. The fact that implementation of either of these policies may be motivated by the ideal of equity restoration fails to insure this outcome. Good intentions do not always spawn good results where social policy is concerned.

Through political pressure, or by dwelling on the guilt feelings of majority liberals toward the disadvantaged minorities, it is sometimes possible to turn policies of preferential treatment into procedures for discrimination-in-reverse. Even by those whose moral values would be equally satisfied by either strategy, the risks inherent in such a shift—performance breakdown, occupational stigmatization, erosion of credentialism, and backlash—need to be assessed against the benefits of this policy. Discrimination-in-reverse would provide immediate and widespread benefits in the form of higher pay and more social power. The economic aspect could, however, also be achieved by alternative methods such as paying more for jobs that are already technically accessible to minority group members or by implementing fiscal policies for income redistribution.

There are also other consequences that warrant consideration. Would preferential treatment bring enough benefits to compensate disadvantaged minorities for the accumulated injustices of the past? Or would it be viewed as merely selective appeasement? Would preferential treatment lead to successive "creaming off" of the leadership cadre which any social group must have in order to achieve political equality? Or would it facilitate the development of this leadership? What are the psychological effects of favoritism? The answers to these questions will largely determine the practical desirability of utilizing policies of preferential treatment and discrimination-in-reverse.

There is also the question of their moral desirability. Historically, efforts to legislate group mobility have been greatly resisted as inconsistent with rugged individualist Protestant Ethic moral values. Minority group favoritism is politically threatening to well entrenched majority groups. Both strategies, preferential treatment and discrimination-in-reverse, will inevitably be judged in the court of social values. These value judgments are likely to be made more calmly and in greater confidence if they could be discussed in terms of concrete evidence of the social consequences of alternative strategies for equity restoration. At this stage, the evidence is meager. A systematic exploration of the assumptions underlying strategies of favoritism is called for if responsible and informed decisions are to guide the imperative quest for social justice and equality.

REFERENCES

Allport, Gordon. *The Nature of Prejudice.* New York: Doubleday Anchor Books, 1958.

Carmichael, Stokely. "What We Want." *New York Review of Books,* September 22, 1966.

Committee on Admissions and Enrollment, University of California. Report to the Berkeley Division, May 12, 1970.

Danzig, David. "In Defense of Black Power." *Commentary* 42, September 1966, pp. 41–46.

Eaton, Joseph W. "Gadna: Israel's Youth Corps." *The Middle East Journal,* Autumn 1969, pp. 471–483. "Reaching the Hard to Reach in Israel." *Social Work,* 15, January 1970, pp. 85–96.

Fleming, Macklin, and Pincus Pollack. "The Black Quota at Yale Law School: An Exchange of Letters." *Public Interest,* Spring 1970, pp. 44–52.

Freud, Sigmund. *Civilization and Its Discontents,* trans. by James Strachey. New York: W. W. Norton, 1926.

Hollingshead, August B., and Frederick Redlich. *Social Class and Mental Illness.* New York: John Wiley, 1958.

Kobrin, Solomon. "The Chicago Area Project—A 25 Year Assessment." *Annals of the American Academy of Political Science,* March 1959.

Lelyveld, Joseph. "India's Students Demand—A Safe Job in the Establishment." *New York Times Magazine,* May 12, 1968.

Lenski, Gerhard. "Status Crystallization: A Non-Vertical Dimension of Social Status." *American Sociological Review,* August 1954.

Leventman, Seymour. "Race and Mental Illness in Mass Society." *Social Problems,* Summer 1968.

Lewin, Kurt. *Field Theory in Social Science,* ed. Dorwin Cartwright. New York: Harper and Row, 1964.

Linton, Ralph. *The Study of Man.* New York: Appleton-Century-Crofts, 1936.

Lipset, Seymour M., and Reinhard Bendix. *Social Mobility in Industrial Society.* Berkeley: University of California Press, 1959.

Mannheim, Karl. *Ideology and Utopia.* New York: Harcourt, Brace, and World, 1936.

Marshall, F. Ray, and Vernon Brigges, Jr. *Remedies for Discrimination in Apprenticeship Programs.* New York: Joint Apprenticeship Program, n.d.

Miller, S. M., and Frank Riessman. *Social Class and Social Policy.* New York: Basic Books, 1968.

Mobilization for Youth. *Action on the Lower East Side.* New York: Mobilization for Youth, 1964.

Newcomb, Theodore. *Social Psychology.* New York: Dryden Press, 1950.

Newsweek. "The Negro in America: What Must be Done," November 20, 1967.

New York Times, August 20, 1967.

Pearl, Arthur, and Frank Reissman. *New Careers for the Poor.* Glencoe: Free Press, 1965.

Rainwater, Lee, and William Yancey (eds.). *The Moynihan Report and the Politics of Controversy.* Cambridge: M.I.T. Press, 1967.

Reiff, Robert, and Frank Riessman. "The Indigenous Nonprofessional." *American Journal of Orthopsychiatry,* July, 1967.

Richard, Michel P. "The Ideology of Negro Physicians: A Test of Mobility and Status Crystallization Theory." *Social Problems,* Summer 1969.

Riesman, David. *Individualism Reconsidered.* New York: Free Press, 1964.

Schrag, Peter. "The Forgotten American." *Harper's,* August 1969, pp. 27–34.

Titmuss, Richard M. *Commitment to Welfare.* New York: Pantheon Books, 1968.

U.S. Department of Labor. *A Report on Manpower Requirements, Resources, Utilization and Training.* Washington, D.C.: U.S. Printing Office, 1965.

C. Factual and research considerations

ERDMAN PALMORE and FRANK J. WHITTINGTON

Differential trends toward equality between whites and nonwhites

The confusion as to whether nonwhites are moving toward equality with whites in various areas can be resolved by the use of an equality index which is a measure of the amount of overlap between two percentage distributions. The EI is the complement of the index of dissimilarity but the EI has the advantages of easier calculation and of positive directionality. Relative to comparisons of central tendency and most other indexes, the EI has the advantages of applying to ordinal as well as interval data, of having less sensitivity to the influence of extreme cases and of reflecting general changes in the distributions. The EI shows that nonwhites have made substantial progress toward equality in income, education, occupation, weeks worked, and quality of housing. Mortality shows little or no movement toward equality since 1960 and marital status has moved away from equality since 1950.

There has been considerable doubt as to whether nonwhites are actually moving toward equality with whites in the various sectors of our society. The Moynihan Report (1965) concluded that the Negro American world is moving toward "massive deterioration of the fabric of society and its institutions." President Johnson (1965) asserted that "For the great majority of Negro Americans—the poor, the unemployed, the uprooted and the dispossessed . . . the walls are rising and the gulf is widening." Carmichael and Hamilton (1967) state specifically "It is a stark reality that the black communities are becoming more and more economically depressed." Pettigrew (1964) concludes that the absolute gains of Negroes are "pale when contrasted with current white standards." Yet most of the available statistics show that Negroes are making substantial progress in most fields.

Part of the confusion is caused by the fact that no one has sys-

This research was supported in part by Grant HD-00668, National Institute of Child Health and Human Development, USPHS.

Source: *Social Forces,* vol. 49 (September 1970), pp. 108–17.

tematically applied a standard index of equality to all the various kinds of statistics available in order to measure trends in equality. There have been many studies which summarize the statistics on the status of Negroes at one point in time (U.S. Department of HEW, 1965; Broom and Glenn, 1967; Glenn and Bonjean, 1969; Price, 1968; Duncan and Duncan, 1969; U.S. Department of Labor, 1966; U.S. Office of Education, 1966; Fein, 1965; Siegel, 1965; Farley and Taeuber, 1968; Moynihan, 1965; Pettigrew, 1964) and some of these present trend data in selected areas. But most of the indexes and the comparisons of central tendencies are either not applicable to much of the data or are inadequate in various ways discussed below. Those that are adequate, such as the index of dissimilarity (Duncan and Duncan, 1955), have not been systematically applied to the wide range of available data. Ginzberg and Hiestand (1968) summarized this problem as follows:

> Instead of being at two distinct levels, the distributions of the two populations (white and Negro) in terms of income, occupation, education, or otherwise, overlap substantially over a broad range. As far as we know, no analyst has yet developed a statistical measure to summarize the degree of overlap. Such a statistic might be called a measure of integration. It is badly needed for then we could begin to answer whether there has been a trend toward more or less integration in income, educational levels, occupations, or other criteria.

Also, the use of different indexes for different sets of data can produce confusing and misleading results. As Duncan and Duncan (1969) point out: "One can discount or exaggerate the trends by manipulating ratios, absolute differences, and Fein gaps."

The purposes of this paper are: (1) to describe a standard index of equality that can be used with ordinal as well as interval data and to discuss its advantages over other measures; (2) to use this equality index to measure the differential trends in income, education, occupation, weeks worked, housing, mortality, and marital status; (3) to discuss briefly some of the possible explanations for the differential trends.

THE EQUALITY INDEX

The *equality index* (EI) is simply the positive complement of the older *index of dissimilarity* (Duncan and Duncan, 1955). It may be described in several ways. It is the proportion of the white and nonwhite percentage distributions that overlap each other. Or, it is the proportion of nonwhites who are equal to the same proportion of whites. It can be thought of as the percent of complete equality, because 100 would mean that there is complete identity, or equality, between the two percentage distributions, and 0 would mean that there is no overlap between the two distributions.

The formula is simply

$$\sum_{i=1}^{n} Min\ W_i\ N_i$$

which means the summation of the smaller of the two percentages, W_i and N_i, where W_i is the percent of whites in the ith category and N_i is the percent of nonwhites in the ith category. Thus, the EI is quite simple to calculate: the percent of all whites in a category is compared to the percent of nonwhites in that category, and the lesser of the two percentages in each category are summed. The index of dissimilarity can be derived from this by subtracting the EI from 100, or the EI can be derived in the same way from the index of dissimilarity.

Figure 1 shows graphically the curves of the white and nonwhite income distributions superimposed upon one another with the area of overlap shaded. The EI is the measure of the shaded overlap area as a percentage of the total area underneath the two curves. Thus the EI would increase if more Negroes shifted to the upper end of the distribu-

FIGURE 1

Percentage distribution of whites and nonwhites by income for 1967

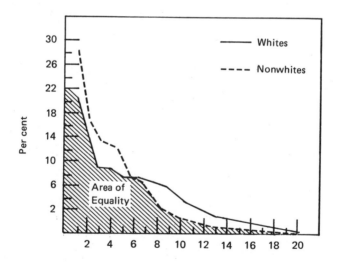

Income in thousands

tion or more whites shifted to the lower end, thereby increasing the amount of overlap.

There are several advantages of the EI (and of its complement, the index of dissimilarity) over the other measures that have been used.

1. The EI can be used with ordinal data such as occupation or quality of housing. The comparisons of central tendency such as means or medians and most of the other indexes cannot be used with ordinal data (Alker and Russett, 1964). The EI can use any data in which the categories can be ranked from higher to lower. The only theoretical limitation on the applicability of the EI is that one of the two groups should have larger percentages in all of the higher categories, and the other group should have larger percentages in all of the lower categories. If this criterion is not met, interpretations of change may become confused. All of the data used in this paper meet this criterion.

2. The EI is not subject to the heavy influence of a few extreme cases as in a comparison of means and in most of the other indexes. Thus, the EI does not require accurate information on extreme cases (which is often impossible to get). For example, it does not matter which of the higher categories a person is placed in, so long as he does belong in one of the higher categories. This is also related to the convenient fact that the EI is unaffected by the broadness of the categories unless the category at the crossover point of the two distributions is so broad that it obscures the inequality within that category. In that case, the EI would be overstated by whatever percent of the total populations are within that category and do not fall under the area of overlap.

3. The EI usually reflects general changes in the shape of the distributions such as changes in range, standard deviation, kurtosis, and skewness. A comparison of means or of medians often does not reveal such changes. The EI does not reflect isolated changes which are not related to the general distribution, but it is probably not important to measure such minor changes anyway.

In addition, the EI has two minor advantages over its complement, the index of dissimilarity:

1. The EI is simple and therefore easier to understand and calculate than the other indexes. The index of dissimilarity requires three steps to calculate: (*a*) subtract the smaller percent from the larger percent in each category, (*b*) sum these differences, and (*c*) divide by 2. In contrast, the EI requires only one step: sum the smaller percent in each category.

2. The EI is a positive measure of equality so that increases in value mean an increase in equality. In contrast, the index of dissimilarity is a negative measure of equality because increases in its value mean decreases in equality.

A few comparisons of the EI with the ratio of nonwhite to white medians will show how these measures behave differently. In 1967 the ratio of nonwhite median income to white median income was .60, indicating that the average nonwhite income was only 60 percent as great as the average white income. However, the EI for that same year was 80 (see Table 1 below), indicating that actually 80 percent of the nonwhites had incomes equal to 80 percent of the whites. Thus, the EI revealed substantially greater equality between white and nonwhite incomes than one would infer from the ratio of median incomes.

For another contrast, the ratio of median incomes indicates that since 1960 the ratio has increased by .013 (the equivalent of 1.3 EI points) per year which is a faster increase than in any other decade. In contrast the EI shows that the percent of nonwhites achieving equality with whites in income increased by only 0.6 of a point per

TABLE 1

Equality indexes from 1940 to present by sex

	1940	1950	1960	1966–68
Income:				(1967)
Total	57.5	70.7	76.6	80.8
Male	56.9	65.6	69.7	73.3
Female	55.2	75.6	83.3	89.4
Education:				(1968)
Total	56.5	63.2	72.7	74.9
Male	56.3	62.3	70.5	73.2
Female	59.8	65.2	74.0	76.2
Occupation:				(1967)
Total	52.7	59.1	61.3	66.4
Male	57.5	63.4	64.1	67.0
Female	39.2	47.9	55.1	65.9
Weeks worked:				(1967)
Total	*	88.0	88.0	92.8
Male	*	88.8	85.8	90.9
Female	*	90.9	95.0	98.0
Housing:				(1968)
Total	*	58.6	67.1	72.6
Mortality:				(1966)
Total	79.2	80.8	83.3	82.9
Male	82.2	84.0	85.8	86.2
Female	75.7	76.4	79.5	78.4
Marital status:				(1967)
Total	*	88.5	85.3	84.8
Male	*	89.7	85.7	85.1
Female	*	87.2	84.8	84.7

* Data not available.
Sources: Edwards, 1943; U.S. Bureau of the Census, 1943a, 1943b, 1953a, 1953b, 1953c, 1963a, 1963b, 1963c, 1968, 1969a, 1969b, 1969c; U.S. Bureau of Labor Statistics, 1969; U.S. Public Health Service, 1953, 1963, 1969.

year, which is less than half the 1940–50 rate (see Table 2 below). Similarly, the ratio of nonwhite median years of education to white median years of education shows the same rate of increase in this decade as for any of the preceding periods. However, according to the EI, movement toward equality in education in this decade was less than one-third the rate of increase for 1950 to 1960 (Table 2). Thus, the use of medians often produces different conclusions from the use of EI as a measure of equality and trends toward equality. One measure is not necessarily more accurate or valid than the other, but it is our contention that the EI is more broadly useful, for the reasons discussed above.

It should be recognized that for certain purposes a comparison of central tendencies is more appropriate than the EI. For example, to compute the per capita amount of money it would take to bring nonwhite incomes up to white incomes, a comparison of mean incomes would provide a closer estimate.

TABLE 2

Annual rate of change in equality indexes for three periods since 1940, by sex

	1940–50	1950–60	1960–66–68
Income:			
Total	1.32	.59	.60
Male	.87	.41	.51
Female	2.04	.77	.87
Education:			
Total	.67	.95	.28
Male	.60	.82	.34
Female	.54	.88	.28
Occupation:			
Total	.64	.22	.73
Male	.59	.07	.41
Female	.87	.72	1.54
Weeks worked:			
Total	*	.00	.69
Male	*	−.30	.73
Female	*	.41	.43
Housing:			
Total	*	.85	.69
Mortality:			
Total	.16	.25	−.07
Male	.18	.18	.04
Female	.07	.31	−.18
Marital status:			
Total	*	−.33	−.05
Male	*	−.40	−.06
Female	*	−.24	−.01

* Data not available.

The data presented in this paper all compare equality between whites and nonwhites rather than between Negroes and whites. The reason for this is that much of the census data used is not available specifically for Negroes, and it was decided to use the nonwhite category consistently so that the EI would be exactly comparable from year to year and from one variable to another. When data for whites and Negroes are used, the EI is about one or two points lower than the EI for whites and nonwhites, because more of the non-Negro nonwhites have equality with whites than do the Negroes. However, the differences between using data on nonwhites versus Negroes is so small that the two indexes may be used interchangeably for most purposes. This is true because the non-Negro nonwhite population is so small relative to Negroes (less than 8 percent of nonwhites were non-Negro in 1960).

U.S. Census data were used to compute all the EI. The income EI was computed from a percentage distribution of white and nonwhite income by $500 intervals up to $5,000, $1,000 intervals up to $8,000, a $2,000 interval to $10,000, a $5,000 interval to $15,000, and all over $15,000 in the final interval. The education EI was based on the following occupation groups: professional and technical, manager and proprietor, farmers and farm managers, clerical, sales, craftsmen and foremen, operatives, private household, service workers, farm laborers and foremen, and nonfarm laborers. The weeks worked EI was based on the following intervals: 13 or less, 14–26, 27–39, 40–49, and 50–52. The housing EI for 1960 and 1968 was based on the following categories: sound housing with all plumbing facilities, sound housing lacking some or all facilities, deteriorating housing with all facilities, deteriorating housing lacking some or all facilities, and dilapidated housing. The EI for 1950 housing was based on somewhat different, but comparable, categories: sound housing with private bath and hot water, sound housing with private bath and cold water, sound housing with running water but no private bath, sound housing with no running water, dilapidated housing with private bath and hot water, dilapidated housing lacking bath or running water.

The EI for mortality was more complex than the others. It was computed on the basis of the percent of death in ten-year age intervals standardized against the white age structure. It is necessary to standardize the nonwhite deaths by applying the death rate to the white age structure in order to control for differences between the white and nonwhite age structures which, in turn, are affected by differential birth rates. If the age structure is not standardized, the EI is about six to nine points lower because nonwhites have a larger proportion of the population in the younger age categories. This age-standardized mortality EI can be thought of as the percent of nonwhite deaths which occurred at the same age as a similar percent of white deaths, after the white and nonwhite age structures have been equated.

The marital status EI is based on the following categories: married with spouse present, married but separated, married but spouse absent for other reasons, widowed, divorced, and single. Marital status was conceived of as an ordinal variable in the sense of declining degrees of "marriedness" from married with spouse present, through ex-married categories, to the never-married category.

FINDINGS

Table 1 presents the EI for income, education, occupation, weeks worked, quality of housing, mortality and marital status, for 1940, 1950, 1960, and for the most recent year in which data are available (1966–68). Table 2 converts these EI to annual rates of change for the three periods since 1940.

These tables show that income had the greatest overall increase in equality with a rise of over twenty-three points between 1940 and 1967 (Table 1). Furthermore, the *rate* of increase has remained stable at about 0.6 of a point per year since 1950 (Table 2). At this rate it would take about thirty years to achieve complete equality of income.

Females started at about the same level of income equality in 1940 but have been increasing at a substantially faster rate than men ever since. By 1967 the women had an EI which was sixteen points greater than the men's. This is probably due primarily to the large proportion of nonwhite women who are employed and now earn substantial incomes. It is not due to any greater equality in education nor in occupation among women because the EI in these areas are almost the same between men and women. In a sense, the high EI for women is somewhat deceptive because more of the white women are living on the greater incomes of their husbands.

Equality in years of education completed shows the second greatest gain, with a rise of over eighteen points. But in contrast to income, there has been a substantial slowdown in the rate of increase between 1960 and 1968. For some reason, the attempts at integration and improvement of education among nonwhites is producing less effect during the 1960s than at any time since 1940. It is true that the absolute amounts of education among both whites and nonwhites are still rising, and the gap between whites and nonwhites is still shrinking, but the rate at which this gap is closing has slowed to about a quarter of a point per year.

Duncan and Duncan (1969) found in a regression analysis of school years completed that the increased equality seems to be related to both increasing similarity between whites and nonwhites in background variables and to a decrease in residual differences due to "color" which may be taken to measure decreases in discrimination.

By contrast with the slowdown in the education EI changes, equality in occupation shows a faster rate of increase in this decade compared to the previous one. The women especially have shown a fast increase with a gain of over ten points in the past seven years. The fact that women show greater rates of increase in each decade is related to their low occupational equality in 1940 (39.2). This low level of equality in 1940 was due primarily to the concentration of nonwhite women in the occupation of private household workers. Fifty-eight percent of the nonwhite women were in this category in 1940 compared to only 11 percent of the white women. By 1967, the percentages in this occupation were less than one-half as great. Since the women's rate of increase in occupational equality is over three times as high as the men's, the amount of equality among women will soon be substantially higher than among men, if this rate of increase continues.

Nathan Hare (1965) earlier noted the decline in progress toward occupational equality during the 1950s. He also found that the higher the educational level, the greater the equality in occupations. Our analysis shows that movement toward equality in the 1960s has again stepped up, now progressing at a rate even higher than in the 1940s. Perhaps this is a result of the earlier high increases in educational equality.

The EI for weeks worked assumes that the smaller percentage of nonwhites who work 50 or more weeks per year represents the greater amount of unemployment among nonwhites. While there was a mixed pattern in this index between 1950 and 1960, with the men showing a decrease and the women showing an increase, there have been consistent increases for both sexes in this decade. The EI for women in 1967 was so high (98.0) that for practical purposes it might be said that complete equality in number of weeks worked has been achieved by women. However, it is true that more of the nonwhites with less than 50 weeks of work were unemployed during part of the year while more of the whites with less than 50 weeks of work did not want work when not employed. Thus, the unusually high EI in weeks worked is somewhat deceptive in not reflecting the distinction between voluntary and involuntary lack of employment.

The housing EI shows a fairly steady improvement from 1950 (the first census in which comparable data were collected) to the present. In 1968 almost three-quarters of the nonwhites had housing rated as equal in quality to three-quarters of the whites'. Thus, the quality of nonwhite housing has improved steadily, even relative to white housing, despite the evidence that segregation has increased during this period, especially in southern cities (Farley and Taeuber, 1968). Apparently the migration of nonwhites to the cities and their general economic gains have enabled nonwhites to substantially improve the quality of their housing despite continued discrimination and segregation.

The mortality EI shows a small increase for men and a small decrease for women since 1960. This decrease among women is not due to increased mortality among nonwhites, but reflects the somewhat larger decline in mortality among white women than among nonwhite women. In other words, while early mortality decreased among both groups, it decreased faster among the white women. Thus, it appears that in the area of health and longevity, progress toward equality between whites and nonwhites has come to a virtual standstill in this decade.

Finally, the EI for marital status shows a consistent decline since 1950. On the other hand, the rate of decline has slowed almost to a standstill since 1960, which may indicate that the EI will soon begin to rise. The Moynihan Report (1965) documents the many factors related to the decline in family stability among Negroes, such as high rates of unemployment, poverty, high rates of mobility from rural areas to city slums and within city slums, etc. Presumably, if these factors were reduced, family stability would increase and the EI for marital status would climb.

DISCUSSION

It is clear that nonwhites have made substantial, though somewhat uneven, progress toward equality in the economic areas of income, occupation, and weeks worked, as well as in education and equality of housing, which are largely dependent on economic status (Figure 2). Thus, those who claim that the economic gap between whites and nonwhites is increasing or that "the black communities are becoming more and more economically depressed" are incorrect, at least on the national level. Despite a slowdown in the rate of change toward equality in education, progress continues to be made on all of these fronts. In most of these areas, complete equality could be reached in thirty to forty years at present rates. Progress toward equality in education has slowed so that it would take ninety years to achieve full equality. Faster progress would require extensive adult education for nonwhites.

On the other hand, it is also clear that in the social variable of marital status and in the socio-environmentally related area of mortality, there has been almost no movement toward equality in this decade. Mortality had shown small increases in equality up to 1960 and perhaps with the

FIGURE 2

Changes in equality indexes since 1940

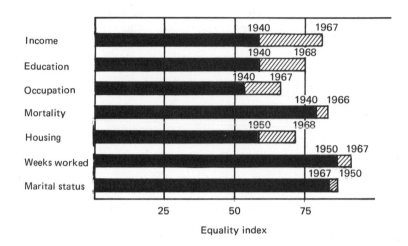

Equality index

advent of such public health programs as Medicare and Medicaid, movement toward equality in this area will soon be resumed. The deterioration in marital status shows signs of leveling off and may begin to climb if the economic gains begin to have a delayed effect on marital status.

It might be argued that a basic reason for the slowdown in movement toward equality in education, as well as a reason for the lack of progress in mortality and marital status, is the fact that all these EI are in the mid-seventies or higher and that it may become more difficult to achieve progress the closer we move to complete equality. Perhaps the remaining inequality is more "hard-core" and is more resistant to change. On the other hand, one might argue that it should become easier to achieve rapid progress as we near complete equality because we could concentrate our resources on the smaller remaining inequality. We are of the opinion that there is no necessary reason why progress must slow down, but that the amount of progress toward equality is directly related to the amount of attention and resources our nation is willing to devote to achieving equality. The facts that the EI for income and weeks worked are also high, but have not slowed, support this view.

There are only small differences between men and women in the indexes for education, occupation, and marital status. But women have substantially greater equality in income and in weeks worked, while men have substantially greater equality in mortality. We believe these sex differentials can be explained by one general principle: greater equality among the inferior category. Thus, women generally make less income and, therefore, constitute the inferior category in this dimension and have a higher income EI. Women work less weeks per year and are "inferior" in the sense of having less of this variable and so have a higher weeks worked EI. In mortality, men are the inferior category because they have less longevity and, therefore, have the higher EI. We believe the reason this principle holds is that the inferior category has a constricted range and variation because they have less of the given variable, and thus there is less room for as much discrepancy between whites and nonwhites within that category. This principle also applies in other areas as shown by the fact that white and nonwhite incomes are closer to equality among the aged than among younger persons (Orshansky, 1964). In this case, aged persons are in the inferior category with less income than others.

It might be argued that there are implicit value judgments in each of these EI: that higher income is judged better than lower income, that more education is better than less education, that higher-status occupations are better than lower, that year-round work is better than part-time work, that sound housing with all facilities is better than deteriorating or dilapidated housing, that longer life is better than shorter life, and that being married with spouse present is better than having spouse absent or being single. It could be argued that these judgments use middle-class standards and that many may well prefer having less education, having a lower-status occupation, working less than 50 weeks a year, or not being married, etc. However, if one is uncertain about the desirability of nonwhites reaching equality in these areas, he can think of the EI as simply an index of similarity, thus removing the question of whether similarity is desirable or not.

The implication of these findings for relative deprivation theory are clear. The rising discontent among Negroes cannot be explained by changes in their absolute or relative socioeconomic position because the EI shows that Negroes are gaining in most areas, both absolutely and relative to whites. Therefore, the rising discontent must be related to rising expectations which apparently are moving faster than the actual gains.

There are several avenues for future research with the EI. One would be to attempt controls or standardization on the basis of such factors as age, region, occupation, or education, in order to see what effect these factors have on the EI. For example, if white and nonwhite populations were standardized by age, would the income EI be greater or lower? There are reasons for expecting that it could be higher, lower, or remain the same. Another avenue would be to compute the EI for other areas, such as health measures, birth rate, regional distributions, and mobility rates. The reader should be aware that the aggregated data on which these EI are based can show only main trends and that detailed analysis of the various reasons for changes at various levels of the distributions is a massive and complex task which has begun in only a few areas. A third use of the EI would be to compute the equality between sexes, between different age groups, between different regions of the country, between countries, etc. We believe there are vast bodies of data to which the EI could be applied to reveal important practical and theoretical information on the present degree of equality and trends toward or away from equality between many types of groups and social categories.

REFERENCES

Alker, H. R., Jr., and B. M. Russett. "On Measuring Inequality." *Behavioral Science,* 9 (July 1964): 207–218.

Broom, L., and N. Glenn. *Transformation of the Negro American.* New York: Harper & Row, 1967.

Carmichael, S., and C. V. Hamilton. *Black Power.* New York: Random House, 1967.

Duncan, O. D., and B. Duncan. "A Methodological Analysis of Segregation Indexes." *American Sociological Review,* 20 (April 1955): 210–217.

———. "Discrimination Against Negroes." Pp. 352–374 in B. M. Gross (ed.), *Social Intelligence for America's Future.* Boston: Allyn & Bacon, 1969.

Edwards, A. M. *Comparative Occupation Statistics for the United States, 1870–1940.* Washington, D.C.: Government Printing Office, 1943.

Farley, R., and K. E. Taeuber. "Population Trends—Residential Segregation Since 1960." *Science,* 159 (March 1968): 953–956.

Fein, R. "An Economic and Social Profile of the Negro American." *Daedalus,* 94 (1965): 815–846.

Ginzberg, E., and D. L. Hiestand. *Mobility in the Negro Community.* Washington, D.C.: United States Commission on Civil Rights, 1968.

Glenn, N., and C. Bonjean (eds.). *Blacks in the United States.* San Francisco: Chandler, 1969.

Hare, N. "Recent Trends in the Occupational Mobility of Negroes, 1930–1960: An Intracohort Analysis." *Social Forces,* 44 (December 1965): 166–173.

Johnson, L. B. "To Fulfill These Rights." Remarks of the President at Harvard University, June 4, 1965.

Moynihan, D. P. *The Negro Family: The Case for National Action.* Washington, D.C.: Government Printing Office, 1965.

Orshansky, M. "The Aged Negro and His Income." *Social Security Bulletin,* 27 (1964): 3–13.

Pettigrew, T. F. *A Profile of the Negro American*. Princeton, N.J.: Van Nostrand, 1964.

Price, D. "Occupational Changes among Whites and Nonwhites, with Projections for 1970." *Social Science Quarterly*, 49 (December 1968): 563–572.

Siegel, P. M. "On the Cost of Being Negro." *Sociological Inquiry*, 35 (1965): 41–57.

U.S. Bureau of the Census, *U.S. Census of Population: 1940*, Vol. 2, *Characteristics of the Population*, Part 1, *United States Summary*. Washington, D.C.: Government Printing Office, 1943. (a)

————. *Vital Statistics of the United States, 1940*, Part 1. Washington, D.C.: Government Printing Office, 1943. (b)

————. *U.S. Census of Population: 1950*, Vol. 2, *Characteristics of the Population*, Part 1, *United States Summary*. Washington, D.C.: Government Printing Office, 1953. (a)

————. *U.S. Census of Housing: 1950*, Vol. 1, Part 1, *United States Summary*. Washington, D.C.: Government Printing Office, 1953. (b)

————. *U.S. Census of Population: 1950, Subject Reports, Marital Status*. Washington, D.C.: Government Printing Office, 1953. (c)

————. *U.S. Census of Population: 1960*, Vol. 2, *Characteristics of the Population*, Part 1, *United States Summary*. Washington, D.C.: Government Printing Office, 1963. (a)

————. *U.S. Census of Housing: 1960*, Vol. 1, Part 1, *United States Summary*. Washington, D.C.: Government Printing Office, 1963. (b)

————. *U.S. Census of Population: 1960, Subject Reports, Marital Status*. Washington, D.C.: Government Printing Office, 1963. (c)

————. "Marital Status and Family Status: March 1967." *Current Population Reports*. Series P-20, No. 170. Washington, D.C.: Government Printing Office, 1968.

————. "Educational Attainment: March 1968." *Current Population Reports*. Series P-20. No. 182. Washington, D.C.: Government Printing Office, 1969. (a)

————. "Income in 1967 of Persons in the United States." *Current Population Reports*. Series P-60, No. 60. Washington, D.C.: Government Printing Office, 1969. (b)

————. "Housing Units by Condition and Plumbing." Unpublished preliminary release, 1969. (c)

U.S. Bureau of Labor Statistics. *Handbook of Labor Statistics, 1968*. Washington, D.C.: Government Printing Office, 1969.

U.S. Department of Health, Education and Welfare. *White-Nonwhite Differentials in Health, Education and Welfare*. Reprinted from *Indicators*. Washington, D.C.: Government Printing Office, 1965.

U.S. Department of Labor. *The Negroes in the U.S.* Bureau of Labor Statistics Bulletin No. 1511. Washington, D.C.: Government Printing Office.

U.S. Office of Education. *Equality of Educational Opportunity*. Washington, D.C.: Government Printing Office, 1966.

U.S. Public Health Service. *Vital Statistics of the United States: 1950,* Vol. 3. Washington, D.C.: Government Printing Office, 1953.

————. *Vital Statistics of the United States: 1960,* Vol. 2, *Mortality, Part A.* Washington, D.C.: Government Printing Office, 1963.

————. *Vital Statistics of the United States: 1966,* Vol. 2, *Mortality, Part A.* Washington, D.C.: Government Printing Office, 1969.

D. Policy and practice considerations

JOHN KENNETH GALBRAITH, EDWIN KUH, and
LESTER C. THUROW

Toward greater minority employment

One of the plain lessons of the last 20 years is that where equality for blacks, other minorities and those so treated is concerned, good intentions are not enough. Nor is a serious commitment to reform which fails to specify the exact change to be achieved. Nor is any measure which does not have the force of law. Twenty years ago, most Americans, including many Southerners, accepted the principle of equality in educational opportunity and believed school segregation should some day be brought to an end. And most affirmed the right of all citizens (all literate citizens, in any case) to vote—sometime. And most believed that discrimination in access to restaurants, hotels and other public facilities should some day be ended. There was no lack of speeches affirming these goals. Nothing happened, however, until exact requirements were specified, and timetables for compliance were laid down, and those that did not comply were made subject to the force of law. Had such action not been taken, Southern schools and public facilities would still be wholly segregated and black voters south of the Mason-Dixon Line would still be few and courageous.

The lesson on schools, voting and public facilities is one we here bring to bear on the most egregious discrimination that still remains in American society, which is the virtually complete monopoly by white males (literally white, non-Spanish-speaking males) of the good jobs in commerce, industry and government, and the virtually complete denial of these jobs to blacks, Spanish-speaking citizens and women. The remedy we offer involves a wide-spectrum use of the word "minority" —we propose to call it the Minorities Advancement Plan (MAP). It is flexible in design and nonarbitrary in its application. But it is clear as to the ultimate requirement—and it has the force of law. It will occur to quite a few people to plead that what is here proposed is excellent and should be left to the voluntary efforts of those involved. This, however well-meant, holds forth little more promise than did voluntary desegregation in the South. But first a word on the problem.

Source: *Current*, No. 133 (October 1971), pp. 22–29.

In the last 10 years, concern for equality in employment has been all but exclusively confined to what may be called entry-level jobs— jobs, good or bad, that a man or woman gets coming off the street or upon leaving school, as an alternative to unemployment. That blacks, Puerto Ricans, Mexican-Americans and (where they are not disbarred for clear physical reasons) women should be equally prepared for such jobs and have an equal chance to obtain them is now widely agreed in principle and extensively affirmed by law. Much remains to be done about equality in hiring as the current statistics on black and female unemployment graphically affirm. But it is far from being the worst area of discrimination. The worst discrimination is not in the jobs at which the many enter but in the better jobs beyond.

In the better salary corporation, women, blacks, Spanish-speaking citizens and American Indians have only token representation. For all practical purposes, jobs here are monopolized by white males. The figures are uncompromising. In 1969, white males accounted for only 52 percent of all wage-and-salary-earners in private and public employment. They had 96 percent of the jobs paying more than $15,000 a year. Women make up about 30 percent of the full-time labor force; only 2 percent of the women so employed had incomes over $15,000.

The occupational classifications show an equally striking discrimination. Of the male labor force in 1969, 8 percent had jobs as salaried managers and officials. Only 2 percent of the female labor force had jobs that were so classified. Of the male managers and officials, 30 percent—not far short of a third—earned more than $15,000. Of the women managers and officials, only 4 percent—one in 25—earned that much.

But even these figures give an unduly favorable picture of private industry. The various levels of government, though no model of equality, give women and minorities a much better break than private corporations. In the public sector in 1969, white males had "only" 89 percent of the good jobs—i.e., those paying more than $15,000. Women had 6 percent and nonwhite males had 5 percent. In the private economy, by contrast, white males had 98 percent of the good jobs. Nonwhite males and women divided the remaining 2 percent. (In the Federal Government last November, blacks, Spanish, Indians and Oriental Americans held 53.4 percent of the jobs in the GS 1, or lowest white-collar category, and 2 percent of those in the GS 18, or highest classification.)

We see no reason why anyone should try to suppress his indignation over these figures. They are appalling. They show that the American economy is run by—and extensively for the benefit of—a white male elite. We accept it only because, as was once true of segregated lunch counters, and Jim Crow hotels, it has existed for so long. But there is also good reason to consider the practical consequences. The people subject to this discrimination are no longer mute or helpless; one can hardly imagine that they will permanently and peacefully accept their subordinate status. There is, accordingly, a choice between eliminating this discrimination or leaving it to later and much more angry remedy.

One cannot be altogether sanguine that those now favored will see the wisdom of such pre-emptive reform. Most elites, in the past, have considered their supremacy part of the natural order of things when not a matter of divine right. So it may well be with this privileged class. But there is a practical way of ending the present discrimination and perhaps, on this occasion, foresight and common sense will rule. As members ourselves of the elite (something of which we are more than conscious) we would like to urge others to join in showing that, for once, reform can come, at least in part, from the privileged as well as the abused.

FOR A MINORITIES ADVANCEMENT COMMISSION

We propose that the Congress now enact legislation declaring it to be national policy that employment of women, blacks, American Indians and Spanish-speaking minorities be in accord, throughout the various salary brackets in industry and government, with the numbers in the working force. To enforce this we propose that there be created a competently staffed body, fully representative of the minority groups to be assisted, called the Minorities Advancement Commission.

The law would empower the commission to require any firm that has employed more than 5,000 people during the previous five years to submit a plan for bringing the distribution of women, blacks and Spanish-speaking workers in its salary hierarchy into conformity with the representation of these groups in the working force of the community or communities in which it operates. The time allowed for full compliance would be 10 years. Firms with fewer employers and, in consequence, somewhat less flexibility in promotion and employment, would be given more time: We suggest an extra year for each thousand fewer employes; so that a firm with 4,000 workers would have 11 years, one with 3,000 would have 12 years and one with 2,000 would have 13 years. Firms with fewer than 2,000 employes would be exempt from the application of the law.

A similar requirement would be made binding by law on the Federal Government. State and local governments would be invited similarly to bind themselves by law, and would be encouraged to this end by the educational assistance to be mentioned presently. Educational institutions in the above employment categories—in practice, the very large ones—would be subject to similar inducement. In the case of private corporations, we would suggest exempting a maximum of three top positions from the operations of this legislation on the theory that, in the very senior positions, selection of talent should be subject to a minimum of constraint.

In the case of corporations, legislation would apply from just under the top positions down to a salary level set at 150 percent of the national average earnings of fully employed male workers. (In 1969, this was $10,000; so $15,000 would now be the lower limit.) This part of the corporate hierarchy would be divided into five layers, or quintiles, each with one-fifth of the total salary payments. Compliance would be achieved when the appropriate share of salary in each quintile is paid to female, black or Spanish-speaking executives or other salaried workers.

Geographically, women are distributed fairly evenly over the population and also over the working population. For compliance here, we suggest using the expected proportion of women in the full-time labor force. This is now approximately 30 percent. In the last 10 years this proportion has risen by 4 percentage points so, assuming a similar increase in the next 10 years, this requirement would be satisfied by paying 34 percent of the salary income in each quintile to women.

Blacks and Spanish-speaking minorities are not uniformly distributed throughout the country. Here we propose that executive and other salary payments conform to the proportion of the minority-group members in the working force (those employed and seeking employment) in the principal areas of operation of the firm in question. These figures, based on the Standard Metropolitan Statistical Areas as defined by the United States Bureau of the Census, would be supplied by the commission.

We are sensitive to a reaction that this proposal will already have elicited from many executives, including some who are not hostile to the objective. Surely, it will be said, this puts an impossible straitjacket upon the hiring of executives, specialists and other salaried personnel. Not merit but sex, color and ethnic origins would become the overriding considerations. Accordingly, we come now to the elements of flexibility in MAP which, we believe, meet any such legitimate objection.

A firm, it has already been noted, is given 10 years to comply, with added time for smaller (although by no means small) concerns. But we further propose that each firm be allowed to file with the commission its preferred "track" for meeting this objective 10 years (or more) hence. Subject to a minimum level of progress—after two years, not less than 5 percent of the eventual goal in each of the quintiles—the corporation would be permitted to follow any route to ultimate compliance that it deemed desirable. The early years could thus be devoted to recruiting, training and promoting the women and minority group members whose advancement, at the end of the period, would put the firm in full compliance.

Having filed its track, the firm would be subject to penalties for failing to meet its requirements. The fine should be something more than the difference between what it is actually paying to women and minority group members, and what is required under its plan. However, we would favor a hearing procedure that would allow a corporation, after notice and for good reason, to petition for an alteration in its track, providing always that it reached its required goal in the specified time and did not fall below its minimum annual rate of improvement.

American Indians, in many respects the most disadvantaged of minorities, are too few in most areas to be dealt with as a special category. We suggest, as a partial solution, that salary paid to American Indians might count double for compliance in any of the three categories —women, blacks or Spanish-speaking—that we do recognize. Black or Spanish-speaking women could count for compliance as women or as members of the relevant minority—whichever category a firm prefers. Over-compliance in a higher quintile would always be a credit for the same amount (measured by salary) of undercompliance in the next lower quintile.

For smaller employers (those with fewer than 5,000 employes) the number of salary categories, i.e., the quintiles, might well be reduced. Without damaging the ultimate outcome, we believe that these provisions eliminate any legitimate complaint based on the rigidity of the procedures here employed. What remains is the need for aggressive planning and effort to develop executive and other talent among women and the minorities. But that, precisely, is our purpose.

MAP would be binding on all departments and agencies of the Federal Government, subject to special regulations for women in the Armed Forces and a declaration of intent as to minority representation instead of compelled procedures in the case of the judiciary. As with corporations, each department or agency, in conjunction with the Civil Service Commission, would file a track designed to bring it into compliance in the 10-year period.

A word need now be said about the development of the requisite talent. More may be available than is commonly imagined. As long as it is assumed that the better jobs belong to white males, the search for talent is extensively confined to white males. But certainly there will be need for an increase in executive and specialized training to fill the demand for women, blacks and Spanish-speaking personnel that MAP would create. To this we would expect business, engineering and law schools to respond.

But we also propose a system of grants by the Federal Government to states for the support of such training by public and private institutions, and for the special recruitment and preparation that the black and Spanish-speaking students would require. We see these grants as the device for overcoming Constitutional difficulties in compelling compliance by state governments and educational institutions. Such aid would be contingent on legislation by the state governments applying MAP to their own employment policies and to the localities with employment large enough to bring them within the range of MAP. States foregoing such assistance and the resulting training would be subjecting corporations and other employers within their boundaries to a possible shortage of executive and specialized personnel, and prejudicing their own development. Acceptance of MAP by state and local governments and the filing of a track could also be a condition for the receipt of other Federal aid.

Enacted now or in the near future, MAP will mean that 10 years hence the most glaring and indefensible form of discrimination remaining in the American society will have been largely, though not yet completely, erased. Our purpose is not to do the impossible but to insure the possible. What of the objections? There will be many. There are none, we believe, that cannot be answered.

ON ANSWERING OBJECTIONS

It will be claimed that, to meet the requirements of MAP, American corporations (and public bodies) will be loaded with a great deal of inferior talent. There is, we suggest, no clear evidence that women, blacks or Spanish-speaking people are intellectually inferior to white males. There will have to be accelerated development of executive and specialist talent in these groups. But that is an important purpose of MAP and it is for this that time is provided.

It will be asked why we confine MAP to firms (and governmental units) employing more than 2,000 people. That is because larger firms and institutions have more flexibility in their employment policies than smaller firms, and have more highly organized procedures for executive development. Also, in these firms, owners and members of owning families have given way to professional executives. And we are exceedingly conscious of the political resistance we would encounter with a measure that would seem to interfere with the prerogatives of the small-business man. As proposed here, MAP would apply to somewhat fewer than 2,000 corporations, but those 2,000 account for roughly half of all production of goods and services in the private sector of the economy.

It will be suggested that 10 years for the big firms is too long. If equality is right, why not now? We think it important to differentiate between solid progress and appealing rhetoric. Ten years to equality is far better than never, which is the present prospect.

It will be said that the plan will engender hostility on the part of deserving white males who will see female, black, Puerto Rican or Mexican employes advanced to meet the requirements of the law. This seems to us inevitable. But we note that the present discrimination engenders anger on the part of women and the minorities, and that this anger is certain to grow. Equality would seem to be the optimal situation for minimizing anger.

It will be asked why other newly arrived ethnic groups—Italians, Poles, Germans, Jews—are not given similar preference. Although these ethnic groups think of themselves as minorities and, on occasion, believe themselves subject to discrimination, United States Census studies show that they have higher incomes than fully rooted Americans. Such is specifically the case with Russians, Poles, Italians, Germans, Irish—and English. White males of such ethnic origins belong to the club.

It will be said that MAP will weaken the competitive position of the business firm. This is a variant of the argument that women, blacks and Spanish-speaking personnel are either inherently inferior or suffer from inferior educational opportunity. The first cannot be defended; the second is something MAP is meant to correct. But it might also be remarked that MAP will apply to all sizable firms. If there are costs, all firms will be more or less equally affected.

It will be asked why MAP is confined to the higher income jobs. Why not make it applicable to the shop floor? The answer is that no reform can accomplish everything. Existing government legislation and union rules are all but exclusively focused on the production worker and we seek to avoid conflict with these regulations, including any tangle with the unions. It is also important that our present willingness to act at the bottom be matched by a similar willingness to act at the top. As things now stand, a white construction worker can be kept out of a job by regulations that require the contractor to employ blacks. He must wonder, if he stops to think about it, why the white executive has no similar worry. Also, if women and members of the minority groups are properly represented at the top, it would seem reasonably certain that they will suffer less discrimination at the bottom.

Finally, it will be said (and said and said and said) that MAP is an unjustified interference with private business, an improper abridgment of the first rule of free enterprise which holds that everyone should be tested by his ability to contribute to earnings and nothing else. The answer is that the present monopoly of good jobs by white males is indefensible and if it continues will one day result in much more drastic and disagreeable interference with private enterprise. That MAP seeks to forestall. Also no one is now disturbed by an order requiring construction and other firms to hire black workers roughly in accordance with their representation in the community. It would be unfortunate were there to be worry about free enterprise only as the good jobs become involved.

We do endorse promotion by merit. But we do not have promotion by merit so long as women, blacks, Indians, Puerto Ricans and Mexican-Americans are excluded from the competition. After 10 years of MAP, promotion will be much more nearly equal for everyone.

In this connection, we would urge all critics to keep one final point in mind. The choice is not between MAP and a perfect world. The choice is between MAP, or something very like it, and the indefensible discrimination that it seeks to correct.

Chapter 3

INTEGRATION VERSUS LOCAL COMMUNITY CONTROL IN EDUCATION

A. Introduction

The sixties and seventies have been eventful and uncertain years in the field of education. Community pressures and social developments have increasingly intruded into the sedate environment of the schoolhouse, which traditionally has been secluded from such strife by its claim of professionalism. Just how set apart the school actually was in the past is an open question, but concerning the present there is little doubt. Race and ethnic issues are among the most prominent social areas to demand the attention of today's educational personnel.

The 1954 *Brown* vs. *Board of Education* decision provided a momentous impetus for change within education. In this historic case the Supreme Court firmly discarded the "separate but equal" Plessy-Ferguson doctrine of 1896 in favor of "all deliberate speed" toward integration in the classroom. In 1969 a subsequent ruling, which might be characterized as "integration now," increased the tempo and reinforced the mandate for school integration. Metropolitanwide busing began to emerge as an important instrument for attaining that goal. The Supreme Court, the major judicial institution of the United States, had become an unswerving advocate of intergroup association and educational equality in the school setting.

A revolution of a kind within the existing institutional framework has been taking place, not, however, without the resistance of significant segments of society, including some Southerners, middle-class suburbanites, and white ethnic working-class communities. Another source of opposition, ironically, has developed among blacks and in other minority constituencies. The Black Power movement, with its orientation toward separate political and social institutions, became an articulate protagonist for local community control as an alternative to school integration. In part this posture grew out of a sense of despair for the tangible prospects of achieving real integration in what was perceived to be a racist and basically cynical society. Black Power advocates maintain that only black teachers and parents possess the compassion and unique skills required to communicate with and educate black young people.

The school issue has also been coupled with a larger political question in minority development. Internal strength and cohesion are necessary if minority communities are to acquire the power necessary to make an impact in the political realm. Control of the local educational apparatus is an aspect of such an accumulation of strength, and only minority teachers are seen as able to stimulate the type of ingroup identification and commitment among the young that would support minority-group social and economic development. The approach clearly symbolizes a group solidarity and power analysis. A general outline of this position is articulated in Charles Hamilton's article, "Race and Education."

Local community control, however, is not attainable without obstacles, including intense communal warfare, as epitomized in the large-scale, nationally prominent Brownsville–Ocean Hill experience in New York City. Opposition within the educational structure, within the minority community itself, and within the broader urban political system has thrown up formidable barriers to movement along these lines. David Cohen, an educator highly favorable to minority aspirations, sets forth some of the limitations of local community control and touches on a range of alternatives in "The Price of Community Control."

In addition to ideological and political considerations, there are more strictly educational, and to an extent factual, matters to be addressed. In practical terms, or regarding demonstrable educational achievements, does a separate or integrated school environment yield greater benefits for minority children? The most significant statement in recent years regarding this question was contained in the much-discussed Coleman report.[1] The report was impressive, first of all, in documenting the pervasiveness of segregation and inequality in education. In evaluative terms, it found that blacks in integrated settings possess a greater sense of efficacy, namely, a conviction that they can control their own environment and future. More important to our immediate concern, the study states: "This analysis of the test performance of Negro children in integrated schools indicates positive effects of integration."[2] While indicating that greater academic achievement was realized in mixed situations, the report also points out that the statistical differences that were found were generally small.

A subsequent extensive study by the U.S. Commission on Civil Rights (*Racial Isolation in the Public Schools*) arrived at generally similar conclusions.[3] Taking all other factors into account, it states, black children do better in mixed racial settings. Disadvantaged black students attain better academic outcomes when they attend school with a majority of either advantaged *or* disadvantaged white students, as compared with a majority of other disadvantaged blacks.

---

[1] James Coleman et al., *Equality of Educational Opportunity*, Office of Education (Washington, D.C.: U.S. Government Printing Office, 1966).

[2] Ibid., p. 28.

[3] *Racial Isolation in the Public Schools: A Report of the United States Commission on Civil Rights* (Washington, D.C.: U.S. Government Printing Office, 1967).

It should be recognized that the Coleman report, in particular, has provoked much controversy and has been subjected to extensive critique regarding its methodology. Coleman himself has shifted his views, for example on the value of busing as a means of promoting integration. Both reports delineate a number of surrounding variables which play a role in educational attainment, such as family background, socioeconomic status, the quality of teaching, and the resources and facilities in the school. Further, these studies basically compared integrated settings with what might be termed segregated settings, *rather than with majority black settings which were operating substantially under the philosophy and conditions of local community control.*

Additional background research exploring various aspects of intergroup relations and education will be found in the selection by Nancy St. John and Ralph Lewis, "The Influence of School Racial Context on Academic Achievement." They report on their own studies and those of others with respect to academic achievement. An interesting finding is that the effects of integration or separation may not be general; separate subject areas such as math or reading can be influenced differentially.

Parenthetically, an influential, more recent study by Christopher Jencks and his colleagues at the Harvard School of Education places a cloud of doubt on educational arrangements as an avenue of advancement for racial and ethnic groups.[4] In *Inequality: A Reassessment of the Effect of Family and Schooling in America,* Jencks et al. argue against the assumption that the school system is an important vehicle for equalizing status and income. Although this assumption has had a central place in various social policy approaches, including the War on Poverty program and its ramifications, evidence is presented from disparate sources which refutes the assumption. In Jencks's view, if society is really serious about promoting equality, it should create procedures to redistribute income directly rather than awaiting the dubious day when education will equalize earning power. The Jencks position is more complex than this in its general presentation, however. Like most group relations matters, it has inspired heated controversy and criticism.

The Jencks statement leads directly to questions of policy, strategy, and practice. In "Community Control versus School Integration," William Grant gives a lucid description of how the issue of local community control vs. school integration was played out in decentralization planning in one large urban center. The dynamics of community politics, including activities of various actors and factions, and the reactions of

---

[4] Christopher Jencks et al., *Inequality: A Reassessment of the Effect of Family and Schooling in America* (New York: Basic Books, 1972).

the school bureaucracy are graphically presented. The article suggests a number of factors that will have to be dealt with by any group attempting to influence educational policies along one of these lines.

In recent disputes concerning school integration, the question of busing has received increasing emphasis as a critical issue. For an enlightening review of the salient considerations on this matter, see the relevant statements by I. F. Stone and Nathan Glazer, who present lucid arguments on different sides of the issue.[5]

---

[5] I. F. Stone, "Moving the Constitution to the Back of the Bus," *The New York Review of Books,* vol. 18 (April 20, 1972), pp. 4–11; Nathan Glazer, "Is Busing Necessary?" *Commentary,* vol. 53 (March 1972), pp. 39–52.

B. Theoretical and philosophical considerations

CHARLES V. HAMILTON

Race and education: A search for legitimacy

The author asserts that the educational questions and issues being raised by many black parents, students, and teachers today are substantially different from the traditional concerns of experts. The black spokesmen are questioning the *legitimacy* of the educational institutions; they no longer believe that it is sufficient to try to increase the *effectiveness* of those institutions. This difference has caused a tension between those who have been victims of indifferent and inefficient policies and practices and those who believe it is still possible to make the existing institutions operable. Black people are calling for community control, not for integration. They are focusing as much on Afro-American culture and awareness as they are on verbal and arithmetic skills. Some black people are thinking of entirely new, comprehensive forms of education, based on substantially different normative values.

An article on public policy, race, and education in the United States in the late 1960's cannot overlook the clear existence of tremendous ferment taking place in the various black communities in this country. The nature of that ferment is such that, if we would devise relevant policy for educating vast numbers of black people today, we cannot focus merely, or even primarily, on achievement in verbal and mathematical skills as criteria for educational improvement. At one time, possibly to the mid-1960's, it was possible to talk about educational policy largely in terms of "integration" (or at least, desegregation) and assume that plans to implement integration would be dealing with the core of the problem of educational deficiency. This is no longer the case.

Today, one hears wholly different demands being raised in the black community. These demands are better represented by the kinds of resolutions coming out of the workshops of the newly formed (June, 1968) National Association of Afro-American Educators than by the

Source: Charles V. Hamilton, "Race and Education: A Search for Legitimacy," *Harvard Educational Review*, 38, Fall 1968, 669–684. Copyright © 1968 by President and Fellows of Harvard College.

conclusions reached by the report on *Equality of Educational Opportunity* (Coleman Report). These demands are reflected more clearly in the demonstrations of black high school students in many cities for more emphasis on Afro-American history and culture and for better science lab facilities than by the findings of the United States Commission on Civil Rights (*Racial Isolation in the Public Schools*). These demands are more clearly illustrated in the positions taken by the Harlem chapter of the Congress of Racial Equality (CORE), calling for an independent school system for Harlem, and by many of the Concerned Black Parents groups than in policy recommendations found in the statement issued by the Board of Education of Chicago, Illinois in August, 1967 (Redmond Report).

First, I would like to indicate why it is more important at this time, from a socio-political point of view, to put more credence in the wishes of the black community than in the statements and findings of the experts. Second, I would like to give examples of the kinds of things on the minds of some of those black people taking an active interest in new directions for education in the black community. Third, I want to present a sketch of a proposal for dealing with some of the problems in some of the large, urban areas. I am not sanguine that the proposal will be applicable in all places (I assume it will not be), but neither do I believe it possible or necessary to develop one model to fit all occasions. My proposal attempts to combine some of the fervent wishes of a growing number of black people with the clear need to think in wholly new institutional terms. I am fully aware that public policy in this area has been influenced by such dichotomies as "integration vs. segregation" (*de jure* and *de facto*) and "integrated education vs. quality (compensatory) education." My presentation will not use these terms as primary focal points, but it is clear that the main thrust of my proposal will support the involvement of more parents in the school system and the improvement of educational opportunities within the black community. Some critics will view this as an "enrichment" proposal, or as an effort at "compensatory" education, or even as a black power move to maintain and further divisiveness in the society. I simply acknowledge these criticisms at the outset and intend to let my proposal stand on its own merits.

A CRISIS OF EDUCATIONAL LEGITIMACY

It is absolutely crucial to understand that the society cannot continue to write reports accurately describing the failure of the educational institutions *vis-à-vis* black people without ultimately taking into account the impact those truths will have on black Americans. There comes a point when it is no longer possible to recognize institutional failure and then merely propose more stepped-up measures to overcome those failures—especially when the proposals come from the same kinds of people who administered for so long the present unacceptable and dysfunctional policies and systems. Professor Seymour Martin Lipset once wrote:

> Legitimacy involves the capacity of the system to engender and maintain the belief that the existing political institutions are the most appropriate ones for the society. The extent to which contemporary democratic political systems are legitimate depends in large measure upon the ways in which the key issues which have historically divided the society have been resolved.
>
> While effectiveness is primarily instrumental, legitimacy is evaluative. Groups regard a political system as legitimate or illegitimate according to the way in which its values fit with theirs.[1]

And in another place, he has written:

> All claims to a legitimate title to rule in new states must ultimately win acceptance through demonstrating effectiveness. The loyalty of the different groups to the system must be won through developing *in them* the conviction that this system is the best—or at least an excellent—way to accomplish their objectives. And even claims to legitimacy of a supernatural sort, such as "the gift of grace," are subjected on the part of the populace to a highly pragmatic test—that is, what is the payoff?[2]
>
> The United States gradually acquired legitimacy as a result of being *effective*.[3]

The important point here is that loyalty, allegiance, is predicated on performance. What decision-makers *say* is not of primary importance, but it is important what black people *believe*. Do they *believe* that the school systems are operating in their behalf? Do they *believe* that the schools are *legitimate* in terms of educating their children and inculcating in them a proper sense of values? With the end product (i.e., their children graduating from high school as functional illiterates) clearly before their eyes at home and with volumes of reports documenting lack of payoff, it is not difficult to conclude that black people have good reason to question the legitimacy of the educational systems.

They begin to question the entire process, because they are aware that the schools, while not educating their children, are at the same time

---

[1] Seymour Martin Lipset, *Political Man: The Social Bases of Politics* (New York: Doubleday, 1963), p. 64.

[2] Seymour Martin Lipset, *The First New Nation: The United States in Historical and Comparative Perspective* (New York: Basic Books, 1963), pp. 45–46. (Emphasis added.)

[3] Ibid, p. 59. (Emphasis in original.)

supporting a particularly unacceptable situation. They know that the schools are one of the major institutions for socializing their children into the dominant value structure of the society. Professor V. O. Key, Jr. concluded in his book, *Politics, Parties and Pressure Groups:*

> In modern societies the school system, in particular, functions as a for-midable instrument of political power in its role as a transmitter of the goals, values, and attitudes of the polity. In the selection of values and attitudes to be inculcated, it chooses those cherished by the dominant elements in the political order. By and large the impact of widely ac-cepted goals, mores, and social values fixes the programs of American schools. When schools diverge from this vaguely defined directive and col-lide with potent groups in the political system, they feel a pressure to conform.[4]

The relevance of all this is that makers of policy and their advisers must recognize that there is a point beyond which vast numbers of black people *will* become alienated and will no longer view efforts on their behalf, however well-intentioned, as legitimate. When this happens, it behooves decision-makers, if they would search for ways of restoring faith, trust, and confidence, to listen to the demands of the alienated. The "experts" might see integration as socially and educationally sound and desirable, but *their* vision and empirical data might well be, at this juncture, irrelevant. Unless this is understood, I am suggesting that public policy might well find itself in the position of attempting to force its programs on a reluctant black community. And this is hardly a formula for the development of a viable body politic.

A clear example of a paternalistic, objectionable policy is contained in the report of the Chicago Board of Education, *Increasing Desegrega-tion of Faculties, Students, and Vocational Education Programs,* issued August 23, 1967. The Report called for busing black children into all- or predominantly white schools. It contains the very revealing para-graph:

> The assignment of students outside their neighborhood may be objected to by Negro parents who prefer that their children attend the segregated neighborhood school. This viewpoint cannot be ignored. Prior to imple-mentation of such a transfer policy the administration must take steps to reassure apprehensive sending area parents that transfer will be beneficial not only in terms of integration but of improved education for their chil-dren. The generation of a favorable consensus in the designated sending area is important. *If such a consensus is unobtainable, the transfer pro-gram would have to proceed without a popular base.* In the light of the

[4] V. O. Key, Jr., *Politics, Parties and Pressure Groups* (New York: Thomas Y. Crowell Company, 1964), pp. 12–13.

dismal alternatives such a program perhaps should proceed even without consensus, but every effort should be made to attain it.[5]

This is a perpetuation of the pattern of telling the black community what is best for it. My point is that this position will only increase alienation, not alleviate it. At the present time, when the educational systems are perceived as illegitimate, it is highly unlikely that such a policy could lead to success. In order for the program to work, support *must* be obtained from the black community. This means that educational achievement must be conceived more broadly than as the mere acquisition of verbal and mathematical skills. Very many black parents are (for good reason) quite concerned about what happens to the self-image of their black children in predominantly white schools—schools which reflect dominant white values and mores. Are these schools prepared to deal with their own white racism? Probably not, and a few summer institutes for white, middle-class teachers cannot prepare them. Are these schools prepared to come to terms with a young black child's search for identity? Will the black child indeed acquire certain skills which show up favorably on standardized tests, but at the same time avoid coming to grips with the fact that he or she should not attempt to be a carbon copy of the culture and ethos of another racial and ethnic group? Virtually all the social scientists, education experts, and public policy-makers who emphasize integration overlook this crucial, intangible, psychological factor. Many concerned black parents and teachers do not overlook it, however. And their viewpoint has nothing to do with black people wanting to perpetuate "separate but unequal" facilities, or with attitudes of "hate whitey." This concern is simply a necessary reaction to the fact that many white (and black) liberal, integration-oriented spokesmen are tuned in to a particular result and overlook other phenomena. They fail to understand that their criteria for "educational achievement" simply might not be relevant anymore.

What I am stating (in as kind a way as possible) is that setting criteria for measuring equal educational opportunity can no longer be the province of the established "experts." The policy-makers must now listen to those for whom they say they are operating; which means of course that they must be willing to share the powers of policy-making. The experts must understand that what is high on the liberal social scientist's agenda does not coincide with the agenda of many black people. The experts are still focusing on the effectiveness of existing educational institutions. Many black people have moved to the evaluation of the legitimacy of these institutions.

---

[5] *Increasing Desegregation of Faculties, Students, and Vocational Education Programs* (Board of Education, City of Chicago, August 23, 1967), p. B–20. (Emphasis added.)

American social scientists generally are unable to grasp the meaning of alienation when applied to certain groups in this country. (Most of the recent perceptive literature on alienation and modernization deals with new nations of Africa and Asia.)[6]

Consequently, Grant McConnell, in an important book, *Private Power and American Democracy,* could write:

> In general the use of government has depended on a particular group's capacity to isolate the relevant governmental agency from influences other than its own and to establish itself as the agency's constituency—at once giving an air of validity to its own ends and endowing it with the added disciplinary power of public authority over its own members.[7]

And later:

> . . . farm migrant workers, Negroes, and the urban poor have not been included in the system of "pluralist" representation so celebrated in recent years.[8]

Then finally:

> It can be readily agreed that if explosive mass movements are a genuine threat to America, a politics of narrow constituencies might be desirable to counter the danger. Small associations probably do provide order and stability for any society. In the United States some associations may serve in this manner to a greater degree than others. The American Civil Liberties Union and the League of Women Voters have given notable service to American democracy. Trade unions and farm organizations have undoubtedly also been similarly useful at various times. Nevertheless, it should be clear that a substantial price is paid for any guarantee against mass movements provided by a pattern of small constituencies. That price is paid in freedom and equality. Although the price would be worth paying if the danger were grave, it can hardly be argued that such an extremity is present.[9]

There are voices in the black community (accompanied, as we well know, by acts of expressive violence) saying precisely that the danger *is*

---

[6] See: Myron Weiner, ed., *Modernization: The Dynamics of Growth* (New York: Basic Books, 1966); David Apter, *The Politics of Modernization* (Chicago: University of Chicago Press, 1965); S. N. Eisenstadt, *Modernization: Protest and Change* (Englewood Cliffs, N.J.: Prentice-Hall, Inc., 1966); Edward Shils, *Political Development in the New States* (New York: Humanities Press, 1964); Thomas Hodgkin, *Nationalism in Colonial Africa* (New York: New York University Press, 1957); K. H. Silvert, *Expectant Peoples: Nationalism and Development* (New York: Random House, 1964); Lucian W. Pye, *Politics, Personality and Nation Building: Burma's Search for Identity* (New Haven: Yale University Press, 1962).

[7] Grant McConnell, *Private Power and American Democracy* (New York: Random House, 1965), pp. 346–347.

[8] Ibid., p. 349.

[9] Ibid., pp. 355–356.

grave and that the extremity *is* present. The educational systems are particularly vulnerable, because of their very conspicuous inability to "pay-off."

AN ALTERNATIVE AGENDA

It is instructive, then, to examine some of the major items presented by certain voices in the black community. Clearly, one source of constructive ideas would be black teachers, those persons who not only teach in ghetto schools, but whose children attend those schools (in most instances), who, themselves, grew up in the black community, and who, for the most part, still live in black communities.[10] Approximately 800 such teachers met in Chicago, June 6–9, 1968, in a national conference and formed the National Association of Afro-American Educators. They did not spend the four days discussing the Coleman Report or the report of the U.S. Civil Rights Commission. One could identify four particular areas of concern at that conference, and these areas coincide to a great extent with the issues raised by associations of Concerned Black Parents as well as various Afro-American History clubs in the high schools around the country.

1. Control

It was generally concluded that the existing educational systems were not responsive to the wishes of the black community. Therefore, those structural arrangements now operating should be changed substantially. The decision-making process in most ghetto school systems was challenged. The workshop on the black school and the black community issued the following statement:

—Whereas, the educational systems of this nation have criminally failed the Black youth of this country,

—Whereas, Black parents have not had a voice in determining the educational destiny of their youth,

—Whereas, the Black youth and Black parents are demanding relevant education to meet their needs,

---

[10] In a column entitled "Quality Teaching in Decentralized Slum Schools," Fred M. Hechinger, education editor of *The New York Times,* wrote: "It seems more realistic and, for the long pull, more constructive to face the fact that part of the answer to the crisis must come through the efforts of Negro teachers. If young Negro college graduates can be channeled into these schools and if their greater identification with the children's and the parents' own background can more easily gain the pupils' confidence and attention, then to sacrifice some of the present licensing requirements may be a small price to pay" (*The New York Times,* April 29, 1968).

—Therefore, be it resolved that we encourage, support and work to organize local communities to control their own schools through local or neighborhood school boards and further that this organization go on record to immediately implement such plans.
—The goal of the National Association of Afro-American Educators should be Black control of the Black Community schools.[11]

One hears these kinds of statements increasingly among newly politicized people in the black communities. The focus has shifted; emphasis is now on viable ways to gain enough leverage to drastically revise a system. Black people, having moved to the stage of questioning the system's very legitimacy, are seeking ways to create a new system. This is difficult for most Americans to understand precisely because they have assumed the continuing legitimacy of the present educational system.

2. Parent involvement and alliance with black teachers

It is becoming clearer and clearer that the major agents of control should be black parents in the community working closely with the teachers in the school. For this reason, if no other, many black spokesmen do not favor various compulsory plans for busing black children out of their communities into white schools, in some instances, miles away from home. Are we to assume that black parents, likewise, will travel miles across town in the evenings to attend PTA meetings—frequently to be surrounded by a sea of white faces, more articulate and with more organized voting strength? The principle of busing overlooks the very important factor of facilitating black parent participation in the child's schooling. If in fact the home has a critical role to play in the educational process, then we would be well advised not to pursue policies which would make that role more difficult.

The participation of black parents in the child's schooling is one of the points high on the agenda of some black people. And it is clearly at odds with one of the stated objectives of the Redmond Report: to bus black children into white schools, but to maintain a quota (no white elementary school would be over 15 percent black; no high school over 25 percent black), in order to guard against the possibility of a white exodus. James Redmond, Superintendent of Schools in Chicago, said: "Chicago will become a predominantly Negro city unless dramatic action is taken soon . . . School authorities (must) quickly achieve

---

[11] Excerpt from notes of discussion and reports of workshops of National Association of Afro-American Educators (Chicago, Illinois, 1968). (Mimeographed).

and maintain stable racial proportions in changing fringe areas."[12] Trying to placate whites simply is not a matter of top (or high) priority to many black people, especially if it must be done by manipulating black children.

Discussion of parental involvement and control has serious implications for the standards of professionalism we adopt. Black parents might well have different notions about what is methodologically sound, what is substantively valuable. They might well be impatient with some of the theories about teaching reading and writing. And at this stage who is to say that their doubts are not valid? The present approaches have hardly proved efficacious. Therefore, when we get sizeable black parental participation, we are opening up the profession to question and challenge about what constitutes educational legitimacy. No profession welcomes such intrusion from laymen. This is quite understandable; professionals have a vested self-interest. All those years of college courses and practice teaching and certifying exams, all those credentials of legitimacy may be going by the board. But that is precisely what happens in societies which are modernizing, in societies where new groupings—alienated from traditional norms—rise to make new normative demands. It is disturbing, disruptive, painful. It is change. And this is the phenomenon American social science has been unable to come to terms with in the latter half of the twentieth century—especially with reference to the issue of race relations.

3. Psychological impact

A third matter of concern to these new black voices is the psychological impact of educational institutions on the black children. Many black people are demanding more black principals in predominantly black schools, if only because they serve as positive role models for the children. Children should be able to see black people in positions of day-to-day power and authority. There is a demand to have the schools recognize *black* heroes with national holidays. There is concern for emphasizing group solidarity and pride, which is crucial for the de-

---

[12] Quoted in an editorial in *Chicago Sun-Times,* January 12, 1968, p. 27. The editorial, which favored the Redmond Plan, further stated: "That part of the Redmond Plan that has excited opposition calls for fixing immediately a balanced racial enrollment in those all-white schools that are in the way of the Negro expansion. It would be roughly 90 percent white, 10 percent Negro. The Negro pupils (who are from middle-class families) would be acceptable to white families and keep them anchored in the neighborhood, whereas they would flee to the suburbs if the Negro proportion became greater than 25 percent. The plan may not work. If it does it is at best only a holding action until the entire metropolitan area faces up to the demographic realities of our time. But it should be tried."

velopment of black Americans. And there is very serious question whether a predominantly white, middle-class ethos can perform this function. Again, the Coleman data measure verbal skills and mathematical abilities, but there are other areas of equal importance. One should not assume that symbols of cultural pride are unimportant. Professor Lipset was correct when he described the impact of these symbols, but he was incomplete when he applied them to the United States—when the growing awareness of black Americans is taken into account. He wrote:

> A major test of legitimacy is the extent to which given nations have developed a common "secular political culture," mainly national rituals and holidays. The United States has developed a common homogeneous culture in the veneration accorded the Founding Fathers, Abraham Lincoln, Theodore Roosevelt, and their principles.[13]

The schools serve as a major instrument to transmit such a common homogeneous culture. And yet, we are beginning to see black Americans call for the recognition of other heroes: Frederick Douglass, Martin Luther King, Jr., Malcolm X, and so forth. Students are demanding that the traditional Awards Day programs at their schools include such awards as a Malcolm X Manliness Award, a Marcus Garvey Citizenship Award, and Frederick Douglass and Martin Luther King, Jr. Human Rights Awards. We see black writers challenging the idea of a common secular political culture. John Oliver Killens and Lerone Bennett, Jr. are two prominent examples. Killens captured the mood when he wrote:

> We (black Americans) even have a different historical perspective. Most white Americans, even today, look upon the Reconstruction period as a horrible time of "carpetbagging," and "black politicians," and "black corruption," the absolutely lowest ebb in the Great American Story . . .
>
> We black folk, however, look upon Reconstruction as the most democratic period in the history of this nation; a time when the dream the founders dreamed was almost within reach and right there for the taking; a time of democratic fervor the like of which was never seen before and never since . . .
>
> For us, Reconstruction was the time when two black men were Senators in the Congress of the United States from the State of Mississippi; when black men served in the legislatures of all the states in Dixie; and when those "corrupt" legislatures gave to the South its first public-school education . . .[14]

---

[13] Lipset, *Political Man*, p. 68.
[14] John Oliver Killens, *Black Man's Burden* (New York: Trident Press, 1965), pp. 14–15.

Even our white hero symbols are different from yours. You give us moody Abe Lincoln, but many of us prefer John Brown, whom most of you hold in contempt as a fanatic; meaning, of course, that the firm dedication of any white man to the freedom of the black man is *prima-facie* evidence of perversion or insanity.[15]

And Lerone Bennett, Jr. challenged much of American historical scholarship when he challenged the role and image of Abraham Lincoln:

Abraham Lincoln was *not* the Great Emancipator. As we shall see, there is abundant evidence to indicate that the Emancipation Proclamation was not what people think it is and that Lincoln issued it with extreme misgivings and reservations.[16]

A growing number of black Americans are insisting that the schools begin to reflect this new concern, this new tension. We simply cannot assume a common secular political culture. If we continue to operate on such false assumptions, we will continue to misunderstand the very deep feeling of alienation in the black community. And misunderstanding cannot be a viable basis for enlightened public policy. Likewise, it is not only important that Afro-American history be taught in the black schools, but that it also be incorporated into the curriculum of white schools throughout this country. It is not sufficient that only black children be given an accurate historical picture of the race; all Americans must have this exposure—in the inner city, the suburbs, the rural schools.

Who can predict what the "tests" will show when we begin to expose black children to these kinds of innovations? What sort of impact will this have on the motivation of those "slow learners," those "high risks," those (and here is the misnomer of them all) "culturally deprived"? The legitimacy of the "standardized tests" must be questioned as long as they overlook these very essential components.

4. Curricula and instructional materials

Closely related to the third point is a concern with the kinds and content of materials used, especially in black schools. How are black people portrayed? Do the textbooks reflect the real experience of black Americans in history and in contemporary society? The workshop on instructional materials at the Afro-American Educators Conference concluded:

In each local community black educators must develop a criteria for selection of materials which will be presented to the Board of Education,

---

[15] Ibid., p. 17.
[16] Lerone Bennett, Jr., "Was Abe Lincoln a White Supremacist?" *Ebony,* 23, No. 4 (February, 1968), p. 35.

to local textbook committees, and to the major publishing houses which provide text and supplemental materials to that community. It is incumbent upon us, if we are to serve this society, that instructional material which we select be both educationally sound and incorporate a strong black orientation.

Black classroom teachers must help black students to speak the language of the market place and assist them as they move back and forth between "their own thing and a white American thing." Since all groups usually speak two languages, one at home and within their group and another in the economic world, by nurturing and respecting our own language and effectively manipulating the other we will become a truly bilingual people. This is necessary to achieve a viable economic base . . .

Black teachers must become connected with major textbook publishing firms as authors, editors and consultants to create the materials available on the market. We must pressure major publishers to reflect the needs of black children in schools. We will work for a factual inclusion of the scientific contribution of black scientists to medical and scientific advancement. For example, Dr. Daniel Hale Williams (open heart surgery) and Dr. Charles Drew (developer of blood plasma) must receive their rightful place in elementary and secondary science texts.[17]

These are some of the things on the agenda of many black people as they consider possible solutions of our vast educational problems. It is far too soon to evaluate the results of most of these proposals—in some instances they have not even been implemented. And in most cases they are in the embryonic stage. We are without precedent in these matters, and it would be presumptuous of American social scientists to attempt to prejudge results, or even to suppose that they could. Black people are searching for new forms of educational legitimacy, and in that kind of modernizing atmosphere the traditional criteria for measuring effectiveness might well be irrelevant and anachronistic.

AN ALTERNATIVE MODEL

The rhetoric of race and education, as stated earlier, is prolific with dichotomies of segregation vs. integration, quality education vs. integrated education, compensatory programs vs. busing, and so forth. Too much is assumed by these simplistic terms, and a superficial use of these labels frequently restricts and predetermines discussion at the outset. While this is unfortunate, it is probably unavoidable, given the historical context and the highly emotional atmosphere. Those persons favoring "neighborhood" schools and opposing busing have traditionally been, in the North, white parents and taxpayer groups, usually identified as anti-

---

[17] Excerpt from notes and discussion and reports of workshops of National Association of Afro-American Educators (Chicago, Illinois, 1968). (Mimeographed).

Negro in their basic racial views. These groups would normally be found opposing open housing laws as well. Therefore their motivations are questioned when they argue that they are essentially concerned about "educational standards" and property values. When it is pointed out to them that white students do not suffer academically and (if panic selling is avoided) property values do not go down, they do not listen. And their intransigence leads their opponents to label them as racial bigots and segregationists.

Proponents of busing and integration see a positive academic and social value in racially heterogeneous classrooms. Integration to these people is virtually synonymous with quality. And black people who once worked for desegregated schools but who no longer do so are viewed as having given up the fight, as having joined the white racists, and, indeed, as having become black racists and advocates of "Black Power separatism."[18]

I state this simply to acknowledge an awareness of some of the positions taken before I proceed to suggest an alternative educational plan. The fact that my ideas would appear more closely akin to the views of some white segregationists whose ultimate goal is to deny educational opportunity to black people is an *appearance* I cannot avoid. It is important, however, to point out that a close examination of the ultimate goals of my suggestions will indicate a clear divergence from views held by the segregationists. In other words I am motivated by an attempt to find an educational approach which is relevant to black people, not one that perpetuates racism. The plan I am suggesting is not a universal panacea; it is not applicable in all black ghettos. Where it is feasible— particularly in the large urban communities—I strongly propose it for consideration.

This is a model which views the ghetto school as the focal point of community life. The educational system should be concerned with the entire family, not simply with the children. We should think in terms of a Comprehensive Family-Community-School Plan with black parents attending classes, taking an active, day-to-day part in the operation of the school. Parents could be students, teachers, and legitimate members of the local school governing board. A similar plan is already in operation in Chicago: the Family Education Center. There are two centers,

---

[18] An example of this attitude was contained in the report of the President's civil disorders commission (Kerner Commission). "The Black Power advocates of today consciously feel that they are the most militant group in the Negro protest movement. Yet they have retreated from a direct confrontation with American society on the issue of integration and, by preaching separatism, unconsciously function as an accommodation to white racism" (*Report of the National Advisory Commission on Civil Disorders* [New York: E. P. Dutton & Company, 1968], p. 235).

the Westinghouse and Doolittle Centers, which provide basic adult education, prevocational and vocational training, and work experience programs.

Mr. William H. Robinson, Director of the Cook County Department of Public Aid, has stated:

> The Center's most unique feature is the Child Development Program for the students' (parents') pre-school children, who come to school with their mothers and spend the day in a well-equipped, professionally staffed nursery school. Mothers can attend classes with the assurance that their children are receiving proper care and mental stimulation. Thus, the program makes participation in an educational program possible for many recipients who were prevented previously because they could not obtain adequate child care services.[19]

Since the inception of the program two years ago, 1,300 adults and 500 children have been involved in the centers.

This concept should be expanded to include fathers as well, those unemployed and willing to obtain skills. Many of these parents could serve as teachers, along with a professional staff. They could teach courses in a number of areas (child care, auto mechanics, art, music, home economics, sewing, etc.) for which they are obviously now trained. The Comprehensive Plan would extend the school program to grades through high school—for adults and children—and it would eliminate the traditional calendar year of September to June. (There is no reason why the educational system could not be revised to take vacations for one month, say in December of post-Christmas, and another month in August. The community educational program would be a year-round function, day and evening.)

The school would belong to the community. It would be a union of children, parents, teachers (specially trained to teach in such communities), social workers, psychologists, doctors, lawyers, and community planners. Parent and community participation and control would be crucial in the hiring and firing of personnel, the selection of instructional materials, and the determination of curriculum content. Absolutely everything must be done to make the system a functioning, relevant part of the lives of the local people. Given the present situation of existing and growing alienation, such involvement is essential.

If it can be demonstrated that such a comprehensive educational institution can gain the basic trust and participation of the black community, it should become the center of additional vital community functions. Welfare, credit unions, health services, law enforcement, and

---

[19] Cook County Department of Public Aid, *The Challenge of Change* (Annual report, Chicago, 1967), p. 11.

recreational programs—all working under the control of the community —could be built around it. Enlightened private industry would find it a place from which to recruit trained, qualified people and could donate equipment and technical assistance. The several advantages of such a plan are obvious. It deals with the important agencies which are in daily, intimate contact with black people; it reduces a vast, fragmented service bureaucracy which now descends on the black community from many different directions, with cumbersome rules and regulations, uncontrolled by and unaccountable to the community. It provides the black people with a meaningful chance for participation in the very important day-to-day processes affecting their lives; it gives them educational and vocational tools for the future. All these things reflect the yearnings and aspirations of masses of black people today.

The Comprehensive Plan envisions the local school as a central meeting place to discuss and organize around community issues, political and economic. All of the establishments functioning under the plan would provide relevant intermediary groups to which the people could relate. The size of the community involved would vary, with several factors to be considered: geography, number of participating agencies, available funds (from federal, state, and local governmental sources), and manageability. At all times, the primary concern would be about the active involvement of people and about their possession of real power to make decisions affecting the Comprehensive Plan. They would hire consultants and experts whose legitimacy would be determined by their relevance to the community, not by a predetermined set of criteria superimposed from outside.

The proposed Comprehensive Plan attempts to come to grips with the understandable alienation discussed in the first section and with the appropriateness of the agenda items described in the second section of the paper. This plan is better understood when one keeps in mind the premise presented earlier: black people are questioning, evaluating the *legitimacy* of existing educational institutions, not simply searching for ways to make those institutions more *effective*. I am suggesting that we are at a point in the process of modernization and social transformation when we must begin to think and act in wholly new normative and structural terms.

DAVID K. COHEN

The price of community control

Like everything else in the cities, education seems to defy both management and comprehension. The struggle over urban schools has in recent years grown progressively more ferocious, with the casualties mounting accordingly. Discussions of underachievement and psychological damage have given way to cries of genocide. No longer are anger and criticism confined to the malfeasance of an occasional superintendent; the arena of contention now includes entire educational programs—integration, school improvement, community control—each designed in its own way to remedy conditions in slum schools. Meanwhile, the schools remain segregated, student achievement shows no sign of change, and the distribution of power is no different from what it used to be. Yet while we appear to have been on a treadmill with respect to basic educational reform, the ideological scenery has been going by at a furious rate; at present, the main issue no longer appears to be whether segregation should be eliminated, or more money allocated to schools, but who shall control what exists.

How has this change come about? Until about a year ago, most people would have agreed that the main purpose of school reform was to eliminate racial disparities in educational achievement; this, in turn, was regarded as the best way to reduce racial disparities in jobs and income. The debate, by and large, centered on the question of how the schools should go about accomplishing that task. Many Negroes and white liberals supported an emphasis on integration, arguing that segregated schools impaired motivation and achievement, and thereby damaged Negroes' chances for occupational success and full citizenship. Educators, on the other hand, typically located the problem not in the racial organization of public education but in the intellectual and cultural "deprivation" of Negro children; hence, they advocated educational programs aimed at compensating for those deficiencies.

Recently, two new educational proposals have been advanced—decentralization and community control. In the form in which they were initially made, these proposals did little to disturb the assumptions underlying earlier efforts at reform. Thus, increased accountability to the local community was presented as another way of unlocking a school's potential for raising the educational attainment of its pupils. Although other issues have since arisen, the original claims for decentralization

Source: *Commentary*, vol. 48 (July 1969), pp. 23–32. Reprinted from *Commentary*, by permission; copyright © 1969 by the American Jewish Committee.

rested on the belief that the traditional "liberal" approaches to school reform—integration and/or compensatory education—had been tried and had failed.

Behind this notion lay three major assumptions. One was that government had in fact redistributed resources—in the form of students, teachers, dollars, or whatever—in order to eliminate the racially unequal distribution of results in schooling. A second was that the programs of integration and compensatory education had been evaluated, and it had been demonstrated that they did not work: i.e., test scores had not changed. Finally, the reason for this failure was perceived to be administrative or political in nature: the school bureaucracy was opposed to reform, the teachers were racist, or the entire structure was hopelessly unresponsive. From these assumptions flowed the conclusion that any new policy proposal—be it bloc grants, administrative decentralization, or community control—must center on transforming fundamental political relationships.

Before taking up the merits of these new proposals, I should like to discuss the assumptions on which they rest. For it is by no means self-evident: (*a*) that liberal programs of educational reform were in fact tried on a significant scale; (*b*) that where they were tried, they failed; or (*c*) that political and administrative change is necessarily a precondition for change in the distribution of educational achievement.

II

Hard evidence on the effectiveness of educational strategies has never been easy to come by. Until 1966, for example, when the Coleman Report was published,[1] virtually no direct evidence existed on the relationship between a school's racial composition and how well its students performed. What the Coleman Report revealed turned out to be at some variance with integrationist ideology: Negro students in mostly white schools were indeed higher achievers than those in mostly Negro schools, but this apparently bore no intrinsic relation to a particular school's racial composition. Rather, in those mostly white schools where Negroes performed well, the white students were typically from more advantaged homes; Negro students in a middle-class white school would do no better than Negro students in an equally middle-class Negro school. As a practical matter, integrationists could reassure themselves that the relative lack of a Negro middle class meant that social-class integration would inevitably entail racial integration as well, but in view

---

[1] James S. Coleman, et al., *Equality of Educational Opportunity* (Washington, D.C.: U.S. Department of Health, Education, and Welfare, 1966).

of this finding they could no longer embrace the notion that a school's racial composition *per se* affected achievement.

Of course, the absence of unequivocal evidence on achievement was never the main obstacle to school integration, and in many communities where integration was tried, achievement gains seem indeed to have followed. In most communities, however, the attempt was never even made. The blame for this may be placed primarily on the indifference, inertia, and opposition of school officials, and on the general political sentiment which they reflected. Although committed educational leadership in places like Berkeley, Evanston, and Syracuse showed that organized white resistance could be overcome, most school systems—in the hundreds of communities whose size and demography put integration within easy reach—never reached that stage. Even fewer efforts were made in the large cities, where national attention was riveted.

Integrationists responded to this situation by devising a strategy which promised to reduce white opposition by coupling integration with a variety of beguiling educational attractions: educational parks, magnet schools, special education centers, and the like. If most white parents, the reasoning went, were forced to choose between inferior all-white schools and educationally superior integrated facilities, they would not hesitate to choose the latter. The problem was that educational innovations are as expensive as school budgets are tight; the strategy required new legislation which would allocate much more money to city schools.

In any event, the strategy was never really tried, since most professional educators chose a different response altogether. They saw that Negro parents wanted better schools and higher achievement, and therefore offered programs of remedial and compensatory education in the existing segregated schools. When this counter-strategy was embodied in local programs, and in Title I of the Elementary and Secondary Education Act of 1965, it put a premium on the perpetuation of segregated schools. It paid educators to maintain schools in the slums rather than create the integrated, educationally superior facilities envisioned in integrationist rhetoric.

Thus it is incorrect to say that school integration failed; what failed was the politics required to bring it about. Like most liberal strategies for social change, integration is politically viable only on the assumption that it is in the interest of whites to reduce the status disparity between themselves and Negroes. Inducing whites to choose integration by creating educationally irresistible schools was a clever effort to create such an identity of interest. The only flaw was that before white parents could be presented with the choice, vast new funds would have had to be appropriated, with the explicit proviso that they would be used to create these schools. And naturally the money itself could not be obtained without substantial white support. In political terms this meant that in order to make the strategy work one had to presume the prior existence of that very identity of educational interests which the strategy was designed to bring into being. In this case, circular reasoning proved to be as deadly in politics as it usually is in logic: only a few of the integrationists' schools have ever been created.

The concept of compensatory education favored by most educators represented an effort to avoid this fatal circularity. Since compensatory programs operated only in slum schools, they seemed indeed to offer a happy political alternative. Whites could assume a progressive stance by supporting improved ghetto education—and better schools for poor whites, too—while opposing or remaining neutral on demands for busing, Princeton plans, and other politically volatile integration tactics. For these reasons—to say nothing of the substantial Negro support the remedial programs enjoyed—a powerful coalition of moderate and liberal reformers and schoolmen came together behind such legislation as Title I of the Elementary and Secondary Education Act.

How did these programs fare? Over the past two years a succession of evaluations has been unable to find much evidence of improved achievement. To be sure, their sponsors have proclaimed the programs a success: the litanies of praise that have been issued cite improved school conditions, brighter attitudes, better attendance, reduced vandalism, happier teachers, etc. Nonetheless, to judge by the main criterion the programs were designed to satisfy, the general absence of gains in achievement makes all these claims seem trivial or disingenuous.

What accounts for this unhappy record? In a strict sense the question cannot be answered, for as long as we don't know what works, it is impossible to make the comparisons which might suggest the reasons for failure. Comparisons aside, however, one *can* assess in a general way the actual impact on slum schools of the millions of federal dollars that have been appropriated for their improvement. Title I increased instructional expenditures for each participating child by about $60 a year in 1966–67, and last year by about $65. Since the nation annually spends an average of about $450 per pupil for instruction, the increment (10 to 15 percent) from Title I can only be described as modest. The simplest way to figure the amount of educational improvement that an increase like that can buy is in terms of the time a teacher devotes to her children. If a teacher has thirty students and works a five-hour day (and if we imagine that she divides the day into a series of tutorials), then each student receives a ten-minute daily tutorial. An increase of 10 percent in the teaching staff would add one minute to the daily individual attention a student receives. That does not exactly constitute an educational revolution.

There is more. For one thing, the compensatory moneys have often been used to make up for existing differences between black and white schools, rather than for creating better-than-equal black schools. For another, the funds made available under Title I frequently have been so dispersed that their budgetary impact—which is clear enough on a balance sheet—is undetectable in the target schools themselves. As a result, in many cases the infusion of money has had the opposite effect from the one intended. If, on the one hand, the funds are concentrated only on the neediest children, a noticeable change does occur in these children's school program, but only for an hour or so a day, or a day a week. Teachers who work in the school but not in the program often become hostile or jealous, and those who do work in the program, since their colleagues are unfriendly and their students unsuccessful, grow frustrated and discouraged. They explode and leave, or somehow adjust cynically to the situation; neither reaction is particularly productive. If, on the other hand, the funds are diffused widely over a variety of children and schools, intense frustration on the part of a few teachers is traded off for a more generalized low level of despondency or indifference. Then there is the added problem of turnover in both teaching staff and in the programs themselves, which occurs partly as a result of the conditions I have just outlined, partly for political or administrative reasons. Continuity is rare and knowledge noncumulative: the same basic lessons are often learned over and over again, either by new teachers in the same program, or by the same teachers in new programs. No one benefits perceptibly.

There have been a few experiments which involved rather larger sums than those provided by Title I, but here too one would be hard put to say unequivocally that they resulted in improved achievement. Some interpretations of evidence from the More Effective Schools program in New York City, for example, suggest that there may have been achievement gains for children who were exposed to the program over long periods of time, but other interpretations suggest the opposite; similarly with the tutoring program conducted by New York's Mobilization for Youth and a few other programs. In all cases, reports of improvement are open to serious question.

Finally there are pre-school programs, which vary in content and direction from traditional classroom situations, to parent-training programs, to programs giving individual attention to two-year-olds. A number of these programs have reported substantial gains. Two things, however, should be noted about them. The first is that the gains appear to dissipate quickly if things are allowed to return to normal; the second is that those programs which are school-centered are very expensive, costing between $1,000 and $1,500 per child per annum.

Now, research on pre-school education seems to indicate that it is indeed possible, although it is by no means easy, to affect patterns of intellectual development if pervasive changes in a child's environment are instituted a good deal earlier than the age at which schooling now begins, and if they are continued on into the elementary school years. But the prospect of undertaking such a course of action raises many problems in its turn. One of these relates to the political and cultural implications of further extending the school's dominion over children; I will take this up later. Another is suggested by the price that is likely to be exacted for such reform: if the cost of improving achievement will be an additional one or two thousand dollars per pupil per year, and if our main goal is to eliminate racial disparities in adult income and occupation, then why not spend the money directly on family income maintenance, or on creating socially useful and important jobs? Perhaps the best way to change existing inequalities in income and occupation is to change them, not to use schooling as a means of deferring reform.

The costliness of programs of intensive education in early childhood is politically crucial in another way, too, for a ghettoized approach to school improvement assumes that whites will trade off the programs' cost for the maintenance of segregation. Although to some extent that is doubtless true, there is no guarantee that the commitment of whites to existing patterns of segregation will stretch to the point where they would be willing to spend on black children two or three times what is typically spent on whites. It is precisely here that the "failure" of compensatory education resides. As a recent publication of the U.S. Office of Education dolefully pointed out, a really serious effort in compensatory education would ". . . require a mobilization effort more far-reaching than any now envisioned by any community." It would, in other words, imply a level of white support for ghetto development which—in light of the past eight years' experience—is as difficult to conceive as the amount of white support that would be required for integration.

III

What has failed, then, is not the traditional "liberal" educational technologies—whether of the integrationist or compensatory variety; these technologies have been tried too sporadically and haphazardly to permit a careful assessment. Rather, the deficiency lies in the absence of operational political strategies which would bind up the interests of blacks and whites in such a way as to elicit white support for programs that would improve the relative status of black children. That is a primitive political defect, an inability to apply what might be called the politics of common interest to basic social reform.

But if it is incorrect to say that integration and compensatory education have been tried and found wanting, politically it all seems to amount to the same thing: the relative educational status of Negro and white children in metropolitan areas is little different now from what it was in 1954. The persistence of this dreary contrast has in recent years provided a major impetus to movements for decentralization and community control.

Decentralization and community control refer to a variety of notions about schooling and school reform, not all of them related to the problem of disparities in achievement. One of these is that the potentially effective components of city school systems—parents, teachers, and inquisitive children—are walled off from each other by a Byzantine bureaucratic maze; before the elements can function to the children's best advantage, the argument runs, the walls must be broken down and the bureaucracy brought under control. Another view is that the entire educational system is racist, from the way it allocates resources, to the attitudes of its teachers and the character of its textbooks; according to this view the remedy is not to make the system more accessible but to transfer control of the enterprise altogether: until the schools are operated by the parents of their young black clients (or those who legitimately stand *in loco parentis*), they will not be responsive to the needs of Negro children. A third view is that the problem resides in the psychological consequences of powerlessness. As things now stand, it is argued, the central fact of life for black Americans is that they do not control their personal and collective destinies. All the significant ghetto institutions—schools, government, welfare, etc.—are controlled by whites. Unless these whites are replaced by Negroes, black children will lack a sense that the world will respond to their efforts, and their achievement will languish as a consequence. The last two ideas roughly comprise the meaning of community control, the first, decentralization.

Of the three, the notion that the root problem is bureaucracy probably has the broadest appeal. For one thing, the complexity and unresponsiveness of many big-city school systems is legendary; no client of any class or color happily accepts the reign of the clerk, and increasing numbers reject the inflexible style and pedagogy of the schools. For another, we have long been accustomed to the idea that the very size of institutions inevitably produces a kind of social arteriosclerosis, and assume that the remedy lies not in reaming out the conduits, but in reducing the distance between the vital organs and the extremities. Finally, the anti-bureaucratic critique is almost always couched in irresistible contrasts between extreme situations—Scarsdale as opposed to Bedford-Stuyvesant, or Winnetka as opposed to the West Side of Chicago.

Unfortunately, however, there is no evidence that the level of parent participation in schools is related to students' achievement. It is true that parents in suburban communities are somewhat more likely to participate in school affairs than those in central cities, but this seems to have more to do with the consequences of affluence than with anything else; analysis of the data in the Coleman Report fails to reveal any association between the level of parental participation and achievement. Nor is there any evidence that smaller school districts—which we all presume to be less bureaucratized and more responsive to parents and children—produce higher levels of achievement than larger ones. With a few outstanding exceptions, public education in the U.S. runs on the assumption that administrative decentralization, small and homey school districts, and local control are educational essentials; literally thousands of school jurisdictions stand as testimony to this creed, against only a handful of urban monoliths. Yet here again there appears to be no relation whatsoever between the size of a school district (or whether its board is elected or appointed) and the achievement of the students in its schools.

On the other hand, there is abundant evidence that parents who are involved in a direct way in their children's education tend to have children who achieve at higher levels. Involvement of this sort includes reading to children, taking them to libraries, talking to them, explaining things, and otherwise providing lots of cognitive stimulation and support for intellectual accomplishment. Thus, when poor parents are trained to behave toward their children in the way middle-class parents do, the children's level of achievement rises. This should not come as a surprise, except perhaps to those hardy souls who believe that the intellectual deprivation associated with poverty can be traced exclusively to genetic makeup. It does, however, argue for the establishment of parent-training efforts, like the one that has been operating in Ypsilanti, Michigan, rather than programs aimed at eliminating bureaucracy in schools.

Advocates of community control (as opposed to administrative decentralization) might raise the objection here that the source of underachievement is not bureaucratic inertia in the first place, but institutional racism. There is, in fact, no dearth of evidence that city school systems discriminate against the poor in general and Negroes in particular. Studies of resource allocation almost always reveal that predominantly black schools suffer by comparison with white schools, in terms of such things as teacher experience, tenure, and certification. In addition, the attitudes of many teachers are influenced by class and racial antagonisms; in the Coleman sample of Northern urban elementary schools, between 10 and 20 percent of teachers in ghetto schools overtly expressed a preference for schools with all or nearly all white student bodies. It should be noted, however, that Negro children whose teachers are as good as or better than the average for whites and have better than average racial attitudes, do not show higher achievement than their less fortunate counterparts in ghetto schools.

Here it may be countered that it is not a teacher's racial attitudes which affect performance, but his expectations of his students' academic success. And indeed, this idea appears to make intuitive good sense. It seems reasonable to believe that bigoted white teachers—or Negroes who accept white stereotypes—will somehow communicate to their students the sense that black children are academically less capable. If that is so, then it might well follow that the most efficient way to deal with such teachers, short of large-scale psychotherapy, would be to sharpen dramatically their responsibility to the parents of Negro children, on the theory that they would then have to shape up or ship out.

Let us assume for the moment that this hypothesis is correct.[2] Let us also grant that community control would transform academic expectations that have been distorted over the years by bigotry or brainwashing. Would it also eliminate underachievement in ghetto schools? The latter is unlikely, for most achievement differences appear to be related not to a student's race or to his school's racial composition, but to factors having to do with social class. Correcting the consequences of racist distortions in teachers' expectancies is not the same thing as correcting the vast class differentials which produce differences in achievement in the first place. The notion that bigoted teachers depress the academic performance of black children is based on the premise that these teachers fail accurately to perceive and/or to act upon the children's real potential, *because the children are black.* Yet it has been shown that differences in achievement are of roughly the same magnitude at grade six or nine as they are at the time children enter school, and are relatively insensitive to variations in *anything* about schools. All the research of the last four decades points to the conclusion that differences in nutrition, general health, and access to intellectual and cognitive stimulation —which, of course, vary widely by social and economic status, and therefore by race—are the chief environmental determinants of children's intellectual performance. Eliminating racial distortions in teacher expectations would improve ghetto education, but it would probably not eliminate disparities in achievement that are ultimately due to differences in social class.

Both of the theories that I have discussed so far suffer from the obvious defect of presuming that schools have an impact upon students'

---

[2] It has been argued most persuasively by Robert Rosenthal and Lenore Jacobson in *Pygmalion in the Classroom* (New York: Holt, Rinehart & Winston, 1968). In a review published in the *American Educational Research Journal* (November 1968), Robert L. Thorndike cast serious doubt on the author's research.

achievement, when most evidence on this point tends in the opposite direction. The third—the fate-control theory—does not so presume. Its premise is the notion that the central educational problem for black children is not poor pedagogy, but powerlessness, a political condition in the ghetto which is not at all unique to the schools. Now, it takes only a modicum of political insight to notice that Negroes do not control most of the institutions which directly affect their lives, and little ideological originality to argue that hence they are a subject people, dominated in colonial fashion by a foreign white ruling class. This argument has been advanced with increasing strength since World War II, but until publication of the Coleman Report there was no way to link the political fact of powerlessness with students' performance in school. One of that report's major findings, however, was that the extent to which black students felt they could master their destiny was a powerful determinant of their achievement, more important than all the measures of family, social, and economic status combined.

That provided the necessary link. If a student's sense of environment control strongly influenced his achievement, black control of ghetto schools, it seemed to follow, would produce a sense of personal efficacy which would in turn lead to improved performance. The idea now enjoys enormous popularity, primarily because it seems entirely consistent with reality. First of all, political and cultural emasculation has been a dominant element of the black experience in America. Secondly, all the precedents of American ethnic history are supposed to demonstrate that group political and economic solidarity is the touchstone of personal status and mobility. Finally, it seems to make eminent sense that people who feel in control of their destiny will be high achievers; the sense of mastery leads to mastery.

But try it the other way: mastery leads to the sense of mastery; high achievers are more likely to have a stronger sense of environment control than low achievers. It sounds just as persuasive one way as the other, a perplexity which is amply reflected in research. Some studies suggest that the sense of efficacy causes achievement, some suggest that it works the other way around, and others find no association whatsoever. We have no studies of the relationship between parents' political efficacy (or their sense thereof) and their children's test scores; the few studies that relate parents' general sense of environment control to their children's achievement are inconclusive and contradictory. Here as elsewhere, the results of scientific research provide a firm basis for nothing but further research.

In summary: a good deal has been made of the various ways in which decentralization and community control will improve achievement, but a review of what we know turns up confused, contradictory, or discouraging evidence. This does not mean that greater participation, less bureaucracy, greater openness, and more accountability are not worthwhile goals; I happen to think they are crucial. In my view, however, these are essentially political and administrative issues, and one's assessment of their significance or desirability should be determined by theory and evidence particular to those realms of experience. The one thing my brief review of the educational evidence *does* mean is this: if one were guided solely by research on achievement and attitudes, one would not employ community control or decentralization as the devices most likely to reduce racial disparities in achievement.

IV

But the gathering momentum for community control and decentralization is unlikely to be diminished by this news. On the contrary, advocates of these policies argue that evidence derived from the existing situation is not simply inadequate but altogether inapplicable. More important, the major pressures for decentralization and community control now have less to do with the failure of educational strategies than with the failure of what I referred to earlier as the politics of common interest.

As a historical matter, it is of course true that one of the underlying causes of the movement for community control has been the persistence of racial disparities in achievement. Yet the nature of the current situation is best illustrated by the fact that within the last year, the persistence of these disparities has not simply produced more militant demands for higher achievement but has created a profound crisis of authority in ghetto schools, a sense that these schools lack legitimacy as educational institutions. This feeling is strongest among Negroes—especially the young, the activists, and the professionals—but it is reinforced by the many middle- and upper-middle-class whites who reject the public schools' regimentation and authoritarianism for other reasons. For some blacks and whites, the notion that only parents and community residents are legitimately empowered to operate schools rests on what is taken to be the objective inadequacy of those in authority; scarcely anyone with access to print denies that the schools have failed to correct ghetto educational problems. Repeated for years, this assertion has led effortlessly to the idea that the established agencies lack the special competence upon which most educational authority is assumed to rest.

There is, however, more to the crisis of authority than that. The illegitimacy of ghetto education is more and more often proclaimed to reside not in the failure of that education to produce achievement equal to that of white schools—had it done so, according to the earlier logic, the criterion of legitimacy need never have been challenged—but in the defective nature of the social contract between black and white America. One manifestation of this position is the attack that has been launched on the instruments—achievement test results, rates of college acceptance, etc.—typically used to determine if the older, "rational" criterion of authority was being satisfied; not only that, but the intellectual and cultural content of those instruments has been dismissed as irrelevant or antithetical to the black community's political and cultural aspirations. A second, and politically more explosive, manifestation of this view is the assertion that school officials and teachers whose ideas or activities suggest the absence of political and cultural identification with the black community therefore also lack the qualifications requisite to educate black children. This is entirely consistent with the new criterion of authority, which assumes that the task of educators in the ghettos is to establish the basis for a valid social contract between Negroes and the institutions in their communities. Hence it becomes not at all strange to substitute for the old, "rational" tests of educational competence a subjective test of political consensus, for in a sense the situation is presumed to have reverted to the precontract state of nature, wherein the main issue is one of defining the body politic that is about to come into being, and deciding who shall be its citizens.

This "anti-colonial" position is, in the technically correct sense of the term, revolutionary; it asserts that the established authorities and the principles upon which their dominion rests are fundamentally and irreparably illegitimate, and that the only way they can continue to command is by the use of naked power. In such a situation the minimum task of the revolutionary is to bring that fact into the open, to "expose" the illegitimacy by provoking the authorities to violence.

Although only a relatively few Negroes consciously hold this position, their political strength is multiplied enormously by the fact that there are *very* few who explicitly hold the opposite view. Most blacks have an acute sense of the injustice which white society has visited upon them, so that if white authorities should attempt to suppress an openly revolutionary cadre, the best response they could hope for from the general community would be one of sullen hostility. In the case of the struggle over the schools, this makes it functionally impossible to distinguish those who want community control as a means of fulfilling the achievement criterion from those who want it as the basis for a new social contract. The two groups will remain pretty much identical so long as the achievement criterion remains unsatisfied.

It is easy to see why the anti-colonial position is anathema to the established authorities. Among other things, in selecting school personnel advocates of this position seek to substitute what amounts to a test of political loyalty for a series of universalistic "professional" standards. In last year's school dispute in New York, for example, the Ocean Hill Board was accused of racism and of violating due-process guarantees for teachers, but whether or not this was true, the real issue was the Board's effort to apply a test of political consensus to educators. Since—as in Africa—there are always whites who can pass such a test, the Ocean Hill Board could maintain that it was not guilty of racism at the same time that it sought to expel teachers for what *it* called racism—i.e., non-consensus.

But whatever the local variations, the crucial fact is that the crisis in urban education is passing into a phase in which only a change in the locus of authority will bring peace. How long the present transition period will last is hard to say, but the main elements of the domestic political situation appear to favor an increase rather than a diminishing of the anti-colonial impulse. Those elements include: the inability of the liberal/labor/civil-rights coalition to secure legislation that would mount a broad and basic attack upon black-white disparities in income and occupation; an unprecedented (but hardly unheralded) upsurge of black nationalism; the emergence of a black professional class in Northern cities as a political force.

Since the collapse of the Johnsonian consensus on domestic affairs, which can be roughly dated to the 1966 White House Conference "To Fulfill These Rights," these three elements have come into high relief, reinforcing one another. After the White House Conference, it became increasingly clear that Congressional liberals were light-years away from the political strength required to legislate fundamental change in the economic and social status of Negroes. The resources lost to the war effort in Vietnam were of course partly to blame, but there was more to it than that: as the White House Conference report suggested, fundamental change would require social spending on an absolutely unprecedented scale. Even without a war in Vietnam the Congressional struggle would have been titanic in its proportions; it was clearly impossible under conditions of large-scale defense spending.

In the cities, therefore, where no real effort has been made to deal with the underlying problems of jobs and income, attention remains where it has been since 1954. The schools are visible and accessible, in the sense that the political nexus of employment and housing is not; their performance has been obviously out of harmony with the ideology of education expounded by all moderates and liberals since *Brown vs. Board of Education;* and the inability in the last decade to effect widespread educational reforms has insured that existing frustrations would grow as performance fell farther and farther behind expectations.

As a result, the primary urban activity since late 1967 has been a struggle for the division and control of what already exists. Although one may argue that this is a rational response if one believes there is no hope for new social legislation, it has the notable drawback of creating political divisions which even further diminish the likelihood of such legislation. The greatest division of this kind has occurred between Negroes and white liberals. (To be sure, the peace between them had never been easy. Aside from the inevitable element of paternalism—whites in the movement were cooperating to solve what was typically seen as "the Negro problem"—there was the problem generated by rivalry for jobs and leadership once the movement began to score some successes.) In the recent disasters in New York City, many of the same white liberals who had championed the cause of civil rights suddenly found themselves under attack because they happened to inhabit those institutions toward which urban Negroes were now turning with hungry eyes. In a sense, the social-welfare bureaucracies—schools, welfare, anti-poverty programs—were the least strategic places to attack. They have, after all, been among the most liberal institutions, they have a common interest with blacks in the expansion of social-welfare legislation, and they are typically populated by whites who are noticeably more liberal than the average. But they were close at hand, they were the institutions Negroes knew about, they were (or seemed) easier to approach than others more remote and conservative, they were located in the ghettos rather than downtown, and they were even sympathetic to the situation which produced the movement for black control.

Add to this the politicization of the cultural and psychological upsurge known as black nationalism, which began in the mid-1960's and was well underway long before black power became a political and ideological reality. Renewed interest on the part of blacks in Afro-American culture and "Negritude" produced basic and legitimate demands upon white America, in the schools and elsewhere. The written materials of education are typically bigoted, and there is virtually no important aspect of public education in the cities, from the distribution of money to the attitudes of teachers, which is untouched by discrimination or racial antagonism. These problems, however, are as amenable to remedy by integration as by black separatism.

But in the absence of genuine integration, or of much evidence of fundamental economic and social change, nationalism became wedded to the demand for a piece of the action, and was forged into a program for change. This is not the place to argue the merits of the position as a general matter; what is important is that black nationalism offered a system of ideas which seemed to correspond with the interests of the emerging class of black professionals, and to explain the need for black community control. Even in itself integration is a difficult path: it promises strain, tension, and unfamiliarity to black and white administrators and teachers equally, and hence it has never inspired real enthusiasm except among a few. Community control, on the other hand, avoids these pitfalls. It offers concrete gains long overdue—jobs and promotion to administrative and supervisory positions, without the accompanying discomfort of venturing into foreign schools and neighborhoods—under the ideological aegis of assisting in the development of one's own community. A more perfect coincidence of ideology and self-interest can hardly be imagined.

The coming-of-age of the black professional class, a potent aspect of the struggle for community control, may turn out in the end to be the most important element in the battle over the schools, more significant than the substitution of parent for citywide boards, or community for bureaucratic control. The enfranchisement of a black elite, long overdue, should indeed help to improve education. In the short run, however, it has poured fuel on an already raging fire. Frustration, hostility, ambition, and concern for children long neglected is a potent combination, especially when applied generously to the complicated gear-works of big-city civil-service labor relations. The results have been spread depressingly over more editions of the New York *Times* than one cares to contemplate. As the struggle continues—and it surely will—the Lindsays of the world will seek to maintain civil peace —and their positions—by accommodating as many black demands for a slice of the action as they find possible, while the Albert Shankers will seek to maintain life by holding on to what they have. In so doing, the Lindsays will find themselves alienating lower-class and sometimes liberal white constituents, and the Shankers will find themselves making alliances with and concessions to conservative elements. The liberals will find themselves in the position of having to defend those portions of the social-welfare bureaucracies they control against black demands; all they can do, aside from hanging on for dear life, is to assume a principled position against segregation and for the application of vastly greater resources. However one may sympathize with that position, it is no more likely to be useful in the next day's struggle to keep afloat politically than it is either to reduce segregation or to increase the available resources.

V

Is there a way out of our present morass? The difficulty here is twofold. One might still imagine that a massive assault on status disparities would shift attention away from the question of legitimacy, but it is hard to conceive of such an assault being mounted. Producing the needed legislation would require sustained political mobilization of blacks and whites, a prospect which seems remote so long as: (a) they are so fatally preoccupied with each other; (b) new money cannot be found to reduce the competition and allow recruitment of a broader constituency; and (c) many powerful whites and ambitious blacks, for their separate reasons, prefer a political settlement to economic and social justice.

I do not mean to imply, however—and this is the second difficulty—that the way out would be clear if only more resources were available. That, unfortunately, is only the converse of the argument for decentralization: it makes no more sense to pretend that removing social and economic disparities will solve all the problems of city schools than to argue that political rearrangement will eliminate achievement disparities. The point can be conveniently illustrated: the liberal ideology of educational improvement tells us that since schooling is the least divisive and best way to insure equal chances for jobs and income, we should provide more of it for Negroes. School reforms based on this notion typically include heavy doses of those disciplined activities which are thought to yield high scores on achievement tests. But the same middle-class liberals who advocate this medicine for the poor often cannot stomach administering it to *their* children; they enroll them instead in more open, permissive, and pedagogically diversified private schools. This paradox suggests in practice what many advocates of school reform cannot admit as a matter of principle: that there exists presently a fundamental tension between the sorts of educational changes which are thought to improve achievement, and those designed to diversify pedagogy, reduce routine, and allow for individual and cultural creativity.

As an ideological matter, school reformers have dealt with this tension by placing exclusive stress on either diversity or achievement; the practical political consequence has been to behave as though solving one problem would solve the other. Many liberals have therefore supported programs designed to extend the dominion of the schools over children's lives, and have advocated such things as twelve-month school years, preschools and kindergarten for all, afternoon school centers, and the like. Under any circumstances serious questions could be raised about the desirability of a further intrusion of state institutions into a child's cultural and intellectual development; given the current circumstances—in which the institutions in question suffer from an advanced form of political, cultural, and pedagogical atrophy—the problems are terrific. Although one can easily imagine a program of extended schooling being executed well, with concern for diversity and individuality, there is a big difference between what one can imagine and what one can actually do with the materials at hand. The extension of schooling means the extension of the schooling that happens to exist, as the history of Headstart and Title I—to say nothing of the compulsory education movement—makes abundantly clear. Thus, liberals who advocate such measures run the risk of overtly or covertly subverting other educational values they hold dear.

In the case of decentralization—as the recent events in New York reveal—the same insistence on unitary solutions to separate problems has led to the widespread idea that political and administrative change will remedy racial achievement differences, an idea which, as I have tried to show, flies in the face of all past experience and knowledge concerning the determinants of achievement. As for the aim of creating diversity in the schools, decentralization and community control can be described only as half-hearted and incomplete attempts in that direction.

Consider the various proposals for decentralizing the New York City schools. All, from the Bundy plan to the most radical proposals for community control, assume that the necessary and sufficient condition for producing diversity is the imposition of new control on existing institutions and resources. But this amounts to nothing more than a system of educational laissez-faire, which is hardly the same thing as diversity, especially when schools are segregated by race and class. In the competition for school resources, the net effect of such a system would be to institutionalize the political disadvantages of blacks and poor people, isolate them in the competition for money, and thereby establish in custom, law, and administrative code those failures of the politics of common interest which led to the demands for control in the first place.

More important, however, is the fact that the need for diversity— for alternative cultural and pedagogic styles in schooling—cannot be satisfied by racial division or changes in administrative structure alone. Diversity and excellence in schools are qualities not likely to appear unless a premium is put upon them. Creating such diversity would entail the recruitment of new people to education, and new institutions to schooling: not just neighborhood boards, but universities, labor unions, churches, and voluntary associations formed for the purpose of education. The business of attracting, organizing, funding, and maintaining such institutions cannot be accomplished by further provincializing the existing structure, any more than regulating it can be left to essentially free competition.

Real diversity would be costly both politically and fiscally, and would require a somewhat different view of the relationship between the state and the schools from the one now regnant. At the moment we think of the state not only as the sole regulator of public education, but as exclusive operator of the schools; this greatly restricts, for political and constitutional reasons, the extent to which the schools can be diverse. Were the state to continue its role as regulator but take less of a hand in actually running the schools, greater diversity might be possible; under such conditions that state would concern itself with maintaining essential principles of interest regulation, civil liberties, civil rights, and educational standards.

The form that such an arrangement would take is uncertain. There have been proposals to put money on the heads of children—or in the pockets of their parents—but they raise problems related to segregation, and to the well-known fact that the poor usually exercise choice in a less strategic fashion than do the affluent. Another proposal has been to create alternative *institutions;* this might obviate the problem of choice to a certain extent, but like the tuition proposals, it raises questions about the interests of parties that are presently involved in the educational enterprise.

All these alternative proposals deserve careful consideration, whether one is concerned with pedagogy, political participation, or the possibilities for a democratic culture. They deserve consideration not only as to their intrinsic merits, but because they serve as a counterbalance to the idea that diversity and openness in the schools can be produced solely through political arrangements designed to settle an authority crisis arising from long-standing grievances of quite another sort. One might also hope that a discussion of these issues would contribute to repairing some of the deep political divisions within the democratic Left. These fissures have sprung in part from the fact that organizations and individuals that would in a more civilized atmosphere have tended to take different stands on different issues—racial identity, pedagogic diversity, political participation, reduction of racial disparities in income and occupation—have in the current climate been forced to take a single stand on all at once. The resulting schizophrenia has been widely displayed in the columns of all serious publications which either originate in or recognize the existence of New York City.

Finally, attention to alternative forms of education might help to set in clear relief another idea currently simmering at the edges of the liberal political consciousness, namely that the best way to reduce racial disparities in children's school achievement might be to reduce the disparities in their parents' social and economic status. Support for this notion, as I pointed out earlier, arises from a variety of considerations: the dependence of achievement on parental status; the potential political, cultural, and emotional dangers of extending the system of schooling that now exists; the inherent risks of presuming that profound social change can be purchased cheaply with a bit of improved schooling.

VI

It should be plain by now that I myself am persuaded by the soundness of this analysis, yet I am also aware that its intellectual cogency is strongly and negatively related to its chances for political life and prosperity. We are presently at an important crossroad, both in education and in race relations, and the path we take will probably influence the shape of things for many, many years. Roughly speaking, the issue is how to settle an increasingly severe crisis of authority. On the one hand, by carving up existing institutions and resources in such a way as to arrange a viable contract between blacks and the institutions in their neighborhoods, we can work out a political settlement of the tensions that have arisen from a long-standing failure to remedy basic social and economic injustice. Thereby, perhaps, we can purchase peace, or, if not peace, at least the confinement of the conflict and noise within the ghetto. On the other hand, we can resolve the authority crisis by attacking the fundamental disparities which produced it.

It would be easy to overestimate in alarmist fashion the consequences of choosing the easier path; a good deal of this has unfortunately already been done. It would be silly, or worse, to argue that educational disaster will ensue from whatever decentralization and community control can be politically arranged. There will be problems, but there are problems now. It seems to me much more likely that under community control the basic disparities would remain more or less intact, while the atmosphere and conduct of the schools would show improvement.

A good deal has also been said to the effect that the movements for decentralization and community control are provoking a general rightward trend in American politics. That such a trend exists is clear, and it also seems reasonable to believe that it feeds upon the wilder and more vociferous elements in the movement for community control. But we should remember that this trend was first noticed years ago as a reaction to the movement for *integration,* and that it probably manifests the underlying reality of white attitudes in a limited-resource situation, not a response to particular strategies. It is unhappy and frustrating to witness the present spiral of distrust, and the struggle for control of what exists; these contribute their share to the general poisoning of the political atmosphere. But they are symptoms of the underlying political weakness, not its primary cause.

Of the two alternatives, it takes no great vision to see where the political chips lie. The second alternative is costly, whether we measure cost in dollars allocated, status lost, stereotypes shattered, or political effort expended. The first has a certain political price—as the convulsions in New York revealed—but it gives the appearance of costing little otherwise. In addition to this enormous political advantage, it has behind it the gathering momentum of profound changes in black politics, culture, and society. Although the politicization of these forces, and their arrangement behind the banner of community control, results chiefly from the failure of the society at large to deal directly with social and economic inequality, political facts cannot be wished away, either by dreams of what might have been or strategies on paper about what might be: unless the inequalities are swiftly attacked, these forces will not be denied.

C. Factual and research considerations

NANCY ST. JOHN and RALPH LEWIS

The influence of school racial context on academic achievement

Examination of effects on academic achievement of racial and SES components of social context. Sample: 900 black and white pupils in 36 inner-city sixth grade classrooms of various racial and SES mixtures. Cross-tabular analysis reveals higher achievement for children of both races in schools over 50 percent white. With individual and peer SES and prior achievement controlled through multiple regression, significant positive relationship is found for blacks between school percent white (current and cumulative) and achievement in Math but not Reading, and for whites between cumulative percent white and achievement in both Reading and Math. For whites, but not for blacks, a significant effect remains when more powerful controls on social class, available for a subsample, are entered into regression equations.

INTRODUCTION

The influence of social context on attitudes or behavior has long intrigued social scientists. The past decade has seen an impressive series of studies which tackle the methodological problems involved and attempt to separate the effects of group and individual characteristics (Davis, Spaeth, and Huson, 1961; Tannenbaum and Bachman, 1964; Hauser, 1970). A usual sample is composed of high school students, and a common finding is that the behavior (college aspirations) of an individual is affected not only by his own background (SES) but also by that of his school mates (Wilson, 1959; Michael, 1961; Ramsøy, 1961; Turner, 1964; Boyle, 1966; Kandel and Lesser, 1969).

A number of alternative explanatory or intervening variables have been tested: mobility values (Turner, 1964), characteristics of close friends (Campbell and Alexander, 1965), intellectualism of school environment (McDill, Meyers, and Rigsby, 1967). An important issue

Note: This is a revision of a paper presented at the annual meeting of the Eastern Sociological Association, New York, April 1971. The research reported here was supported in part by U.S. O.E. Grant No. OE6-1-70-0011 (509).

Source: *Social Problems,* vol. 19 (Summer 1971), pp. 68-79. Reprinted by permission of The Society for the Study of Social Problems, and the authors.

is whether scholastic ability should be considered a contaminating or intervening variable when estimating the influence of school or neighborhood context on educational outcomes. Sewell and Armer (1966) found that, when IQ (as well as sex and family SES) was controlled, the effect of neighborhood context on college plans disappeared. Turner, Michael, and Boyle (1966) in their separate critiques of Sewell and Armer's analysis argue that IQ is more properly considered, not as a contaminating independent variable to be controlled, but rather as another effect of context or part of a causal chain. This series of contextual studies has tended to be restricted, not only in choice of measures of input, of outcome, and of intervening variables, but also in that differential effects for ethnic sub-groups are not examined and past social context is ignored.

The effect of school racial composition on academic achievement can be seen as one aspect of this general topic. The 1954 Supreme Court decision stressed other dimensions of segregation, the stigma attached, and the impossibility of equal (if separate) schooling. But desegregation may do more than equalize schooling and remove stigma. It may also change many characteristics of the individuals that compose the school group. A study of the effects of racial composition must, therefore, deal with the same methodological problems that concern those who investigate other aspects of social context. In turn, the techniques and findings of desegregation research may contribute to our understanding of contextual effects in general.

Since 1954 there have been a fair number of investigations of the relation of school racial composition and academic achievement, but no definitive findings. Small-scale cross sectional studies comparing children in naturally segregated and integrated settings have not succeeded in establishing the original equivalence of subjects; and bussing studies that measure children before and after desegregation usually do not control on the quality of schooling. (See St. John, 1970, for a review of this research.) Moreover these studies tend to be limited in that most investigators have focussed on black pupils rather than pupils of both races, on aspiration or on verbal ability rather than on academic achievement, and on racial context at one moment, rather than over time.

The Report of the massive Equality of Educational Opportunity Survey (Coleman, 1966) found that the SES background of his school mates had a large effect, beyond that of his own background, on the verbal achievement of a child, but that the race of school mates had no independent effect. One limitation of the EEOS is that it was in no sense longitudinal. Achievement was tested once in early fall, rather than before and after exposure to current school context. School racial experience since grade one undoubtedly varied from child to child, but these previous experiences go largely unmeasured.[1] Reanalysis of the EEOS data by the U.S. Commission on Civil Rights (1967), by McPartland (1968), and by Smith (1972) clarifies many of the relationships reported by Coleman, but cannot go beyond the basic limitation of survey data referring to one point in time.

A study by Wilson (1967) has the advantage of two types of longitudinal data, first grade IQ scores and measures of the school social class and racial mix for each student at each educational level, primary to senior high. Wilson reported a strong relationship for both blacks and whites between the social class of school mates and achievement, but no relationship for either group between the race of school mates and achievement.

In Pittsburgh, St. John and Smith (1969) found that, controlling for social class, the arithmetic achievement of black ninth graders was significantly higher if they had attended integrated schools over all or most of their elementary years. The stronger effect for longitudinal than for current racial context and for arithmetic than for reading suggests that the focus of the Coleman Report on current context and verbal ability may explain its finding of no independent effect for school racial composition.

This paper explores the relation of the academic achievement of children to the current and past racial composition of their schools in inter-racial sixth grade classrooms in a large Northern city. Four principal questions guided the analysis:

1. Is there a significant positive relation between school percentage white and achievement?
2. Is the relation the same whether the independent variable is measured over time or at one point in time (cumulative or current school percentage white)?
3. Is the relation the same whether the dependent variable is reading or arithmetic achievement?
4. Is the relationship the same for black and for white children?

PROCEDURES—THE SAMPLE

The 46 elementary schools in the city enrolling five or more black sixth graders were classified according to social class and racial composition. A stratified random sample of 18 schools was drawn from this

---

[1] Students' reports of first grade in which they had classmates of another race does show a zero-order relationship with verbal achievement in EEOS data (Coleman, 1966; U.S. Office of Education, 1967).

matrix. Two sixth grade classrooms were selected from each school (again randomly). The final sample included all white (497) and black (411) children in these 36 rooms. The classes varied from seven to 100 in the percentage of black children enrolled and from lower to middle socioeconomic status (SES). School SES and racial mixture were to a degree independent: among the schools of lowest SES, half were majority white, and among those with many middle-class pupils one was all black.

THE DATA

The data with which to measure the dependent, independent, and control variables of this study were obtained from school cumulative records:

Reading (Fall, 3)—the grade equivalent score for average of paragraph and word meaning sub-tests of the Metropolitan Achievement Test administered in the fall of the third grade—the earliest test score available.

Reading (Spring, 6)—ditto, for the test administered in the spring of the sixth grade.

Math (Spring, 5)—grade equivalent score on the Metropolitan Achievement Test in arithmetic, administered in the spring of the fifth grade year.

In the analyses that follow, Reading (Spring, 6) and Math (Spring, 5) are the dependent variables. Since no measure of IQ in Grade One was available, Reading (Fall, 3) is entered into the regression equations as an independent variable in order to control on initial ability or early achievement.

The main independent variables of the study are sixth grade classroom percentage white (Class percent W[6]), fifth grade school percentage white (School percent W[5]) and average school percentage white for grades one to five (School percent W[1–5]). State school racial censuses established the racial composition of schools in the city, year by year. For each child the racial composition of the school attended in each of the first five grades was noted and an average was calculated.

The two variables most likely to contaminate the relation between racial composition and achievement are school quality and family socioeconomic status (SES). In this study some degree of control on school quality is achieved by confining the sample to schools in a single system. Moreover week-long observations in each school did not reveal large or consistent differences by racial mix in plant, equipment, cur-

TABLE 1

Correlation matrix for measures of achievement, SES, and school racial mix for whites[1] and blacks[2]

Blacks \ Whites	1	2	3	4[3]	5	6	7	8	9
1. Reading (Spring, 6)	—	.49**	.62**	-.03	.15*	.33**	.40**	.17**	.37**
2. Math (Spring, 5)	.46**	—	.40**	.00	.13*	.26**	.26**	.22**	.36**
3. Reading (Fall, 3)	.53**	.29**	—	.05	.15*	.29**	.33**	.21**	.31**
4. Sex[3]	.03	.06	.17**	—	.04	.00	-.01	-.04	.05
5. Family SES	.27**	.24**	.24**	-.05	—	.40**	.32**	.02	.16**
6. Class SES (6)	.17**	.21**	.12*	.01	.27**	—	.57**	.33**	.26**
7. School SES (1–5)	.14**	.16**	.10	.00	-.03	.10	—	.47**	.69**
8. Class percent W (6)	.06	.22**	.02	.03	-.05	.30**	.36**	—	.61**
9. School percent W (1–5)	.08	.19**	.08	.04	.07	.14**	.39**	.57**	—

[1] N's vary from 344 (Reading, 3) to 497 (Sex and Class percent W).
[2] N's vary from 309 (Reading, 3) to 412 (Sex and Class percent W).
[3] Boys were coded 1; Girls were coded 2.
* Statistically significant at the .05 level.
** Statistically significant at the .01 level.

riculum, or characteristics of teachers. The most noticeable differences were those associated with the SES of pupils.

The only measure of family SES recorded on the cumulative record card was occupation of one or both parents. For this study *Family SES* is the average occupational level (coded according to Hollingshead's seven-point scale, reversed) of a child's own father if he were present and of the child's mother if she were employed. Families presumed to be on welfare were assigned to the lowest SES category. This index of SES was chosen after home interviews with a random subsample of mothers indicated that it correlated with other measures of SES[2] better for blacks than did occupational level of the father alone or of the male head of household (in many cases the child's stepfather). For the white sample the latter measure might have represented the family status somewhat more accurately than the index used. We discuss below the consequent difficulty of controlling on family background when examining the effect of racial context on white achievement. *Class SES (6)* is Family SES aggregated over all pupils in each classroom. Since the two measures have the same source of data, they are not wholly independent. *School SES (1–5)*, on the other hand, is quite independent of Family SES. It is the average SES rank of the schools a child attended in his first five years, the rank order based on 1960 Census education and income data for the census tracts within each school district. *School SES (5)* is this same statistic for the fifth grade only.

As is usual in studies which depend on cumulative school records for a very transient population, data is missing on up to a quarter of the sample on some measures. We decided against cleaning the sample by eliminating any cases on which any data is missing and instead have employed the missing data correlation matrix (Table 1) for the regressions. Since pupils for whom data is missing tend to be low both in achievement and in neighborhood SES and percentage white, failure to include them in the analyses should lead to a conservative estimate of the relation between the independent and dependent variables of the study.

FINDINGS

Correlational, cross-tabular and multiple regression analyses were used to test the relation between school racial composition and academic achievement. The correlation matrix (Table 1) shows that for whites there is a statistically significant positive relationship between both cumulative and current school percentage white and achievement in

---

[2] Condition of housing, person/room ratio, parental educational level.

arithmetic and reading. For blacks there are significant positive relationships for arithmetic, but none for reading. However, the significant coefficients for various measures of social class with measures of racial mix, on the one hand, and with achievement, on the other hand, warn us that for either race any apparent relation between racial mix and achievement may be spurious and due to the influence of social class.

Cross-tabular analysis allowed us to examine the linearity of the relation between school racial composition and achievement. Table 2 shows the percentage of pupils with high achievement[3] according to the racial composition of current or former schools. The chi square statistics indicate the same significant relationships revealed by zero order correlations. For whites the positive effect of cumulative school percent white appears to be linear, but in several of the other tables a boundary effect is discernible. White pupils achieve more if present schools are over 50 percent white; black pupils if present or past school are over 50 percent white. Up to that point a larger or smaller percentage of own race appears to make little difference in achievement.

Three-way cross-tabular analysis was also performed, controlling on (a) sex and (b) family SES, with essentially the same results (not shown). For whites in 14 out of 16 tables the chi square statistic reached the .01 level of significance, and in each case, in addition to a linear relationship, a boundary effect at 50 percent white was discernible. For blacks, the only consistently significant relationships were math scores by current racial composition; but in each case being in schools more than 50 percent white appeared to be crucial.

The absence of perfect linearity in the independent-dependent variable relationship argued against use of multiple regression analysis. On the other hand, regression avoids the danger, characteristic of tabular analysis, of spurious effects due to imprecise categories (see Tannenbaum and Bachman, 1964) and also allows simultaneous control on several variables. In this analysis sex, third grade reading achievement, and family SES were controlled and the equations run twice, once with cumulative School SES (1–5) and School percent White (1–5) as independent variables, and once with current school SES and percent white[4] as independent variables. The results are shown in Table 3.

For whites we find that under these controlled conditions cumulative racial context is still significantly related to achievement—at the .05 level for reading and at the .01 level for arithmetic—but current racial context is not related to achievement in either subject. For black chil-

---

[3] Top third of total distribution (races together), or 6.6–11.4 for Reading (6) and 6.1–9.2 for Math (5).

[4] School percent W(5) and School SES (5) for Math; Class percent W(6) and Class SES (6) for Reading.

TABLE 2

Percent of pupils on grade level in reading and math, by current or cumulative school percentage white

Percent on grade level[2]	Current % W (5 or 6)[1]				School % W (1–5)			
White pupils	1–50	51–80	81–100	p <*	1–50	51–80	81–100	p <*
Reading (Spring, 6)	11	39	37	.01	6	25	49	.01
	(57)	(218)	(173)		(34)	(88)	(208)	
Math (Spring, 5)	4	29	29	.01	0	21	35	.01
	(46)	(119)	(217)		(31)	(90)	(184)	
Black pupils	1–19	20–49	50–100	p <*	1–19	20–49	50–100	p <*
Reading (Spring, 6)	15	23	19	not sig.	15	16	31	.05
	(89)	(82)	(144)		(129)	(101)	(48)	
Math (Spring, 5)	4	3	17	.01	6	6	18	.05
	(83)	(106)	(123)		(106)	(95)	(50)	

[1] Current percent W is Class percent W (6) for Reading (6) and School percent W (5) for Math (5).
[2] Top third of total distribution (races together), or 6.6–11.4 for Reading and 6.1–9.2 for Math.
* Chi square statistic with 4 degrees of freedom was significant at this level.

TABLE 3

Unstandardized (b) and standardized (β) regression coefficients for achievement scores in reading and math on current and cumulative school percent W, with sex, Reading (3), family SES and current or cumulative school SES entered in all equations

| | Whites | | | | Blacks | | | |
| | Reading (6) | | Math (5) | | Reading (6) | | Math (5) | |
	b	β	b	β	b	β	b	β
Current Context								
Sex	(−.18)	−.06	(−.08)	−.03	(−.15)	−.06	(.04)	.02
Reading (Fall, 3)	(+.02)	.57**	(.56)	.34**	(.89)	.50**	(.35)	.25**
Family SES	(.00)	.00	(.10)	.08	(.16)	.13**	(.14)	.13**
Class SES (6)[1]	(.57)	.16**	(.01)	.06	(.21)	.06	(.01)	.05
Class percent W (6)[2]	(.00)	.01	(.01)	.09	(.00)	.04	(.01)	.21**
R²		.41		.18		.31		.16
Cumulative Context								
Sex	(−.18)	−.06	(−.09)	−.03	(−.14)	−.05	(.05)	.02
Reading (Fall, 3)	(.96)	.54**	(.52)	.32**	(.88)	.50**	(.30)	.22**
Family SES	(.01)	.01	(.06)	.06	(.19)	.15**	(.20)	.20**
School SES (1–5)	(.02)	.15**	(−.01)	−.06	(.01)	.08	(.01)	.08
School percent W (1–5)	(.01)	.10*	(.02)	.29**	(.00)	.02	(.01)	.15**
R²		.43		.22		.32		.15

[1] School SES (5) for Math (5).
[2] School percent W (5) for Math (5).
* Significant at .05 level.
** Significant at .01 level.

dren both measures of the independent variable are related to achievement in math, but neither to achievement in reading.

In view of the controversy (referred to above) over the appropriateness of controlling on scholastic ability when testing the effects of social context on educational outcomes, we examined the regression coefficients for achievement on school percent white both with and without third grade reading scores entered into the equations. Table 4 shows that for white pupils the effect is greater when the early score is left out but is significant either way. For black pupils it makes no difference whether or not the early score is entered.

TABLE 4

Standardized regression coefficients for achievement on cumulative school percent white, with sex, family SES, and school SES controlled, and Reading (3) either in or out of equations

	Reading (3) Out		Reading (3) In	
	R^2	β	R^2	β
White				
Reading	.23	.19**	.43	.10*
Math	.13	.35**	.22	.29**
Black				
Reading	.10	.05	.32	.02
Math	.11	.16**	.15	.15**

* Significant at .05 level.
** Significant at .01 level.

Table 3 also shows that for black children family SES, but not school SES, is significantly related to reading achievement with other variables controlled, whereas for white children, the opposite is true. The lack of relationship for black children between social class context and verbal achievement is quite contrary to the findings of Coleman and Wilson. It is possible that use of a social class index appropriate to the situation in many black families has allowed us to assign to family SES variance that would otherwise be assigned to peer SES. As mentioned above, the family SES score apparently reflected differences in family background less accurately for white children, with the result that school SES, class SES and third grade reading scores pick up some of the variance in white achievement not accounted for by individual family background.[5]

[5] Separate analyses of the white sample by sex, SES, achievement, and parochial school experience suggest a complex interaction of these variables, such that the white sample is slightly biased by the inclusion of a number of low achieving boys of middle-class background. Their sisters and their high-achieving brothers are presumably in parochial school. This phenomenon may be typical of racially changing neighborhoods.

These effects on achievement for measures of SES suggest the possibility that even with regression analysis the apparent relationship between racial context and achievement may be spurious and due to inadequate control on SES. The regressions were, therefore, rerun for the 200 children whose mothers had been interviewed, entering into the equations first the same SES measures (more accurately measured for this sub-sample) and then additional measures of SES (parental educational level and mother's verbal ability). (See Table 5.) For

TABLE 5

Standardized (β) regression coefficients in reading and math on cumulative school percent white with three extra measures of SES added to the equations for the sub-sample whose mothers were interviewed

	Whites		Blacks	
	Reading	Math	Reading	Math
Sex........................	−.02	−.04	.02	.06
Reading (Fall, 3)............	.62**	.43**	.44**	.31**
Family SES[1]................	−.02	.07	.20*	−.06
Father's Education..........	.10	.20	−.00	−.00
Mother's Education.........	.10	−.07	−.25*	−.20
Mother's Verbal Ability.......	.08	.12	.31**	.33*
School SES (1–5)............	−.00	−.22	.10	−.09
School percent W (1–5)......	.21*	.46**	−.05	.10
R[2]....................	.63	.43	.40	.17
d.f....................	92	80	104	89

[1] Mean parental occupation level.
* Significant at .05 level.
** Significant at .01 level.

whites the original findings are confirmed; although the several measures of SES now together explain more variance in achievement than do the regressions for the total sample, the relation between school percentage white and achievement is undisturbed: scores in reading and arithmetic rose significantly with school percent white. For blacks, however, the beta for arithmetic on school percent white drops from .15 to .10 and is no longer statistically significant.

CONCLUSION AND DISCUSSION

In answer to the questions with which this paper started, we have found that:

1. There *is* a positive relation between school percentage white and academic achievement, but
2. The relationship is more consistently significant if the dependent variable is mathematics rather than reading.

3. The relation is more consistently significant if the independent variable is cumulative rather than current school percentage white.
4. The relationship between cumulative racial context and achievement is stronger for white children than for black children.

The tabular analysis tables showed a jump in the achievement of children of both races in schools over 50 percent white, a finding which suggests that the effect of racial context on achievement may in fact be greater than appears in regression analyses without correction for nonlinearity. However, a hasty conclusion that racial context has more influence on the achievement of white than black children could be an "ecological fallacy," since a selective factor may be responsible. It is probable that whereas housing discrimination and loyalty locks black families of all social class levels in the ghetto, white families who remain in a racially changing neighborhood do so because age, illness, desertion, or poverty prevents them from moving. In other words, their SES may be lower than appears and this, rather than the racial mix of the neighborhood, may explain the low achievement of their children. Analysis of the subsample with more accurate and more powerful measures of SES did not reduce the relation for whites between school racial composition and achievement. However, the stronger relationship for whites than for blacks may still be due to other aspects of home background and not entirely to differential effects of school race on black and white children.

The stronger effect of context on arithmetic than on reading for children of both races is more impressive, but also may be an artifact of inadequate measurement. Third grade reading scores seem to be appropriate Time 1 measurements for later achievement in reading but less appropriate for achievement in arithmetic. The zero order correlations for Reading (3) with Reading (6) and Math (5) were .62 and .40 respectively for whites and .53 and .29 respectively for blacks. Thus the early reading score was a more stringent control on growth in reading than in arithmetic.

On the other hand, the greater effect for math may be because (at the fifth grade level) it is a school-learned skill, as compared with reading, which can be picked up at home, in libraries, or from street signs. This leads to the questions with which this paper started: Is the quality of teaching (of math) especially poor in ghetto schools?[6] Or does the stigma of segregated education discourage white and black children alike? Or do the attitudes and habits of a group of children (many of whom have suffered deprivation of one sort or another) affect all children, regardless of individual racial or social class background? This

---

[6] See Wilson's discussion of this point (1967, p. 183).

paper cannot answer these questions. Adequate answers would involve objective measurement and testing of such intervening variables as the quality of segregated and integrated education,[7] pupils' perception of the stigma attached to segregated and integrated schools, and the differential school-related attitudes of black and white children. We have found a statistically significant effect associated with school racial context. Further research will be needed to determine whether this effect can properly be called "contextual" and what aspects of the context are crucial.

REFERENCES

Boyle, Richard P. "The effect of high school on students' aspirations." *American Journal of Sociology,* 71 (1969): 628–639.

Campbell, Ernest Q., and C. Norman Alexander. "Structural effects and interpersonal relationships." *American Journal of Sociology,* 71 (November 1965): 284–289.

Coleman, James S., et al. *Equality of Educational Opportunity.* Washington, D.C.: U.S. Department of Health, Education and Welfare, 1966.

Davis, James A., Joe L. Spaeth, and Carolyn Huson. "A technique for analyzing the effects of group composition." *American Sociological Review,* 26 (April 1961): 215–225.

Hauser, Robert M. "Context and consex: A cautionary tale." Part 2, *American Journal of Sociology,* 75 (January 1970): 645–664.

Kandel, Denise B., and Gerald S. Lesser. "Parental and peer influences on educational plans of adolescents." *American Sociological Review,* 34 (April 1969): 213–223.

McDill, Edward L., Edmund D. Meyers, and Leo C. Rigsby. "Institutional effects on the academic behavior of high school students." *Sociology of Education,* 40 (Summer 1967): 181–199.

McPartland, James. *The Segregated Student in Desegregated Schools: Sources of Influences on Negro Secondary Students.* Baltimore: Johns Hopkins University, 1968.

Michael, John A. "High school climates and plans for entering college." *Public Opinion Quarterly,* 25 (Winter 1961): 585–595.

Ramsøy, Natalie Rogoff. *American high schools at mid-century.* New York: Bureau of Applied Social Research, Columbia University, 1961.

St. John, Nancy H. "Desegregation and minority group performance." *Review of Educational Research,* 40 (February 1970): 111–134.

St. John, Nancy H., and Marshall S. Smith. "School racial composition, achievement and aspiration." Cambridge: Center for Educational Policy Research, 1969 (mimeo).

---

[7] The findings of Coleman et al. (1966) suggest that such an endeavor is not likely to be easy.

Sewell, William H., and J. Michael Armer. "Neighborhood context and college plans." *American Sociological Review*, 31 (April 1966): 159–168.

Smith, Marshall S. "A replication of the EEOS Report's Regression Analysis," in *On Equality of Educational Opportunity*, ed. Frederick Mosteller and Daniel P. Moynihan. New York: Vintage Books, 1972.

Tannenbaum, Arnold S. and Jerald G. Bachman. "Structural versus individual effects." *American Journal of Sociology*, 69 (1964): 585–595.

Turner, Ralph H. *The Social Context of Ambition*. San Francisco: Chandler Publishing Co., 1964.

Turner, Ralph H., John A. Michael, Richard P. Boyle. "Communications on 'neighborhood context and college plans.' " *American Sociological Review*, 31 (October 1966): 698–707.

U.S. Commission on Civil Rights. *Racial Isolation in Public Schools*. Washington, D.C.: U.S. Government Printing Office, 1967.

Wilson, Alan B. "Residential segregation of social classes and aspirations of high school boys." *American Sociological Review*, 24 (December 1959): 836–845.

1967 "Educational consequences of segregation in a California community," in U.S. Commission on Civil Rights, *Racial Isolation in Public Schools*, Volume II, 1967.

D. Policy and practice considerations

WILLIAM R. GRANT

Community control versus school integration: The case of Detroit

New York and Detroit are the only big cities in America that have decentralized their public school systems in order to establish community control. Many people can still recall the bitter conflict over decentralization that raged in New York during the autumn and winter of 1968, involving an extended teachers' strike, intense racial and ethnic hostility, and a bewildering tangle of educational, political, and legal issues. The experience of Detroit—with the nation's fourth largest public school system of 290,000 students—in 1969 and 1970 is less widely known but perhaps even more important. For here the central issue was framed—and resolved—with a directness and clarity unusual in American politics. The issue was simply whether, as a practical matter, community control is compatible with racial integration. And the unequivocal answer in Detroit was no.

DECENTRALIZATION PROPOSED

The story of school integration and community control in Detroit is symbolized by the rise, success, and sudden demise of the political career of A. L. Zwerdling, the president of the city's board of education until 1970. After graduation from law school in 1939, Zwerdling, the son of a poor Central European immigrant who became a wealthy furrier, went to work as an assistant to Walter Reuther and soon rose to associate general counsel of the UAW. In 1946 he set up a flourishing private labor law practice, and although many unions wanted his services he found time to be active in the Americans for Democratic Action and in the Stevenson for President campaigns.

In 1964, Reuther persuaded Zwerdling to run for a seat on the Detroit Board of Education. The civil rights movement was then at its zenith, and three school board members were not running for reelection. Convinced that this was the time to put a liberal majority on the

Source: *The Public Interest*, No. 24 (Summer 1971), pp. 62–79, copyright © 1971 by National Affairs Inc.

board, Detroit's liberal groups formed a coalition, recruited candidates, organized a campaign—and won. In the years that followed, the board changed school boundaries to promote integration, hired black teachers and administrators, and demanded from publishers textbooks giving a fairer portrayal of the races. Every decision, every appointment, every statement reflected the board's overriding commitment to the goal of racial integration.

In the summer of 1969, however, the civil rights movement was in disarray and the ideas of community control and black power were on the rise. The Michigan legislature then passed a law requiring the decentralization of the Detroit public school system. On the face of it, this action did not seem particularly momentous. The school board was already on record in favor of decentralization, or "increased community involvement," as most members preferred to call it, in the belief that decentralization would help to persuade blacks that the system was fair.

But the liberal board majority still viewed integration as their primary goal, and they were determined that any decentralization would be of a sort that would promote that overriding aim. Zwerdling was also aware, as he told a meeting of school administrators in Washington, D.C. in 1969, that "no one who has come to our public meetings on decentralization is interested in integration. Everyone wants segregation so they will be assured a little piece of control." It was his fear, he said, that "you cannot have both integration and community control." And if it came to a choice between the two, there was no question about how he would vote. "I did not become the president of the Detroit Board of Education to preside over the liquidation of an integrated school system," he told the League of Women Voters after he returned from Washington. "Everyone in the City of Detroit could sign a petition asking me to vote for segregation," he told a public board meeting later, "and that still would not change my vote." Under Zwerdling's leadership and with a $360,000 planning grant from the Ford Foundation, the board opted for a decentralization plan that mapped out racially integrated local school districts.

Within nine months, Zwerdling and the rest of the liberal board majority had been recalled from office after a vitriolic campaign with racist overtones, and Detroit voters had elected a new school board with the smallest proportion of black representatives in 15 years. The liberal superintendent had resigned, and the new board talked of "weeding out" other administrators. Detroit had undergone one of the most tumultuous political controversies in its history, and the races were more sharply polarized than at any point since the devastating riots of 1967.

Detroit's experience with decentralization documents the problems involved in reforming even the most progressive and least insulated of the nation's big city school systems. It also offers some important evidence on the incompatibility of integration and decentralization.

AN INTEGRATIONIST'S PROGRESS

As has been noted, the Detroit board had been ruled by a black-liberal-labor coalition since the election in 1964 on an integrationist platform of Zwerdling, Peter F. Grylls, a telephone company executive, and the Rev. Darneau Stewart, a black minister. They joined with Remus Robinson, a surgeon elected in 1955 and the first black member of the school board, to make a pro-integration majority on the seven-member board. Zwerdling was the acknowledged leader and the board's most forceful advocate of integration.

Shortly after taking office, Zwerdling tried to fire the superintendent, Samuel M. Brownell, on the ground that he was not aggressive enough on the integration issue, but Remus Robinson, generally a cautious, conservative man, refused to go along. Brownell soon solved the problem by announcing that he would not seek to renew his contract when it expired in 1966. Zwerdling set out to find a man with a proven record on integration, but after a year-long search, the man the board wanted, Neil V. Sullivan of Berkeley, California, rejected the job. In July 1966, on a split vote, the board named Norman Drachler, Zwerdling's second choice, as acting superintendent. Drachler, then assistant superintendent for community relations, had begun in the Detroit school system as a teacher in 1936. The board made him superintendent by unanimous vote the following March.

No one, except perhaps Zwerdling, expected the quiet, scholarly Drachler to bring a revolution to the school system, but the new superintendent turned out to be just the aggressive integrationist the board had wanted. The proportion of black teachers increased from 31 percent in 1966 to 42 percent in 1970; that of black administrators more than tripled, from 11 percent in 1966 to 37 percent in 1970. Drachler appointed two men from outside the system to be the city's first black deputy superintendents. At Drachler's direction, Detroit became the first big city openly to challenge textbook publishers on the presentation of blacks in their books, and in some cases the school system published its own books in preference to using what the board thought was an inadequate commercial book. As a condition of doing business with the school system, all contractors were required to prove they had a suitable percentage of black employes and executives.

Since 1965, the school board's announced policy had been to integrate school districts. In the early 1960's, the system had been divided into regions, each with its own regional administrators, and when in 1962 the board decided to move the Sherrill School from a mainly white region into a predominantly black one, a group of black parents within the school's district lines brought suit in a federal court to block the move. The case lingered in court until 1965, when the school board won an indefinite adjournment by agreeing to redraw all its region boundaries so that each region contained both black and white neighborhoods.

Despite these efforts, by the fall of 1970, fully three-fourths of Detroit's black pupils were in schools that were still more than 90 percent black. The movement of whites to the suburbs and the increasing size of the black population (a large proportion of them of school age) far outweighed any tinkering that could be done with the school system. The new administration, therefore, made only slight progress in reducing classroom segregation. Drachler altered the school system's open enrollment policy so that students could transfer only if the move furthered integration. The busing policy was similarly revised—but only about 3,000 students were bused, and then only for the purpose of relieving overcrowding. There was little sentiment and no money for city-wide busing, although a 1967 staff report had informed Drachler that massive busing was the only way to integrate the city's schools and classrooms.

AN IDEA WHOSE TIME CAME QUICKLY

Throughout this century, centralization and consolidation have been touchstones in the orthodoxy of American public education. The thrust of school reform has been to enlarge, consolidate, and centralize school systems. This movement culminated when the Compromise School Act of 1896 broke the power of the ward trustees over the highly decentralized New York City school system and placed it in the hands of a central school board. Such was the power of this idea that in the late 1950's Myron Liberman could write: "One of the most important education trends in the next few decades is likely to be the decline of local control of education. Such a development is long overdue. Local control has clearly outlived its usefulness on the American scene. Intellectually, it is already a corpse."

Until the mid-1960's, little notice was paid to the argument, advanced in studies dating back nearly 30 years, that the major urban school systems had become too large and were no less in need of restructuring than small rural systems. This view suddenly came into fashion. At first, reformers urged not community control but rather a larger voice in decisions by *professionals* at the lower levels of the school system. Thus, Marilyn Gittell argued that the New York City school system was incapable of educational reform because of the tight control exercised by a few professionals at the top; the answer, she held, was "decentralization of bureaucratic authority and the expansion of outside professional influence." And in Detroit in 1968, the High School Study Commission, a group of 350 civic leaders formed in the aftermath of some demonstrations by black students, advanced a similar view. Most decisions, the commission recommended, should be made by the school principal. He "should be the one person who combines necessary decision-making with a clear grasp of the needs peculiar to a given neighborhood. He should be given the responsibility for relating the school to its environment; he should be given the authority to do it; he should be held accountable for the results."

In the mid-1960's, as more blacks became disillusioned with integration, decentralization acquired an important new base of political support and in the process underwent an important alteration. From having been a strategy for dispersing administrative authority among school professionals, it soon became as well a strategy for dispersing the school board's policy-making powers among the citizens of local communities—hence the emphasis upon "community control." In Detroit, a major leader of the community control movement was the Rev. Albert Cleage, Jr., a charismatic black minister who had played a key role in the integrationist Sherrill School case. "I did not have a philosophical commitment to integration at any point," Cleage now says. "My primary interest has always been the best possible education for black children. We used the Sherrill case because it was the tactic of the time." Cleage and his followers began turning away from integration and toward community control as early as 1963, when Malcolm X appeared in Detroit at a conference Cleage had helped arrange. Later Cleage, who renamed his Central United Church of Christ the Shrine of the Black Madonna, helped form the Inner City Parents Council and became its chairman. In June 1967, he presented to the school board the council's first formal demand for black control of black schools.

The community control movement soon acquired two advocates in the Michigan legislature. One of these was James Del Rio, a black Democrat with a flair for the dramatic who represented a poor district in Detroit. Early in the 1968 session, Del Rio introduced a bill to divide the system into 16 "subsidiary" and autonomous school systems, each of which would be independent in the eyes of the state and co-equal with the other 650 Michigan school systems. The bill attracted support from Albert Cleage but was heatedly denounced by practically everyone else with any influence in Detroit education—the city-wide PTA, the Board of Commerce, the Detroit Federation of Teachers, Detroit's influential black weekly, the *Michigan Chronicle,* the city's Urban Coalition group, and the board of education itself. After clearing the House education committee, the bill was defeated by a floor vote. Virtually unnoticed during the lively discussion over Del Rio's bill was a second bill introduced by a liberal white Democrat from Detroit, Jack Faxon, which called for division of the school system into regions, each with its own elected school board, but which also retained and enlarged the city's existing central board. Faxon's measure was killed in committee.

This massive opposition was not to community control but to the drastic Del Rio bill. The board of education became more interested in the subject upon the presentation of the High School Study Commission report, which recommended administrative decentralization and also argued for making provision for "the voice of the inner city in the planning and decision-making process of the schools." Zwerdling suggested that a citizens' committee be elected in each of the city's 22 neighborhood high school districts to act as a "liaison" between the school board and the community. But though all board members advocated reform of this type, they were unable to resolve the crucial issue of how much power to turn over to community boards.

In 1968, a city-wide black group, the Citizens for Community Control, organized a number of conferences in which participants in New York City's Ocean Hill–Brownsville experiment spoke. Afterwards, the chairman of this group wrote in the *Michigan Chronicle* that "equality of education through integration is politically and geographically unworkable." He also challenged the school board to stop talking about "community involvement" on the ground that "we already have had that in Detroit. And it doesn't work." Blacks, he declared, would accept nothing less than complete community control. "The principal should have the power to hire and fire the teachers, and the community the power to hire and fire the principal."

Meanwhile, in November, Andrew Perdue, a black attorney, was elected to the board of education with the support of Rev. Cleage and other community control advocates. Perdue was deeply committed to decentralization and community control.

Neither Cleage's Inner City Parents Council nor the Citizens for Community Control developed a particularly large following. Probably they would have if the board had been unwilling to discuss community control. But the board was not unwilling. In fact, it was primarily responsible for making community control and decentralization topics of discussion in the first place. What the board was responding to, in the absence of strong local pressure, was the national discussion of community control that started with the debate over Ocean Hill–Brownsville. Thus, when *The New York Times* interviewed superintendent Drachler during the New York teachers' strike in the fall of 1968, he declared: "Some type of decentralization is inevitable. The question is what is the best method of achieving decentralization?"

The Del Rio and Faxon bills were reintroduced at the beginning of the 1969 session of the state legislature. Almost immediately, one was tabled and the other died in committee. Legislative discussion of decentralization seemed to be dead.

But in Detroit, support for decentralization continued to grow. On April 8, 1969, the Detroit NAACP made its first formal request for decentralization. Its plan for a "community centered school" called for an elected board to oversee each of the city's 330 schools. The boards, whose membership was to be "weighted in favor of parents with children in the school," would in turn name representatives to sit on a board for the entire high school area. "It is our hope that strong state legislative action will not be necessary for creating change in the school system," a NAACP representative said. "However, it appears that legislation or not, we are headed for some form of community control."

Days later, State Senator Coleman Young handed to the Senate clerk a bill which was a polished version of the Faxon proposal. Young, a Democrat from Detroit's inner city and the acknowledged leader of the black legislators, is also the state's Democratic National Committeeman. His support assured that decentralization was a live issue in the legislature.

The board discussed the NAACP plan for more than a month. Four of the seven members indicated they would support it or something like it, but there was no agreement on specifics, and some members were cautious. The board's state lobbyist reported that Senator Young's bill could be killed in the Senate education committee. Most board members were not prepared to oppose the Young bill because they did not oppose decentralization, but neither were they prepared to say what kind of decentralization they favored. The lobbyist was ordered to take a hands-off position on the bill. But he did attempt to protect the board by having Young add a phrase providing that the regional school boards would function "subject to guidelines" adopted by the central board. And at the request of the Detroit Federation of Teachers, which was similarly sitting out the decentralization controversy, Young, an old unionist, added a clause holding that "the rights of retirement, tenure, seniority, and other benefits of any employee transferred to a regional school district or between regional school districts . . . shall not be abnegated, diminished or impaired."

In June, the Young bill was reported out of the education committee, and after virtually no debate the Senate passed it by a vote of 25 to 5. In July, the House passed it by a vote of 83–18. These large margins helped to persuade Republican Governor William G. Milliken, and on August 11 he signed the bill into law.

In Detroit, nobody was particularly happy with the new law. Blacks thought it did not go far enough in securing community control. Many whites believed that decentralization was unnecessary and a waste of money, although some white conservatives were quick to recognize that community control would be a boon to them.

DRAWING THE LINES

For the school board, the first order of business was to establish the boundaries of the new regions, and during the fall it held five public hearings on this issue. It quickly became clear that the black community was less than enthusiastic about creating racially integrated regions. "Consideration should be given to those areas where a sense of community prevails," an NAACP representative stated. "This decentralization bill is not a vehicle for integration." New Detroit, the city's Urban Coalition group, declared: "Elimination of *de facto* segregation should be the result of and not the object of education." The representative of another black group reported that "Throughout all our discussions, integration has been the least sought-after variable." Such sentiments were aptly summed up by a spokesman for the largely black First Congressional District Democratic organization, who said, "Redistricting must guarantee black control of black schools."

The willingness of blacks to forsake integrated regions stemmed from the simple demographic fact that, although 65 percent of Detroit public school students were black, only 44 percent of the city's electorate was black. If the regions were fully integrated—with each region's racial mix duplicating the mix of the city as a whole—they all would have black student majorities and black voter minorities.

When Zwerdling and his fellow board members talked of coupling decentralization with integration, integrated regions were precisely what they had in mind. "It is true that decentralization will not change where anyone goes to school," Zwerdling said in early 1970. "It is not going to end racial isolation. But if we drew boundaries that put blacks into one region and whites into another region there could never be any integration. We would have frozen things. But . . . we seek to achieve integration, and so what we can do is create a situation where blacks and whites working together on region boards can move to end the segregation within their own region." Zwerdling ignored the possibility that a white voter majority might move region boards farther away from integration.

In ordinary circumstances, Zwerdling's plan would have commanded a voting majority of the board. Zwerdling and the other members of his 1964 campaign team, Grylls and Stewart, were prepared to vote for it, and their frequent ally, Remus Robinson, had said that he would go along. But early in 1970 Robinson was hospitalized with cancer and was unable to be present to cast his vote. Zwerdling delayed the vote for weeks in the hope that Robinson would be well enough to appear and vote.

Two other board members, James A. Hathaway and Patrick A. McDonald, refused to support the Zwerdling plan. Hathaway, a white attorney elected in 1968 with Perdue, had decided to vote for black control of black schools because that was what had been demanded in the hearings. McDonald, a young white attorney with an ambitious eye on higher office, had spent most of his term opposing every Zwerdling program—to which the board majority reciprocated by refusing to consider any McDonald suggestion. As usual, McDonald had his own plan, which only he was prepared to vote for.

Andrew Perdue was the swing vote; if he could be won over, Zwerdling's plan would have a majority even in Robinson's absence. But Perdue considered the Zwerdling plan a "smokescreen." If the board were really serious about achieving maximum integration, he insisted, it would have to change school "feeder patterns wherever possible." Unless the board were willing to do that, it should stop talking about integration and draw up the black-controlled and white-controlled regions that every one demanded.

In mid-March, when it became apparent that Robinson would not attend another board meeting, Drachler called in his key aides and told them that Perdue's vote had to be won. To do that, Drachler said, "I need an integration plan." The staff proceeded to give him one. Without altering the regions mapped out by the Zwerdling plan, Drachler's aides redrew the boundaries of many high school districts within five of those regions. The racial composition of half of the city's 22 neighborhood high schools would be substantially affected, and the three remaining all-white schools would become integrated. Cody, a 2.1 percent black school, would become 31.3 percent black; Redford, only 2.2 percent black, would become 29.2 percent black; and Denby, 3.1 percent black, would become 53 percent black. About half of the 9,000 students to be affected by the plan would be white students, who would be sent to predominantly black schools. It was the first time the board had integrated both ways, requiring whites to go to black schools as well as the reverse.

With Zwerdling's approval and Robinson's support, Drachler presented the plan to the board at a secret dinner meeting on March 31, 1970. Perdue gave his assent, and the four votes needed to adopt the plan were assured. "You have spoiled my dinner," McDonald told Drachler.

The next day, McDonald called Drachler to ask for a copy of the plan. Zwerdling had given instructions that no documents were to be distributed, but Drachler decided that McDonald had a right to have a copy of the plan. So on Friday a messenger delivered a full copy of the integration plan and the supporting charts to each board member. McDonald promptly turned over his copy to a favored reporter, and on Sunday both Detroit newspapers carried page one stories about the board's readiness to adopt a "sweeping integration plan."

REACTION IN DETROIT AND LANSING

The reaction was swift and violent. On Monday parents at four junior high schools affected by the plan kept their children home in protest; at one of these, only 50 of 500 students showed up for class. That night, a group of angry white parents met to form a Citizens' Committee for Better Education and elected Edward Zaleski, a policeman, as its temporary chairman. "It will be a tough fight," Zaleski said, "but we are prepared to fight this thing all year, or ten years if necessary."

On Tuesday, as the boycotts continued, the school board held a meeting; white parents jammed the second floor board room at school headquarters, and hundreds more overflowed into hallways and the ground floor lobby. McDonald, whose popularity among the city's white voters was rising, went to the lobby to proclaim himself the champion of the parents' cause and to denounce his fellow board members. He further suggested that anyone unhappy with the school board might study the state's recall law. At one point during the evening, the parents tried to break down the glass doors leading to the meeting room, chanting "Hell no, we won't go." Inside, the board heard more than 30 speakers, most of them against the plan. A spokesman for the Detroit Urban League hailed the action as "the board's finest hour." After five hours, the board, as expected, officially enacted the plan—Zwerdling, Grylls, Stewart, and Perdue in favor; McDonald and Hathaway against.

The turmoil in the schools continued for a week. Detroit officialdom was in confusion. And white parents continued to organize. Aubrey Short, a metallurgical engineer with eight children, was elected permanent chairman of the Citizens' Committee for Better Education. On May 4, the committee held a rally in front of school headquarters to kick off a recall campaign against the four board members who had voted for the integration plan.

Meanwhile, in Lansing, the Michigan legislature had enacted a protest of its own. The day after the integration plan was adopted, two old foes of the board, James Del Rio and E. D. O'Brien, a conservative white from Detroit, pulled out of committee a bill providing for a referendum on decentralization and added an amendment requiring the school board to send every student to the school nearest his home. The next day, the bill as amended passed 68–31. Del Rio was absent and none of Detroit's black legislators voted for the bill, but white Detroit conservatives joined with suburban and rural legislators to make up the huge majority. The Senate voted 22 to 9 to repeal the decentralization law outright. Senator Young declared that "this is capitulation to blind prejudice."

For Young and other supporters of decentralization, the situation was desperate. Clearly there were enough votes to prohibit any form of decentralization and to pass anti-integration legislation as well. Young was furious at the Detroit school board for adopting what he came to call "this chicken shit integration plan." He could be seen walking to sessions of the Senate muttering to no one in particular, "And they thought they could get away with this in an election year."

Young decided that his best tactic was to get the legislature to pass a new law authorizing decentralization but outlawing the integration plan. "You can support that kind of bill," he told his fellow black legislators, "because the anti-integration clause will last only as long as it takes to get this thing into court." Such a strategy was further recommended by the fact that only a third of the 149 candidates who had filed for the regional school board elections were black. The prospect of a white sweep of the elections made Young all the more willing to take up a new decentralization law, which would allow time for more candidates to file.

Young and the House Speaker, another leading liberal, met with conservative legislators from April through June in an effort to reach agreement. The central problem was where to draw the regional boundaries. Conservatives wanted boundaries drawn along legislative district lines because these best served to separate black and white areas. Liberals would not go along with such a blatantly segregationist plan and wanted the boundaries drawn according to school attendance boundaries. Governor Milliken said he would sign no law which did not win approval of the entire Detroit delegation.

After nearly three months of steady work, a compromise was worked out. The legislature would pass a decentralization law with the boundary issue unresolved; if within seven days after the governor signed the bill no agreement on boundaries could be reached, the governor would appoint a three-member boundary commission to do the job. The bill sailed through the House 93–1 and through the Senate 30 to 0 without debate. The governor signed it into law on July 7. When the legislature could not decide on the boundaries, the governor appointed a commission to settle the matter.

In Young's opinion, the new decentralization law was better than the old one. It provided for eight regional school districts, each with a five-member elected board. The top vote-getter in each region would be the regional chairman and would have a seat on the central school board. The central· board would have only five at-large members, so that the regional chairmen would be in the majority. The central board would handle labor negotiations, distribution of lump-sum budgets to the regions, and the building of new schools from the limited construction budget. Most other responsibilities for running the system rested with the regional boards. Unlike New York City, where high schools remain under central board authority, all Detroit schools were turned over to the regional boards except for a handful of specialized, city-wide schools.

The new law also managed to take a few digs at the board majority. It shortened the terms of Zwerdling, Stewart, and Grylls by one year so that they would expire on December 30, 1970. It also restricted the power of the board to fill the vacancy created by the death of Remus Robinson on June 14th. The legislature enacted these provisions on the understanding that, if it did so, the group pressing for the recall of the board majority would call off the campaign. Everyone in state government feared that a recall campaign carried on through the summer could lead to another riot.

But a few days after Governor Milliken signed the new decentralization bill into law, Aubrey Short, chairman of the Citizens' Committee for Better Education, said his group would not call off the campaign after all. "A lot of people have decided they don't like the board of education. If they have changed their minds, then they can vote against the recall on election day," he said.

THE RECALL

The recall campaign is one of the amazing success stories of modern Detroit politics. Within two weeks after the kickoff, a door-to-door campaign had netted 70,000 signatures of the 114,000-plus required (a number equal to 25 percent of the total local vote for governor in the last election). Earlier attempts to recall public officials—most recently it had been Detroit Mayor Jerome Cavanagh—had failed because of the large number of signatures needed. But the school board recall had a momentum which could not be stopped, and on June 15 the committee filed petitions with 130,000 names. A month later the city clerk ordered the issue on the August 4 primary election ballot.

Three separate federal and state suits were filed during the next month in an effort to keep the recall off the ballot. But on July 31, just five days before the election, the Michigan Court of Appeals overruled a lower court decision and ordered the recall question put back on the ballot.

The inconsistent court decisions left little time for a campaign to oppose the recall. After the final court decision, a group of old-line liberals tried to organize against the recall, but they could raise only enough money for one full-page newspaper advertisement. The UAW, now without Walter Reuther at the helm, printed leaflets opposing the recall, but little else was done. "Where have they all gone?" asked Andrew Perdue on election day, "the UAW, the NAACP, the others who supported us."

The election turnout was light—only 23 percent of the city's eligible voters went to the polls—and the recall carried with 60 percent of the vote. Voting was unusually heavy in the city's white neighborhoods, and in some areas where the integration plan would have required whites to go to black schools, the favorable vote on the recall was 90 percent. An equally heavy percentage opposed the recall in black neighborhoods, but voting there was not as heavy as in white precincts.

It was the first successful recall in the 128-year history of the Detroit school system, and when it was over, not even the recall committee was terribly proud of what it had done. Edward Zaleski defensively told an NBC news interviewer: "I had a right to fight. My daughter was being sent to a black school. We knew we were going to win because we were fighting for our children. They were fighting for only an idea."

THE NEW SCHOOL BOARDS

On the day of the recall election, the governor's boundary commission announced its conclusions. The commission members—a prominent black liberal clergyman, a conservative white city councilman, and a little-known Wayne State University law professor—had agreed from the outset that integration of regions would not be a condition. They also agreed to divide political control equally between whites and blacks. With these issues out of the way, they set to work to create four white-controlled and four black-controlled regions. Their deliberations centered on the technical problem of drawing boundaries that kept as close as possible to existing school boundaries while still meeting the one man, one vote test. As a result of the commission's work, which was finished less than two weeks after its appointment, decentralization was at last ready to go into effect—or so it seemed.

But shortly after the recall, the NAACP brought suit against the legislature challenging its right to overturn the school board's April 7 integration plan. The United States District Court refused to reinstate that original plan. Upon appeal, the Federal Circuit Court ruled in mid-October that the section of the decentralization law prohibiting the board from implementing its integration plan was unconstitutional, but it turned back to the District Court the question of whether the board's original plan should be put into effect. The District Court in turn asked the school board, which now included four members appointed by the governor to replace those recalled, to suggest alternative plans, and the board responded by offering three—the original integration plan, a voluntary integration plan suggested by Patrick McDonald, and a plan requiring every high school student to take at least part of his course work at a second school. The Court selected McDonald's plan to create "magnet" high schools designed to attract voluntary student transfers and ordered that the plan be put into effect by September 1971.

Meanwhile, school board elections were under way. Although the new decentralization law canceled the normal primary and opened up the election to new candidates, only 51 additional candidates filed, making a total of 200. These 200 were a diverse group, including 19 teachers, 18 housewives, 7 lawyers, and a sampling of other professions. No consistent city-wide campaign organization was evident during the weeks prior to the election. The UAW, traditionally an important power in Detroit politics, was active and successful in several parts of the city, especially in two black areas. The Citizens' Committee for Better Education was likewise in evidence in areas where feeling against the integration plan had been high. But in general the campaigning was unorganized as a result of which the most important factor in the election seemed to be the candidate's name. As in other Detroit elections, well-known political names often won.

Despite any confusion, the election produced a clear victory for the conservatives. The new 13-member central board included six staunch anti-integrationist conservatives and only three blacks, of whom only one was elected on an at-large basis—giving the board the smallest proportion of blacks in 15 years. Contrary to all expectations, blacks won a voting majority on only two of the eight regional boards, although black students were in the majority in six of the eight regions. In the three regions where opposition to the integration plan was most intense, not a single black was elected. Of the 43 central and regional board seats on the ballot, 13 were filled by blacks, whereas 10 were filled by Polish-Americans (four of them on the central board). Although black voters generally rejected openly separatist black candidates

—a slate headed by Rev. Cleage did poorly in an inner-city region where Cleage is well known—white separatists fared better at the hands of the white electorate.

To anyone who may have doubted it, the conservatism of the new board manifested itself almost immediately after the new members took office on January 1, 1971. A few days later, the board held a special meeting to consider the Appeals Court's decisions to overturn the state's anti-integration law. Six new conservative members wanted to appeal the order to the United States Supreme Court. McDonald, whose support they had expected, refused to vote for the appeal because he feared that the court might overturn his voluntary integration plan. That left the board split 6 to 7 against an appeal which indicated to the conservatives that they could control the board as long as McDonald, whom they considered their spiritual leader on the strength of his opposition to the integration plan and his silent support of the recall, voted with them. At the next meeting they snatched the presidency of the board from James Hathaway, who had presided over the interim board, and handed it over to McDonald—the man who, until a few months earlier, had been the pariah of Zwerdling's liberal board.

As a result of the election, superintendent Drachler found himself in a difficult position. It was clear that, at best, he could command only five or six votes on the 13-member board. Moreover, the new board had suddenly become money-conscious. Whereas the old liberal board had paid little attention to the $29 million deficit in the system's $249 million budget, the new board started cutting programs and firing personnel, including 192 non-contract teachers, in an effort to reduce spending by $12 million within six weeks. Trying—but with little success—to make it sound like a normal event, Drachler announced toward the end of January that he would resign at the end of the school year in order to set up and direct a new program, funded largely by the Ford Foundation, to train future educational leaders.

COMMUNITY CONTROL—OR "DIXIE"?

The early weeks of decentralization produced several issues which could have sparked city-wide confrontations like those experienced in New York. First, a regional board acceded to the demands of a group of black parents to remove a principal in clear violation of the school system's contract with the principal's union. But the principal backed off and was quietly given another assignment. Then, in defiance of the central board's instruction another regional board refused to give students a statewide achievement test. The central board said nothing.

This same regional board also said it would not implement voluntary integration in September. Still no open confrontation occurred. Everyone seemed anxious to avoid what they called "another Ocean Hill," and when a confrontation threatened to escalate to that point, both the regional and central boards backed away.

There was also some evidence in the early weeks that the new boards were less than unanimous in their enthusiasm and commitment to make decentralization work. Some new members had been outspoken in their opposition to the whole idea of decentralization during the campaign, and several of them continued to take this view once in office. They talked of having the legislature end "this foolish experiment" before the next school board election in 1973. And some of the regional boards seemed more interested in avoiding responsibility than in using or expanding it. After a series of high school disruptions, the central board was forced to assume responsibility for handling incidents because the regional boards did not want to have to deal with the messy problem of student unrest.

But it is still too early to determine whether decentralization in Detroit will produce genuine community control or whether it will have a favorable impact on student achievement. It may or it may not. Only time will tell, although it may be a significant portent for the future that at no point during the debate on decentralization was education the prime consideration. The arguments were all political.

About the short-run political consequences of decentralization, some things do seem clear. In Detroit the process of decentralization produced severe racial polarization and a backlash vote which put a conservative school board in office. The blacks who pressed for decentralization were the losers; they ended up with less power and less influence than they had had before decentralization. As a result, some of the city's more conservative black leaders are ready to give up on decentralization before it is even a year old. Meanwhile, the devastating political conflict that accompanied the process of decentralization has not yet quieted down, and the "peace of reconciliation" that Alan Altshuler envisions as the ideal outcome of decentralization has yet to descend upon Detroit.

The national importance of Detroit's experience with decentralization lies in the conflict which developed between decentralization and integration. It can be argued that the board's integration plan, which was developed as a compromise to get needed votes, did not in fact achieve much integration. But there can be no doubt that those who worked to recall the school board did so in order to fight integration no matter how modest its degree. *And in fighting integration during the recall campaign, whites who had opposed decentralization for two years sud-*

denly embraced community control as they realized that segregated regions would protect them forever from the threat of integration that the Zwerdling plan had posed.

It may not be, as one school official observed on the day of the recall election, that "the song is 'community control' but the tune is 'Dixie.' " But the Detroit experience does offer convincing evidence that integration and community control are not easily compatible.

Chapter 4

COALITIONS VERSUS INDEPENDENT ACTION AS A MINORITY STRATEGY

A. Introduction

Almost all movements for social change have at one time or another been faced with the dilemma of whether to join together with potential allies or go it alone. Often such choices result from ideological preferences and biases, personalities of leaders, or the fluctuation of broader events. In sketching the recent historical background of the civil rights movement, Bayard Rustin's article in this chapter points out that the current inward-looking Black Power trend represents a reaction to the failures of earlier coalitional and integrationist policies.

Any activist or planner responsible for strategy decisions must balance the benefits and losses that might accrue from choosing one or the other of these alternatives. It is clear that significant advantages can be derived from consolidating with allies. A small or weak movement can gain increased strength, particularly through the pooling of resources —money, manpower, leadership, facilities and equipment, contacts, political muscle, and the like. The accumulation of sheer numbers of people to turn out at a rally or carry off a demonstration can have an impact or exert a coercive force. Even if such a display of numbers is focused on a single event, the results can be of symbolic import. The moral support and encouragement that members of an unpopular movement can obtain from coalition allies can provide a crucial impetus for forward movement, including continued, invigorated independent activity.

As in all community action, such a course entails potential risks and losses, however. An organization entering into a coalition must ordinarily give up one thing to gain another. Thus its freedom of action may become restricted, and some measure of autonomy in shaping its own destiny may be sacrificed. For racial and ethnic minorities possessing a low level of assertiveness or self-confidence, this can be a vital forfeit, particularly when ingroup solidarity and self-determination are their central objectives. Potential allies that are powerful community groups are likely to be in closer association with the establishment or somewhat conservative in outlook. Coordinated planning with such organizations may necessitate a reduction in militancy or the abandonment of unpopular, self-oriented programs by minority organizations.

Interorganizational alliances also require a fundamental outlay of energy to maintain linkages. These energy costs are consumed in the time required to exchange information, allot responsibility, persuade dissident units, or overcome the inertia of a disinterested or divided confederation. Such internal organizational activities are often at the expense of outwardly directed efforts aimed at the targets of change. Strained interpersonal relations, the paternalistic attitudes of majority participants, and hidden conflicts of interest may all diminish the values to be gained from coalitions.

Two classic statements which differ on the merits of coalitions for racial minorities are included in this chapter. Because both were written at precisely the point when Black Power was emerging as a significant force, they convey the urgency and particular historical circumstances associated with this development. Stokely Carmichael and Charles V. Hamilton, in "The Myths of Coalition," argue against coalitions and for independent action; Bayard Rustin, in " 'Black Power' and Coalition Politics," makes the case for coalitions.

This issue opens up a range of critical, complex strategy questions. Under what circumstances is it appropriate to form coalitions, and when is this inadvisable? Should linkages be ad hoc or permanent, formal or informal, single issue or cross-cutting, and with what kind of allies should they be made? In part, the consideration of coalitions depends on the characteristics of the power structure or target group. What is the extent of its strength? Does it possess a monolithic unity, or is it itself fragmented and pluralistic? To what degree is it sympathetic to the antagonist's view, and how open or closed is it generally to outside communication? Such an analysis of the opposition can contribute to determination of the need for and composition of coalitions.

Even those who are committed to a philosophy of independent action must acknowledge the need for coalition-building skills *within* a given minority movement. It has been pointed out that most social movements have centrifugal tendencies, in terms of competing leaders and factions.[1] Coalitional activities and skills are necessary in order to maintain a reasonable degree of cohesion, if not unity, within such organizations.

Coalitions among different minority movements may also be problematical; varying patterns of consensus, disagreement, and indifference may appear, depending on the specific issues being addressed. For example, taking blacks, Chicanos, and women as a point of reference, the following relationships may appear:

1. *Competition* between black males and women advocates on procedural decisions regarding preferential treatment in employment.
2. *Mutual agreement* among all groups as concerns better health care services.

---

[1] Luther P. Gerlach, "Movements of Revolutionary Change: Some Structural Characteristics," *American Behavorial Scientist*, vol. 14 (July–August 1971), pp. 812–36.

3. *Disagreement* between women and traditionally minded Chicano groups concerning abortion reform.
4. *Indifference* or lack of mutual concern on a matter such as bilingual education, which is of moment only to Chicanos.

The trick in shaping such coalitions would appear to be to emphasize those issues on which there is agreement and reasonable expectations of mutual benefit, such as health services, welfare rights, and child care, while playing down divisive matters or those of little salience, except as tradeoffs.

Another way of addressing this matter is to consider the preconditions of meaningful coalitions. Carmichael and Hamilton suggest several in their selection, including: (1) mutual recognition of respective self-interests, (2) attention to specific identifiable goals, and (3) the existence of independent power bases within the units of the coalition. Questions concerning such matters as what preconditions are connected up with what types of outcomes for member units of a coalition, move the discourse from a theoretical and philosophical plane to an empirical one. Inquiries framed in such a fashion are susceptible to investigation through existing social research methods.

An example of one type of research investigation on the subject of coalitions is "Majority Involvement in Minority Movements," by Gary T. Marx and Michael Useem, who use a historical methodology to study three differing minority movements—civil rights, the Abolitionists, and the campaign against Untouchability in India. In particular, Marx and Useem assess the effects of majority member participation in such minority movements. General strains and types of action preferences among minority and majority members in all three instances are described, and implications are suggested. Survey research methods have also been used, as in interviews of a sample of blacks to determine their typical mode of reaction to situations of intergroup difficulty. Characteristics of those who lean toward separatism (avoidance) and those who seek a resolution to such problems through intergroup engagement (assimilation) were discerned in one such study.[2] Knowledge of this type could determine who to recruit for different forms of participation or what types of strategies might be acceptable to different minority constituencies. Other traditions of investigation on this subject that may be of interest are field studies of ongoing community processes[3] and

---

[2] Donald L. Noel, "Minority Responses to Intergroup Situations," *Phylon,* vol. 30 (Winter 1969), pp. 367–74.

[3] Tilman C. Cothran and William Phillips Jr., "Negro Leadership in a Crisis Situation," *Phylon,* vol. 22 (Summer 1961), pp. 107–18.

laboratory-type investigations using structured tasks or game procedures with small groups.[4]

Turning from research data to more pragmatic concerns, John Florez, of the National Urban Coalition, in "Chicanos and Coalitions as a Force for Social Change," recommends a specific strategy for the Chicano community. This strategy, which is comprised of a series of temporary unions between Chicanos and existing power blocks, can be evaluated in the light of the theoretical and research articles that precede it. Florez appears to blend a strategy of group solidarity and power with aspects of a cultural pluralism perspective (see Chapter 1).

---

[4] Theodore Caplow, "A Theory of Coalitions in the Triad," *American Sociological Review,* vol. 21 (August 1956), pp. 489–93.

B. Theoretical and philosophical considerations

STOKELY CARMICHAEL and CHARLES V. HAMILTON

The myths of coalition

There is a strongly held view in this society that the best—indeed, perhaps the only—way for black people to win their political and economic rights is by forming coalitions with liberal, labor, church and other kinds of sympathetic organizations or forces, including the "liberal left" wing of the Democratic Party. With such allies, they could influence national legislation and national social patterns; racism could thus be ended. This school sees the "Black Power Movement" as basically separatist and unwilling to enter alliances. Bayard Rustin, a major spokesman for the coalition doctrine, has written:

> Southern Negroes, despite exhortations from SNCC to organize themselves into a Black Panther Party, are going to stay in the Democratic party—to them it is the party of progress, the New Deal, the New Frontier, and the Great Society—and they are right to stay.[1]

Aside from the fact that the name of the Lowndes County Freedom Party is *not* the "Black Panther Party," SNCC has often stated that it does not oppose the formation of political coalitions per se; obviously they are necessary in a pluralistic society. But coalitions with whom? On what terms? And for what objectives? All too frequently, coalitions involving black people have been only at the leadership level; dictated by terms set by others; and for objectives not calculated to bring major improvement in the lives of the black masses.

In this [article], we propose to reexamine some of the assumptions of the coalition school, and to comment on some instances of supposed alliance between black people and other groups. In the process of this treatment, it should become clear that the advocates of Black Power do *not* eschew coalitions; rather, we want to establish the grounds on which we feel political coalitions can be viable.

Source: *Black Power,* by Stokely Carmichael and Charles V. Hamilton, pp. 58–84. Copyright © 1967 by Stokely Carmichael and Charles V. Hamilton. Reprinted by permission of Random House, Inc.

[1] Bayard Rustin, "Black Power and Coalition Politics," *Commentary* (September, 1966). [Reprinted as the second article in this chapter.]

The coalitionists proceed on what we can identify as three myths or major fallacies. *First,* that in the context of present-day America, the interests of black people are identical with the interests of certain liberal, labor and other reform groups. Those groups accept the legitimacy of the basic values and institutions of the society, and fundamentally are not interested in a major reorientation of the society. Many adherents to the current coalition doctrine recognize this but nevertheless would have black people coalesce with such groups. The assumption—which is a myth—is this: what is good for America is automatically good for black people. *The second myth* is the fallacious assumption that a viable coalition can be effected between the politically and economically secure and the politically and economically insecure. *The third myth* assumes that political coalitions are or can be sustained on a moral, friendly, sentimental basis: by appeals to conscience. We will examine each of these three notions separately.

The major mistake made by exponents of the coalition theory is that they advocate alliances with groups which have never had as their central goal the necessarily total revamping of the society. At bottom, those groups accept the American system and want only—if at all—to make peripheral, marginal reforms in it. Such reforms are inadequate to rid the society of racism.

Here we come back to an important point made in the first chapter: the overriding sense of superiority that pervades white America. "Liberals," no less than others, are subjected and subject to it; the white liberal must view the racial scene through a drastically different lens from the black man's. Killian and Grigg (1964) were correct when they said in *Racial Crisis in America:*

> . . . most white Americans, even those white leaders who attempt to communicate and cooperate with their Negro counterparts, do not see racial inequality in the same way that the Negro does. The white person, no matter how liberal he may be, exists in the cocoon of a white-dominated society. Living in a white residential area, sending his children to white schools, moving in exclusively white social circles, he must exert a special effort to expose himself to the actual conditions under which large numbers of Negroes live. Even when such exposure occurs, his perception is likely to be superficial and distorted. The substandard house may be overshadowed in his eyes by the television aerial or the automobile outside the house. Even more important, he does not perceive the subjective inequalities inherent in the system of segregation because he does not experience them daily as a Negro does. Simply stated, the white American lives almost all of his life in a white world. The Negro American lives a large part of his life in a white world also, but in a world in which he is stigmatized. (p. 73)

Our point is that no matter how "liberal" a white person might be, he cannot ultimately escape the overpowering influence—on himself and on black people—of his whiteness in a racist society.

Liberal whites often say that they are tired of being told "you can't understand what it is to be black." They claim to recognize and acknowledge this. Yet the same liberals will often turn around and tell black people that they should ally themselves with those who can't understand, who share a sense of superiority based on whiteness. The fact is that most of these "allies" neither look upon the blacks as co-equal partners nor do they perceive the goals as any but the adoption of certain Western norms and values. Professor Milton M. Gordon, in his book, *Assimilation in American Life,* has called those values "Anglo-conformity" (p. 88). Such a view assumes the "desirability of maintaining English institutions (as modified by the American Revolution), the English language, and English-oriented cultural patterns as dominant and standard in American life." Perhaps one holding these views is not a racist in the strict sense of our original definition, but the end result of his attitude is to sustain racism. As Gordon says:

> The non-racist Anglo-conformists presumably are either convinced of the *cultural* superiority of Anglo-Saxon institutions as developed in the United States, or believe simply that regardless of superiority or inferiority, since English culture has constituted the dominant framework for the development of American institutions, newcomers should expect to adjust accordingly. (pp. 103–104)

We do not believe it possible to form meaningful coalitions unless both or all parties are not only willing but believe it absolutely necessary to challenge Anglo-conformity and other prevailing norms and institutions. Most liberal groups with which we are familiar are not so willing at this time. If this is the case, then the coalition is doomed to frustration and failure.

The Anglo-conformity position assumes that what is good for America—whites—is good for black people. We reject this. The Democratic Party makes the same claim. But the political and social rights of black people have been and always will be negotiable and expendable the moment they conflict with the interests of their "allies." A clear example of this can be found in the city of Chicago, where Mayor Daley's Democratic "coalition" machine depends on black support and unfortunately black people vote consistently for that machine. Note the results, as described by Banfield and Wilson in *City Politics* (1966):

> The civic projects that Mayor Daley inaugurated in Chicago—street cleaning, street lighting, road building, a new airport, and a convention hall, for example—were shrewdly chosen. They were highly visible; they

benefited the county as well as the city; for the most part they were non-controversial; they did not require much increase in taxes; and they created many moderately paying jobs that politicians could dispense as patronage. The *mayor's program conspicuously neglected the goals of militant Negroes,* demands for the enforcement of the building code, and (until there was a dramatic exposé) complaints about police inefficiency and corruption. *These things were all controversial, and, perhaps most important, would have no immediate, visible result; either they would benefit those central-city voters whose loyalty could be counted upon anyway or else* (as in the case of police reform) *they threatened to hurt the machine in a vital spot.* (p. 124; author's italics)

As long as the black people of Chicago—and the same can be said of cities throughout the country—remain politically dependent on the Democratic machine, their interests will be secondary to that machine.

Organized labor is another example of a potential ally who has never deemed it essential to question the society's basic values and institutions. The earliest advocates of unionism believed in the doctrine of *laissez-faire.* The labor organizers of the American Federation of Labor (AFL) did not want the government to become involved in labor's problems, and probably for good reason. The government then—in the 1870's and 1880's—was anti-labor, pro-management. It soon became clear that political power would be necessary to accomplish some of the goals of organized labor, especially the goals of the railroad unions. The AFL pursued that power and eventually won it, but generally remained tied to the values and principles of the society as it was. They simply wanted in; the route lay through collective bargaining and the right to strike. The unions set their sights on immediate bread-and-butter issues, to the exclusion of broader goals.

With the founding and development of mass industrial unionism under the Congress of Industrial Organizations (CIO), we began to see a slight change in overall union orientation. The CIO was interested in a wider variety of issues—foreign trade, interest rates, even civil rights issues to an extent—but it too never seriously questioned the racist basis of the society. In *Politics, Parties and Pressure Groups* (1964), Professor V. O. Key, Jr. has concluded: ". . . on the fundamental question of the character of the economic system, the dominant labor ideology did not challenge the established order." Professor Selig Perlman wrote: ". . . it is a labor movement upholding capitalism, not only in practice, but in principle as well."[2] Organized labor, so often pushed as a poten-

---

[2] Selig Perlman, "The Basic Philosophy of the American Labor Movement," *Annals of the American Academy of Political and Social Science,* vol. 274 (1951), pp. 57–63.

tial ally by the coalition theorists, illustrates the pitfalls of the first myth; as we shall see later in this chapter, its history also debunks the second myth.

Yet another source of potential alliance frequently cited by the exponents of coalitions is the liberal-reform movement, especially at the local political level. But the various reform-politics groups—particularly in New York, Chicago and California—frequently are not tuned in to the primary goals of black people. They establish their own goals and then demand that black people identify with them. When black leaders begin to articulate goals in the interest of black people *first,* the reformers tend, more often than not, to term this "racist" and to drop off. Reformers push such "good government" programs as would result in posts being filled by professional, middle-class people. Wilson stated in *The Amateur Democrat,* "Blue-ribbon candidates would be selected, not only for the important, highly visible posts at the top of the ticket, but also for the less visible posts at the bottom" (p. 128). Black people who have participated in local reform politics—especially in Chicago—have come from the upper-middle class. Reformers generally reject the political practice of ticket balancing, which means that they tend to be "color blind" and wish to select candidates only on the basis of qualifications, of merit. In itself this would not be bad, but their conception of a "qualified" person is usually one who fits the white middle-class mold. Seldom, if ever, does one hear of the reformers advocating representation by grass-roots leaders from the ghettos: these are hardly "blue-ribbon" types. Again, when reformers push for elections at large as opposed to election by district, they do not increase black political power. "Blue-ribbon" candidates, government by technical experts, elections at large—all these common innovations of reformers do little for black people.

Francis Carney concludes from his study of California's liberal-reform Democratic clubs[3] that although those groups were usually strong on civil rights, they were nonetheless essentially middle-class oriented. This could only perpetuate a paternalistic, colonial relationship—doing *for* the blacks. Thus, even when the reformers are bent on making significant changes in the system, the question must be asked if that change is consistent with the views and interests of black people—as perceived by those people.

Frequently, we have seen that a staunch, militant stand taken by black leaders has frightened away the reformers. The latter could not understand the former's militancy. "Amateur Democrats (reformers)

---

[3] Francis Carney, *The Rise of the Democratic Clubs in California,* Eagleton Institute Cases in Practical Politics. New York: McGraw-Hill, 1959.

are passionately committed to a militant stand on civil rights, but they shy away from militant Negro organizations because they find them 'too race-conscious' " (p. 285), says Wilson in *The Amateur Democrat,* citing as one example the Independent Voters of Illinois, who felt they could not go along with the desire of some black members to take a very strong, pro-civil rights and anti-Daley position. The liberal-reform politicians have not been able fully to accept the necessity of black people speaking forcefully and for themselves. This is one of the greatest points of tension between these two sets of groups today; this difference must be resolved before viable coalitions can be formed between the two.

To sum up our rejection of the first myth: . . . [T]he political and economic institutions of this society must be completely revised if the political and economic status of black people is to be improved. We do not see how those same institutions can be utilized—through the mechanism of coalescing with some of them—to bring about that revision. We do not see how black people can form effective coalitions with groups which are not willing to question and condemn the racist institutions which exploit black people; which do not perceive the need for, and will not work for, basic change. Black people cannot afford to assume that what is good for white America is automatically good for black people.

The second myth we want to deal with is the assumption that a politically and economically secure group can collaborate with a politically and economically insecure group. Our contention is that such an alliance is based on very shaky grounds. By definition, the goals of the respective parties are different.

Black people are often told that they should seek to form coalitions after the fashion of those formed with so-called Radical Agrarians—later Populists—in the latter part of the nineteenth century. In 1886, the Colored Farmers' Alliance and Cooperative Union was formed, interestingly enough, by a white Baptist minister in Texas. The platform of this group was similar to that of the already existing Northern and Southern Farmers' Alliances, which were white. But upon closer examination, one could see substantial differences in interests and goals. The black group favored a Congressional bill (the Lodge Federal Elections Bill) which aimed to guarantee the voting rights of Southern black people; the white group opposed it. In 1889, a group of black farmers in North Carolina accused the Southern Alliance of setting low wages and influencing the state legislature to pass discriminatory laws. Two years later, the Colored Alliance called for a strike of black cotton pickers. Professors August Meier and Elliot Rudwick ask a number of questions about these two groups, in *From Plantation to Ghetto* (1966):

Under what circumstances did Negroes join and to what extent, if any, was participation encouraged (or even demanded) by white employers who were members of the Southern Alliance? . . . Is it possible that the Colored Alliance was something like a company union, disintegrating only when it became evident that the Negro tenant farmers refused to follow the dictates of their white employers? . . . And how was it that the Alliance men and Populists were later so easily led into extreme anti-Negro actions? In spite of various gestures to obtain Negro support, attitudes such as those exhibited in North Carolina and on the Lodge Bill would argue that whatever interracial solidarity existed was not firmly rooted. (pp. 158–59)

The fact is that the white group was relatively more secure than the black group. As C. Vann Woodward writes in *Tom Watson, Agrarian Rebel,* 1963, "It is undoubtedly true that the Populist ideology was dominantly that of the landowning farmer, who was, in many cases, the exploiter of landless tenant labor" (p. 18). It is difficult to perceive the basis on which the two could coalesce and create a meaningful alliance for the landless, insecure group. It is no surprise, then, to learn of the anti-black actions mentioned above and to realize that the relation of blacks to Populists was not the harmonious arrangement some people today would have us believe.

It is true that black people in St. Louis and Kansas backed the Populists in the election of 1892, and North Carolina blacks supported them in 1896. But it is also true that the Populists in South Carolina, under the leadership of "Pitchfork" Ben Tillman, race-baited the black man. In some places—like Georgia—the Populists "fused" with the lily-white wing of the Republican Party, not with the so-called black-and-tan wing.

Or take the case of Tom Watson. This Populist from Georgia was at one time a staunch advocate of a united front between Negro and white farmers. In 1892, he wrote:

You are kept apart that you may be separately fleeced of your earnings. You are made to hate each other because upon that hatred is rested the keystone of the arch of financial despotism which enslaves you both. You are deceived and blinded that you may not see how this race antagonism perpetuates a monetary system which beggars both.[4]

But this is the same Tom Watson who, only a few years later and because the *political* tide was flowing against such an alliance, did a complete turnabout. At that time, Democrats were disfranchising black people in state after state. But, as John Hope Franklin recorded in *From Slavery to Freedom* (1957):

---

[4] Tom Watson, "The Negro Question in the South," *Arena,* vol. 6 (1892), p. 548.

Where the Populists were unable to control the Negro vote, as in Georgia in 1894, they believed that the Democrats had never completely disfranchised the Negroes because their votes were needed if the Democrats were to stay in power. This belief led the defeated and disappointed Tom Watson to support a constitutional amendment excluding the Negro from the franchise—a complete reversal of his position in denouncing South Carolina for adopting such an amendment in 1895. (p. 218)

Watson was willing to ally with white candidates who were anti-Democratic-machine Democrats. With the black vote eliminated, the Populists stood to hold the balance of power between warring factions of the Democratic Party. Again C. Vann Woodward spells it out in his book, *Tom Watson, Agrarian Rebel:*

> He [Watson] . . . pledged his support, and the support of the Populists, to any anti-machine, Democratic candidate running upon a suitable platform that included a pledge to "a change in our Constitution which will perpetuate white supremacy in Georgia."
> How Watson managed to reconcile his radical democratic doctrine with a proposal to disfranchise a million citizens of his native state is not quite clear.
> "The white people dare not revolt so long as they can be intimidated by the fear of the Negro vote," he explained. Once the "bugaboo of Negro domination" was removed, however, "every white man would act according to his own conscience and judgment in deciding how he shall vote." With these words, Watson abandoned his old dream of uniting both races against the enemy, and took his first step toward the opposite extreme in racial views. (pp. 371–72)

At all times, the Populists and Watson emerge as politically motivated. The history of the period tells us that the whites—whether Populists, Republicans or Democrats—always had their own interests in mind. The black man was little more than a political football, to be tossed and kicked around at the convenience of others whose position was more secure.

We can learn the same lesson from the politics of the city of Atlanta, Georgia today. It is generally recognized that the black vote there is crucial to the election of a mayor. This was true in the case of William B. Hartsfield, and it is no less true for the present mayor, Ivan Allen, Jr. The coalition which dominates Atlanta politics has been described thus by Professor Edward Banfield in *Big City Politics:*

> The alliance between the business-led white middle class and the Negro is the main fact of local politics and government; only within the limits that it allows can anything be done, and much of what is done is for the purpose of holding it together. (p. 35)

Mayor Hartsfield put together a "three-legged stool" as a base of power. The business power structure, together with the "good government"-minded middle class that takes its lead from that power structure is one leg. The Atlanta press is another. The third leg is the black community. But something is wrong with this stool. In the first place, of course, the third leg is a hollow one. The black community of Atlanta is dominated by a black power structure of such "leaders" as we [have already] described: concerned primarily with protecting their own vested interests and their supposed influence with the white power structure, unresponsive to and unrepresentative of the black masses. But even this privileged group is economically and politically insecure by comparison with the other two forces with whom they have coalesced. Note this description by Banfield:

> Three associations of businessmen, *the leadership of which overlaps greatly,* play important parts in civic affairs. The Chamber of Commerce launches ideas which are often taken up as official city policy, and it is always much involved in efforts to get bond issues approved. The Central Atlanta Association is particularly concerned with the downtown business district and has taken the lead in efforts to improve expressways, mass transit, and urban renewal. Its weekly newsletter is widely read and respected. *The Uptown Association is a vehicle used by banks and other property owners to maintain a boundary line against expansion of the Negro district. To achieve this purpose it supports nonresidential urban renewal projects.* (pp. 31–32, author's italics)

Atlanta's substantial black bourgeoisie cannot compete with that line-up.

The political and economic interests causing the white leaders to enter the coalition are clear. So is the fact that those interests are often diametrically opposed to the interests of black people. We need only look at what the black man has received for his faithful support of politically and economically secure "alliance partners." Banfield puts it succinctly: "Hartsfield gave the Negro practically nothing in return for his vote" (p. 30). That vote, in 1957, was nine-tenths of the 20,000 votes cast by black people.

In 1963, a group of civic leaders from the black community of Southeast Atlanta documented the injustices suffered by that community's 60,000 black people. The lengthy list of grievances included faults in the sewerage system, sidewalks needed, streets which should be paved, deficient bus service and traffic control, substandard housing areas, inadequate parks and recreation facilities, continuing school segregation and inadequate black schools. Their report stated:

> Atlanta city officials have striven to create an image of Atlanta as a rapidly growing, modern, progressive city where all citizens can live in

decent, healthful surroundings. This image is a blatant lie so long as the city provides no health clinics for its citizens but relies entirely upon inadequate county facilities. It is a lie so long as these health clinics are segregated and the city takes no action to end this segregation. Because of segregation, only one of the four health clinics in the South side area is available to over 60,000 Negroes. This clinic . . . is small, its equipment inadequate and outdated, and its service dangerously slow due to general overcrowding.

In 1962, the city employed 5,663 workers, 1,647 of them black, but only 200 of those did other than menial work. The document lists twenty-two departments in which, of 175 equipment operators in the Construction Department, not one was black. The city did not even make a pretense of belief in "getting ahead by burning the midnight oil": there was only one public library in the community, a single room with 12,000 volumes (mostly children's books) for 60,000 people.[5]

This is what "coalition politics" won for the black citizens of one sizeable community. Nor had the situation in Atlanta's ghettos improved much by 1966. When a so-called riot broke out in the Summerhill community, local civic groups pointed out that they had deplored conditions and called the area "ripe for riot" many months earlier.

Black people must ultimately come to realize that such coalitions, such alliances have *not* been in their interest. They are "allying" with forces clearly not consistent with the long-term progress of blacks; in fact, the whites enter the alliance in many cases precisely to impede that progress.

Labor unions also illustrate very clearly the treacherous nature of coalitions between the economically secure and insecure. From the passage of the Wagner Act in 1935 (which gave unions the right to organize and bargain collectively), unions have been consolidating their position, winning economic victories for their members, and generally developing along with the growing prosperity of the country. What about black workers during this time? Their status has been one of steady deterioration rather than progress. It is common knowledge that the craft unions of the AFL (printers, plumbers, bricklayers, electrical workers) have deliberately excluded black workers over the years. These unions have taken care of their own—their white own. Meanwhile, the unemployment rate of black workers has increased, doubling, in some cases, that of white workers. The unions themselves were not always innocent bystanders to this development:

---

[5] "The City Must Provide. South Atlanta: The Forgotten Community," Atlanta Civic Council, 1963.

. . . The war has been over twenty years now, and instead of more Negroes joining labor unions, fewer are doing so; for the Negro, increased unionization has in too many instances meant decreased job opportunity. . . .

When the International Brotherhood of Electrical Workers became the collective bargaining agent at the Bauer Electric Company in Hartford, Connecticut in the late forties, the union demanded and got the removal of all Negro electricians from their jobs. The excuse was advanced that, since their union contract specified "whites only," they could not and would not change this to provide continued employment for the Negroes who were at the plant before the union was recognized. Similar cases can be found in the Boilermakers' Union and the International Association of Machinists at the Boeing Aircraft Company in Seattle.[6]

Precisely *because* of union recognition, black workers *lost* their jobs.

The situation became so bad that in 1959 black workers in the AFL–CIO, under the leadership of A. Philip Randolph, organized the Negro American Labor Council (NALC). Some black workers, at least, finally accepted the reality that they had to have their own black representatives if their demands were to be made—not to mention being met. The larger body did not particularly welcome the formation of this group. Randolph told the NAACP convention in June, 1960 in St. Paul, Minnesota that "a gulf of misunderstanding" seemed to be widening between the black community and the labor community. He further stated:

It is unfortunate that some of our liberal friends, along with some of the leaders of labor, even yet do not comprehend the nature, scope, depth, and challenge of this civil rights revolution which is surging forward in the House of Labor. They elect to view with alarm practically any and all criticisms of the AFL–CIO because of racial discrimination.[7]

It has become clear to many black leaders that organized labor operates from a different set of premises and with a different list of priorities, and that the status of black workers does not occupy a high position on that list. In fact, they are highly expendable, as in the political arena. Note the following observation:

. . . the split has even deeper causes. It arises out of the Negro's declaration of independence from white leadership and white direction in the civil rights fight—the Negro view today is that the whites, in labor or in other fields, are unreliable race campaigners when the chips are down, and that only the Negro can carry through to race victories.

---

[6] Myrna Bain, "Organized Labor and the Negro Worker," *National Review* (June 4, 1963), p. 455.

[7] "Labor-Negro Division Widens," *Business Week* (July 9, 1960), p. 79.

"Negro trade unionists and workers must bear their own cross for their own liberation. They must make their own crisis decisions bearing upon their life, labor, and liberty," Randolph told the NAACP.[8]

The Negro American Labor Council itself, however, suggests that such realizations may not be sufficient. It is our position that a viable group cannot be organized *within* a larger association. The sub-group will have to acquiesce to the goals and demands of the parent; it can only serve as a conscience-pricker—because it has no independent base of power from which to operate. Coalition between the strong and the weak ultimately leads only to perpetuation of the hierarchical status: superordinance and subordinance.

It is also important to note that the craft unions of the AFL were born and consolidating their positions at the same time that this country was beginning to expand imperialistically in Latin America and in the Philippines. Such expansion increased the economic security of white union workers here. Thus organized labor has participated in the exploitation of colored peoples abroad and of black workers at home. Black people today are beginning to assert themselves at a time when the old colonial markets are vanishing; former African and Asian colonies are fighting for the right to control their own natural resources, free from exploitation by Western and American capitalism. With whom will economically secure, organized labor cast its lot—with the big businesses of exploitation or with the insecure poor colored peoples? This question gives additional significance—a double layer of meaning —to the struggle of black workers here. The answer, unfortunately, seems clear enough.

We cannot see, then, how black people, who are massively insecure both politically and economically, can coalesce with those whose position is secure—particularly when the latter's security is based on the perpetuation of the existing political and economic structure.

The third myth proceeds from the premise that political coalitions can be sustained on a moral, friendly or sentimental basis, or on appeals to conscience. We view this as a myth because we believe that political relations are based on self-interest: benefits to be gained and losses to be avoided. For the most part, man's politics is determined by his evaluation of material good and evil. Politics results from a conflict of interests, not of consciences.

We frequently hear of the great moral value of the pressure by various church groups to bring about passage of the Civil Rights Laws of 1964 and 1965. There is no question that significant numbers of clergy and

---

[8] Bain, op. cit.

lay groups participated in the successful lobbying of those bills, but we should be careful not to overemphasize the value of this. To begin with, many of those religious groups were available only until the bills were passed; their sustained moral force is not on hand for the all-important process of ensuring federal implementation of these laws, particularly with respect to the appointment of more federal voting registrars and the setting of guidelines for school desegregation.

It should also be pointed out that many of those same people did not feel so morally obliged when the issues struck closer to home—in the North, with housing, as an example. They could be morally self-righteous about passing a law to desegregate southern lunch counters or even a law guaranteeing southern black people the right to vote. But laws against employment and housing discrimination—which would affect the North as much as the South—are something else again. After all, ministers—North and South—are often forced out of their pulpits if they speak or act too forcefully in favor of civil rights. Their parishioners do not lose sleep at night worrying about the oppressed status of black Americans; they are not morally torn inside themselves. As Silberman said, they simply do not want their peace disrupted and their businesses hurt.

We do not want to belabor the church in particular; what we have said applies to all the other "allies" of black people. Furthermore, we do not seek to condemn these groups for being what they are so much as we seek to emphasize a fact of life: they are unreliable allies when a conflict of interest arises. Morality and sentiment cannot weather such conflicts, and black people must realize this. No group should go into an alliance or a coalition relying on the "good will" of the ally. If the ally chooses to withdraw that "good will," he can do so usually without the other being able to impose sanctions upon him of any kind.

Thus we reject the last myth. In doing so, we would re-emphasize a point mentioned [previously]. Some believe that there is a conflict between the so-called American Creed and American practices. The Creed is supposed to contain considerations of equality and liberty, at least certainly equal opportunity, and justice. The fact is, of course, that these are simply words which *were not even originally intended* to have applicability to black people: Article I of the Constitution affirms that the black man is three-fifths of a person.[9] The fact is that people live their daily lives making practical day-to-day decisions about their jobs,

---

[9] "Representatives and direct Taxes shall be apportioned among the several States which may be included within this Union, according to their respective Numbers, which shall be determined by adding to the whole Number of free Persons, including those bound to Service for a Term of Years, and excluding Indians not taxed, three-fifths of all other Persons."

homes, children. And in a profit-oriented, materialistic society, there is little time to reflect on creeds, especially if it could mean more job competition, "lower property values," and the "daughter marrying a Negro." There is no "American dilemma," no moral hang-up, and black people should not base decisions on the assumption that a dilemma exists. It may be useful to articulate such assumptions in order to embarrass, to create international pressure, ,to educate. But they cannot form the basis for viable coalitions.

What, then, are the grounds for viable coalitions?

Before one begins to talk coalition, one should establish clearly the premises on which that coalition will be based. All parties to the coalition must perceive a *mutually* beneficial goal based on the conception of *each* party of his *own* self-interest. One party must not blindly assume that what is good for one is automatically—without question—good for the other. Black people must first ask themselves what is good *for them,* and then they can determine if the "liberal" is willing to coalesce. They must recognize that institutions and political organizations have no consciences outside their own special interests.

Secondly, there is a clear need for genuine power bases before black people can enter into coalitions. Civil rights leaders who, in the past or at present, rely essentially on "national sentiment" to obtain passage of civil rights legislation reveal the fact that they are operating from a powerless base. They must appeal to the conscience, the good graces of the society; they are, as noted earlier, cast in a beggar's role, hoping to strike a responsive chord. It is very significant that the two oldest civil rights organizations, the National Association for the Advancement of Colored People and the Urban League, have constitutions which specifically prohibit partisan political activity. (The Congress of Racial Equality once did, but it changed that clause when it changed its orientation in favor of Black Power.) This is perfectly understandable in terms of the strategy and goals of the older organizations, the concept of the civil rights movement as a kind of liaison between the powerful white community and the dependent black community. The dependent status of the black community apparently was unimportant since, if the movement proved successful, that community was going to blend into the white society anyway. No pretense was made of organizing and developing institutions of community power within the black community. No attempt was made to create any base of organized political strength; such activity was even prohibited, in the cases mentioned above. All problems would be solved by forming coalitions with labor, churches, reform clubs, and especially liberal Democrats.

[Later we] will present in detail case studies showing why such an approach is fallacious. It should, however, already be clear that the building of an independent force is necessary; that Black Power is necessary. If we do not learn from history, we are doomed to repeat it, and that is precisely the lesson of the Reconstruction era. Black people were allowed to register, to vote and to participate in politics, because it was to the advantage of powerful white "allies" to permit this. But at all times such advances flowed from white decisions. That era of black participation in politics was ended by another set of white decisions. There was no powerful independent political base in the southern black community to challenge the curtailment of political rights. At this point in the struggle, black people have no assurance—save a kind of idiot optimism and faith in a society whose history is one of racism —that if it became necessary, even the painfully limited gains thrown to the civil rights movement by the Congress would not be revoked as soon as a shift in political sentiments occurs. (A vivid example of this emerged in 1967 with Congressional moves to undercut and eviscerate the school desegregation provisions of the 1964 Civil Rights Act.) We must build that assurance and build it on solid ground.

We also recognize the potential for limited, short-term coalitions on relatively minor issues. But we must note that such approaches seldom come to terms with the roots of institutional racism. In fact, one might well argue that such coalitions on subordinate issues are, in the long run, harmful. They could lead whites and blacks into thinking either that their long-term interests do *not* conflict when in fact they do, or that such lesser issues are the *only* issues which can be solved. With these limitations in mind, and a spirit of caution, black people can approach possibilities of coalition for specific goals.

Viable coalitions therefore stem from four preconditions: (*a*) the recognition by the parties involved of their respective self-interests; (*b*) the mutual belief that each party stands to benefit in terms of that self-interest from allying with the other or others; (*c*) the acceptance of the fact that each party has its own independent base of power and does not depend for ultimate decision-making on a force outside itself; and (*d*) the realization that the coalition deals with specific and identifiable—as opposed to general and vague—goals.

The heart of the matter lies in this admonition from Machiavelli, writing in *The Prince:*

> And here it should be noted that a prince ought never to make common cause with one more powerful than himself to injure another, unless necessity forces him to it. . . . for if he wins you rest in his power, and princes must avoid as much as possible being under the will and pleasure of others.[10]

---

[10] Niccolo Machiavelli, *The Prince and the Discourses,* New York: Random House (Modern Library), 1950, p. 84.

Machiavelli recognized that "necessity" might at times force the weaker to ally with the stronger. Our view is that those who advocate Black Power should work to minimize that necessity. It is crystal clear that such alliances can seldom, if ever, be meaningful to the weaker partner. They cannot offer the optimum conditions of a political *modus operandi*. Therefore, if and when such alliances are unavoidable, we must not be sanguine about the possibility of their leading to ultimate, substantial benefit for the weaker force.

Let black people organize themselves *first,* define their interests and goals, and then see what kinds of allies are available. Let any ghetto group contemplating coalition be so tightly organized, so strong, that— in the words of Saul Alinsky—it is an "indigestible body" which cannot be absorbed or swallowed up.[11] The advocates of Black Power are not opposed to coalitions per se. But we are *not* interested in coalitions based on myths. To the extent to which black people can form *viable* coalitions will the end results of those alliances be lasting and meaningful. There will be clearer understanding of what is sought; there will be greater impetus on all sides to deliver, because there will be *mutual* respect of the power of the other to reward or punish; there will be much less likelihood of leaders selling out their followers. Black Power therefore has no connotation of "go it alone." Black Power simply says: enter coalitions only *after* you are able to "stand on your own." Black Power seeks to correct the approach to dependency, to remove that dependency, and to establish a viable psychological, political and social base upon which the black community can function to meet its needs.

At the beginning of our discussion of Black Power, we said that black people must redefine themselves, state new values and goals. The same holds true for white people of good will; they too need to redefine themselves and their role.

Some people see the advocates of Black Power as concerned with ridding the civil rights struggle of white people. This has been untrue from the beginning. There is a definite, much-needed role whites can play. This role can best be examined on three different, yet interrelated, levels: educative, organizational, supportive. Given the pervasive nature of racism in the society and the extent to which attitudes of white superiority and black inferiority have become embedded, it is very necessary that white people begin to disabuse themselves of such notions. Black people, as we stated earlier, will lead the challenge to old values and norms, but whites who recognize the need must also work in this sphere. Whites have access to groups in the society never reached by

---

[11] Saul Alinsky speaking at the 1967 Legal Defense Fund Convocation in New York City, May 18, 1967.

black people. They must get within those groups and help perform this essential educative function.

One of the most disturbing things about almost all white supporters has been that they are reluctant to go into their own communities— which is where the racism exists—and work to get rid of it. We are not now speaking of whites who have worked to get black people "accepted," on an individual basis, by the white society. Of these there have been many; their efforts are undoubtedly well-intended and individually helpful. But too often those efforts are geared to the same false premises as integration; too often the society in which they seek acceptance of a few black people can afford to make the gesture. We are speaking, rather, of those whites who see the need for basic change and have hooked up with the black liberation movement because it seemed the most promising agent of such change. Yet they often admonish black people to be non-violent. They should preach non-violence in the white community. Where possible, they might also educate other white people to the need for Black Power. The range is great, with much depending on the white person's own class background and environment.

On a broader scale, there is the very important function of working to reorient this society's attitudes and policies toward African and Asian countries. Across the country, smug white communities show a poverty of awareness, a poverty of humanity, indeed, a poverty of ability to act in a civilized manner toward non-Anglo human beings. The white middle-class suburbs need "freedom schools" as badly as the black communities. Anglo-conformity is a dead weight on their necks too. All this is an educative role crying to be performed by those whites so inclined.

The organizational role is next. It is hoped that eventually there will be a coalition of poor blacks and poor whites. This is the only coalition which seems acceptable to us, and we see such a coalition as the major internal instrument of change in the American society. It is purely academic today to talk about bringing poor blacks and poor whites together, but the task of creating a poor-white power block dedicated to the goals of a free, open society—not one based on racism and subordination—must be attempted. The main responsibility for this task falls upon whites. Black and white *can* work together in the white community where possible; it is not possible, however, to go into a poor Southern town and talk about "integration," or even desegregation. Poor white people are becoming more hostile—not less—toward black people, partly because they see the nation's attention focused on black poverty and few, if any, people coming to them.

Only whites can mobilize and organize those communities along the lines necessary and possible for effective alliances with the black communities. This job cannot be left to the existing institutions and agencies, because those structures, for the most part, are reflections of institutional racism. If the job is to be done, there must be new forms created. Thus, the political modernization process must involve the white community as well as the black.

It is our position that black organizations should be black-led and essentially black-staffed, with policy being made by black people. White people can and do play very important supportive roles in those organizations. Where they come with specific skills and techniques, they will be evaluated in those terms. All too frequently, however, many young, middle-class, white Americans, like some sort of Pepsi generation, have wanted to "come alive" through the black community and black groups. They have wanted to be where the action is—and the action has been in those places. They have sought refuge among blacks from a sterile, meaningless, irrelevant life in middle-class America. They have been unable to deal with the stifling, racist, parochial, split-level mentality of their parents, teachers, preachers and friends. Many have come seeing "no difference in color," they have come "color blind." But at this time and in this land, color *is* a factor and we should not overlook or deny this. The black organizations do not need this kind of idealism, which borders on paternalism. White people working in SNCC have understood this. There are white lawyers who defend black civil rights workers in court, and white activists who support indigenous black movements across the country. Their function is not to lead or to set policy or to attempt to define black people to black people. Their role is supportive.

Ultimately, the gains of our struggle will be meaningful only when consolidated by viable coalitions between blacks and whites who accept each other as co-equal partners and who identify their goals as politically and economically similar. At this stage, given the nature of the society, distinct roles must be played. The charge that this approach is "anti-white" remains as inaccurate as almost all the other public commentary on Black Power. There is nothing new about this; whenever black people have moved toward genuinely independent action, the society has distorted their intentions or damned their performance.

REFERENCES

Banfield, Edward C. *Big City Politics.* New York: Random House, 1965.
Banfield, Edward, and Wilson, James Q. *City Politics.* New York: Random House (Vintage Books), 1966.
Franklin, John Hope. *From Slavery to Freedom.* New York: Alfred A. Knopf, 1957.

Key, V. O., Jr. *Politics, Parties and Pressure Groups.* New York: Thomas Y. Crowell, 1964.

Killian, Lewis, and Grigg, Charles. *Racial Crisis in America.* Englewood Cliffs, N.J.: Prentice-Hall, 1964.

Meier, August, and Rudwick, Elliot M. *From Plantation to Ghetto.* New York: Hill and Wang, 1966.

Woodward, C. Vann. *Tom Watson: Agrarian Rebel.* New York: Oxford University Press, 1963.

BAYARD RUSTIN

"Black Power" and coalition politics

There are two Americas—black and white—and nothing has more clearly revealed the divisions between them than the debate currently raging around the slogan of "black power." Despite—or perhaps because of—the fact that this slogan lacks any clear definition, it has succeeded in galvanizing emotions on all sides, with many whites seeing it as the expression of a new racism and many Negroes taking it as a warning to white people that Negroes will no longer tolerate brutality and violence. But even within the Negro community itself, "black power" has touched off a major debate—the most bitter the community has experienced since the days of Booker T. Washington and W. E. B. Du Bois, and one which threatens to ravage the entire civil-rights movement. Indeed, a serious split has already developed between advocates of "black power" like Floyd McKissick of CORE and Stokely Carmichael of SNCC on the one hand, and Dr. Martin Luther King of SCLC, Roy Wilkins of the NAACP, and Whitney Young of the Urban League on the other.

There is no question, then, that great passions are involved in the debate over the idea of "black power"; nor, as we shall see, is there any question that these passions have their roots in the psychological and political frustrations of the Negro community. Nevertheless, I would contend that "black power" not only lacks any real value for the civil-rights movement, but that its propagation is positively harmful. It diverts the movement from a meaningful debate over strategy and tactics, it isolates the Negro community, and it encourages the growth of anti-Negro forces.

In its simplest and most innocent guise, "black power" merely means the effort to elect Negroes to office in proportion to Negro strength within the population. There is, of course, nothing wrong with such an objective in itself, and nothing inherently radical in the idea of pursuing it. But in Stokely Carmichael's extravagant rhetoric about "taking over" in districts of the South where Negroes are in the majority, it is important to recognize that Southern Negroes are only in a position to win a maximum of two congressional seats and control of eighty local counties.[1] (Carmichael, incidentally, is in the paradoxical position of

Reprinted from *Commentary,* by permission; vol. 42 (September 1966), pp. 35–40. Copyright © 1966 by the American Jewish Committee.
[1] See "The Negroes Enter Southern Politics" by Pat Waters, *Dissent,* July–August 1966.

screaming at liberals—wanting only to "get whitey off my back"—and simultaneously needing their support: after all, he can talk about Negroes taking over Lowndes County only because there is a fairly liberal federal government to protect him should Governor Wallace decide to eliminate this pocket of black power.) Now there might be a certain value in having two Negro congressmen from the South, but obviously they could do nothing by themselves to reconstruct the face of America. Eighty sheriffs, eighty tax assessors, and eighty school-board members might ease the tension for a while in their communities, but they alone could not create jobs and build low-cost housing; they alone could not supply quality integrated education.

The relevant question, moreover, is not whether a politician is black or white, but what forces he represents. Manhattan has had a succession of Negro borough presidents, and yet the schools are increasingly segregated. Adam Clayton Powell and William Dawson have both been in Congress for many years; the former is responsible for a rider on school integration that never gets passed, and the latter is responsible for keeping the Negroes of Chicago tied to a mayor who had to see riots and death before he would put eight-dollar sprinklers on water hydrants in the summer. I am not for one minute arguing that Powell, Dawson, and Mrs. Motley should be impeached. What I am saying is that if a politician is elected because he is black and is deemed to be entitled to a "slice of the pie," he will behave in one way; if he is elected by a constituency pressing for social reform, he will, whether he is white or black, behave in another way.

Southern Negroes, despite exhortations from SNCC to organize themselves into a Black Panther party, are going to stay in the Democratic party—to them it is the party of progress, the New Deal, the New Frontier, and the Great Society—and they are right to stay. For SNCC's Black Panther perspective is simultaneously utopian and reactionary—the former for the by now obvious reason that one-tenth of the population cannot accomplish much by itself, the latter because such a party would remove Negroes from the main area of political struggle in this country (particularly in the one-party South, where the decisive battles are fought out in Democratic primaries), and would give priority to the issue of race precisely at a time when the fundamental questions facing the Negro and American society alike are economic and social. It is no accident that the two main proponents of "black power," Carmichael and McKissick, should now be co-sponsoring a conference with Adam Clayton Powell and Elijah Muhammad, and that the leaders of New York CORE should recently have supported the machine candidate for Surrogate—because he was the choice of a Negro boss—rather than the candidate of the reform movement. By contrast, Martin Luther King is

working in Chicago with the Industrial Union Department of the AFL–
CIO and with religious groups in a coalition which, if successful, will
mean the end or at least the weakening of the Daley-Dawson machine.

The winning of the right of Negroes to vote in the South insures the
eventual transformation of the Democratic party, now controlled primarily by Northern machine politicians and Southern Dixiecrats. The
Negro vote will eliminate the Dixiecrats from the party and from Congress, which means that the crucial question facing us today is who will
replace them in the South. Unless civil-rights leaders (in such towns as
Jackson, Mississippi; Birmingham, Alabama; and even to a certain extent Atlanta) can organize grass-roots clubs whose members will have a
genuine political voice, the Dixiecrats might well be succeeded by black
moderates and black Southern-style machine politicians, who would do
little to push for needed legislation in Congress and little to improve
local conditions in the South. While I myself would prefer Negro machines to a situation in which Negroes have no power at all, it seems to
me that there is a better alternative today—a liberal-labor–civil-rights
coalition which would work to make the Democratic party truly responsive to the aspirations of the poor, and which would develop support for programs (specifically those outlined in A. Philip Randolph's
$100 billion Freedom Budget) aimed at the reconstruction of American
society in the interests of greater social justice. The advocates of "black
power" have no such programs in mind; what they are in fact arguing
for (perhaps unconsciously) is the creation of a *new black establishment.*

Nor, it might be added, are they leading the Negro people along the
same road which they imagine immigrant groups traveled so successfully in the past. Proponents of "black power"—accepting a historical
myth perpetrated by moderates—like to say that the Irish and the Jews
and the Italians, by sticking together and demanding their share, finally
won enough power to overcome their initial disabilities. But the truth
is that it was through alliances with other groups (in political machines
or as part of the trade-union movement) that the Irish and the Jews
and the Italians acquired the power to win their rightful place in American society. They did not "pull themselves up by their own bootstraps"
—no group in American society has ever done so; and they most certainly did not make isolation their primary tactic.

In some quarters, "black power" connotes not an effort to increase
the number of Negroes in elective office but rather a repudiation of non-
violence in favor of Negro "self-defense." Actually this is a false issue,
since no one has ever argued that Negroes should not defend themselves

as individuals from attack.[2] Non-violence has been advocated as a *tactic* for organized demonstrations in a society where Negroes are a minority and where the majority controls the police. Proponents of non-violence do not, for example, deny that James Meredith has the right to carry a gun for protection when he visits his mother in Mississippi; what they question is the wisdom of his carrying a gun while partici-pating in a demonstration.

There is, as well, a tactical side to the new emphasis on "self-defense" and the suggestion that non-violence be abandoned. The reasoning here is that turning the other cheek is not the way to win respect, and that only if the Negro succeeds in frightening the white man will the white man begin taking him seriously. The trouble with this reasoning is that it fails to recognize that fear is more likely to bring hostility to the surface than respect; and far from prodding the "white power structure" into action, the new militant leadership, by raising the slogan of black power and lowering the banner of non-violence, has obscured the moral issue facing this nation, and permitted the President and Vice President to lecture us about "racism in reverse" instead of proposing more mean-ingful programs for dealing with the problems of unemployment, hous-ing, and education.

"Black power" is, of course, a somewhat nationalistic slogan and its sudden rise to popularity among Negroes signifies a concomitant rise in nationalist sentiment (Malcolm X's autobiography is quoted nowadays in Grenada, Mississippi as well as in Harlem). We have seen such na-tionalistic turns and withdrawals back into the ghetto before, and when we look at the conditions which brought them about, we find that they have much in common with the conditions of Negro life at the present moment: conditions which lead to despair over the goal of integration and to the belief that the ghetto will last forever.

It may, in the light of the many juridical and legislative victories which have been achieved in the past few years, seem strange that despair should be so widespread among Negroes today. But anyone to whom it seems strange should reflect on the fact that despite these vic-tories *Negroes today are in worse economic shape, live in worse slums, and attend more highly segregated schools than in 1954.* Thus—to recite the appalling, and appallingly familiar, statistical litany once again —more Negroes are unemployed today than in 1954; the gap between the wages of the Negro worker and the white worker is wider; while the

---

[2] As far back as 1934, A. Philip Randolph, Walter White, then executive secre-tary of the NAACP, Lester Granger, then executive director of the Urban League, and I joined a committee to try to save the life of Odell Waller. Waller, a share-cropper, had murdered his white boss in self-defense.

unemployment rate among white youths is decreasing, the rate among Negro youths has increased to *32 percent* (and among Negro girls the rise is even more startling). Even the one gain which has been registered, a decrease in the unemployment rate among Negro adults, is deceptive, for it represents men who have been called back to work after a period of being laid off. In any event, unemployment among Negro men is still twice that of whites, and no new jobs have been created.

So too with housing, which is deteriorating in the North (and yet the housing provisions of the 1966 civil-rights bill are weaker than the anti-discrimination laws in several states which contain the worst ghettos even with these laws on their books). And so too with schools: according to figures issued recently by the Department of Health, Education and Welfare, 65 percent of first-grade Negro students in this country attend schools that are from 90 to 100 percent black. (If in 1954, when the Supreme Court handed down the desegregation decision, you had been the Negro parent of a first-grade child, the chances are that this past June you would have attended that child's graduation from a segregated high school.)

To put all this in the simplest and most concrete terms: the day-to-day lot of the ghetto Negro has not been improved by the various judicial and legislative measures of the past decade.

Negroes are thus in a situation similar to that of the turn of the century, when Booker T. Washington advised them to "cast down their buckets" (that is to say, accommodate to segregation and disenfranchisement) and when even his leading opponent, W. E. B. Du Bois, was forced to advocate the development of a group economy in place of the direct-action boycotts, general strikes, and protest techniques which had been used in the 1880's, before the enactment of the Jim-Crow laws. For all their differences, both Washington and Du Bois then found it impossible to believe that Negroes could ever be integrated into American society, and each in his own way therefore counseled withdrawal into the ghetto, self-help, and economic self-determination.

World War I aroused new hope in Negroes that the rights removed at the turn of the century would be restored. More than 360,000 Negroes entered military service and went overseas; many left the South seeking the good life in the North and hoping to share in the temporary prosperity created by the war. But all these hopes were quickly smashed at the end of the fighting. In the first year following the war, more than seventy Negroes were lynched, and during the last six months of that year, there were some twenty-four riots throughout America. White mobs took over whole cities, flogging, burning, shooting, and torturing at will, and when Negroes tried to defend themselves, the violence only increased. Along with this, Negroes were excluded from unions and pushed out of jobs they had won during the war, including federal jobs.

In the course of this period of dashed hope and spreading segregation —the same period, incidentally, when a reorganized Ku Klux Klan was achieving a membership which was to reach into the millions—the largest mass movement ever to take root among working-class Negroes, Marcus Garvey's "Back to Africa" movement, was born. "Buy Black" became a slogan in the ghettos; faith in integration was virtually snuffed out in the Negro community until the 1930's when the CIO reawakened the old dream of a Negro-labor alliance by announcing a policy of non-discrimination and when the New Deal admitted Negroes into relief programs, WPA jobs, and public housing. No sooner did jobs begin to open up and Negroes begin to be welcomed into mainstream organizations than "Buy Black" campaigns gave way to "Don't Buy Where You Can't Work" movements. A. Philip Randolph was able to organize a massive March on Washington demanding a wartime FEPC; CORE was born and with it the non-violent sit-in technique; the NAACP succeeded in putting an end to the white primaries in 1944. Altogether, World War II was a period of hope for Negroes, and the economic progress they made through wartime industry continued steadily until about 1948 and remained stable for a time. Meanwhile, the non-violent movement of the 1950's and 60's achieved the desegregation of public accommodations and established the right to vote.

Yet at the end of this long fight, the Southern Negro is too poor to use those integrated facilities and too intimidated and disorganized to use the vote to maximum advantage, while the economic position of the Northern Negro deteriorates rapidly.

The promise of meaningful work and decent wages once held out by the anti-poverty programs has not been fulfilled. Because there has been a lack of the necessary funds, the program has in many cases been reduced to wrangling for positions on boards or for lucrative staff jobs. Negro professionals working for the program have earned handsome salaries—ranging from $14,000 to $25,000—while young boys have been asked to plant trees at $1.25 an hour. Nor have the Job Corps camps made a significant dent in unemployment among Negro youths; indeed, the main beneficiaries of this program seem to be the private companies who are contracted to set up the camps.

Then there is the war in Vietnam, which poses many ironies for the Negro community. On the one hand, Negroes are bitterly aware of the fact that more and more money is being spent on the war, while the anti-poverty program is being cut; on the other hand, Negro youths are enlisting in great numbers, as though to say that it is worth the risk of being killed to learn a trade, to leave a dead-end situation, and to join the only institution in this society which seems really to be integrated.

The youths who rioted in Watts, Cleveland, Omaha, Chicago, and Portland are the members of a truly hopeless and lost generation. They can see the alien world of affluence unfold before them on the TV screen. But they have already failed in their inferior segregated schools. Their grandfathers were sharecroppers, their grandmothers were domestics, and their mothers are domestics too. Many have never met their fathers. Mistreated by the local storekeeper, suspected by the policeman on the beat, disliked by their teachers, they cannot stand more failures and would rather retreat into the world of heroin than risk looking for a job downtown or having their friends see them push a rack in the garment district. Floyd McKissick and Stokely Carmichael may accuse Roy Wilkins of being out of touch with the Negro ghetto, but nothing more clearly demonstrates their own alienation from ghetto youth than their repeated exhortations to these young men to oppose the Vietnam war when so many of them tragically see it as their only way out. Yet there is no need to labor the significance of the fact that the rice fields of Vietnam and the Green Berets have more to offer a Negro boy than the streets of Mississippi or the towns of Alabama or 125th Street in New York.

The Vietnam war is also partly responsible for the growing disillusion with non-violence among Negroes. The ghetto Negro does not in general ask whether the United States is right or wrong to be in Southeast Asia. He does, however, wonder why he is exhorted to non-violence when the United States has been waging a fantastically brutal war, and it puzzles him to be told that he must turn the other cheek in our own South while we must fight for freedom in South Vietnam.

Thus, as in roughly similar circumstances in the past—circumstances, I repeat, which in the aggregate foster the belief that the ghetto is destined to last forever—Negroes are once again turning to nationalistic slogans, with "black power" affording the same emotional release as "Back to Africa" and "Buy Black" did in earlier periods of frustration and hopelessness. This is not only the case with the ordinary Negro in the ghetto; it is also the case with leaders like McKissick and Carmichael, neither of whom began as a nationalist or was at first cynical about the possibilities of integration.[3] It took countless beatings and 24 jailings—that, and the absence of strong and continual support from the liberal community—to persuade Carmichael that his earlier faith in coalition politics was mistaken, that nothing was to be gained from

---

[3] On Carmichael's background, see "Two for SNCC" by Robert Penn Warren in the April 1965 *Commentary*.

working with whites, and that an alliance with the black nationalists was desirable. In the areas of the South where SNCC has been working so nobly, implementation of the Civil Rights Act of 1964 and 1965 has been slow and ineffective. Negroes in many rural areas cannot walk into the courthouse and register to vote. Despite the voting-rights bill, they must file complaints and the Justice Department must be called to send federal registrars. Nor do children attend integrated schools as a matter of course. There, too, complaints must be filed and the Department of Health, Education and Welfare must be notified. Neither department has been doing an effective job of enforcing the bills. The feeling of isolation increases among SNCC workers as each legislative victory turns out to be only a token victory—significant on the national level, but not affecting the day-to-day lives of Negroes. Carmichael and his colleagues are wrong in refusing to support the 1966 bill, but one can understand why they feel as they do.

It is, in short, the growing conviction that the Negroes cannot win—a conviction with much grounding in experience—which accounts for the new popularity of "black power." So far as the ghetto Negro is concerned, this conviction expresses itself in hostility first toward the people closest to him who have held out the most promise and failed to deliver (Martin Luther King, Roy Wilkins, etc.), then toward those who have proclaimed themselves his friends (the liberals and the labor movement), and finally toward the only oppressors he can see (the local storekeeper and the policeman on the corner). On the leadership level, the conviction that the Negroes cannot win takes other forms, principally the adoption of what I have called a "no-win" policy. Why bother with programs when their enactment results only in "sham"? Why concern ourselves with the image of the movement when nothing significant has been gained for all the sacrifices made by SNCC and CORE? Why compromise with reluctant white allies when nothing of consequence can be achieved anyway? Why indeed have anything to do with whites at all?

On this last point, it is extremely important for white liberals to understand—as, one gathers from their references to "racism in reverse," the President and the Vice President of the United States do not—that there is all the difference in the world between saying, "If you don't want me, I don't want you" (which is what some proponents of "black power" have in effect been saying) and the statement, "Whatever you do, I don't want you" (which is what racism declares). It is, in other words, both absurd and immoral to equate the despairing response of the victim with the contemptuous assertion of the oppressor. It would, moreover, be tragic if white liberals allowed verbal hostility on the part of Negroes to drive them out of the movement or to curtail their support for civil rights. The issue was injustice before "black power" became popular, and the issue is still injustice.

In any event, even if "black power" had not emerged as a slogan, problems would have arisen in the relation between whites and Negroes in the civil-rights movement. In the North, it was inevitable that Negroes would eventually wish to run their own movement and would rebel against the presence of whites in positions of leadership as yet another sign of white supremacy. In the South, the well-intentioned white volunteer had the cards stacked against him from the beginning. Not only could he leave the struggle any time he chose to do so, but a higher value was set on his safety by the press and the government—apparent in the differing degrees of excitement generated by the imprisonment or murder of whites and Negroes. The white person's importance to the movement in the South was thus an ironic outgrowth of racism and was therefore bound to create resentment.

But again: however understandable all this may be as a response to objective conditions and to the seeming irrelevance of so many hard-won victories to the day-to-day life of the mass of Negroes, the fact remains that the quasi-nationalist sentiments and "no-win" policy lying behind the slogan of "black power" do no service to the Negro. Some nationalist emotion is, of course, inevitable, and "black power" must be seen as part of the psychological rejection of white supremacy, part of the rebellion against the stereotypes which have been ascribed to Negroes for three hundred years. Nevertheless, pride, confidence, and a new identity cannot be won by glorifying blackness or attacking whites; they can only come from meaningful action, from good jobs, and from real victories such as were achieved on the streets of Montgomery, Birmingham, and Selma. When SNCC and CORE went into the South, they awakened the country, but now they emerge isolated and demoralized, shouting a slogan that may afford a momentary satisfaction but that is calculated to destroy them and their movement. Already their frustrated call is being answered with counterdemands for law and order and with opposition to police-review boards. Already they have diverted the entire civil-rights movement from the hard task of developing strategies to realign the major parties of this country, and embroiled it in a debate that can only lead more and more to politics by frustration.

On the other side, however—the more important side, let it be said —it is the business of those who reject the negative aspects of "black power" not to preach but to act. Some weeks ago President Johnson, speaking at Fort Campbell, Kentucky, asserted that riots impeded reform, created fear, and antagonized the Negro's traditional friends. Mr. Johnson, according to the *New York Times,* expressed sympathy for the plight of the poor, the jobless, and the ill-housed. The government, he noted, has been working to relieve their circumstances, but "all this takes time."

One cannot argue with the President's position that riots are destructive or that they frighten away allies. Nor can one find fault with his sympathy for the plight of the poor; surely the poor need sympathy. But one can question whether the government has been working seriously enough to eliminate the conditions which lead to frustration-politics and riots. The President's very words, "all this takes time," will be understood by the poor for precisely what they are—an excuse instead of a real program, a cover-up for the failure to establish real priorities, and an indication that the administration has no real commitment to create new jobs, better housing, and integrated schools.

For the truth is that it need only take ten years to eliminate poverty —ten years and the $100 billion Freedom Budget recently proposed by A. Philip Randolph. In his introduction to the budget (which was drawn up in consultation with the nation's leading economists, and which will be published later this month), Mr. Randolph points out: "The programs urged in the Freedom Budget attack all of the major causes of poverty—unemployment and underemployment, substandard pay, inadequate social insurance and welfare payments to those who cannot or should not be employed; bad housing; deficiencies in health services, education, and training; and fiscal and monetary policies which tend to redistribute income regressively rather than progressively. The Freedom Budget leaves no room for discrimination in any form because its programs are addressed to all who need more opportunity and improved incomes and living standards, not to just some of them."

The legislative precedent Mr. Randolph has in mind is the 1945 Full Employment bill. This bill—conceived in its original form by Roosevelt to prevent a postwar depression—would have made it public policy for the government to step in if the private economy could not provide enough employment. As passed finally by Congress in 1946, with many of its teeth removed, the bill had the result of preventing the Negro worker, who had finally reached a pay level about 55 percent that of the white wage, from making any further progress in closing that discriminatory gap; and instead, he was pushed back by the chronically high unemployment rates of the 50's. Had the original bill been passed, the public sector of our economy would have been able to insure fair and full employment. Today, with the spiralling thrust of automation, it is even more imperative that we have a legally binding commitment to this goal.

Let me interject a word here to those who say that Negroes are asking for another handout and are refusing to help themselves. From the end of the 19th century up to the last generation, the United States absorbed and provided economic opportunity for tens of millions of immigrants. These people were usually uneducated and a good many could not speak English. They had nothing but their hard work to offer and they labored long hours, often in miserable sweatshops and unsafe mines. Yet in a burgeoning economy with a need for unskilled labor, they were able to find jobs, and as industrialization proceeded, they were gradually able to move up the ladder to greater skills. Negroes who have been driven off the farm into a city life for which they are not prepared and who have entered an economy in which there is less and less need for unskilled labor, cannot be compared with these immigrants of old. The tenements which were jammed by newcomers were way-stations of hope; the ghettos of today have become dead-ends of despair. Yet just as the older generation of immigrants—in its most decisive act of self-help—organized the trade-union movement and then in alliance with many middle-class elements went on to improve its own lot and the condition of American society generally, so the Negro of today is struggling to go beyond the gains of the past and, in alliance with liberals and labor, to guarantee full and fair employment to all Americans.

Mr. Randolph's Freedom Budget not only rests on the Employment Act of 1946, but on a precedent set by Harry Truman when he believed freedom was threatened in Europe. In 1947, the Marshall Plan was put into effect and 3 percent of the gross national product was spent in foreign aid. If we were to allocate a similar proportion of our GNP to destroy the economic and social consequences of racism and poverty at home today, it might mean spending more than 20 billion dollars a year, although I think it quite possible that we can fulfill these goals with a much smaller sum. It would be intolerable, however, if our plan for domestic social reform were less audacious and less far-reaching than our international programs of a generation ago.

We must see, therefore, in the current debate over "black power," a fantastic challenge to American society to live up to its proclaimed principles in the area of race by transforming itself so that all men may live equally and under justice. We must see to it that in rejecting "black power," we do not also reject the principle of Negro equality. Those people who would use the current debate and/or the riots to abandon the civil-rights movement leave us no choice but to question their original motivation.

If anything, the next period will be more serious and difficult than the preceding ones. It is much easier to establish the Negro's right to sit at a Woolworth's counter than to fight for an integrated community. It takes very little imagination to understand that the Negro should have the right to vote, but it demands much creativity, patience, and political stamina to plan, develop, and implement programs and priorities. It is one thing to organize sentiment behind laws that do not disturb consensus politics, and quite another to win battles for the redistribution of wealth. Many people who marched in Selma are not prepared to support a bill for a $2.00 minimum wage, to say nothing of supporting a redefinition of work or a guaranteed annual income.

It is here that we who advocate coalitions and integration and who object to the "black-power" concept have a massive job to do. We must see to it that the liberal-labor–civil-rights coalition is maintained and, indeed, strengthened so that it can fight effectively for a Freedom Budget. We are responsible for the growth of the "black-power" concept because we have not used our own power to insure the full implementation of the bills whose passage we were strong enough to win, and we have not mounted the necessary campaign for winning a decent minimum wage and extended benefits. "Black power" is a slogan directed primarily against liberals by those who once counted liberals among their closest friends. It is up to the liberal movement to prove that coalition and integration are better alternatives.

C. Factual and research considerations

GARY T. MARX and MICHAEL USEEM

Majority involvement in minority movements: Civil rights, abolition, untouchability

Social movements seeking to change the subordinate status of ethnic minorities have drawn activists from both the minority and dominant groups. Conflict has at times developed between movement members of these two groups. In a comparative analysis of three movements—the civil rights movement, the anti-slavery cause in the U.S., and the movement to abolish Untouchability in India—the sources of tension appear quite similar. Ideologically, minority group activists viewed themselves as more radical and committed to that particular cause than did their dominant group co-workers and were more for a strategy of minority group self-help. Organizational conflict arose as majority members disproportionately assumed decision-making positions in the movement. A third source of tension developed because some movement members were carriers of prejudices and hostilities of the larger social milieu. Outsiders frequently played essential roles in the early phases of these movements, but pressures developed on majority members to reduce involvement or withdraw altogether.

An issue that leftist movements in America have continually confronted concerns the disadvantaged position of various racial and ethnic groups. Awareness of the discrimination, exploitation, and indifference long faced by black Americans was a primary catalyst in the creation of the New Left in the past decade. However, as the history of the civil rights movement of the sixties has shown, this concentration of energy on the situation of an oppressed minority was not without severe problems. In particular, sharp conflict developed over the participation of whites in organizations whose resources were primarily devoted to working for and within the black community. As the civil rights effort evolved, the position of whites in the movement took on an increasingly

Note: A number of colleagues graciously offered useful comments on this paper but we are particularly indebted to August Meier, Elliot Rudwick, and David Riesman for their extensive critiques. We are grateful to the Joint Center for Urban Studies and the Clark Fund for support. An earlier version of this paper was read at the annual meeting of the American Sociological Association, Washington, D.C., 1970.
Source: *Journal of Social Issues*, vol. 27, no. 1 (1971), pp. 81–104.

ambiguous nature, eventually culminating in the exclusion or voluntary withdrawal of whites from central roles in the struggle and the emergence of the ideology of Black Power. Was this development entirely unique to the civil rights movement? Perhaps there are structural elements in this type of political movement which would inevitably lead to acute tension between dominant and subordinate group activists.

One manner in which to deal with this question is through the comparative analysis of similar movements. Our interest is in the role played by "outsiders" in other people's struggles, individuals who do not share the stigma or socially debilitating attribute and who do not stand to gain in the same direct way from the desired social change. There are of course an immense variety of political movements in which both insiders and outsiders played important roles. However, for direct contrast with the civil rights effort we sought movements whose primary concern was altering the depressed condition of a minority group defined along racial or ethnic lines. Two efforts seemed particularly well-suited for a comparative analysis: the movement to end Untouchability in India, and the 19th century abolitionist movement in this country. In a cursory examination of these movements and of the civil rights effort, we were struck by the poignant and ironic parallels in the conflict that often developed between blacks and whites, or Untouchables and caste Hindus, working together in a common movement to bring about change. All three movements were intensely committed to ending the oppression of a relatively small ethnic or racial minority (whose condition was also of significant societal-wide concern), all were predominantly left-liberal in ideology and strategy but included strong radical currents, all had histories stretching over at least several decades, all took on a variety of organizational forms involving large numbers of people, all had both minority and dominant group members active in the struggle, and all were plagued by recurrent tensions between these two groups. In this paper we attempt to draw out several sociological themes which appear to be typically associated with outsider involvement in minority movements.[1]

The recent American civil rights movement originated in the deteriorating situation confronting blacks as the nineteenth century drew to a close and the weakness of Booker T. Washington's accommodationist strategy became apparent. The National Association for the Advancement of Colored People (NAACP), formed in 1909 as an interracial

---

[1] Another interesting and relevant question, but one totally apart from the purpose of this paper, is the question of certain intellectual and ideological *continuities* tying together these three movements. For example, a strong early influence on SNCC was that of Martin Luther King, who was a disciple of Gandhi, who was, in turn, an avid reader of Thoreau.

organization to promote more aggressive action, reflected the growing impatience. Over the decades it has primarily been concerned with legal attacks on discriminatory practices. Since the Second World War, however, a variety of organizations [e.g., Congress of Racial Equality (CORE), Southern Christian Leadership Conference (SCLC), Student Nonviolent Coordinating Committee (SNCC)] have crystallized around more direct offensives against general social conditions facing blacks, such as poverty, inadequate education, and segregated public facilities. Strategies became more militant, nonviolent direct action in various forms spread widely, particularly in the early sixties, and the movement attracted a new generation of less affluent blacks and young northern whites. More recently the radicalization has led to the emergence of black nationalist and socialist ideologies within the movement, and whites have assumed a much more marginal role.

The antislavery crusade followed a course extending over a comparable period, with early abolitionist sentiment finding organizational expression by the time of independence. In 1817 a major effort to facilitate the return of free blacks and manumitted slaves to Africa was formalized in the American Colonization Society, but few departed and this solution to slavery was discredited by the prevalence of anti-black motives underlying the involvement of many advocates. By the 1830s more direct attacks on bondage were current, and the New England and American Anti-Slavery Societies founded in that decade amalgamated diverse political strains under a common desire to end slavery immediately and unconditionally. In the following decades the numerical strength of the movement increased dramatically; by the fifties, the several thousand abolitionist societies claimed a membership in the hundreds of thousands. Abolition of slavery was the unifying cause, but serious schisms rent the movement throughout its history, in some cases resulting in separate organizations. Until the movement's demise during the Civil War, the issues revolved around whether abolition was to be viewed as a reformist end in itself or as a means to a broader transformation of American society, the type of political action to be pursued, how to present the movement's image to an initially unsympathetic public, and the degree to which problems facing free blacks should be incorporated into movement concern.

In India the more than sixty million Untouchables, culturally and religiously excluded from the Hindu fold, and economically very depressed, have thrust upon a variety of protest movements, ranging from Sanskritization to religious cults to struggles for political power. Early in this century their plight received the attention of the Congress movement as it agitated for independence and for a reformed social order that was to include an uplifted Untouchable community. In 1932, for instance, a number of caste Hindus, including Gandhi, established the

Harijan Sevak Sangh, a service organization aimed at ameliorating the Untouchable condition through propaganda, Untouchable education, and unionization. Concurrently a segment of the Untouchable community was becoming politically self-conscious and interested in solving its problems on its own political strength. Prior to independence this led to such strategies as symbolic transgression of religious codes (e.g., temple entry) and pressure to secure special guarantees in the Indian constitution. Since then Untouchable action has included the formation of a regular political party (the Republican party), and, beginning in the mid-fifties, a dramatic protest against Hindu society through mass conversion to Buddhism.

Before examining these movements, several possible problems of method and evidence should be noted. The empirical foundation on which our argument rests could be appreciably stronger. Historical material on the Untouchable movement is sketchy, and sociological analysis of all three developments is limited. This has necessitated reliance on observations and personal accounts of movement participants, especially activists from the minority group. Using subjective assessments presents certain problems, although such evaluations reflect an important social reality. The degree of accuracy in personal accounts may vary considerably between observers, and more systematic data are needed to transform the suggestive findings of this paper into firm conclusions. For example, assertions about ideological differences between insiders and outsiders require verification through standard survey methods. It should also be noted that we will be discussing modal tendencies and do not mean to imply that all involvement of whites in black movements, or of caste Hindus in Untouchable movements, has met with conflict, nor that differences characterizing the insider and outsider groups apply to all members taken individually, nor that other sources of conflict unrelated to race were not often present (e.g., class-based tensions have often been attendant). In addition we are dealing with relations among *activists,* not among uninvolved minority or majority group members, and we are not dealing with the way in which the movements relate to the broader society. We have tried not to magnify the degree of internal tension in these movements by considering only extreme examples, but in emphasizing certain themes only material bearing on these has been presented. A paper focusing on intergroup cooperation in these movements would no doubt deal with a number of issues and data which we neglect.

FOUR CONFLICT THEMES

A comparative assessment of these three movements—abolition, civil rights, Untouchability—will be undertaken along four themes. The first considers lines of *ideological disagreement* which have often distinguished insiders from outsiders. Frequently (though certainly not always) minority group activists have held somewhat more radical and militant attitudes than their majority group colleagues, at least with respect to the struggle over the oppression of that particular racial or caste group. Outsiders, on the other hand, have often affiliated with a broader set of political causes and movements. Even if there is a consensus on questions of ideology and strategy, second and third sources of conflict stem from the fact that social movements are in many ways microcosms of the larger society. The *divergent background and experiences of activists* from the two groups may have important effects on the internal structure and culture of the movements. Structural conflict at times has arisen because dominant group activists, usually from more privileged backgrounds, have tended to come to the movement with more of the skills and experience which are important for the success of the movement, such as writing, internal organizing, planning strategy, and fund raising, but perhaps a lesser commitment to the goals of that particular struggle (though not necessarily a lesser commitment to changing the system). These initial differences may result in disproportionate numbers of outsiders being in decision-making positions and may inhibit the development of similar skills among insiders. A third source of tension, *cultural conflict,* may arise because movement members have often been the carriers, if in a somewhat diluted form, of the prejudices and hostilities of the larger social milieu from which they came. Suspicion, distrust, and scapegoating on the part of the minority group and stereotyping, patronization, and paternalism on the part of the dominant group have often resulted. The final theme to be considered concerns the *development of these conflicts over time.* Outsiders frequently have played critical roles in the early phases of these movements, but as the struggle has gained strength (and/or failed to bring about meaningful change), the latent conflicts between the two groups have tended to become more visible. Pressures develop on outsiders to reduce their level of involvement or to withdraw altogether.

Ideological conflict between oppressed minority and outsiders

In the civil rights, abolition, and Untouchable movements, political divisions have been pervasive, perhaps a characteristic of most intense political movements. Some differences were benign and readily resolved, but others remained sharp and created considerable internal conflict. At times these ideological divisions paralleled the internal social cleavage between activists from the dominant and subordinate groups. A theme running through all three movements has been the occasional tendency for minority-group activists to adopt a somewhat less reformist and more revolutionary perspective on the liberation of their own group, or at least to develop critiques of dominant group activists in these terms. Many instances of conflict between the two groups of activists could be traced to disagreements over the timetable for change, how far one should go in compromises, and the extent to which non-institutionalized protest means were acceptable. There has also been a tendency for outsiders to maintain interest in a wider variety of causes, which have often included the situation of women, the working classes, the poor, depressed castes and other ethnic minorities; they have lacked strong personal identification with any single issue.

Within the civil rights movement, for instance, this pattern was evident in CORE from its original inception until the middle 1960s. Meier and Rudwick (1969) observe that at the time of CORE's founding in 1942 the whites had interests ranging from nonviolence to racial equality, whereas involved blacks were primarily concerned with fighting racism. Two decades later this ideological divergence was still evident in CORE, as a study in the sixties reports:

> Whites generally came to the movement with fairly stable, well-defined liberal views . . . Their participation in the movement, which usually overshadowed other commitments, was one of a range of liberal political activities . . . Negroes, however, required no elaborate liberal conditioning to bring them into the movement. The movement was their cause . . . Negroes were always under direct emotional pressure resulting from segregation and discrimination. Therefore, the potential for great radicalism was present in their personal relationship to the issue. (Bell, 1968, pp. 126–127)

The Untouchable movement evidences a parallel source of tension. B. R. Ambedkar, the foremost leader in the Untouchable movement until his death in the mid-1950s and himself an Untouchable, and Mahatma Gandhi, a caste Hindu, were frequently at odds over the proper solution of Untouchability. Gandhi was associated with a wide variety of causes including ending British colonialism, encouragement of village industry, and uplifting the Untouchables and women, while Ambedkar was concerned almost entirely with the condition of the Untouchables and related depressed classes in India. The two leaders also differed on the amount of change needed to improve the situation of the Untouchables. Gandhi felt that caste Hindus could be persuaded to accept the depressed classes as part of the Hindu fold, but Ambedkar maintained that the prospects for this were dim and that only through the application of political pressure could the rights of Untouchables be secured (Zelliot, 1966; Kerr, 1962). Disagreements also occurred over the effectiveness and acceptability of various protest means. In the 1920s and 1930s direct action campaigns were often conducted against various restrictions faced by the Untouchables. Typical action included the collective drinking from community wells normally off-limits to Untouchables, and the entry into temples reserved for use by caste Hindus. These tactics were less acceptable to caste Hindus engaged in the movement than to their Untouchable allies. The series of events surrounding these steps of direct action are remarkably similar in form to the events and aftermath of the freedom rides of CORE and sit-ins of SNCC in the early sixties.

Within the abolitionist movement white militancy was not lacking, as evidenced by the actions of John Brown, but many black abolitionists at times urged more radical strategies on the movement and expressed a greater sense of urgency for the termination of slavery. In 1829 an early call to arms was issued by the black abolitionist, David Walker, which was frank in its encouragement of violent forms of action if circumstances were appropriate. Walker's "Appeal" was widely circulated and caused much consternation in the white antislavery camp. "A more bold, daring, inflammatory publication, perhaps never issued from the press of any country," asserted the white abolitionist publisher Benjamin Lundy (quoted in Litwack, 1961, p. 234); "I can do no less than set the broadest seal of condemnation on it." Though the position was denounced by many whites in the antislavery cause, a little over a decade later another black abolitionist, Henry Highland Garnet, delivered an address before a national black antislavery convention which strongly echoed Walker's tone and included the exhortation: "It is your solemn and imperative duty to use every means, both moral, intellectual, and physical that promises success" (Garnet, 1843).

Black abolitionists tended to have a shorter timetable for change than did their white co-workers. This difference became sharper as the antislavery movement increasingly sensed that its decades of effort had made little headway, particularly with the Dred Scott decision (1857) and the Fugitive Slave Act of 1850. Militancy increased among blacks as they wearied of "exhortations to be patient and await that 'impartial and just God' who would inevitably rid the nation of slavery" (Litwack, 1965, p. 151). By the critical decade of the 1850s, black circles were openly discussing the encouragement of slave insurrections and forceful opposition to such legislation as the Fugitive Slave Law, and some even advanced the view that the entire political structure of the country should be overturned if necessary for the abolition of slavery. The more radical orientation of blacks in the movement extended beyond the issue of formal bondage to the situation of the free black in America. Many blacks in the antislavery crusade felt that the reformist instincts (in some cases encompassing a variety of issues) of their white colleagues prevented them from confronting subtler but nonetheless pervasive forms of racial oppression faced by those not in formal bondage. White abolitionists were quite sensitive about advocating or evidencing a belief in full social equality and interracial mixing, and even black membership in some abolitionist societies was at times a hotly debated issue (Meier & Rudwick, 1966; Litwack, 1965).

A major strategic fracture, at times overlapping the division between insiders and outsiders, resulted from attitudes toward self-help. Minority group activists have often argued that the process of struggling for one's freedom is a necessary prerequisite for fully ending oppression. Conversely, outsiders have tended to stress the strategic advantages of involving majority group activists. This is seen as increasing the legitimacy of the movement, as well as offering essential resources, such as financial backing.

Frederick Douglass expressed a view shared by many black abolitionists that "the man who has *suffered the wrong* is the man to *demand redress*—that the man *STRUCK* is the man to *CRY OUT*—and that he who has *endured the cruel pangs of Slavery* is the man to *advocate liberty*" (1847). At times white support was viewed more favorably since white activists were essential for gaining further white converts to the antislavery cause. However, as momentum gathered in the decades just prior to the Civil War, black activists increasingly asserted their special standing within the movement. A black abolitionist conference announced in 1854:

> The time is come when our people must assume the rank of a first-rate power in the battle against caste and Slavery; it is emphatically our battle; no one else can fight it for us, and with God's help we must fight it ourselves. (Litwack, 1965, p. 155)

White abolitionists, on the other hand, often conceived of the black role as essentially symbolic—useful at ceremonial occasions, but secondary to the real political effort.

Similar themes are present in the Indian movement. Many Untouchable leaders felt that the efforts of high status Hindus were inherently crippling because their presence meant the Untouchables would be denied control over even their own movement (Rudolph & Rudolph, 1967). Ambedkar adamantly opposed top-down reform and was strongly committed to the central involvement of Untouchables in the struggle. In his own acrid assessment:

> The work of Harijan Sevak Sangh is not to raise the Untouchables. Gandhi's main object, as every self-respecting Untouchable knows, is to make India safe for Hindus and Hinduism. He is certainly not fighting

the battle of the Untouchables. On the contrary, by distributing through the Harijan Sevak Sangh petty gifts to petty Untouchables he is buying, benumbing and drawing the claws of the opposition of the Untouchables which he knows is the only force which will disrupt the caste system and will establish real democracy in India. (Ambedkar, 1943, p. 69)

Similar tensions have been present throughout the recent history of the civil rights movement, culminating in the ascendancy of the idea of Black Power and the partial withdrawal of white activists. A variety of arguments have been advanced against having outsiders engaged in a movement working primarily in black communities (though combating racism in white contexts may be seen as appropriate). As in the case of the Untouchable leaders, black activists were fearful that reform from above would ultimately leave black communities in a state of dependency.

It was argued that the society's dominant white institutions had yielded only limited reform in the past and there was little reason to expect them in the future to be a major impetus behind the more massive changes critically needed. Furthermore, whatever improvement in the condition of black people could already be credited to these institutions was viewed as little more than a response to pressures from below. The mobilization of the black community was therefore viewed as essential at minimum for prodding those with power to create reformist changes. But if the mustering was effectively accomplished, there were additional benefits which were not achievable under top-down reform. For instance, such mobilization may help produce a new sense of pride, self-reliance, and confidence. In addition, the new political awareness may eventuate in more intense and lasting pressure for radical change. White activists of course did not formally represent the dominant white power structure, but they did symbolically to many; their presence in the movement was seen to impede the creation of the desired self-confidence and political consciousness. The civil rights movement was attempting to relate to black people, but blacks had difficulty shaking loose from deferential tendencies around whites, no matter how well-intentioned the whites were. White workers, for instance, were at times able to get rural blacks to register to vote after black workers had failed. Many of the negative aspects of outsider involvement are summarized in a position paper of a SNCC-affiliated group (written just prior to the emergence of the Black Power ethos), which argues strongly for a black-led, black-staffed, and black-financed movement for organizing within their own communities. The rationale includes:

The inability of whites to relate to the cultural aspects of Black Society; attitudes that whites, consciously or unconsciously, bring to Black communities about themselves (western superiority) and about Black people (paternalism); inability to shatter white-sponsored community myths of Black inferiority and self-negation; inability to combat the views of the Black community that white organizers, being "white," control Black organizers as puppets; . . . whites, though individual "liberals," are symbols of oppression to the Black community—due to the *collective* power that whites have over Black lives. (Vine City Project, 1967, p. 97)

The privileged position of the outsiders

Almost by definition, outsiders in these movements tended to have privileges and opportunities that were systematically denied most members of the subordinate group. Consequently outsiders were often more skilled in a variety of ways relevant to the needs of the movement, and this initial difference often created a situation in which outsiders occupied a disproportionate share of high status positions and exerted what was seen as an excessive influence on decision-making. In this respect the internal structure of the movements reflected in microcosm many of the intergroup patterns typical of the broader society. This was tolerated and even accepted as necessary for a limited period, but many minority group activists came to conclude that such an arrangement inhibited the growth of the movement, was incongruent with its basic aims, dampened militancy, and reduced the opportunity for developing political competence among minority-group activists.

This pattern is most apparent in the antislavery cause. In the signing of the constitution establishing the New England Anti-Slavery Society, only a quarter of the signers were black; only three blacks were officially present at the 1833 conference which formed the American Anti-Slavery Society. In the early phases of the abolitionist effort those organizations that were integrated were prone to relegate blacks to peripheral roles requiring little more than a black skin or a personal history of former bondage. As people truly representative of those in bondage they performed useful symbolic functions on ceremonial occasions, but most other roles, such as propagandizing, organizing forums and conventions, and raising financial support, were assumed by whites. With the exception of the underground railway (which involved comparatively few whites) this marginal role for blacks persisted throughout the antislavery movement. Black abolitionists painfully sensed their exclusion; Martin Robinson Delany (1852) critically observed that white abolitionists "have each and all, at different times, presumed to *think* for, dictate to, and *know* better what suited colored people, than they knew for themselves . . ." Frederick Douglass corroborates this view as late as 1855: "Our oppressed people are wholly ignored . . . in the generalship of the movement to effect our redemption" (quoted in Meier & Rudwick, 1966, p. 105).

There are similarities, if less extreme and more benign, in the civil rights efforts of the 1960s. Writing of his own experience in the South, Staughton Lynd notes that

> many of us had drifted into administrative roles . . . not because we wanted to be leaders, but because we were obviously better able to write press releases and answer the telephone than to approach frightened black people in remote rural communities. The objective result, however, was that we made more decisions than we should have made. . . . (Lynd, 1969, p. 14)

Several participant observers noting the same pattern suggest that an additional factor may lie in differences in cultural style revolving around the supposed greater emphasis whites placed on punctuality, structure, and organization (Keller, Mabutt, & Ruhe, 1965). The influx of skilled whites into the movement and their assumption of authority roles created considerable resentment. In some cases local activists withdrew from the movement and many blacks came to feel that, as always, whites were trying to take things over to serve their own ends. An important role in decision-making by whites dates far back in the civil rights movement; for instance, Ralph Bunche in the early 1940s saw white involvement as having a powerful indirect effect on keeping interracial organizations moderate, since blacks in the organizations often felt compelled to defer to white opinion (Myrdal, 1944).

A second structural source of tension in such movements may lie in what is perceived as the differential levels of commitment of the two types of activist. Regardless of background, people enter social movements for a variety of reasons and these may change over time. Yet the minority group activist is working for the liberation of himself and the community with which he is politically, culturally, and personally identified. In most cases he can never leave his ascriptive minority group status, and, should he wish to give up full-time involvement, he may have fewer opportunities in the larger society. He thus may be seen as more reliable and accountable for his actions than an outsider who can leave the struggle more easily. For dominant group activists, abstract moral principles may be more important as a guiding motive since neither they, nor their community of origin, stand to gain in the same direct way from involvement. Furthermore the very political principles that brought the outsiders to the ethnic movement in question may at a later date direct their energies into other causes. The overall commitment of outsiders to the creation of social change may be equivalent to that of the minority group activists, but it may be less identified with any single movement.

Adequate empirical evidence on differential commitment is lacking;

yet common to all three movements is a questioning of the motives and degree of commitment of activists from the dominant group. In the case of the southern civil rights movement there are data indicating that many whites had a short period of activism. According to one study, only seven percent of whites who went South during the summer of 1965 remained there during the fall. Only one out of four white volunteers definitely planned to return to the South to work with the movement, and only a tenth of those in the study reported considerable guilt about leaving the struggle (Demerath, Marwell, & Aiken, 1968, 1971). Unfortunately, comparable turnover rates for blacks are not available. Even when whites remained in the South there was resentment over the perception that they could more readily play two roles. Julius Lester comments:

> Sure whites came South. They got a little taste of jail, got beaten, but they were white. That meant they could go back home and not have to worry as they walked down the street. . . . [N]o matter where they were in the South, they could sneak off and go to a nice white restaurant or the movie theatre. . . . They could drive down the highway and if they were not known as civil rights workers, their minds could be easy. (1968, p. 103)

Furthermore, some whites became engaged in civil rights for reasons only indirectly relevant to the concrete struggle of blacks. In one study, among reasons given by whites for their involvement were: "the opportunity for active rebellion against everything from the oppression of capitalism . . . to my own parents"; or "I like Negroes . . . relationships with them are not neurotic and are free of deception"; and "to make a witness to what I believe" (Pinkney, 1968, pp. 97, 98, 180). Though similar motives might characterize some blacks, they were not as apparent or suspect because of the minority group members' direct personal stake in the struggle. Some blacks felt they were being used as therapy by conscience-stricken white activists.

The abolitionist movement also saw some whites involved for diverse reasons and short periods of time. An historian reports the presence of those for whom the movement represented "a release for private devils," and the cause was not without its "summer soldiers who after a season disappeared in the shadows" (Quarles, 1969, p. 53). There was a tendency for the commitments of some whites to be dictated more by a general social conscience than by a deep radical determination to overthrow slavery, and at times this led to a greater concern with assuming a proper moral posture than with obtaining the movement's goals. A prominent white abolitionist observed, "My friends, if we never free a slave, we have at least freed ourselves, in the effort to emancipate our brother man" (quoted in Quarles, 1969, p. 53). Such sentiments were a factor in the widespread dismay blacks felt with their white allies in the later decades of the movement. Speaking in 1837, a black minister declared that in the early days there were few white antislavery advocates and their commitments were clear and deep, but "now a man may call himself an abolitionist and we know not where to find him" (Wright, 1837).

Many Untouchable leaders were also suspicious of caste Hindus concerned with the condition of the Untouchables. They felt their commitment was never transformed into anything but promises after Gandhi assumed leadership in the 1920s. This led to considerable disillusionment among Untouchable activists (Heimsath, 1964). Suspicion of caste Hindus' motives was manifest, for instance, in debates over whether Untouchables ought to have separate reserved seats in various electoral schemes under consideration by the British government. Ambedkar adamantly favored separate representation as a way of insuring that Untouchables would have their interests and grievances voiced by Untouchables (Ambedkar, 1943). This deep distrust of outsiders is also evident in the politically conscious sector of a large Untouchable community recently studied by Lynch (1969). He notes a widespread feeling that only Untouchable leaders could "really understand and achieve empathy" with the community, a sentiment reflected in the strong identification with Ambedkar's movement at the national level.

Bringing in cultural prejudices

Independent of the structural conflicts in the movement, interpersonal relations within the movement may inadvertently manifest many of the social patterns of the greater society. Though the most virulent and blatant forms of group prejudice were not evident in any of the three movements, mild negative group attitudes and a sense of inferior or superior group status were manifest; and condescension, patronization, paternalism, and stereotyping on the part of the outsiders were also frequently noted. Like Captain Lingard in Joseph Conrad's *The Rescue,* the dominant group activist too often "prided himself upon having no color prejudice and no racial antipathies . . . only he knew what was good for them." At times this was reciprocated by passive acceptance of an inferior social position on the part of activists from the subordinate group, although enmity toward the dominant group co-workers has often been a simultaneous development. All of this was further exacerbated by a feeling among insiders that many dominant group activists behaved hypocritically; they espoused a creed of egalitarianism within the movement, yet often denied it in practice. Many of these deeply felt tensions between the two types of activists were sharpened by a tendency, noted by Coser (1956), for conflict to be particularly pronounced in close-knit groups.

There is much evidence that the internal culture of the abolitionist movement was pervaded by both racial and class prejudice to a much greater extent than was true in the civil rights movement. The sense of racial superiority was retained by many of even the most ardent white abolitionists, and the "patronizing air of the uplifter" toward the "downtrodden and unwashed" frequently characterized the manner in which whites in the movement related to free blacks (Pease & Pease, 1965). Whites often offered advice and observations on a variety of matters in a fatherly and demeaning style to black activists. An exceptional black received effusive praise from some white abolitionists, perhaps reflecting a mild astonishment in encountering a black person of any caliber. The effects were not lost on the black abolitionist, who often complained that the antislavery cause itself was psychologically oppressive. Racial prejudice pervaded much of the atmosphere. A black minister warned an antislavery convention that "abolitionists must annihilate in their own bosoms the cord of caste. We must be consistent—recognize the colored man in every respect as a man and brother" (Wright, 1837). Another source of tension was the feeling that white abolitionists oftentimes were guilty of discrimination outside of the movement. Many abolitionists bitterly denounced the system of slavery and devoted much energy to its eradication, but drew back from behavior that suggested social acceptance of the free black. In some public places and in the home and other private settings white abolitionists often were sensitive to charges of racial mixing, and their private associations were something less than fully integrated. Furthermore, free blacks in the North faced serious economic discrimination. Many whites active in the antislavery struggle were successful businessmen, but they frequently failed to make efforts to hire blacks, or did so only for the most menial positions (Litwack, 1965).

A caste Hindu activist frankly assessed the lingering prejudices many brought to the Untouchable movement.

> It will take some time before *even the best amongst us* begin to look upon Harijans [Untouchables] as an important and integral part of the great Hindu community. *Even the most enlightened amongst us* perfectly unconsciously recognize inwardly the distinction between Harijans and non-Harijans. (quoted in Sanjana, 1946)

Accusations of hypocrisy and inconsistency were also directed at caste Hindus. Like some of the white abolitionists, various Congress spokesmen were quick to denounce the sins of Untouchability but were hesitant to transgress traditional taboos against socially mingling with Untouchables. Some simply refused to share dinners with members of the depressed classes when invited or, if unavoidable, shunned too close a seating arrangement (Natarajan, 1959). When they did join in such dinners they often later underwent symbolic acts of disavowal. Gandhi insisted that orthodox Hindu communities should not be distressed by the process of reform, and when he made the removal of Untouchability a part of the Congress program, he explicitly excluded interdining.

Similar sources of friction along racial lines have also been evident in the civil rights movement. On a number of projects whites felt themselves to be more skilled than their black leaders and refused or were reluctant to follow orders they perceived as unnecessary or wrong. One activist (quoted in Poussaint, 1966) indicated that she felt like "the master's child come to free the slaves," a feeling sometimes revealed in behavior. Levy (1968) reports the case of a civil rights office that was managed by a black activist but which included some white workers. When several whites unfamiliar with the office entered they directed their initial queries for information to the white person rather than to the black in charge. Even with the best of intentions race has a persistent relevance that is hard to overcome. Traditional social forms and etiquette, as well as stereotypes, facilitate (or at least do not directly counter) usual patterns of dominant-subordinate relations, even among those committed to a more equalitarian society. One volunteer recalls: "A white man never turns black in Mississippi . . . [Y]our secret belief [does not disappear] . . . that you are, after all, superior . . . you're still college educated, still play-acting, and still white" (Sutherland, 1965, p. 58). Everyday language in an interracial setting often came to have unintended implications. "Following a marvelous dinner at the house of your local landlord, you hear yourself say, 'Boy, was that a great dinner' and you choke involuntarily on the expletive. You can't forget that you're still white" (Sutherland, 1965, p. 59).

However, social expectations may also ensnarl even the most tolerant, if in a reverse fashion, in the process Goffman (1963) has called "deminstrelization." Some whites overcompensated in trying to deny their outsider and middle-class backgrounds. Whites, in over-reacting to the racism of the larger society, occasionally adopted a subordinate position and hid skills that would be inconsistent with it, or refused to argue with blacks even if strongly provoked. Some gave away personal possessions and were unable to deny any black request. A white volunteer in the South recalls, "we've sort of laid down and let them run over us." In another case a white took over the job of toilet cleaning in a civil rights office to prevent blacks from assuming a stereotyped role (Levy, 1968). The effort to appear as non-white as possible may also be seen in the adoption of aspects of black and working-class culture (Marx, 1967a; Warren, 1965). Hard work by whites for the movement, partly inspired by a desire to prove their commitment, was sometimes seen instead as proof that they were trying to take things over. Interracial sexual affairs were seen by some as a way of transcending race and, for whites, a way of demonstrating their lack of prejudice; but often such affairs appeared to be strategically unwise, were a source of anxiety and jealousy, and were perhaps detrimental to the development of black pride. Activists were also affected by some of the sexual mythology and fears of the larger society. Thus a white staff member of an organization dedicated to the accomplishment of a completely integrated society, on hearing the screams of a girl at an evening conference, reports that his "immediate reaction was that one of the Negroes was raping the shit out of her" (Levy, 1968, p. 81).

In addition to being suspicious of outsiders, some minority group activists displaced their general anti-white feelings onto the white workers. Robert Moses notes that "it's very hard for some of the students who have been brought up in Mississippi and are victims of this kind of race hatred not to begin to let all of that out on the white staff" (quoted in Warren, 1965). In the face of numerous frustrations, these whites were accessible and provided a relatively safe target, unlike most members of the dominant group. The sense of collective guilt which initially brought many outsiders into the movement in some cases predisposed them to accept passively this scapegoating, or even to seek it.

Even if, in their face-to-face interaction, whites and blacks can relate authentically and avoid the kinds of conflict mentioned here, the culture of the outside world, as it impinges on the movement, may create internal conflicts. For instance, in the South, white activists when arrested often faced more tolerable jail conditions, and national indignation over the few whites martyred in the civil rights struggle has been far greater than over the much larger number of blacks. Though one reason for involving whites in the summers of 1964 and 1965 was the desire to draw national attention, when this attention came, many blacks were resentful and took it as one more manifestation of American racism. Survey data reveal that many white activists sensed distrust and hostility from black activists (Demerath, Marwell, & Aiken, 1968; Pinkney, 1968). However, the attitudes of black activists on these issues may be very different from those of the masses of uninvolved blacks. Thus, surveys frequently find that the overwhelming majority of the black population look favorably on white participation in civil rights activity (Marx, 1967b; Campbell & Schuman, 1968).

The changing role of outsiders—Independence needs of oppressed minority

Thus far we have focused primarily on the static question of insider-outsider discord. Certain structural features of the movement have been seen to have various consequences. We now turn briefly to the more dynamic social process question of the evolution of conflict over time.

Rarely have oppressed minorities been entirely responsible for their own liberation. Privileged groups played prominent roles in the ending of slavery in Greece and Rome, were conspicuous in the French and Russian revolutions, and, at least since the time of Karl Marx, observers have noted a tendency for some among the privileged to defect and take up the cause of the oppressed. In the movements examined here, and in others of a similar type, it appears that the role of outsiders may be critical in the early phases of the struggle. The more oppressed the minority group, the more essential may be aid from members of the dominant group in initiating the liberation movement. However, as the movement gathers strength, the importance of outsiders is often greatly reduced, at times leading to their complete withdrawal. Caste Hindus initiated many of the early efforts aimed at ameliorating the condition of the Untouchables, and white abolitionists were primarily responsible for the formation of many of the early antislavery societies, and for hooking these into a national system. In the case of civil rights, whites played a crucial role in the founding of the NAACP, the Urban League, and CORE, although not in organizations emerging later, such as SNCC and the Black Panthers (Kellogg, 1967; Meier & Rudwick, 1969; Farmer, 1966).

Outsiders generally have had greater command over resources, have been freer to act, were likely to be closer to centers of power, and have often had essential "organizing" experience. Their presence in the struggle may add an aura of legitimacy to the protest movement's goals, and when they are harassed or killed in the cause, the situation is dramatized far beyond what happens when minority group members themselves face similar brutalization. In addition, in the germinal phase many members of the oppressed group may be isolated from alternative definitions of the situation, and, in the absence of a strong protest tradition, may not actively question the legitimacy of the system; and of course some may have a vested interest in maintaining the status quo. Thus the important, often even predominant, role of outsiders in the beginning stages of these movements is not surprising. However, an additional factor in the early involvement of outsiders in some organizations such as CORE and the British Committee Against Racial Discrimination (CARD) is an ideology that defined interracial cooperation as an end in itself.

Once outsiders are involved in this type of effort, however, their presence is potentially problematic for reasons discussed above. Some of the virtues of the involved outsiders in the beginning stages may come to be seen as liabilities as the movement evolves. Several developments facilitate the separation of minority and majority group activists. First of all, with engagement in the movement, insiders acquire necessary skills and confidence and become less dependent on outsiders. Second, the latent structural conflicts become more manifest with continued interaction of the two groups. Third, as the objectives are not reached or even approached despite intense activity and sacrifice, militancy and susceptibility to new strategies may increase, as well as internal scapegoating. Finally, as the movement recruits new members from the oppressed group and the character of its membership shifts, it may become increasingly less dependent on manpower from outsiders. Thus, structural aspects of such movements are likely to give rise to severe conflict, and this in turn helps generate beliefs justifying the separation of minority and dominant group activists. On the other hand, the adoption of such beliefs may in some cases precede internal conflict and hasten the division of the movement. Ideology may diffuse between movements, as seems to have occurred in Britain, where a Black Power perspective has been adopted by some blacks in an effort to oust whites from CARD, the major civil rights organization.

The processes noted here are not irreversible. The American Left has vacillated between emphasizing the uniquely racial, as against the shared economic class-aspects, of the situation of blacks in America. At times in the 1930s and in the past two decades, the class component has been ascendant, but at other times the racial line has been considered prime. Concomitantly, tactics have shifted between a racially separate movement and a common integrated struggle. In the mid-1960s with the rise of the Black Power movement, the unique ethnic aspects of black subordination were stressed. Associated with this trend has been the tendency among whites who left the black movement to become engaged in social movements in which they no longer were defined as outsiders (e.g., campus issues, the anti-war movement, draft resistance, women's liberation, ethnic associations). More recently much leftist thought has argued that the problems of blacks and other ethnic groups, the white working class, females, and to some degree even those of students stem from shared economic and political oppression. With this perspective goes an emphasis on cooperation in a common struggle. Similarly, various periods in American history show blacks moving toward and then away from inclusion, depending on the receptiveness of the dominant group. Beyond the internal sources of tension noted here, when the dominant group's supposed receptiveness proves illusory, blacks have increasingly turned inward and in a separatist direction. For instance, the hopes raised by the Civil War and World War I led to an initial emphasis on inclusion; the shattering of those hopes facilitated the ascendancy of separatist leaders such as Booker T. Washington and Marcus Garvey.

The future of the relationship between the white left and the black movement in America is hardly clear at the present. Tensions and impediments to interracial cooperation remain present. Yet movements do not exist in a vacuum. While both the white left and the black movement are made up of highly diverse groups, important segments of each are coming to reflect a growing ideological similarity which stresses the presence of a common enemy and the need for cooperation to build an interracial society free of exploitation and racism. This is apparent in the coalition ties which have been developing over the past few years between the Black Panthers and various white racial groups, though the relationship yet remains an ambivalent one. Thus the tendency for interracial movements to splinter along racial lines may be followed by a tendency to regroup as the limits of independent action and separatism are realized, and because of solidarity created by shared repression at the hands of the government and other powerful institutions in the society.

IN CONCLUSION

A comparative look at these three movements reveals several recurrent themes of intergroup tension. There is much variation depending on the time period and on the segment of the movement involved; yet ideological cleavage frequently exists between dominant and minority-group activists. When conflict of an ideological nature along this line emerged, there was a tendency for insiders to seé themselves as more radical and committed than outsiders, more eager to create changes immediately than gradually, less willing to compromise their program for the sake of expediency, less hesitant to use non-institutionalized protest means, less concerned with a variety of political movements, and more likely to espouse a creed of self-help. As microcosms of society, these movements often developed internal authority- and skill-structures resembling, in diluted form, the subordinate-dominant relations characteristic of the broader societal context, as well as atmospheres containing many of society's intergroup hostilities and prejudices. Over time many of these latent conflicts became manifest, and dominant group activists who played an important role in the formative phases of the movement were excluded or forced to assume greatly reduced roles.

In making inferences about these patterns to still other social movements, generalizations must be undertaken with caution, for the civil rights, Untouchable, and abolitionist causes all represent responses to somewhat common forms of oppression. However, a very impressionistic look at related movements, such as those of Mexican-Americans in this country, the Burakumin in Japan, blacks in South Africa and in the Caribbean, and Asians and Africans in England, suggest many of the same themes. The interaction between insiders and outsiders in a variety of other movements not involving race or ethnicity may also show similarities. It would be interesting to examine movements where the source of outsiderness stems from characteristics such as sex, class, age, religion, or even past experience (e.g., the activity of those without records of confinement in reform movements for prisons or mental hospitals, non-working-class activists in the labor movement, men in the feminist movement, and colonials in nationalist movements). In the case of class struggles, for instance, outsiders (activists without working-class backgrounds) may exhibit more militancy and commitment than insiders. Commentators with viewpoints ranging from Lenin (1943) to Selig Perlman (1928) have argued that conditions facing members of the working class will at best lead to the emergence of a job-oriented consciousness. The "intellectual organizer" as outsider plays a crucial role in interpreting and placing the work experience in a generalized critique of the social order, and thus he tends to formulate more radical and comprehensive programs than the workers. Lenin attributes this primarily to the greater freedom and capacity which the socialist intelligentsia possess for careful analysis of the society's structure, ills, and potential for change. Coser (1956), drawing on the work of Simmel, has suggested another factor. Those who identify with the interests of the entire group, and view themselves as carrying forward the group's mission, tend to become more committed to the goals of the movement than do those who see it primarily as a solution to oppressive conditions personally faced. This objectification of the struggle and consequent generation of militancy has probably been more likely to characterize outsider "intellectuals" active in the labor cause than the workers, although many workers, of course, do translate their immediate situation into a collective solidarity with all workers. In the three movements examined here, the whites and caste Hindus were typically well educated, and in many instances they were experienced political analysts whose coming to these movements paralleled, in some respects, the highly ideological approach of revolutionary intellectuals in labor unions. But we have already discovered that blacks and Untouchables in these minority movements in fact tended at least to believe that insiders were more radical and committed to the cause than their outsider counterparts.

Several additional factors must be taken into account with respect to ethnic movements and outsider militancy, however. First of all, the most active insiders were also frequently highly educated and very aware of the complex social issues involved in their liberation struggles, with many performing the role of the "intellectual" within their own movements. Furthermore, this capacity was built on a commitment stemming from an oppression personally experienced, which served to reinforce rather than undermine a more depersonalized identification with the collective cause. Finally, the intensity of commitment to a particular movement may be mitigated if involvement is shared with other political movements—and in the Untouchability, abolition, and civil rights movements, outsiders were much more prone to be active in other causes or to shift their allegiances from movement to movement. Such factors help to explain why the radicalizing role for outsider-organizers anticipated from Lenin's and Coser's analysis might be reversed in these movements; and this suggests that a variety of conditions must be specified in dealing with the ideological role outsiders may be expected to assume in political movements.

A variety of other issues might also be pursued. We have focused mainly on factors conducive to conflict and separation of insiders from outsiders. Some important additional questions for analysis might be what factors facilitate *cooperation* among inside and outside activists, and in what stages in a movement's life history such conditions might occur. For instance, strong external pressures from an unsympathetic, and occasionally repressive, dominant society have often been conducive to inter-group solidarity. Numerous examples of interracial cooperation are described in the growing literature on the civil rights movement (Zinn, 1965; Pinkney, 1968; Sutherland, 1965; Sugarman, 1966; Belfrage, 1966). Another important question has to do with differences in the extensiveness of conflict and the separation of activists in the different organizations that are part of the same general social movement, such as NAACP, CORE, and SNCC. Rudwick and Meier note that, beyond differences in constituency and in top leadership, the strong bureaucratic structure of the NAACP may have made it more stable and resistant to the separatist thrust that completely changed CORE (Rudwick & Meier, 1970). Finally, it would be interesting to explore whether the internal tensions of a movement portend broader societal changes. The activists' awareness of ideological and interpersonal strains in their movement may encourage many people outside of the cause to become conscious of similar factors in their own lives.

In contrast to the Untouchable and abolitionist movements, the civil rights struggles of this decade are still very much with us. Perhaps one indirect benefit of comparing these three movements is to make our own period of history a little more intelligible, though this is a comment on neither the morality nor strategic value of these developments. Many whites who had contributed much to the civil rights movements were initially shocked, angered, and bewildered at the development of the Black Power movement. Some sought explanations in terms of the presumed unstable personalities of radical blacks, rather than in terms of the social structure of the movement. However, similar processes in the three movements examined here suggest that tension among activists, and the concomitant rise of the Black Power movement, were partly, at least, in response to political differences and interpersonal conflicts common to this *type* of social movement. An identification of historically recurring conflict generated by the structure of such movements might also help future movements avoid or minimize the conflict that ironically may develop among those of different backgrounds committed to common goals of social change.

REFERENCES

Ambedkar, B. R. *Mr. Gandhi and the emancipation of the Untouchables.* Bombay: Thacker, 1943.

Bell, I. P. *CORE and the strategy of non-violence.* New York: Random House, 1968.

Belfrage, S. *Freedom summer.* Greenwich, Conn.: Fawcett Publications, 1966.

Campbell, A., & Schuman, H. *Racial attitudes in fifteen American cities.* Ann Arbor: Survey Research Center, 1968.

Coser, L. *The functions of social conflict.* New York: Free Press, 1956.

Delany, M. R. *The condition, elevation, emigration and destiny of the colored people of the United States, politically considered.* Philadelphia: Author, 1852. Preface reprinted in H. Aptheker (Ed.), *A documentary history of the Negro people in the United States: From colonial times through the Civil War.* New York: The Citadel Press, 1968.

Demerath, N. J., III, Marwell, G., & Aiken, M. Tactics and tensions in a summer of yesteryear: Results of a panel analysis of 1965 southern civil rights workers. Paper presented at the annual meeting of American Sociological Association, Boston, Massachusetts, 1968.

Demerath, N. J., III, Marwell, G., & Aiken, M. T. Criteria and contingencies of success in a radical movement. *Journal of Social Issues,* 1971, *27* (1).

Douglass, F. *The North Star* (editorial), December 3, 1847. In H. Aptheker (Ed.), *A documentary history of the Negro people in the United States: From colonial times through the Civil War.* New York: The Citadel Press, 1968.

Farmer, J. *Freedom when?* New York: Random House, 1966.

Garnet, H. H. An address to the slaves of the United States (1843). In H. Aptheker (Ed.), *A documentary history of the Negro people in the United States: From colonial times through the Civil War.* New York: The Citadel Press, 1968.

Goffman, I. *Stigma: Notes on the management of spoiled identities.* Englewood Cliffs, N.J.: Prentice-Hall, 1963.

Heimsath, C. *Indian nationalism and Hindu social reform.* Princeton: Princeton University Press, 1964.

Keller, A., Mabutt, F., & Ruhe, D. Summer 1965: The white "freedom fighters" in the south. *Kansas Journal of Sociology,* 1965, *1,* 119–122.

Kellogg, C. *NAACP: A history of the National Association for the Advancement of Colored People.* Baltimore: Johns Hopkins, 1967.

Kerr, D. *Dr. Ambedkar: Life and mission.* (2nd ed.) Bombay: Popular Prakashan, 1962.

Lenin, V. I. *What is to be done? Burning questions of our movement.* New York: International Publishers, 1943.

Lester, J. *Look out whitey! Black power's gon' get your mama!* New York: Grove Press, 1968.

Levy, C. *Voluntary servitude: Whites in the Negro movement.* New York: Appleton-Century-Crofts, 1968.

Litwack, L. *North of slavery: The Negro in the free states, 1790–1860.* Chicago: University of Chicago Press, 1961.

Litwack, L. The emancipation of the Negro abolitionist. In M. Duberman (Ed.), *The antislavery vanguard: New essays on the abolitionists.* Princeton: Princeton University Press, 1965.

Lynch, O. M. *The politics of Untouchability: Social mobility and social change in a city of India.* New York: Columbia University Press, 1969.

Lynd, S. The movement: A new beginning. *Liberation,* May 14, 1969, 7–20.

Marx, G. The white Negro and the Negro white. *Phylon,* 1967, *28,* 168–177. (a)

Marx, G. *Protest and prejudice: A study of belief in the black community.* New York: Harper and Row, 1967. (b)

Meier, A., & Rudwick, E. M. *From plantation to ghetto: An interpretive history of American Negroes.* New York: Hill and Wang, 1966.

Meier, A., & Rudwick, E. M. How CORE began. *Social Science Quarterly,* 169, *49* (March) 789–799.

Myrdal, G. *An American dilemma.* New York: Harper and Row, 1944. 2 vols.

Natarajan, S. *A century of social reform in India.* Bombay: Asia Publishing House, 1959.

Pease, W., & Pease, J. H. Antislavery ambivalence: Immediatism, expediency, race. *American Quarterly,* 1965, *17,* 682–695.

Perlman, S. *A theory of the labor movement.* New York: The Macmillan Co., 1928.

Pinkney, A. *The committed: White activists in the civil rights movement.* New Haven: College and University Press, 1968.

Poussaint, A. F. The stresses of the white female worker in the civil rights movement in the south. *American Journal of Psychiatry,* 1966, *123,* 401–405.

Quarles, B. *Black abolitionists.* New York: Oxford University Press, 1969.

Rudolph, L. I., & Rudolph, S. H. *The modernity of tradition: Political development in India.* Chicago: University of Chicago Press, 1967.

Rudwick, E. M., & Meier, A. Organizational structure and goal succession: A comparative analysis of the NAACP and CORE, 1964–68. *Social Science Quarterly,* 1970, *51* (June), 9–24.

Sanjana, J. E. *Caste and outcaste.* Bombay: Thacker, 1946.

Sugarman, T. *Stranger at the gates.* New York: Hill and Wang, 1966.

Sutherland, E. (Ed.) *Letters from Mississippi.* New York: McGraw Hill, 1965.

Vine City Project. Whites in the movement. In M. Cohen and D. Hale (Eds.), *The new student left.* Boston: Beacon Press, 1967.

Warren, R. P. Two for SNCC. *Commentary,* 1965, *39,* 38–48.

Wright, T. S. Address to the New York State Anti-Slavery Society convention. Utica, New York, September, 1937. In H. Aptheker (Ed.), *A documentary history of the Negro people in the United States: From colonial times through the Civil War.* New York: The Citadel Press, 1968.

Zelliot, E. Buddhism and politics in Maharashtra. In D. E. Smith (Ed.), *South Asian politics and religion.* Princeton: Princeton University Press, 1966.

Zinn, H. *SNCC: The new abolitionists.* Boston: Beacon Press, 1965.

D. Policy and practice considerations

JOHN FLOREZ

Chicanos and coalitions as a force for social change

During the past decade this country experienced more attempts at social change than during any previous period. For the first time the federal government—through, for example, community action programs and the President's Committee on Juvenile Delinquency and Youth Crime—sanctioned the use of community organization strategies to change existing social institutions. Private foundations also became more active in funding projects aimed at social change, as evident in the Ford Foundation's 'grey area' projects. During the decade of the 1960s, many people began to have great expectations and hopes for the future. For the first time we were going to improve the quality of living for many and conduct an all-out effort to eliminate poverty and to enfranchise those who previously had been disenfranchised.

In Chicano communities throughout the country we also saw hopes raised, although it was not readily acknowledged that we were having problems. In spite of the "benign neglect" we experienced, we made attempts to become involved. We attended board and committee meetings and tried to make the "maximum feasible participation" concept work. We told our people to talk about their problems and to participate in studies. As our own civil rights movement began to gather momentum and we realized that the established methods of causing change were ineffective, we began to employ other strategies and tactics to bring about change. More important, however, we renewed alliances with our traditional friends.

THE OLD ALLIANCES

It is the purpose of this article to examine these old alliances as they pertain to the Chicano movement and to suggest new alliances through coalitions. It is important first to examine these old alliances, to know who they were, and to ascertain the position in which they have left us.

Source: Copyright © 1971 by Family Service Association of America. Reprinted by permission from *Social Casework,* vol. 52 (May 1971), pp. 269–71. This article also appears in *La Causa Chicana: The Movement for Justice* (New York: Family Service Association of America, 1972).

Liberals

When we reached out for allies to help us, we turned initially to our old liberal friends who were sympathetic listeners and more than eager to identify with our cause. Among them were those liberals who would identify with any new movement or any cause that involved oppressed people. There were other liberals who were more interested merely in attacking the establishment for its own sake, regardless of the consequences. They not only alienated the establishment but also exploited our cause for their own purposes. In addition, they frequently tried to enlist the Chicano in attempts to advance their own agenda. Many Chicanos equated strong rhetoric with genuine concern. The more antiestablishment the rhetoric, the greater their identification with our cause; however, when it actually came to enlisting their support on hard issues, they were nowhere to be found—*se volvían puro polvo* (they would turn to dust)!

The unfortunate outcome of forming these alliances with liberals was that it lulled us into complacency and prevented us from seeking other allies. They could neither provide our people with needed resources themselves nor influence others who possessed these resources.

Other liberals who expressed interest in helping the Chicano frequently hurt more than they helped. Their help was paternalistic and they tended to perpetuate the status quo. Among them were the do-gooders and social workers who adhered to the values of the predominant social system that has long maintained racist stereotypes of the Chicano.

Social workers

In the past, we also looked to social workers for assistance because they were the professionals who knew how to deal with social problems. Among them were some Chicano social workers who were supposed to be sensitive to our problems. The unfortunate outcome, however, was that they led us into dealing with our problems with traditional methods. They too had been victims of inadequate schools of social work. They practiced the archaic and crystallized social work concepts long established in the social work profession. These concepts included the need for cooperation, nonduplication of services, adherence to the worker-client relationship, assimilation, and allegiance to agency policy (field work evaluations included questions about how well the student supported and interpreted agency policy). They believed that men were basically of good will and would do the right thing if only they were told what needed to be done.

By their traditional practices, they frequently counseled our people into a state of deeper resignation and acceptance. They were the first to say we should go through channels and resign ourselves to administrative decisions. Consequently, social workers have frequently hurt our people more than they have helped. As the late Senator Robert F. Kennedy stated:

> We need to create new remedies to deal with the multitude of daily injuries that persons suffer in this complex society simply because it is complex.
>
> I am not talking about persons who injure others out of selfish or evil motives. I am talking about the injuries which result simply from administrative conveniences, injuries which may be done inadvertently by those endeavoring to help—teachers and social workers and urban planners.[1]

Many Chicano social workers frequently found themselves caught in the conflict between the traditional social work concepts they had learned and what they knew from personal experiences needed to be done. Some found themselves being oppressed; others found themselves seeking new employment; still others have become more effective as they developed clearer understanding of the roles they must play.

Middlemen

During the past decade we also saw a proliferation of new agencies and greater support given to old agencies with the understanding that they should seek greater citizen participation. We attempted to ally ourselves with these agencies and to participate in their boards and committees. For example, we saw more manpower programs to help minorities and United Funds to help the poor. The programs were funded and staffed, but there were no visible results. Housing programs for the poor were initiated, but somehow the poor seldom profited. More minority children appeared in United Fund posters, but there were no programs for minorities. Current United Fund policies, which exclude new groups from being funded, make it impossible for Chicano programs to be started. Those that have been initiated are frequently suppressed and meticulously monitored.

Our alliance with these middlemen has often given credibility to their projects and allowed them to demonstrate to the taxpayer that they are doing something for the Chicano. They are able to say that they are professional and have the public interest in mind. If the programs fail,

---

[1] Robert F. Kennedy, Address on Law Day, University of Chicago Law School, Chicago, Illinois, May 1, 1964.

they can blame the failure on the lack of adequate numbers of professionals and sufficient money.

COALITIONS AND CHICANOS

It has become increasingly clear that if social change that will improve the living conditions of Chicanos is to occur, that change must be championed by Chicanos. Peter Marris and Martin Rein, after their study of the projects sponsored by the Ford Foundation and the President's Committee on Juvenile Delinquency, make the following statement.

> This is perhaps the most important general conclusion of our study: that no movement of reform in American society can hope to supplant the conflicts of interest from which policy evolves. It can only act as an advocate, not as judge. If it is to be persuasive, it must be single-minded about the interests it represents, and so willing to surrender any claim to universal authority.[2]

The issues of concern to the Chicano will never be articulated in the American democratic social arena that operates through pressures of vested interests unless the Chicano does it himself. The social experiments of the past decade have demonstrated this point. These experiments have proved that there must be a resolve and a commitment to a cause. Liberals, middlemen, and disinterested reformers are too easily led into nonpartisan positions and collapse for lack of a strong community base. Nonpartisan liberals are with us one day if the cause is popular; the next day they are "turned on" to something new. Four years ago they were concerned about the poor; now they are concerned with the environment.

This statement does not imply, however, that we should *not* seek the support of others, but simply that if we *ourselves* do not constantly press for the interests of our people, no one else will. As Marris and Rein state:

> A reformer in American society faces three crucial tasks. He must recruit a coalition of power sufficient for his purpose; he must respect the democratic tradition which expects every citizen, not merely to be represented, but to play an autonomous part in the determination of his own affairs; and his policies must be demonstrably rational. These criteria are not peculiar to the United States—nor irrelevant even to totalitarian societies—but each gains in America a particular emphasis. In the first place, the distribution of authority is uniquely complicated.[3]

---

[2] Peter Marris and Martin Rein, *Dilemmas of Social Reform: Poverty and Community Action in the United States* (New York: Atherton Press, 1967), p. 230.

[3] Ibid., p. 7.

It is this writer's contention that if change is to come about for the improvement of the masses of our people, we must redefine our strategies, our priorities, and our alliances. We must ask ourselves the following questions: When do we sit in as members of a community committee? Which is more important—more Chicano social work instructors and Chicano Studies or better health services for our people? As one Chicano *tecáto* (an addict) said to a group of Chicano college students, "You guys are more concerned with Brown Studies than you are with us who are dying daily because of an overdose of heroin."

Chicano coalitions

Today we are an aware group of people and are coming closer together to deal with the problems facing Chicanos. We are coming closer together because of a new hope that flows not from being accepted on an advisory board but rather from a sense of identification with a cause. We are now aware enough to know that *no one* will express the concerns of Chicanos except Chicanos.

For some time we labored under the notion that "we needed to get ourselves together" and that when we were unified under one Mexican-American organization, our problems would be solved. Today we realize that, although we are a group of people—diversified in our concerns—who often differ in our methods of dealing with our problems, we have common threads that bind us together. In essence, within our own communities we have formed our own Chicano coalitions. We may not always agree on everything—for example, the youth as opposed to the elderly, the professional as opposed to the activist—nevertheless, we embrace a common philosophy based on self-determination and expressed through the following goals:

1. To bring to the Chicano individual all the resources available so that he can express his right of self-determination through the control of every phase of his life.
2. To identify all institutions and their agencies that prohibit the expression of our rights and potentialities. Identify avenues and methods of action to change such institutions.
3. To mobilize groups to advocate and articulate the need for change.
4. To develop communication networks at all levels of the Chicano social structure that will allow quick mobilization of groups to initiate change based on well thought-out specific goals and expertise available to carry through such goals.[4]

---

[4] Marta Sotomayor, The Chicano Movement and Power Strategies (paper delivered at the Urban Coalition Conference for Mexican-Americans, Denver, Colorado, March 21, 1970).

More and more we are working together and minimizing the debate. We are utilizing the diverse skills we possess—including political know-how, technical skills, professional competence, program development, and activist strategies—toward *la Causa*. For example, in one community in the Southwest, all these skills were combined to develop a community-based organization that now is managing its own programs, competing with older established institutions for resources, and becoming an advocate for Chicanos. It required the activists to bring the need to the attention of the community, the professionals to package the idea, and those persons with political know-how finally to make the project a reality. Such examples are now becoming more frequent and are indicative of the Chicano's ability to work with one another in common concerns.

Coalitions with new allies

Our past traditional alliances with other groups have at times hurt rather than helped our cause. We must, therefore, reevaluate our past alliances and redefine our relationships with them. Will the middleman consider himself as an all-benevolent but authoritarian *patron,* or will he see himself in a position for stewardship? Will the liberal sacrifice "doing his thing" for the sake of our people? More important, we must seek out those new allies who actually hold the power and resources to deal with our problems. We must learn to identify those "power blocks" and attempt to seek their support and with them form coalitions —temporary unions for a common purpose. In addition, we should identify those issues for which we can gain the support of those power blocks.

In the past, we have sacrificed action for debate over political philosophies (men often do the right thing for the wrong reasons). At times we failed to seek the support of key groups because we were told by our old allies that they would not support us, but we never bothered to find out for ourselves. We too were "hung up" about our stereotypes about the power structure. In *To Seek a Newer World,* Senator Kennedy said:

> Too often in the past we have been enmeshed in the traditional debate between liberals and conservatives over whether we should or should not spend more government funds on programs. What we have failed to examine with any thoroughness is the impact of these programs on those we sought to assist, indeed whether they have had any impact at all.[5]

---

[5] Robert F. Kennedy, *To Seek a Newer World* (New York: Doubleday & Co., 1968), pp. 32–33.

Recent experiences in the coalition process with new allies have demonstrated some successes. In one city, for example, a Chicano tenant union, a bank president, and other members of the power structure coalesced to replace an old-time public housing authority director with a more responsive individual. In other cities, corporation presidents have supported Chicano issues and provided financial support. Although these are isolated examples, it is important to note that within the power structure of a community there are potential allies, but we have failed to seek their support. In the past we have allowed the middlemen professionals to tell those in power what needed to be done. The outcome was more of the same kind of programs and the same kind of attitudes being maintained by the public. This writer advocates the elimination of the middleman wherever possible.

Increasingly, we are seeing some changes in the leadership of the power structure. We should, however, be in a position to understand and define the nature of the relationship into which we enter with our new allies. We should realize that, although they may agree with us on certain issues, they may disagree completely on many others. In some instances the power structure may coalesce with us in wresting resources from the middlemen on such issues as welfare reform, school problems, and legal issues. In other instances they may provide resources from their own private sector for economic development and special projects. At the same time, however, this same group may not support us in *la huelga.* Does their lack of support in some areas mean that we will not work with them if they do not totally agree with us all the time? All too frequently some Chicanos have failed to recognize this difference and consequently have been responsible for the denial of needed help to our people. In short, while some of us are "doing our thing" (as are the liberals), we use our own people in the process.

Too frequently we have heard, "I do not want to deal with the establishment because I'll lose my credibility with my people." This writer is not certain that the "people" who are unemployed and suffer from inadequate housing, ill health, inadequate courts, and a high rate of incarceration are concerned about anyone's credibility. Although these issues are not romantic and are not readily solved, they are, nevertheless, some of the problems with which we must cope if we are to help the masses of our people. Can we not find allies to help us deal with these problems without losing our integrity?

Finally, we must be sufficiently flexible to dissolve current relationships and form new ones as we define new objectives. If we understand and accept the terms of the relationship with these individuals or groups as being specific and for a definite objective, there is no loss of integrity.

CONCLUSION

Although there is no question that the Chicano must look after the interests of Chicanos, there are times when the Chicano can coalesce with other groups for a common purpose. We have failed in the past to examine more closely the composition of those groups, and we have failed to see that rhetoric does not always produce action. For too long we have missed opportunities to relate directly to power blocks and instead have related to middlemen and other "nice guys." If we are to be successful in solving the great problems of our people, we must have the ability to deal with them by using many kinds of methods. The coalition process is only one of these methods but it is one that we have not fully explored. Can we have the vision to use this process in the interest of our people?

Chapter 5

THE WHITE ETHNIC: OPPRESSOR OR VICTIM?

A. Introduction

The term "backlash" entered the political vocabulary of America in conjunction with the 1968 Presidential campaign of George Wallace. This development was viewed with disquiet by those working for racial equality. It reflected an increased polarization in the nation on racial and social issues, as well as a strengthening of traditionally retrograde forces. While the militancy of oppressed minorities had been seen favorably as a useful and even necessary step toward social justice, the rising countermilitancy of the right among white nationality ethnic groups had an ominous cast. The "silent majority" of "middle Americans" was beginning to speak with an awesome voice.

White ethnics in particular became a symbol of backlash. The group is usually defined as composed of Caucasian peoples of Eastern and Central European descent (such as Italians, Irish, Poles, Germans), with a lower-middle-class socioeconomic standing and blue-collar factory and trade occupations. The prototypical white ethnic owns his own home and resides in an old central-city neighborhood or on the urban fringe. It has been estimated that roughly 60 million people (including 20 million workers) are included among their ranks.

White ethnics had not been embraced as a group in the recent past by liberal and radical factions, including racial minorities, students, social critics, and the media. Often a member of this group was depicted as manning the front lines of racism and was symbolized by such descriptive epitaphs as "rednecks," "hard hats," "Wallacites," and "backlashers." Working-class ethnic neighborhoods have received intensive press coverage for roughly resisting such measures as open housing in Cicero, Illinois, and school bussing in Boston. Hard-hat unionists were condemned for their vocal advocacy of military oppression overseas in Vietnam and "law and order" police repression in the ghettos at home.

In "A Black View of the White Worker," James Boggs portrays blue-collar unionists as particularly vitriolic. Trade unions keep their doors shut to membership by racial minorities. The union establishment has made a cozy accommodation with the political establishment, maintaining the status quo and ensuring that racial groups are frozen in inferior roles. Rather than aiding their less advantaged fellow workers, blue-collar unionists conspire against them, presumably as a way of protecting their own meager gains. Indeed, they populate in disproportionate numbers the vigilante organizations that have been formed to illegally and undemocratically harass aspiring racial movements. Boggs sees white ethnic workers on an irreversible collision course with black advancement. This assessment, not lightly made, is informed by Boggs's long years of active personal involvement as a black in the labor movement.

Gus Tyler, like Boggs a labor activist and radical writer, presents a starkly different portrait of the white ethnic worker in "White Worker/ Blue Mood." This image emerges from a growing literature sympathetic to the position of white ethnics which describes "forgotten Americans" caught in an economic squeeze and social cross fire.[1] Most are above the minimum poverty level, but high prices continually erode their economic position. They feel locked in a struggle to maintain their standing and preserve their values in the face of severe pressures aimed at displacement by groups just below them on the social scale. All this appears to be taking place in an atmosphere of lawlessness and anarchy on all sides, and ineffectual and corrupt governmental officials seem incapable of containing it.

The white ethnic feels it is his fringe neighborhood that is overrun and broken up, and his cherished home that is threatened by the paths of racial migration and programs of integration. Property values suffer and equities are endangered, while the school program deteriorates amid intergroup hostility and strife. Meanwhile, the cost of health care soars, city services bypass him, he is engulfed by pollution, and all the while he is manipulated by the "big shots"—city hall, corporations, the "better people." It is on him that the weight of disproportionate taxation falls, forcing him to carry everyone else on his back—both welfare chiselers and affluent connivers who take advantage of every tax loophole.

He finds it difficult to understand the privileged treatment extended to racial minorities in the competition for jobs, housing, and education. After all, his immigrant ancestors had it rough; nevertheless, they got ahead, despite ethnic discrimination and without the aid of handouts. Why, he asks, should the burden of making America right again be on his shoulders? Marvin Novak, an articulate spokesman for this group, states it pungently: "Racism is not our invention; we did not bring it with us; we found it here. And why should we pay the price of American guilt? Must all the gains of the blacks, long overdue, be chiefly at our expense? Have we, once again, no defenders but ourselves?"[2]

The white nationality member, like his black, red, and brown counterpart, feels himself to be powerless and overshadowed, a disregarded, disadvantaged minority. Because of his great frustration and often modest education, he is often not up to understanding the nation's troubles

---

[1] "White Ethnic America: A Selected Bibliography," compiled by Judith M. Herman, American Jewish Committee, Institute of Human Relations, October 1969.

[2] Marvin Novak, "White Ethnics," *Harpers,* September 1971, pp. 44–50.

perceptively, and he is left vulnerable to the simplistic explanations offered by charismatic spokesmen of organized political reaction.

In his analysis Tyler particularly emphasizes the common economic victimization of both ethnic whites and racial minorities, reflecting the marginal–working class concept described by Tabb in Chapter 1. The top 1.4 percent of the population, he tells us, captures 10 percent of the annual income—more than all those in the bottom 34 percent combined. When wealth is the referent, economic maldistribution is still more pronounced; in 1962, 1 percent of the population held 33.3 percent of the wealth of the nation. These patterns of economic inequality have remained constant since the beginning of the century. White ethnics and racial minorities, Tyler holds, grapple with one another for more of the crumbs near the bottom, while the economic elites at the top escape responsibility for sharing the burden of promoting racial justice. Rather, they benefit all the while from the mutual antagonisms and confusions of those at the foot of the socioeconomic pyramid.

Boggs and Tyler represent polar interpretations of the white ethnic position. However, it is possible to discern at least five different interpretations of the white ethnic backlash:

1. As a racist response to just demands by blacks (Boggs).
2. As an expression of the needs of another neglected and deprived population.
3. As an ethnic, cultural reawakening and pluralistic response to increased ingroup identity and pride on the part of racial minorities.
4. As a natural political and economic power struggle among interest groups for scarce resources.
5. As a clash among common victims of an unjust economic system (Tyler).

These varying interpretations have significant ramifications in terms of bringing policy and strategy to bear on this issue.

There is a long tradition of scholarly study of ethnic matters in sociology and anthropology, including subbranches such as ethnology. This body of research is available to aid those attempting to deal with contemporary ethnic problems. A representative selection is provided here. In a study of Irish and Italians, John Goering discovered a reemergence of ethnic interests in the third generation. Ironically, there are indications that such a resurgence can in part be correlated with opposition to demands for equal rights by racial minorities. This return to ethnicity, however, appears also to provide a vehicle for focusing discontent and skepticism regarding the "American dream." While white ethnics may view demands for equal rights negatively from a group relations standpoint, the resurgence of ethnicity offers them a platform for community organizing and political mobilization. Guidelines for those with particular interests in organizational work with white ethnics may be derived from another study which delineates patterns of organizational affiliation and participation.[3] Other research studies having potential usefulness treat areas such as the degree to which the experience of white ethnic immigrants and racial minorities is similar or different,[4] the extent to which white ethnics do or do not support rightist candidates at the polls,[5] value systems and lifestyles of working-class families,[6] and participation of ethnics in city politics.[7]

A program of action with working-class middle Americans requires, first, a strategy, and second, an approach to organizing. Irving Levine, director of the Institute on Pluralism of the American Jewish Committee, delineates the outlines of a proposed strategy. He accepts the problems and grievances of this group as compelling and suggests an approach responsive to their needs which would be geared to working on such issues as better police protection, tax reform, and public education. An addendum to his statement enumerates a series of issues which speak to the various needs of white ethnics. While his thrust is toward independent programming for this group, in later writings Levine has also articulated a strategy of "something for everybody" which would open up possibilities for coalitions between lower-class and blue-collar constituencies and would provide common benefits for both. The Ethnic Heritage Studies Act is an acknowledgment by Congress of the political necessity to be responsive to the needs of this group. Levine combines a cultural pluralist analysis with a political strategy of intergroup attitudes and relationships, in terms of the policy options categorized in Chapter 1.

The organizing problem is complicated by the past tendencies of professionals and intellectuals to avoid nationality communities, partly

[3] Djuro J. Vrga, "Differential Associated Involvement of Successive Ethnic Immigrations: An Indicator of Ethno-Religious Fractionalism and Alienation of Immigrants," *Social Forces*, vol. 50 (December 1971), pp. 239–48.

[4] Karl E. Taeuber and Alma F. Taeuber, "The Negro as an Immigrant Group: Recent Trends in Racial and Ethnic Segregation in Chicago," *American Journal of Sociology*, vol. 69 (1964), pp. 374–82; Nathan Glazer, "Blacks and Ethnic Groups: The Difference and the Political Difference it Makes," *Social Problems*, vol. 18 (Spring 1971), pp. 444–61.

[5] Richard Hamilton, "Liberal Intelligentsia and White Backlash," *Dissent*, Winter 1972, pp. 225–32; "The Marginal Middle Class: A Reconsideration," *American Sociological Review*, vol. 31 (April 1966), pp. 192–99.

[6] Irving Tallman and Ramona Morgnes, "Life Style Differences among Urban and Suburban Blue Collar Families," *Social Problems*, vol. 49 (March 1970), pp. 334–48.

[7] Daniel N. Gordon, "Immigrants and Munipical Voting Turnout: Implications for Changing Ethnic Inpact on Urban Politics," *American Sociological Review*, vol. 35 (August 1970), pp. 665–81.

because these did not seem to have a priority claim for attention and partly because they appeared inimical to the progress of racial minorities. Now that there also appears to be a need to reach white ethnics, professionals find themselves isolated—without points of contact. The change agent is handicapped additionally because these communities are often tight ethnic enclaves which are resistant to outside influence and possess unique cultural forms with which he may not be familiar. One suggestion is that practitioners entering such communities should work through and seek sanctions from dominant local institutions such as churches, political clubs, and unions.[8] It is clear that outsiders need to show respect for local norms and that appeals must acknowledge white-ethnic regard for the solidarity of the family, neighborhood stability, mutual aid, and sympathy with the underdog. Typical liberal language conveying abstract ideas and lofty morality is likely to be perceived as foreign and threatening.

This combination of strategy and organizing tactics should be evaluated in terms of its potential effectiveness in reaching and motivating middle Americans. What do the research studies suggest in this connection? Further, what are the consequences likely to be with respect to the position of racially oppressed minorities, both in the short run and in the long run? Should we opt for an alternative strategy geared to increasing the power and resources of racial minorities in preparation for the eventual clash with white ethnics prognosticated by Boggs? How do these approaches square with Tyler's analysis, which asserts that the real villain is the system as a whole? Can locality-based organizing efforts impact national policy and affect structural aspects of economic inequality? If not, what options exist?

---

[8] Charles F. Grosser, "Organizing the White Community," *Social Work*, vol. 16 (July 1971), pp. 25–31.

B. Theoretical and philosophical considerations

JAMES BOGGS

A black view of the white worker

In my book *The American Revolution* I traced the decline of organized labor in the United States from a *movement* (which once launched the social productive forces of this highly advanced society onto the road of control of production) to a *bureaucracy* that does not move today except in support of the Establishment. Its relationship to the Establishment in every sphere—industrial, political and military—is that of a force that accepts the American capitalist system as the best in the world and only wants it reformed and refined a little to give workers a bigger share of the pie.

When we speak of the labor movement in the United States, it is necessary to remember that we are talking primarily of a Northern movement. Organized labor never really could or would tackle the question of the division of labor in the South between whites and blacks. Only in the mines and mills, where the ethnic structure was already firmly entrenched, did labor organize in the South.

Until World War II the industrial work force of the United States consisted chiefly of immigrants from Europe who had come to this country to escape regimented and impoverished lives and who had a vision of the United States as a land where one could rise from rags to riches in a few years. With this view of the land to which they were coming, it was only natural that these workers accepted the attitude toward black people held by the whites already here. It is true that these workers waged many militant struggles against the American capitalists, but these struggles were always limited by the workers' acceptance of racist policies by which the blacks were kept beneath them and by the fact that they themselves were willing to keep the blacks down as a basis for their own elevation.

In the early days of the civil rights movement, labor, especially its national leadership and the CIO wing, fought for legislation against

Source: Reprinted from *The White Majority: Between Poverty and Affluence* (New York: Vintage Books, 1970), pp. 103–10.

From *New Generation* magazine, Vol. 51, No. 2. By permission of the National Committee on Employment of Youth of the National Child Labor Committee.

both the poll tax and lynching. Since such legislation had little concrete meaning for rank-and-file Northern workers, they supported these activities passively and without protest. In the early days of the King movement in the South, local unions even sent donations to the civil rights cause, usually under the influence of the few socially conscious radicals who still remained in or around the unions, having weathered the McCarthy witch hunts that virtually purged the labor movement of those with any serious social consciousness.

I am not suggesting that the labor organizations would have been very much different if the socially conscious radicals had not been purged, for not even these radicals ever seriously dreamed of blacks becoming a social force in this country that would be demanding social changes far beyond labor's wildest dreams.

In *The American Revolution* I said that *if* it had been possible, around 1948, to incorporate the black work force into production, and into the labor movement, then it might have been possible to visualize the integration of the races in the United States. That was speculation. What has happened is that blacks themselves have begun to struggle outside the labor apparatus and in so doing have put severe tests and strain on the labor unions.

For when blacks demanded equal job opportunities, the unions replied that, although they were on record as favoring such opportunities, only management and the government had the power to provide jobs. They preferred to shift the responsibility for stimulating jobs, even make-believe ones like the WPA jobs of the thirties, to government, because, as long as it was government's responsibility, the unions would not have to confront their predominantly white memberships on this question. The unions obviously were not prepared to suggest that white workers give up their jobs to blacks. The alternative was to suggest that all suffer together and thus find a basis for struggling together. A few black workers in the labor organizations suggested this, but received no support from the labor leadership. Instead, the leadership evaded the issue and thus allowed the wrath and fears of the white workers to simmer and increase as blacks pressed their demands for equal job opportunities.

Older black workers inside the union tended to become complacent and even now are not a serious factor either inside the labor organizations or in the black movement. They can best be described as conservative, while the older white workers must be characterized as reactionary.

Actually, it is putting it mildly to call white workers reactionary. The AFL is dominated by the skilled trades—construction workers, carpenters, brickmasons, electricians, sheet-metal workers, ironworkers, painters—who for the most part are arrogantly hostile to black workers. The

AFL leadership is comfortable with the counterrevolution at home and abroad. Merely supporting the foreign policy of the United States is not enough for it; it screams for more extreme counterrevolutionary measures. It is not only anticommunist but profascist. AFL workers, spurred on by their leaders and spurring on their leaders, have become the staunchest supporters of the Vietnam war and the most militant enemies of protesting students and pacifists.

The leaders of UAW and CIO unions are little better. Far from guiding their membership in a struggle *against* the war in Vietnam most have encouraged support of the war. The main difference is that the UAW-CIO unions attempt to maintain a liberal image through association with allegedly liberal politicians.

Except where questions of higher pay are involved, the rank-and-file white worker in the United States is more conservative than most politicians and industrialists in relation to the black movement. Many industrialists and politicians see the need to make concessions to blacks for the sake of social peace, at home and abroad. But the average white worker only sees the black movement as a direct threat to himself and his own position and privileges.

Fascism in the United States is unique because it is developing from the grass roots rather than from the top down. Today such organizations as the Minutemen, the White Citizens Council, the America Firsters and scores of others that have been organized to defend the United States against black demands for justice are made up of workers, skilled and unskilled. These workers are the ones who work with blacks inside the shop during the day and then return to their homes in the suburbs at night to organize against the same blacks. Sometimes they will confide in some black worker with whom they have worked for many years that their hostility is not against him but against those "jitterbugs" and "guerrillas" in the black ghetto. They are completely insensitive to the fact that the black jitterbugs and guerrillas to whom they refer are the sons of the black workers in whom they are confiding. They don't seem to care that their unconcealed antagonism is educating even some of the older, passive blacks into more militant positions.

White workers tend to see blacks as threatening their jobs when in fact their jobs are being threatened by automation and cybernation. Instead of accepting the technical progress of automation and using it as a basis to demand the right to a decent livelihood for everyone, working or not, they have chosen the road of fighting blacks not only on the job market but even in other arenas involving the black community, such as schools and police, where white workers are not directly threatened. Often afraid to confront blacks at the point of production, they organize outside the plant with the aim of inflaming not only white workers but other groups in the white population not engaged in the process of production. Thus, side by side with the development of the black revolutionary forces are growing the counterrevolutionary forces of white workers.

Today, when the police force of every major city is actually an occupation army for black people, white workers have become the chief supporters of the "Support Your Local Police" movement. Wherever you find a community consciously excluding blacks on the basis of race, it turns out to be a community of workers. (Bourgeois communities exclude blacks on the basis of economics.) In every major urban center there is a suburb notorious for its exclusion of blacks. In Detroit it is Dearborn, which is composed mainly of Polish workers who fled from Hamtramck, which is inside the Detroit city limits and was once the largest Polish settlement outside of Warsaw. Dearborn's residents are refugees from a Hamtramck encircled by blacks. Dearborn's mayor is elected year after year on the slogan "Keep Dearborn Clean"—meaning, of course, clean from black people. Chicago has Cicero, where Italian workers keep the neighborhoods "clean." Cleveland has a Slavic section and an Italian section, both of which mobilize periodically for pitched battles with blacks. These two ethnic groups stand out, but they only express more dramatically what is deeply embedded in every ethnic grouping of the white working class.

"White working class" does not have the same meaning in the United States as in the classical European interpretation, because white workers, by the very nature of the country's historical development, are in a class above all blacks. "The worker" (i.e., the white worker) supports the system precisely because it has provided him with this superior position even when he is worse off economically than some blacks.

Of all the classes in the United States the worker feels most threatened by the blacks. Today the worst thing that could happen in this country would be the arming of these workers. In fact, fascist tendencies are growing so rapidly among them and they are already arming themselves at such a rapid rate that even the power structure is deeply disturbed, fearful that white workers will turn on it if it makes any concessions to the black movement. At this stage, however, these workers are content to vent their hate and frustration on the blacks. Wherever possible, these workers join the special forces that have been set up by the police or by city administrations to assist in time of emergency in putting the blacks back in their place.

Blacks in the United States have long since bypassed the labor organizations. No one knows this better than the labor leaders themselves, who cannot relate to the young blacks either inside or outside the labor force and find the few old blacks whom they have incorporated into their political machines of little use in trying to relate to young blacks. Younger blacks are extremely sensitive to the antagonism of white workers and cannot distinguish them from oppressors. Already in Detroit, home of the UAW and of the late Walter Reuther, labor's most progressive spokesman, young black workers are rallying to DRUM (Dodge Revolutionary Union Movement). DRUM is made up of young black production workers who have now organized local groups inside the Ford and General Motors plants after a series of successful wildcat strikes at the Chrysler Hamtramck plant. These black workers represent the new street force whose allegiance is to the black community, not to labor. Unlike the older black workers who were grateful for any job, these younger men believe that their confinement to the old back-breaking jobs on the production line is strictly a manifestation of the racism in American society. From their point of view, these jobs, no matter how much they pay, are no better than the field-hand jobs their slave forefathers were forced to perform in the South. What the union and an older generation of workers accept as the company's prerogative, these young blacks challenge. To them, the statement that the "company has the sole right to run the plant as it sees fit" expresses not a truth but a popular prejudice.

The demands and the expectations of these young black workers far exceed the wildest dreams of the labor movement and of earlier generations of workers even in their most militant days. The white workers who monopolize the skilled jobs—plumbers, electricians, tool-and-die men, machine repairmen—think only in terms of more money per hour. The DRUM member, at the bottom of the production ladder, demands the hiring of black plant doctors, fifty black foremen and even a black chairman for the board of directors. He is not satisfied with any old job; he wants control of the plant itself.

Inside the plant, white workers are being shaken up, not just by these demands but by the fact that older black workers who once seemed so docile are becoming increasingly sympathetic and even supportive of the young blacks, thus threatening the peaceful coexistence between white and black inside the plant that was once so comforting to the white workers.

Since white racism is expressing itself at the present time most clearly inside the white work force, and since black power is regarded by the white worker as the main threat to his hard-won comforts, a clash is inevitable. This clash is being staved off today only because the military forces of this country, whether in the form of the police, the National Guard, state troopers or the United States Army, have made it clear that they will be employed to crush the blacks. Thus reassured, the unofficial white forces have not felt it necessary to rush into the ghetto.

The inevitable clash cannot be averted by the labor leaders. In fact, labor leaders are irrelevant to it. They have waited too long to intervene. For too many years they have allowed white workers to go their merry and not-so-merry way, joining and supporting the system until their policies have become indistinguishable from the racist policies of the system and are in fact the system's main prop.

In the United States the alienation of man from man started long before the alienation of man from production. It is from this alienation that blacks and whites of the lowest strata of the society will bleed the most.

GUS TYLER

White worker/Blue mood

"It's us they is always chokin' so that the rich folks can stay fat."
—A 28-year-old Kentucky miner on the [wage and price] "freeze."
New York Times, September 24, 1971

What are the facts about the American workers—especially white workers? Of the 77.902 million gainfully employed in 1969, 28.237 million wore blue collars; that is, 36 percent. But others might as well have worn that collar. Of the 36.844 million "white-collar" workers, about 18 million were in clerical and sales—an added 22 percent of the employed.

TABLE 1

Breakdown of employed persons age 16 and over by occupation and color (in thousands)

	White	Nonwhite
Blue Collar	24,647	3,591
Service	7,289	2,239
Clerical	12,314	1,083
Sales	4,527	166
Professional-technical	10,074	695
Manager, officials	7,733	254
Proprietors, farmers	2,935	356
Total	69,519	8,384

In addition, there were another 9.528 million engaged in service trades —a category that earned less than the blue-collar, clerical, or sales people. The total in all these blue and bluish jobs comes to 69 percent of the employed.

Who, beside farm workers, is not included? There is the class listed as professional, technical, managerial, as officials and proprietors, who make up about a quarter of the employed. Despite their lofty titles millions of these are just plain, worried workers. Consider that Italian "professional" who teaches in Franklin K. Lane High School or that Jewish "proprietor" who owns a candy store in Harlem.

The white worker is currently called "middle American," a description that evokes the image of a man and his family at the center of American affluence. But what is the reality?

The white worker is not affluent—not even near-affluent. The median

Source: *Dissent,* vol. 19 (Winter 1972), pp. 190–96.

family income in 1968 (pre-Nixon) was $8,632, about $1,000 short of what the Bureau of Labor Statistics calls a "modest but adequate" income. That this median family cannot meet the American standard of living refutes the mischievous myth that poor means black, and white means affluent. The myth is mischievous because it turns an ethnic difference into a class struggle and implies—and sometimes states—that the way to end poverty is simply to end racism. This myth, as that of "the vanishing American worker," is based upon a truth that when exaggerated becomes an untruth.

While it is true that a much higher percentage of nonwhites than whites is officially poor, it is equally true that in 1968 two-thirds of the poor were white. Nor is this white poverty limited to Appalachia.

TABLE 2

Percentage of the total employed in various categories of white labor

	White Percentage of Total Employed of All Races
Blue Collar	32%
Service	9.3
Clerical	16
Sales	6
Professional-technical	13
Managers, officials	10
Proprietors, farmers	1.7
Total	88%

Note: Whites, then, make up 88 percent of the employed; nonwhites 12 percent. Of the whites, the categories that compose the blue-mooded (exclude farmers and include about half of those in the professional, proprietor, etc., category) make up about 75 percent of the employed.

Our latest report on who is poor (March 1970) reveals that of the 5.047 million U.S. families listed as living in poverty, 1.363 million or 25 percent are black: only one out of four poor families is black. In the metropolitan areas of America, in 1968, there were 2.477 million poor families of which 777,000 were black: less than one-third. In the central cities of these metropoles, there were 748,000 poor families, of which 358,000 were black: less than half.

The poor are not mainly the unemployed. One-third of the family heads listed as officially poor work full weeks at least 50 weeks a year. Others work part years. Most of the poor have jobs—and are white.

While families with incomes under $3,000 are officially poor, those with incomes above $3,000 are not all rich. Twelve percent of the families in America have an income between $3,000 and $5,000. (A recent Labor Department study found that an urban family of four needed at least $5,895 a year to meet its basic needs. If $6,000 a year were used as a cut-off poverty line, then 29.3 percent of the families in America are living in poverty.) A high 52 percent of the families had an income of less than $9,000 a year—a figure still below the official "modest but adequate" income. Seventy-two percent of the families have an income below $12,000 a year—a sum just above what the BLS considers adequate for a family of four in New York City. In round figures, about three out of four families struggle along.

If so many Americans are nonaffluent, who gets the money in this affluent society? Here are some facts on income distribution.

In 1968, the bottom fifth of the nation's families received 5.7 percent of the country's income; the top fifth received 40.6 percent. The middle three-fifths were bunched between 12 and 23 percent. These figures, from the U.S. Department of Commerce publication *Consumer Income* (December 1969), actually understate the great gap between top and bottom. In calculating income, the Department of Commerce excludes "money received from the sale of property, such as stocks, bonds, a house, or a car . . . gifts . . . and lump sum inheritances or insurance payments." If these items were included, the income of the top fifth would be appreciably increased—and, by the inclusion of these receipts in the total calculation of income, the percentage of income of the other fifths would be automatically decreased.

Between 1947 and 1967, income shares did not change. The bottom moved from 5 percent to 5.4 percent; the top from 43 percent to 41.2 percent. The change is negligible—and, after allowance for other receipts not counted as income, we find that there has been no meaningful redistribution of income in the quarter-century since the end of World War II.

This iron law of maldistribution applies not only to the nation as a whole but also to the nonwhite families of America, which darkly mirror the class structure of the mother culture. Among nonwhite families, in 1968 the lowest fifth got 4.8 percent of the income and the top fifth 43.6 percent; in 1947, the lowest fifth got 4.3 percent and the highest 45.7 percent. In sum, whether we look at white or dark America, in 1947 or 1968, the maldistribution remains almost constant—an economic fact regardless of race, creed, etc.

Recently, a young man at Harvard undertook a study of income distribution reaching all the way back to 1910. Although his findings may be subject to some refinement, his rough conclusions—reached after more than casual digging—tell us a bit more about the rigidities of our class structure. In 1910, he finds, the lowest tenth received 3.5 percent of the income; in 1961, it received a mere 1 percent. The bottom tenth got a smaller share of the GNP in 1961 than it did in 1910. In 1910, the top tenth received 33.9 percent of the income; in 1961, it received 30 percent. The table below records the economic truism that the more times change the more they remain the same.

In a recent study by Herman P. Miller and Roger A. Herriott, in which they recalculated income to include some of the factors excluded from the Commerce Department reports, they found that in 1968 the top 1.4 percent of families and individuals drew 11 percent of the nation's income, while the bottom 16 percent drew only 2 percent and the next-from-the-bottom 18 percent drew only 7 percent of the national income. In sum, a top 1.4 percent drew more than the bottom 34 percent.

TABLE 3

Percentage of national personal income, before taxes, received by each income-tenth

	Highest Tenth	2nd	3rd	4th	5th	6th	7th	8th	9th	Lowest Tenth
1910...............	33.9	12.3	10.2	8.8	8.0	7.0	6.0	5.5	4.9	3.4
1960...............	28.0	16.0	13.0	11.0	9.0	8.0	6.0	5.0	3.0	1.0

Note: In terms of "recipients" for 1910–37 and "spending units" for 1941–59. Data for 1960–61 were available in rounded form only. Figures for 1910 were taken from National Industrial Conference Board *Studies in Enterprise and Social Progress* (New York: National Industrial Conference Board, 1939), p. 125; data for 1960–61 were calculated by the Survey Research Center.

This maldistribution of income is repeated in a maldistribution of wealth (ownership) which is the major cause of our economic inequities. A study by Robert Lampman points out that although there was less concentration of wealth in the period after World War II than after World War I, a creeping concentration began to set in after 1949. That year, the top 1 percent held 21 percent of the wealth. In 1956, this rose to 26 percent—by 1962, to 33.3 percent. (Data are drawn from statistics provided by the Internal Revenue Service, based on estate tax returns that offer loopholes for the most affluent. It is therefore not unreasonable to conclude that all of these figures understate the true concentration of wealth in America.) By 1970, if this trend has continued, we were back to 1929, when the top 1 percent held 36.3 percent of the nation's wealth.

If, however, the maldistribution of income is an inequity of ancient origin, whose persistence we have noted for this whole century, why is the white worker turning restless at this particular moment? The reasons: (1) a quantitative erosion of income, (2) a qualitative erosion of living, (3) a frightening erosion of social order.

Although not living in affluence, the white worker was better off in the '60s than at any other time of this century. In the recovery years following the Great Depression of the early 1930s, he and his family were enjoying an ever-rising standard of living. In 1947, the median family income (in constant 1968 dollars) was $4,716; by 1967, it rose to $8,318, an increase of about $4,000—after allowing for inflation.

During the same period, the percentage of families making under $7,000 a year decreased and the percentage making more increased sharply—again in constant dollars. In 1947, 75 percent of the families had an income of less than $7,000, and 25 percent had an income above that figure. In 1967, on the contrary, 63 percent of the families had an income above $7,000 and only 36 percent had an income below that figure.

All this was happening, however, without any basic redistribution of income in America. Per capita income was growing because the total national income was growing at a rate faster than that of the population. There was more available for everybody.

The rise in income was reflected in a lifestyle based on rising expectations. You mortgaged your life for a home, because you expected to earn more in the days to come. You bought on the installment plan, everything from baby carriage to auto. You planned a future for your kids: a nice neighborhood, a good school, a savings plan to put the kids through one of the better colleges—maybe even Harvard or Vassar. You were out to "make it," no matter how hard you worked, how much you scrimped, how often you borrowed, how late you moonlighted. You had hope!

You didn't even mind paying ever-higher taxes, so long as your take-home pay was bigger. The tax was an investment in the future—a town or a country where things would be better. You would enjoy it tomorrow, and the kids would enjoy it for generations. You were future-minded.

As a result, this numerous class became the mass base of social stability in America. It was not status quo-ish in the sense that it would be happy to have its present frozen forever; it was constantly pushing for change. But it sought change within a system that it felt was yielding more and could continue to yield more. And to keep moving, this class joined unions for economic advance and voted Democratic for socio-economic legislation.

Sometime in the mid-60s, however, this social structure began to fall apart. Almost unnoticed by the media was the decline in the real income of the nonsupervisory employee. Between 1965 and 1969, the buying power of the worker was in steady decline—despite wage increases. Pay envelopes were chewed up by inflation and taxation.

The year 1965 was the first of the escalated involvement in Vietnam, and this imposed a triple burden on the American worker. First, he had to pay a greater tax to help finance the war. Second, he had to pay more for consumer goods because this war, like any other, automatically increases demand without increasing supply. Third, he supplied his sons for the military; the affluent found ways to escape in schools and special occupations, the poor were often too ill or illiterate.

The year 1965 is also the mid-point of a decade in which America began to respond to poverty and discrimination. The Johnson years produced a spate of national legislation to provide income and opportunities for the poor, especially the blacks. Local governments were trying to cope with their crises. At all levels, America began to spend public money to resolve pressing problems.

The American worker supported these social measures, through the unions and the Democratic party. He saw these bits and pieces of socioeconomic legislation as a spur and parallel to his upward effort.

It was not apparent to this same worker that the upside-down system of taxation in the United States placed the cost of these measures on the shoulders of the huge "middle" sector—the sector neither poor nor rich enough to escape taxes. Although the federal income tax supposedly is graduated so as to make the wealthy pay at a higher rate, this expressed intent is annulled by the many loopholes for those who derive income from sources other than wages or salaries. At the local level, it is the small homeowner who pays the tariff through *ad valorem* property taxes and the small consumer who pays through the nose for city, county, and state sales taxes.

The worker feels that he is paying triple: he pays for his own way; he pays for the poor; he pays for the rich. He is ready to do the first; he resists the others.

Finally, this same worker has been squeezed by a system of private taxation, operated through monopoly pricing. Everything from electricity to eggs is manipulated in closed and increasingly enclosed markets. As buying power goes up (current dollars in income), the response of dominant sectors of the economy is not to *increase* supply but to *limit* production (or distribution) to keep the consumer on the same level while increasing profits for the seller.

To add insult to injury, the worker is advised by the media and, more recently, by the Administration, that if prices are going up, it is his own fault: high wages make high prices. If he wants to buy for less, he must work for less. This logic boggles the worker who cannot understand how he can live better by earning less. Once more, he is the victim of a myth. The truth was stated in an editorial by the sober *Wall Street Journal* on August 5, 1968:

> In the past 20 years, there have been three distinct periods in which factory prices climbed substantially over a prolonged interval. In each in-

stance, labor costs per unit of factory output were *declining* when the price climb began—and these costs continued to decline for a considerable period after the price rise was underway. In each case, corporate profits began to increase sharply well before the price climb started.

To keep up with rising prices, workers demand higher wages and salaries—through unions and as individuals. But they never catch up, for in a monopoly-oligopoly conglomerate economy, the man who can fix the prices must always end up winning the game.

The result is that millions of workers feel they are paying more and more for less and less. They are paying for a war—with their sons, their taxes, and their overcharged purchases—only to feel they are losing the war. They are paying more for what they buy—and get more cars doomed for early obsolescence, phones that ring wrong numbers, homes that are jerry-built, doctors who make no home visits. They pay more and more in local taxes—and feel they are subsidizing crime and riot.

Hard work seems to have brought nothing but hard times. After federal taxes are taken out of the pay, after local taxes are paid, and then the rest is used to buy debased goods and services at inflated prices, the worker knows—and his wife knows still better—that he is no longer moving up.

The worker in urban America, however, is the victim not only of income maldistribution—but also of population maldistribution, which is a catastrophe whose impact he cannot stand and whose origin he does not understand. Few city dwellers even suspect that much of their urban crisis started down on the farm.

Since World War II, about a million Americans a year have moved from a rural to an urban culture. This massive shift of about 20 million people in one generation has been described as the most gigantic migration in the history of man. Such a collision of cultures has always meant crowding, crime, and conflict. In the 1960s, history repeated itself— except that the immigrant was invisible because he was an in-migrant.

What set this wave in motion? Two contradictory national policies: to increase agricultural productivity and to restrict its production. Subsidized science found ways to make four stalks grow where one grew before. Subsidies to farmers, then, reversed the process by rewarding growers for nonproduction. The result was less and less need for labor on the soil. Farm workers went jobless; small farm owners went bankrupt or were bought out. Rural Americans were driven from their familiar farms into the unfamiliar cities, from warm earth to cold concrete.

This rural-push–urban-pull has been in motion ever since the turn of the century. But what was once a drift became a flood in the 1960s. The discomfort and disorder that followed set another dynamic in motion: the urban-push–suburban-pull.

If the worker can afford it, he generally flees—to outskirts and suburbs. He does so whether he is black or white. (Between 1964 and 1969, 600,000 blacks fled the central cities for other parts of the metropolitan areas.) Those who cannot flee, stay and get ready for the fight.

A current notion holds that the central cities are black and the suburbs white, dividing metros into separate but unequal societies in geographic separation. Again this is a half-truth which, if it were totally true, might well lessen social conflict. But the truth is that many whites cannot move, because they cannot afford to. Typically, they are white workers of more recent stock; economically unmonied and geographically immobile. Often, their neighborhoods abut black ghettos where—after the flight of the more affluent blacks—there are left, according to James Q. Wilson, "only the most deprived, the least mobile, and the most pathological."

Through the '60s, the crush became a crunch—not simply because there were more bodies in the central cities but also because there were fewer places to put them. By public action, we have torn down about twice as many housing units as we have put up. Private builders have bulldozed slums to erect luxury highrisers. Hundreds of thousands of units are abandoned annually by their landlords, because the rotting property is all pain and no profit. As decay sets in at the ghetto core, rats and rain and fleas and fire take over to deprive the most deprived of their turf. So these newly dispossessed become the latest in-migrants, driven from their holes into the surrounding neighborhoods, spreading panic in their path.

Under these pressures, the ethnics—white and black—move from economic frustration and personal fear to political fury. The physical stage on which this tragedy is unfolding is a tiny piece of turf. Now 70 percent of the people—our urban population—live on 1.6 percent of the total land area. The American worker—white or black—is the victim of maldistribution—of people as well as income and wealth.

In the 1970s fury comes easily to the white worker. It's stylish. He sees it everywhere. In the form of common crime—in the subway, on the street, at his doorstop; in the form of riots in the ghettos or the campus or the prison. The present generation of workers has grown up in an age of war: World War II, Korea, Vietnam. For three decades, they have lived with mass violence, directly and vicariously.

Retribalization reawakens ancient feelings. The white worker has always had the sense of belonging to some special group. There were constant reminders of ethnicity in neighborhood names, groceries, bars, funeral parlors, holidays, papers, ward politics, gang leaders, subtle prides and prejudices. But in an America that was devoted to the mythos of the melting pot and in a period dedicated to the ethos of one world, the white worker tucked his ethnicity up his sleeve. Now, in a retribalized world, he displays his ethnicity—as a pennant to carry into battle.

The young among the white workers, like the young everywhere, add their special stridency to the clamor. They are high on expectations and low on boiling point. To a civilizational distemper, they add their hot tempers, turning ethnic salvation into a moral justification for violence.

Our white worker is ready for battle. But he does not quite know against whom to declare war.

As a child of toilers he holds the traditional view of those who labor about those who don't. He feels that those inflated prices, those high taxes, those inadequate wages are all part of a schema for fattening up the fat. While he rarely, if ever, uses the words "establishment" or "system," he instinctively assumes there's an establishment that exploits him through a devilishly devised system.

Part of the system, his experience teaches, is for the rich to use the poorest to keep the once-poor and the possibly-poor as poor as possible. For generations, employers who demanded protection against foreign imports were importing foreigners to depress wages and break strikes. Out of this arose the Know-Nothing party that threatened, within a couple of years, to become a major national movement. In the mid-19th century, Irish workers (themselves recent immigrants) feared that the Emancipation Proclamation, ending chattel slavery for the blacks, would intensify wage slavery for the whites. Out of this fear rose the sadistic Draft Riot of 1863 with its lynching and burning of blacks. In the 1920s, the white worker opted for immigration legislation to stem the flow of cheap hands.

As we move into the '70s, many workers fear that the Brass is using Underclass to undermine the Working Class. They seldom use this language, but often feel these sentiments. As they hear it, this is what the rich are saying: "We must fight poverty and discrimination to the last drop of *your* blood. Share *your* job; share *your* neighborhood; pay *your* taxes." These moral exhortations come from the high and mighty, economically ensconced in tax havens far from the madding crowd.

In protest against this establishment, the worker turns to strikes for higher wages and revolt against taxes. But neither remedy works. Wage gains are offset by higher prices. Lower taxes mean lower services—schools, streets, travel, sanitation, police, medical care. What looked like a direct way out turns out to be a maze.

Since our worker does not know how to deal with the system, he tries to do the next best thing: to act within the system to protect his own skin. And in our torn and turbulent cities, it is too often his "skin" that determines his mood.

This mood is generally called "backlash," a reawakening of ancient prejudice directed against blacks because they have dared to raise their heads and voices. But to explain the growing tension simply as "backlash" is once more to create a mischievous myth out of partial truth. To deny that prejudice exists is naive; to ascribe rising racial clash to a simple proliferation of prejudice, equally naive. The white worker feels economically threatened, personally imperiled, politically suckered. His anxieties make him meaner than he means to be. Racial suspicion turns into tribal war when people—no matter their color—are oppressed by their circumstances. Maldistribution of income and people must multiply strife. This strife, ironically, tends not to change but to continue the system that produced the conflict. So long as black battles white and poor battle not-so-poor, the establishment can continue to "divide and rule."

The further irony is the innocence of those on top who are, in a depersonalized way, responsible for the turmoil on the shrinking turf. The upper 1 percent rarely suspects that its incredible wealth is the prime reason the lesser people, without urging, are at one another's throats. As the wealthiest see their role, they are the great creators: investing, employing, making. They are the great givers, turning tax exempt funds to do God's work.

In short, there is no devil: those at the top merely move their money around in a depersonalized way through impersonal channels (corporations) to multiply their money so they may do man's and God's work better; those in the middle merely try to lift their real income so they and their family can live—better; those at the bottom merely want what man needs to stay alive and kicking. Yet somehow they all end up in a fight, with the top acting genteelly through finances, and the lesser people resorting intemperately to fists.

If there is a devil, he is—as he always is—invisible, ubiquitous, and working his evil will through the way of all flesh. In our case, he is the inherent imperative in a culture that has badly distributed its wealth and people: the devil still is the system.

C. Factual and research considerations

JOHN M. GOERING

The emergence of ethnic interests: A case of serendipity

This study reports the findings of a study of the emergence of ethnic interests among a sample of 100 Irish and Italians. The failure to find predicted relationships among scale items for a proposed scale of ethnic consciousness led to a consideration of "law" of third-generation return. The reemergence of ethnicity as a salient force in the lives of third-generation ethnics was associated with little organizational activity but significant questioning about the reality of the "American dream" and opposition to the demands of Negroes for equal rights. The declining importance of objective ethnic constraints does not then necessarily imply total assimilation but rather serves as a condition for the emergence, however episodically, of ethnic consciousness.

Contrary to all predictions ethnic interests persist, and to some even appear to have increased in salience (Bernard, 1969; Cinel, 1969; Glazer and Moynihan, 1963; Goldstein and Goldscheider, 1968; Greeley, 1969; Vecoli, 1970; Zochert, 1969). Little is known, however, about the conditions for this persistence while even less is known about the corollary problem of the measurement of ethnic consciousness. This paper relates an attempt to develop a scale for measuring ethnic interests and consciousness with serendipitous attention focused on the notion of "third-generation return."

ETHNICITY: RACE, RELIGION, OR NATIONAL ORIGIN

In the literature in the field of ethnic studies there appear to be two critical distinctions or criticisms which help formulate the basis for developing a scale of ethnic consciousness. The first is the distinction between ethnicity as a descriptive, categoric fact of birthplace, and ethnicity as a subjective property (Wirth, 1964:245–246). Ethnic studies

Note: This study was partly financed by a grant from the National Science Foundation. I wish to thank Joseph A. Kahl for providing valuable criticism of an earlier draft of this paper.
Source: *Social Forces,* vol. 49 (March 1971), pp. 379–84.

have generally been descriptive, with a picture given of the historical movements and events in the lives of one or several nationality groups. The subject to be studied is people of foreign birth; the method of study is an elaborate use of letters, documents, biographies, and personal "understandings." It has recently, however, become increasingly clear that the attribute of national ancestry is only an approximate corollary of social generational changes and the variations in response to opportunity and discrimination. The fact of being Polish or Italian is only part of the collective experiences which condition, in an indeterminate way, various relationships, aspirations, and attitudes. A feeling of both belongingness and rejection becomes both the basis for distinguishing kinds of ethnic identification and the basis for the persistence of ethnicity in American life. This subjective property becomes the basis for the scaling of ethnic consciousness.

A second difficulty is that there is a substantial sphere of interaction between religious and ethnic behavior and belief. It has, in fact, been common for the term "ethnic" to be used to refer to all differences in race, religion, and national origin (Bloom, 1948:171; Glaser, 1958:31; Gordon, 1964:27; Hatt, 1948:36). An example of the overlapping of these referents for ethnicity is in research on the law of third-generation return. This hypothesis about the rise of ethnic interests has generally been studied in terms of changing patterns of religious behavior (Lazerwitz and Rowitz, 1964; Russo, 1969). The result has been that ethnic interests are seen only ambiguously and with a certain amount of confusion (Bender and Kagiwada, 1968:367). It is clearly necessary to separate out the effect of the rise and fall of religious interests from the persistence of ethnic interests.

The basic issue to be discussed will be the problems involved in measuring or scaling ethnic consciousness, while at the same time controlling for religious differences. The study attempts to be an honest reflection of some of the complexities and frustrations of measuring a variable-ethnicity independent of social class pressures, generational changes, and religion. It is clearly only an initial attempt.

METHODOLOGY

The present study is based on interviews with 100 Irish and Italian Catholics living in Providence, Rhode Island. Equal numbers of Irish and Italians were interviewed. Members of ethnic groups from the same religious denomination were selected in order to partly control for the effects of religion on ethnic attitudes and interests. Respondents were selected in a multistage sampling design utilizing census tract information and city directory householder lists. Census tracts with the highest proportions of Irish and Italians were selected from various areas of the city. A systematic sample of names and addresses of ethnic families was drawn from the household section of *Polk's Providence City Directory*. Names with unclear ethnicity were not used. To determine whether the ethnic groups in the city might have undergone a significant number of name changes, thus invalidating the directory lists, all legal name changes recorded in the Probate Court of the City of Providence were checked for the years 1930, 1940, 1950, and 1960. The information on Italian and Irish name changes show that there has never been a significant number of name changes among these groups, and that the number of such changes has not noticeably increased in the thirty-year period. The average number of name changes was only 15 per year and in no year did the number exceed 30. Interviewing was completed in the spring of 1966 with a refusal rate of approximately 17 percent.

PRELIMINARY MEASUREMENT AND FINDINGS

Part of the difficulty in formulating a scale of ethnic consciousness is related to the paucity of research on the types and sources of variation among individuals within any given ethnic group. Rather than ask the somewhat historical question of how one ethnic group differs from another, the logic of scaling would emphasize within-group variations in the quality of group life identified as ethnicity. Ethnic consciousness is clearly not something that is inborn but rather a constituent of many levels of identification and feeling. Operationalizing proposed levels of ethnic consciousness, however, revealed problems that were both unexpected and frustrating. The intention to create a scale of ethnic consciousness was frustrated along several lines. A somewhat chronological listing of the difficulties encountered in the attempt to scale available data will indicate the inherent difficulties in scaling ethnicity as well as the manner in which the research findings influenced reconceptualization.

The first attempt at operationalization led to a distinction between three components of ethnic consciousness. The first element or subtype related to the extent to which ethnic differences were seen or recognized by the individual. Was there a simple awareness of one's own and other ethnic groups within the life of the local community? The second aspect of the proposed scale included identification and interaction with one's ethnic group. Lastly, there would be potential conflict in which there was a clearly defined ethnic "enemy." This last aspect would explore the potential for intergroup conflict and ethnic violence.

These three dimensions seemed to represent logical divisions of the manner in which individuals could be attached to their own ethnic group. At one end of this scale would be those individuals who were aware of the ethnic factor but who had no attachment to it or involvement with its goals. At the other end would be the ethnic militant engaged in organized struggles for his group. Thus, if an individual identified with his group, he could also be expected to show some awareness of ethnicity. The expectation was that knowledge of the individual's attitude or score on one of these elements would indicate a good deal about his position on the other dimensions.

ETHNIC SCALES AND THIRD-GENERATION RETURN

Under the first component we asked, in open-ended form, about the major splits or divisions that characterized the population of the city. Ethnicity was mentioned as a major source of division by 60 percent of the study population. The Irish, more than the Italians, were aware of this division. It had been hoped that this item would be highly associated with other questions asking about the existence or awareness of ethnicity. There were, however, no statistically significant or meaningful relationships among the items proposed for this dimension of the scale, or between these items and other parts of the scale.[1]

The unanticipated lack of association in the data resulted in two classes of difficulties. The first, and clearest, consequence was the necessity to abandon this dimension of the ethnic scale. The proper questions had not been asked; or else—and this is the second difficulty—the awareness of ethnicity may not be directly associated with other components of ethnic consciousness. That is, it may not, for example, be the outside, *minimal* limit of ethnic consciousness. Awareness of ethnicity may not be simply the first element of ethnic consciousness, but may become manifest at another, later stage or in different contexts. A consideration of one of the more intriguing hypotheses in the field of ethnic studies may shed some light on the full implications of this unanticipated finding.

Marcus Lee Hansen, a social historian, formulated as early as 1938 a notion about the development of ethnic awareness in the third generation. This has become popularized as a "law" of the third generation (Hansen, 1966:263–264):

> Whenever any immigrant group reaches the third-generation stage in its development a spontaneous and almost irresistible impulse arises which forces the thoughts of many people of different professions, different positions in life and different points of view to interest themselves in

---

[1] Contingency coefficients based on the chi-square analysis were used to determine statistical association.

that one factor which they have in common: heritage—the heritage of blood.

Hansen suggests that there will be an irresistible tendency toward an increased awareness of ethnicity with the passage of time. The "thoughts" of the third generation become "interested" in ethnicity.

We find interesting reflections on this hypothesis in our data. The respondents were asked two questions to get at what could be termed "self-rated ethnicity." The first question simply asked, "Do you think of yourself as Irish/Italian?" The second question was more evaluative: "Do you feel that being (Irish/Italian) is important to you?" The data show that those who are either first or second generation are about evenly divided in their response to both questions. Roughly, 50 percent of the ethnic groups studied (Irish and Italians), who are not yet third generation, think of themselves as ethnic and believe it is important. There are no significant differences in the responses of the first two generations to these questions.

For the third generation, however, a curious twist appeared in the data. Those who were themselves, and their fathers, born in the United States, reported the largest agreement with the question as to whether they thought of themselves as ethnic. Almost 70 percent of those in the third generation think of themselves ethnically. This response would, then, lend partial support to Hansen's hypothesis. It also signifies a curious pattern in the continuum of ethnic consciousness. There is greater awareness of ethnicity among those who are further removed from the ghetto.

Ethnic verbalization is clearly not the actual first stage in the formation of ethnic consciousness. One component of ethnic consciousness, the awareness or salience of ethnicity, appears most strongly in the third generation. Just at the point when the influence of ethnicity could be expected to be minimized, this awareness raises its head. Ethnicity is not clearly perceived in the ghetto. The boundaries of the ghetto become the boundaries of the real world. The awareness of ethnicity, and its divisiveness, comes with the "children of the uprooted." All forms of ethnic consciousness are not associated with the ethnic ghetto.

ETHNIC "MILITANCE" OR INTOLERANCE

The attempt to scale the supposed first dimension of ethnicity—verbalization—was frustrated by the discovery of a substantive incongruity. When we attempted to scale what we thought might be the opposite end of the continuum—militance—we encountered an equally difficult set of problems. We discovered, or more appropriately encountered, what we may call an inherent foreshortening of the continuum of ethnic consciousness. One conceptualization of the ideally class-conscious worker would, for example, see him as one who was inextricably and consciously involved in warfare against his enemy—capitalists. Organizational activity would be one sign of this militant posture. It does not seem possible to locate corollary patterns of response for ethnic consciousness. There is no enemy, defined primarily in ethnic terms, against whom it is in one's interest to establish permanent organization.

Several items will give a partial indication of the above. We asked the respondents, for example, if they resented the fact that the Irish or Italians were trying to push in "where they were not wanted." The intention was to ascertain whether there was resentment against other groups' intrusions or activities. Almost 90 percent of the Italians felt that the Irish were not all aggressive; and almost 80 percent of the Irish felt the same way towards the Italians. Neither group was seen to be fighting for a new position, implicitly, for its interests. Another aspect of ethnic militance we hoped to explore was resentment against contact with "outsiders." The ethnic militant would prefer to deal only with those of his kind—analogously, proletarians with proletarians. We asked if the respondents preferred to have people they worked with "to be of the same nationality." Ninety-seven percent replied that it made no difference. When asked if they would prefer to spend their leisure time with a member of their own, rather than another, ethnic group, almost one-fourth of the first generation, but only 7 percent of the third generation felt that this was important. Again, when asked whether they liked or disliked other ethnic groups, almost 40 percent of the first generation expressed dislike, compared to less than 10 percent of the third generation. There is a partial exclusion and dislike of other ethnic groups among those in the first generation. The majority, however, are not willing to admit to hostility or to restricting their choice of association only to those within the pale.

Another potential sign of ethnic militance would be participation in ethnic voluntary organizations. Membership in ethnically oriented clubs would be presumptive evidence of the existence of at least the "technical conditions" of conflict group formation (Dahrendorf, 1959:185). In this connection we asked the respondents whether they belonged to "any clubs, organizations, or special groups of any sort." Only 5 respondents reported membership in an ethnic organization. Neither the Irish nor Italians seek membership in organizations with ethnic purposes or charter. There is, then, only slight evidence of interethnic hostility and organization; whatever exists in the insularity of the ghetto disappears with the assimilation of successive generations.[2]

---

[2] An important root of this assimilation is intermarriage. While only 15 percent of the first generation married outside their own ethnic group, over 63 percent of the third generation married exogenously.

While there is less interethnic hostility with successive generations, ethnicity, nevertheless persists—persists, in part, in the individual's perception of himself as ethnic. The emergence of this form of ethnic consciousness is not, however, as natural a process as Hansen would suppose. One of the conditioning factors for its emergence, as it appears in our data, is a growing skepticism about the principles of the "American dream." The ideology of the ethnic ghetto is both more "American" and tolerant than that of the third generation. For example, in response to the statement, "With few exceptions, most Americans have an equal opportunity to make their way in life," almost 90 percent of the first generation but only roughly 70 percent of the third generation indicated agreement. Again, agreement with the statement that "America may not be perfect, but the American way has brought us as close as human beings can get to a perfect society," was stronger among ghetto residents than among the succeeding generations. The third generation returns to the seclusiveness of ethnicity in resentment against unattained promises. A withdrawal from the principles of a universalistic ideology provides the rationale for a new, more heuristic, creed. The new beliefs of the third generation appear less tolerant than those of the first generation. The first generation are stronger adherents of the principles of equal civil rights. When asked for agreement with the statement that "everyone should have a fair chance of getting the best housing available," 92 percent of the first generation but only 82 percent of the third generation agreed. And when asked to agree or disagree with the idea that "Negroes today are demanding more than they have a right to," roughly 35 percent of the third generation but over 45 percent of the first generation disagreed. Ethnicity persists in a confrontation with Negroes' demands for equality and opportunity, demands which earlier generations took for granted.

CONCLUSIONS AND FUTURE RESEARCH

The declining importance of objective ethnic constraints—foreign birth, ethnic endogamy—does not necessarily imply complete assimilation, but rather operates as a condition for the emergence of more subjective or ideological ethnic interests. A typology of subjective and objective ethnic pressures will help to clarify the dynamics of the re-emergence of ethnicity (see Figure 1). Without subjective awareness, ethnic group members would be without clear programs of goals for assimilation. A manifest level of ethnic concerns—ethnic groups for themselves—has only rarely been found in the United States, and then combined with working-class issues (Adamic, 1931; Bimba, 1932). Manifest ethnic interest groups, when viewed from the perspective of

FIGURE 1

Typology of ethnic interests

Subjective Ethnic Constraints \ Objective Ethnic Constraints	Present	Absent
Present	Ethnic groups for themselves	Emergence of ethnic interests in a "new form"
Absent	Passive or latent ethnic interests	Absorption

our data, would not be truly revolutionary because of the implied acceptance by the immigrant generation of underlying American goals and ideology. Ethnic militance would be organized for improved access to the good life. The absence of objective ethnic pressures is a condition for the third-generation concern with new ethnic interests. These interests, due to an uncertain relationship with objective constraints, will wax and wane depending on circumstances. They may serve both the goals of increased political power or resentment against the incursions of racial minorities. A free-floating resentment can be the basis for a variety of new interest groupings. Total absorption may or may not be the final resting place for the assimilation of ethnic and racial minorities; discussion of this point has and will continue for some time (Eisenstadt, 1954; Glazer, 1954; Gordon, 1964; Moynihan, 1969).

Clearly many of the arguments that have been made, could have been made more strongly with larger samples, the study of more minority groups, other communities, and other issues. Further research is needed on the interaction of racial and ethnic consciousness, and on the forms of skepticism and relative deprivation which are at the basis of much recent ethnic hostility. Specific information on the ideology and frustrations involved in the achievement of various ethnic groups and generations would provide a clearer sense of the influence which ethnic consciousness can have on working-class movements, political organizations, and the processes of assimilation. As background, historical research on interethnic group conflicts would provide insights into the role of ethnic leadership, issues, and organization on the course of assimilation.

While the attempt to develop a measure of ethnic consciousness and interests failed, the failure, nevertheless, provided some insight into the complexities of ethnic awareness and militance. The third generation does indeed return to ethnicity, but less as a source of cultural or religious refreshment than as the basis for organizing the skepticism associated with discontent and racial confrontation. All of these reflections are preliminary in that ethnic interests will continue to become articulated in situations of ethnic and racial tension.

REFERENCES

Adamic, L. *Dynamite: The Story of Class Violence.* Gloucester, Massachusetts: Peter Smith, 1931.

Bender, E. I., and G. Kagiwada. "Hansen's Law of Third Generation Return and the Study of American Religio-Ethnic Groups." *Phylon*, 29 (Winter 1968): 360–370.

Bernard, W. S. "Interrelationship Between Immigrants and Negroes: A Summary of a Seminar on Integration." *The International Migration Review*, 3 (Summer 1969): 47–57.

Bimba, A. *The Molly Maguires.* New York: International Publishers, 1932.

Bloom, L. "Concerning Ethnic Research." *American Sociological Review*, 13 (April 1948): 171–177.

Cinel, D. "Ethnicity: A Neglected Dimension of American History." *The International Migration Review*, 3 (Summer 1969): 58–63.

Dahrendorf, R. *Class and Class Conflict in Industrial Society.* Stanford: Stanford University Press, 1959.

Eisenstadt, W. N. *The Absorption of Immigrants.* London: Routledge & Kegan Paul, 1954.

Glaser, D. "Dynamics of Ethnic Identification." *American Sociological Review*, 23 (February 1958): 31–40.

Glazer, N. "Ethnic Groups in America: From National Character to Ideology." Pp. 158–173 in M. Berger et al. (eds.), *Freedom and Control in Modern Society.* New York: Van Nostrand, 1954.

Glazer, N., and D. P. Moynihan. *Beyond the Melting Pot.* Cambridge: M.I.T. Press, 1963.

Goldstein, S., and C. Goldscheider. *Jewish Americans: Three Generations in a Jewish Community.* Englewood Cliffs: Prentice-Hall, 1968.

Gordon, M. M. *Assimilation in American Life.* New York: Oxford University Press, 1964.

Greeley, A. M. "Ethnicity as an Influence of Behavior." *Integrated Education*, 7 (July-August): 33–41, 1969.

Hansen, M. L. "The Third Generation." Pp. 255–271 in O. Handlin (ed.), *Children of the Uprooted.* New York: Harper & Row, 1966.

Hatt, P. "Class and Ethnic Attitudes." *American Sociological Review*, 13 (February 1948): 36–43.

Lazerwitz, B., and L. Rowitz. "The Three-Generations Hypothesis." *American Journal of Sociology*, 69 (March 1964): 529–538.

Moynihan, D. P. *Maximum Feasible Misunderstanding: Community Action in the War on Poverty.* New York: Free Press, 1969.

Russo, N. J. "Three Generations of Italians in New York City: Their Religious Acculturation." *The International Migration Review,* 3 (Spring 1969): 3–16.

Vecoli, R. J. "Ethnicity: A Neglected Dimension of American History." *American Studies in Scandinavia,* 4 (Summer 1970): 5–23.

Wirth, L. "The Problem of Minority Groups." Pp. 244–269 in A. J. Reiss, Jr. (ed.), *Louis Wirth: On Cities and Social Life.* Chicago: University of Chicago Press, 1964.

Zochert, D. "Ethnic Divisions Persist in U.S." *Chicago Daily News,* September 18, 1969.

D. Policy and practice considerations

IRVING M. LEVINE

A strategy for white ethnic America

While the phenomenon of urban white backlash involves the entire spectrum of American groups, the volatility of this backlash and its political implications are most dangerous in the lower middle class. This group, a "have" group only since World War II, consists largely of second- and third-generation European ethnic subgroups.

The ethnic response of basic antipathy to blacks is similar to that of the more established whites in rural, small-town, and southern America. There is, however, a major difference, the consequences of which may prove to be devastating to racial and social progress: Rural and small-town white Americans have traditionally been on the conservative side of issues, but ethnic groups, until now, have been counted on to deliver a rather solid liberal vote. The urban ethnic block has also been the backbone of the American labor movement. It is the fiber of whatever remains of big city political machines, and it previously supplied the largest numerical base of support for social welfare programs.

The current ethnic disaffection on the racial issue, and the proven ability of neoreactionary forces to capitalize on this disaffection, should be seen as a deep threat to America. The fallout from racial conflict is converting many lower-middle-class Americans to a status quo posture on other issues, a posture that may not be in keeping with their economic position or their own self-interest.

A NEW LOOK AT THE ETHNIC WORKING AMERICAN

Much has been said about the negative reaction of ethnic whites to black competition for the jobs, housing, political power, and other benefits which they themselves have only recently begun to enjoy. While indeed an important factor, competition cannot be seen as the single

Source: Paper presented at the Philadelphia Conference on the Problems of White Ethnic America, June 1968.

Written in June 1968, this article was one of the first efforts to speak to the problems of this country's white ethnic working class, and it formed the philosophy for the National Project on Ethnic America, predecessor of the Institute on Pluralism and Group Identity of which Irving M. Levine is presently the director.

cause of group conflict, however. Rather, one must examine the effects of a broader sickness related to the style of life characteristic of all middle-class America. Especially among those without adequate resources, that style of life might be characterized as one in which "the reach far exceeds the grasp."

The appetite and the sense of possibility generated by an affluent society create both the need and the assumption of wherewithal to consume conspicuously and repetitively. The average American is bombarded by the mass media message of abundance. From the radio in the morning, to newspapers and advertisements on the buses, to the evening TV commercials, he or she is told that elegance and luxury are well within the means of any hardworking citizen. But the affluence of lower-middle-class Americans is a tenuous one, historically and even currently, and it does not allow the comforts which the media say they deserve.

In order even to stay relatively free of debts and save for their children's education, it is often necessary for both husband and wife to work. This redefinition of family roles, a relatively new phenomenon, clashes with many traditional values of ethnic group life and contributes to a sense of disorientation and alienation. The bureaucratized, automated nature of modern industrial work similarly limits the availability of constructive outlets for expressing individuality and productiveness. Furthermore, as the leadership of the political machine and the labor union becomes more "professional," neither offers the working class a sense of pride or importance to society.

Lower-middle-class America, then, is comprised largely of individuals who feel almost as powerless in relation to modern society as do the poorest residents of the ghetto. As a group, however, they are able to exert enough influence, at least, to block efforts at social reform. In part because of their own powerlessness, in part because of fear, the white working class sees blacks as the enemy, especially as they begin to demand, march, riot, and obtain political power. Since the black group is also an acceptable symbol of dislike, it is a perfect target for the resentment of a class of rather impotent Americans. By exaggerating the results of black aggressiveness, the white worker is saying, "Why doesn't someone speak up for me?"

NEW STRATEGIES FOR DEPOLARIZATION

What does this projection of anger and frustration mean in the search for a program that not only will attempt to combat a racism deeply imbedded in ethnic America but also will speak with positive relevance to this group? To begin, perhaps there is a need to identify the real problems of lower-middle-class white ethnic groups and speak creatively to their deepest needs. We must certainly speak with more vigor, but we must also include new structure and new semantics that depart from the tired rhetoric of the New Deal.

The progressive elements of society must convince actual or potential backlash groups that alliance and cooperation can yield constructive results for them as well as for blacks. To do this, the traditional exponents of national policy must refocus their rhetoric and modify their priorities to some extent, building the kind of acceptability needed to depolarize the American public. Capitulating to a regressive ideology or slowing down on meeting black demands is not advocated by this strategy. Rather, what is essential is a recognition that certain needs, both rational and irrational, must be met for another large and alienated group of Americans if the country is to escape major—probably violent—clashes.

The following are issues and arguments which should be exploited in the context of this strategy. It should be noted that these are serious agenda items for the nation as a whole. They obviously go beyond ethnicity and would be beneficial to blacks as well as whites and to the upper middle class as well as the lower middle class. In the context of the current politicosocial situation, however, emphasis is on a targeted approach to the "working American." In some instances, these issues might serve as a base around which to organize coalitions with other groups, but each could serve by itself as a progressive rallying point for the energies of lower-middle-class white ethnic America.

1. Law and order

In the past few years liberal forces have so mishandled the issue of law and order that it has been allowed to become the right-wing battle cry. To dismiss the fears which yield such a strong emotional response to the law-and-order issue is to perpetuate the John Birch Society as the organization most responsive to the people. Furthermore, to preach continually that we must eliminate the cause of crime foolishly leads only to a generalized rejection of progressive social programs as encouraging violence.

The issue of crime in the streets must be seen in ways that speak genuinely to the widespread fears for personal security in an urban existence that is anonymous, mobile, transient, technically oriented, and bureaucratic. Concentrating only on the inadequacies of the police adds to dissension and polarization. Instead, *the police function should be reevaluated so that law enforcement and the enhancing of personal security are redefined as problems for the proper kind of community organization.*

Neighborhoods should be encouraged to organize around issues of law enforcement, just as they have organized around schools, housing, health, and welfare. New possibilities for fighting crime—including upgraded police training, sophisticated electronic devices, and advanced communications systems—must become the focus of widespread public demand.

The structure of community involvement must lead to the utilization of neighborhood persons in new and carefully thought-out security roles. Escort services for women, storefront police stations, and direct home-to-police burglar systems ought not to be simplistically stereotyped as vigilantism. Professional community organizers must be put in jobs which develop indigenous leadership in this field. Their role would be to organize local leadership around the goals of better law enforcement, improve community relations with police, fight unprofessional police behavior, advance the rehabilitation of criminal offenders, seek the treatment of narcotics addicts, and defuse tension situations that are not in themselves violative of law but threaten to break out in overt destructive activity.

The specific tactics suggested here are intended as examples of a refocus on the law-and-order issue which can be supported by working-class ethnic Americans. Accepting these notions does not involve repudiating either the demands of black militants or the effectiveness of the police, who are themselves based in these lower-middle-class ethnic groups. Instead, it creates constructive channels for dealing with real fears.

Much of the present fear of crime has more of a rational base than some care to admit, and the spread of that fear is even more dangerous than its original causes. One of the ways to destroy fear is to initiate motion toward solving the problem. Unless we are willing to allow all of the emotion to be expressed through the cult of violence and gun buying, we must be willing to explore new possibilities and strategic approaches.

2. Tax reform, especially on local levels

Ethnic America is comprised largely of steady workers who have only recently become home owners. Almost three fourths of the workers who earn between $6,000 and $7,500 own their own homes, some in older central-city neighborhoods and a growing number in burgeoning working-class suburbs. The AFL–CIO reports that nearly 50 percent of all union members now live in suburbs, and for union members under age 30, the proportion is 75 percent.

For these first-time property owners, one of the major concerns is the spiraling property tax rate. At the same time, they see other taxes increasing without a correspondingly evident increase in the quantity or quality of service they secure. These new homeowners can be rallied into a progressive force for modifying the regressive nature of taxes on every governmental level. It is they who are paying proportionately more through a 10 percent surtax, through sales taxes, and through ever-escalating social security taxes.

Moreover, while living costs have gone up and business has been granted depreciation allowances, the working-class ethnic American still deducts only $600 [now $750] from his taxable income for each dependent. Five years ago it was almost an established fact, sanctioned and supported by a spectrum of groups, that the dependency allowance would be raised to $1,000; Congress seemed about to act, but it never happened, and there has been no persistent lobbying for tax reform on behalf of lower-middle-class America.

If we accept the need for emphasizing new issues which will de-polarize the nation, *we should demand fundamental, long-range tax reform. In the short run, labor, the churches, and community organizations should press for doubling the dependency allowance.* The need is to respond to ethnic America's feeling that they are neglected by government in favor of more militant minority groups. Also, the suburbanization of much of white ethnic America presents this group with continuously escalating local school taxes. The more affluent, professional, and education-minded professional suburban class cannot impose elitist educational tastes on the marginal blue-collar worker. The demand for the replacement of local school taxes by a graduated statewide tax is surely an issue that speaks for the needs of white ethnic America. At the same time it may serve to equalize city and suburban school budgets, bringing benefits to black children as well as white taxpayers.

3. Inadequate public education

With the best of intentions, the education issue has too often been defined in terms of bussing and racial balance, and ethnic America is opposed to both. Here again, liberal rhetoric has become its own worst enemy. Members of the lower middle class, anxious to escape the worst in inner-city education, have been made to feel that it is they who must now sacrifice to remedy these deficiencies. It has not helped, and it will not help, to try to convince them that bringing black children into a school need not affect the quality of education delivered to their own children. We have seen this strategy fail in community after community.

While equality in education is a fighting issue which should occupy our time and involve our conscience, in reality the widespread obsolescence of education is a more inclusive fight. *The possibilities opened up by effective decentralization and community participation, by computer technology, and by a widening of the choice of educational options should be disseminated throughout ethnic America and held up as models for new programs.* The granting of a per-pupil stipend might encourage new, competing educational systems, relieve the failure-oriented public school apparatus of the total burden, and satisfy parents of parochial school children (most of whom are ethnic whites) that their special financial problems are not being totally disregarded.

Another new ingredient, now more universal than ever among lower-middle-class Americans, is a desire for a college education for their children. Next to blacks and poor southern whites, it is the children of ethnic Americans who are not entering the universities. In some cities, high school dropout rates range from 30 to 40 percent in this group. Therefore, instead of continuing to define the educational issue in the polarized terminology of racial issues, we must ask why the system performs so badly for lower-middle-class whites as well as for blacks, and we must project into the future the dire effects of this failure. The political demand should be for an end to educational obsolescence and for universal higher education.

Such a stance need not involve concerned Americans in abandoning integrationist goals. Rather, it suggests a new strategy where multiple options and central superior educational facilities result in integrated experiences in a variety of new educational settings, but without the kind of divisiveness that is rendering integration impossible today.

4. Occupational mobility

The jobs held by this large group of American workers are generally characterized in familiar terms of monotony and lack of creativity. The factory and the shop are not noted for their contribution to the growth of the worker, but there is too often no alternative. Current political emphasis in this area is on training and employment for "hard-core unemployed," but nothing is being offered to the worker in exchange for his support of programs which he sees as aimed at his job. While this perception of impending takeover may be a false one, its existence gives it a reality which must be dealt with.

Speeches which emphasize the availability of jobs for all Americans will not counter the insecurity which is often the base of irrational fear. Instead, *we need programs which will encourage working Americans to broaden their educations for the possibility of second careers.* Too many workers reach a dead end by the age of 35 or 40, with 25 to 30 more years of unproductive employment to look forward to. A program perhaps modeled after the G.I. education bill could attract the positive support of this large group, which is now limited to expressing its resentment of blacks as symbols of its own frustration. Government support for on-the-job training, and for upgrading skills and changing job categories, might make white workers more sympathetic to similar programs for the hard core unemployed. It is also important for government to recognize that leisure ought to be supported in some of the same ways that productivity is stressed. The new housing act's provision for helping to finance vacation homes is a step in the right direction.

5. Personal growth and mental health

If our society in the contemporary period were not facing the effects of an economic crisis, racial polarization, and the aftermath of a divisive war, everyone, not just intellectuals, would be talking about alienation, anomie, and widespread psychological needs. These conditions desperately affect the lower middle class, who have not turned to psychiatry and organized mental health as have the more affluent. Many are closed-up people who are moving in tunnels, frightened of a world where no one seems to be in control—least of all, themselves. *We need to develop the kinds of public mental health programs that, with effective group settings, retreats, and guidance facilities, would help these people open themselves up and deal with their anxieties.*

Also missing in our country today is ample opportunity to experience personal creative growth, especially in the areas of culture and the arts. The upper middle class has traditionally reserved "culture" to itself, and lower-class blacks and Puerto Ricans are beginning to discover indigenous culture, but we have allowed the lower middle class to become totally addicted to the lowest possible cultural common denominator. Television, bowling, and the movies are the limits of entertainment beyond the family. *New forms of entertainment and leisure-time activities which can be organized under the auspices of churches, unions, and ethnic societies are imperative.*

One of the personal cultural lacks for ethnic America is a sense of authentic group identity. Second and third generations are often confused and concerned over the nature of their group membership.

Among Jews, this phenomenon has undergone intensive study, and some programs have been developed to define and strengthen Jewish identity in America. Similar efforts are needed for other ethnic groups to augment this dimension of individual identity.

CONCLUSION

The issues outlined here represent only a few of the kinds of problems which must be dealt with in a new way. They represent a sympathetic approach to lower-middle-class ethnic America, one which recognizes the difficulties this group faces in an increasingly anonymous urban culture. These issues (and others listed in the addendum) obviously go beyond ethnicity to relate to the needs of middle-class America as a whole, in contrast to the recent emphasis on the needs of the so-called underclass. Such a focus has not only left that underclass unsatisfied, it has stimulated in the lower middle class, only a few steps up the success ladder, enough volatile negative reaction to make them the shock troops of anti-black politics.

The emphasis on the working ethnic American is a strategic one, based on the premise that this group is not about to ally itself with either the poor or the upper middle class, no matter how common their goals might be. If such a coalition is impossible, then ethnic America must be dealt with as an entity unto itself, on its own terms. Not to do so can only lead to a continuing, accelerated conflict with the very real danger of victory for a reactionary and repressive majority.

However we might wish to assert the priority of the most disadvantaged, we can no longer define the major problem of America only in terms of blacks. We must include in the definition of the problem white reaction to black demands, and we must act accordingly in seeking solutions. Our rightful but often self-righteous transfixion on black America has developed into a "no-win" policy, hardening the lines of polarization between white and black into a reality that could blow the country apart and frustrate long overdue progress for blacks.

To change this white reaction, some of the brilliance which articulated black demands will have to be similarly developed to speak for and with lower-middle-class America. White ethnic groups must feel the security of recognition by mainstream institutions. Only when we grant this recognition and listen to their insightful spokesmen can we arm ourselves with a strategy that will lessen frustration and polarization.

With new understanding, we can help lower-middle-class whites identify and solve their own problems, often along lines which parallel the self-interests of blacks. Then we can begin to discuss realistically coalitions which transcend the barrier of race.

ADDENDUM

An inclusive listing of issues that speak to the needs of lower-middle-class white ethnic Americans:

1. Crime in the streets.
2. Unfair and burdensome tax structures, especially on local levels.
3. Inadequate and uncomfortable transportation.
4. High credit rates.
5. Excess costs for rentals and home maintenance.
6. High medical costs.
7. Need for beautification and cleanliness of neighborhoods.
8. High cost of entertainment.
9. High cost of automobiles and their maintenance.
10. Poor performance of public education.
11. Burden of parochial education.
12. High cost and lack of opportunity for higher education.
13. Poor mental health, usually unrecognized.
14. Lack of help in child rearing.
15. Poor or overpriced recreational facilities.
16. Poor planning of neighborhood and suburban environment.
17. Inadequate adult education for second and third career possibilities.
18. Lack of occupational mobility.
19. Threat of automation.
20. Lack of a sense of community.
21. Breakdown of local government, its lack of representativeness and distance from the people.
22. American foreign policy and the "mother" country.

Chapter 6

CONFLICT VERSUS CONSENSUS AS A GROUP RELATIONS STRATEGY

A. Introduction

Conflict and protest, concluded the National Advisory Commission on Civil Disorders, have characterized group life throughout American history. Some of this conflict originated from the actions of majority-group exploiters and discriminators, such as slave traders or anti-Catholics who brutalized the Irish and other early immigrant groups. Conflict also characterized some minority social movements, such as slave revolts or terrorist enclaves (the Molly Maguires are a case in point). We have evolved a complex pattern of Stamp Act riots, Indian massacres, and labor disruptions, interlarded with various traditional forms of political process.

Nevertheless, in the group relations field, a tendency has existed in the past for professionals and reformers to stress conciliatory methods. A prevalent human relations orientation has led to the perception of problems in humanistic, interpersonal terms and to the development of programs that emphasize education, tension reduction, and incremental legal action. (Such programs are associated with the strategies of intergroup attitudes and relationships, and group welfare, which were identified as policy options in Chapter 1.) The changing of attitudes has been seen as an accessible, professionally valid, and socially acceptable way of dealing with many race and ethnic matters.

Only in very recent years has this perspective been brought into serious question and has greater attention been paid by group relations professionals and social scientists to conflictual factors. For example, Stanley Eitzen[1] posits a general model of group relations that assumes all majority-minority relationships involve unequal distribution of power, a condition that invariably embodies elements of conflict. (This analysis is predisposed to strategies of group rights and group solidarity and power.)

In addition to its historical real-world presence, conflict has been advocated as a rational and useful tool for social development. Thoreau, Rousseau, and Hume in an earlier period and men such as Gandhi, Camus, Fanon, Malcolm X, and Martin Luther King in more recent times have espoused varying contentious political methods. What are the values of conflict, or in the words of Lewis Coser, its social functions?[2] Coser suggests a series of positive attributes. It has group-

---

[1] Stanley D. Eitzen, "A Conflict Model for the Analysis of Majority-Minority Relations," *Kansas Journal of Sociology,* vol. 8 (Spring 1967), pp. 76–92.

[2] Lewis Coser, *The Functions of Social Conflict* (New York: Free Press, 1956).

binding qualities related to identification of the boundary lines of social collectivities and societies, thereby helping to clarify social definitions and processes. It also provides a group-preserving service by acting as a safety valve which allows tensions and grievances to emerge so that they do not build up and explode abruptly, shattering the fabric of society. As a consequence of conflict, the relative strengths of different groups may be manifested, thereby facilitating social stability around newly defined balances of power. Sometimes this is done through new rules, norms, or institutions which guide social interaction.

Conflict may have special benefits for a minority grappling with an outside antagonist. It can solidify such a group by promoting internal cohesion in the face of an alien threat. Concomitantly, greater internal tolerance, morale, and goodwill among members may develop. Such participation can enhance personal commitment to a particular goal, ideology, or collectivity, or operate as an antidote to despair or alienation.

Elsewhere, Coser writes of the positive functions of violence, a specialized form of conflict.[3] Violence can be a danger signal to a society, indicating grievances or defects of such magnitude that they require urgent attention. It can provide a catalyst, setting in motion a chain of actions which correct injustices or malfunctions in the system. For those who participate, violence can be a form of achievement, especially when other avenues of gratification or recognition are blocked.

Other positive effects of conflict can be cited: the crystallization and clarification of viewpoints, the disruption of institutional inertia, the forcing of creative solutions to problems are examples. In "The Functions of Racial Conflict," Joseph Himes elaborates on the benefits to society that are a unique contribution of racial conflict. The general lines of this argument should, however, have been sufficiently conveyed, and it is useful to balance this position by introducing critiques which point to the limitations and dangers of conflict as a strategy.

As one kind of rejoinder, Melvin Tumin's analysis in "Violence and Democracy" grows out of the context of violent opposition by students to the war in Vietnam. The issue is sharpened in that Tumin firmly agreed with the objective of ending what he considered an immoral and reprehensible foreign intervention. However, he also rejects modes of opposition which involve extreme conflict. In particular, violence is seen as a danger to an open society—detrimental to fair play, free speech, and civil political behavior. In dealing with social questions,

---

[3] Lewis Coser, "Some Functions of Violence," *Annals of the American Academy of Political and Social Sciences,* vol. 364 (March 1966), pp. 8–18.

antagonists, he feels, should be prepared to lose in the marketplace of pluralistic competition. Otherwise, we face the "suspension or the destruction of democracy."

This cardinal concern overshadows other reservations that have been expressed concerning the use of conflict as a tactic:

1. Adherents can become caught up in the excitement and emotional catharsis of the process and use it endlessly, without attention to its effects on target problem conditions.
2. Legitimate opposition can be crushed, and both opponents and innocent bystanders can be seriously damaged.
3. It leads to irrational and inhumane methods of problem solving, involving an oversimplified, single-issue, devil theory perspective.

Obviously, proponents of both views—conflict and consensus—are able to bring persuasive argumentation to bear. The introduction of additional analytical variables can perhaps assist in weighing the alternatives as a course of action. The nature of resistance is one factor which could be considered: How powerful is the opposition, how willing is it to listen, and what is the nature of its response in terms of repression? The character and makeup of the advocacy group are also salient: Does it have sufficient internal strength and external support, are the threats it makes credible, is there a climate of social legitimacy for the use of conflict or has moral justification for such action been established? What is the nature of the goals (and of the demands) being pursued: Do they threaten existing power relations, authority structures, and resource holdings? Are intermediaries available to check the intensity of disruption and to act as brokers? Numerous other considerations could be cited; these suggest the lines of inquiry that permit reasoned judgments to be made.

As with the other issues, empirical data are available to guide the assessment of conflict versus consensus. In "The Organizational Sub-structure of Disorderly Politics," Donald Von Eschen, Jerome Kirk, and Maurice Pinard investigate the question of member participation. They are concerned with engagement in routine politics and in direct-action movements, or "disorderly politics," using the sit-ins of the early 1960s as a case in point. The pattern of previous organizational participation by individuals is examined relative to later involvement in a conflict organization. The study has implications with regard to which individuals may be recruited for such participation and where they can be reached. It also suggests what types of communities, based on organizational makeup, are receptive to conflict or consensus politics.

Policy and practice considerations in this issue are represented in "Disruptive Tactics," by Harry Specht. Specht, a teacher and writer in the field of community organization practice, conceptualizes a spectrum of tactical options ranging from collaboration to violence and delves into the practical aspects of their implementation. In particular, he focuses on the parameters and consequences of conflictual modes of action, which he designates "disruptive tactics."

As we have seen, groups, including minorities, who are seeking to enhance their position of power have tended to use conflict as a necessary tool. A number of instrumental questions come to mind. They should be weighed in conjunction with the analytic variables stated earlier. When can such initiatives be used with success, and when can they lead to failure? What special internal organizational and external situational factors need to be taken into account? What material resources or support in the form of allies are necessary to sustain a confrontation? Should any ethical considerations related to political civility or general community welfare be brought into strategic calculations? These are some of the difficult questions and dilemmas that properly should enter into organizational planning in the choice of conflict or consensus as a strategy.

B. Theoretical and philosophical considerations

JOSEPH S. HIMES

The functions of racial conflict

Social conflict is revealed as both natural and functional in human society. Conflict is called "realistic" when rationally determined means are used to achieve culturally approved ends. In the field of Negro struggle, legal redress, political pressure and mass action meet these defining criteria of realistic conflict.

This study examines some of the social functions of conflict as here defined. It is asked: does realistic conflict by Negroes have any system-maintaining and system-enhancing consequences for the larger American society? The analysis revealed that realistic racial conflict (1) alters the social structure, (2) extends social communication, (3) enhances social solidarity, and (4) facilitates personal identity.

When one contemplates the contemporary American scene, he may be appalled by the picture of internal conflict portrayed in the daily news. The nation is pictured as torn by dissension over Vietnam policy. The people are reported being split by racial strife that periodically erupts into open violence. Organized labor and management are locked in a perennial struggle that occasionally threatens the well-being of the society. The reapportionment issue has forced the ancient rural-urban conflict into public view. Religious denominations and faiths strive against ancient conflicts of theology and doctrine toward unification and ecumenism. Big government is joined in a continuing struggle against big industry, big business, big finance, and big labor on behalf of the "public interest."

The image created by such reports is that of a society "rocked," "split" or "torn" by its internal conflicts. The repetition of such phrases and the spotlighting of conflict suggest that the integration, if not the very existence of the society is threatened. It is thus implied, and indeed

Note: Presidential address delivered at the annual meeting of the Southern Sociological Society, New Orleans, April 8, 1966. I am indebted to Professors Ernst Borinski, Lewis A. Coser, Hylan G. Lewis, and Robin M. Williams, Jr., for their critical reading of this manuscript.

Source: *Social Forces*, vol. 45 (September 1966), pp. 1–10.

often stated, that the elimination of internal conflict is the central problem for policy and action in the society.

These preliminary remarks tend to indicate that there is widespread popular disapproval of social conflict. In some quarters the absence of conflict is thought to signify the existence of social harmony and stability. According to the human relations theme, conflict, aggression, hostility, antagonism and such divisive motives and behaviors are regarded as social heresies and therefore to be avoided. Often the word conflict is associated with images of violence and destruction.

At the same time, in contemporary sociology the problem of social conflict has been largely neglected. As Coser, Dahrendorf and others have pointed out, this tendency issues from preoccupation with models of social structure and theories of equilibrium.[1] Conflicts are treated as strains, tensions or stresses of social structures and regarded as pathological. Little attention is devoted to the investigation of conflict as a functional social process.

However, some of the earlier sociologists employed social conflict as one central element of their conceptual systems. Theory and analysis were cast in terms of a process model. Conflict was viewed as natural and as functioning as an integrative force in society.

To Ludwig Gumplowicz and Gustav Ratzenhofer conflict was the basic social process, while for Lester F. Ward and Albion W. Small it was one of the basic processes. Sumner, Ross, and Cooley envisaged conflict as one of the major forces operating to lace human society together.[2] Park and Burgess employed social conflict as one of the processual pillars of their sociological system.[3]

At bottom, however, the two analytic models of social organization are really not inconsistent. Dahrendorf argues that consensus-structure and conflict-process are "the two faces of society."[4] That is, social integration results simultaneously from both consensus of values and coercion to compliance. Indeed, in the present study it is observed that the two sources of social integration are complementary and mutually supporting.

---

[1] Lewis A. Coser, *The Functions of Social Conflict* (Glencoe, Illinois: The Free Press, 1956), p. 20; Ralf Dahrendorf, *Class and Class Conflict in Industrial Society* (Stanford: Stanford University Press, 1959), chap. 5.

[2] William Graham Summer, *Folkways* (Boston: Ginn, 1906); Edward Alsworth Ross, *The Principles of Sociology* (New York: Century, 1920); Charles Horton Cooley, *Social Process* (New York: Charles Scribner's Sons, 1918), and *Social Organization* (New York: Charles Scribner's Sons, 1909).

[3] Robert E. Park and Ernest W. Burgess, *Introduction to the Science of Sociology* (Chicago: University of Chicago Press, 1924).

[4] Dahrendorf, op. cit., pp. 157–165. Arthur I. Wastow makes the same point in his concepts of "church," "state," and "government" as models of social integration. See *From Race Riot to Sit-In, 1919 and the 1960s: A Study in the Connections Between Conflict and Violence* (New York: Doubleday & Co., 1966).

Coser has led the revival of sociological attention to the study of social conflict. In this task he has injected the very considerable contributions of the German sociologist Georg Simmel into the stream of American sociological thought. Ralf Dahrendorf, among others, has made further substantial contributions to the sociology of social conflict. One latent consequence of this development has been to sensitize some sociologists to conflict as a perspective from which to investigate race relations. Thus race relations have been called "power relations" and it has been proposed that research should be cast in terms of a "conflict model."[5] This approach is consistent with Blumer's thesis that race prejudice is "a sense of group position" and that empirical study involves "a concern with the relationship of racial groups."[6]

In the present discussion the term racial conflict is used in a restricted and specific sense.[7] By racial conflict is meant rational organized overt action by Negroes, initiating demands for specific social goals, and utilizing collective sanctions to enforce these demands. By definition, the following alternative forms of conflict behavior are excluded from the field of analysis.

1. The aggressive or exploitative actions of dominant groups and individuals toward minority groups or individuals.
2. Covert individual antagonisms or affective compensatory or reflexive aggressions, and
3. Spontaneous outbursts or nonrationalized violent behavior.

As here treated, racial conflict involves some rational assessment of both means and ends, and therefore is an instance of what Lewis Coser has called "realistic conflict."[8] Because of the calculating of means and ends, racial conflict is initiating action. It is a deliberate collective enterprise to achieve predetermined social goals. Of necessity, conflict includes a conscious attack upon an overtly defined social abuse.

---

[5] Lewis M. Killian and Charles M. Grigg, *Racial Crisis in America* (Englewood Cliffs, N.J.: Prentice-Hall, 1964), p. 18 ff.; H. M. Blalock, Jr., "A Power Analysis of Racial Discrimination," *Social Forces,* 39 (October 1960), pp. 53–59; Ernst Borinski, "The Sociology of Coexistence—Conflict in Social and Political Power Systems," unpublished, pp. 6–7; Wilson Record, *Race and Radicalism* (Ithaca: Cornell University Press, 1964); Ernst Borinski, "The Litigation Curve and the Litigation Filibuster in Civil Rights Cases," *Social Forces,* 37 (December 1958), pp. 142–147.

[6] Herbert Blumer, "Race Prejudice as a Sense of Group Position," in J. Masuoka and Preston Valien (eds.), *Race Relations* (Chapel Hill: The University of North Carolina Press, 1961), p. 217.

[7] In much authoritative literature the concept conflict in racial relations is used in various other ways. See for example, George Simpson and J. Milton Yinger, *Racial and Cultural Minorities* (New York; Harper & Row, 1965), chap. 4; Killian and Grigg, op. cit.; Leonard Broom and Norval D. Glenn, *Transformation of the Negro American* (New York: Harper & Row, 1965), esp. chaps. 3 and 4.

[8] Coser, op. cit., pp. 48–55.

Merton has pointed out that groups sometimes resort to culturally tabooed means to achieve culturally prescribed ends.[9] Under such circumstances one might assume that if legitimate means were available, they would be employed. But, Vander Zanden has observed, "Non-violent resistance is a tactic well suited to struggles in which a minority lacks access to major sources of power within a society and to the instruments of violent coercion."[10] He goes on to add that, "within the larger American society the Negro's tactic of non-violent resistance has gained a considerable degree of legitimacy."[11] Three principal manifestations of Negro behavior fit this definition of racial conflict.

1. Legal redress, or the calculated use of court action to achieve and sanction specific group goals. Legal redress has been used most often and successfully in the achievement of voting rights, educational opportunities and public accommodations.
2. Political action, or the use of voting, bloc voting and lobby techniques to achieve legislative and administrative changes and law enforcement.
3. Non-violent mass action, or organized collective participation in overt activity involving pressure and public relations techniques to enforce specific demands.

This paper examines some of the social functions of conflict as here defined. It is asked: Does realistic conflict by Negroes have any system-maintaining and system-enhancing consequences for the larger American society? To this question at least four affirmative answers can be given. Realistic racial conflict (1) alters the social structure, (2) enhances social communication, (3) extends social solidarity and (4) facilitates personal identity. Because of space and time limitations, considerations of societal dysfunctions and goal achievements are omitted.

STRUCTURAL FUNCTIONS

H. M. Blalock has noted that within the American social structure race relations are power relations.[12] Thus, realistic social conflict is an enterprise in the calculated mobilization and application of social power to sanction collective demands for specific structural changes. Yet, because of minority status, Negroes have only limited access to the sources of social power. Robert Bierstedt has identified numbers, resources and

---

[9] Robert K. Merton, *Social Theory and Social Structure* (Glencoe, Illinois: The Free Press, 1957), pp. 123–149.
[10] James W. Vander Zanden, "The Non-Violent Resistance Movement Against Segregation," *American Journal of Sociology,* 68 (March 1963), p. 544.
[11] Ibid., p. 544.
[12] Blalock, op. cit., pp. 53–59.

organization as leading sources of power.[13] Of these categories, resources which Bierstedt specifies as including money, prestige, property and natural and supernatural phenomena are least accessible to Negroes.

Perforce then, realistic racial conflict specializes in the mobilization of numbers and organization as accessible sources of power. Thus a boycott mobilizes and organizes numbers of individuals to withhold purchasing power. A demonstration organizes and mobilizes numbers of individuals to tap residual moral sentiments and to generate public opinion. Voter registration and bloc voting mobilize and organize numbers of citizens to influence legislative and administrative processes. Legal redress and lobby techniques mobilize organization to activate legal sanctions or the legislative process.

The application of mobilized social power in realistic racial conflict tends to reduce the power differential between actors, to restrict existing status differences, and to alter the directionality of social interaction. First, in conflict situations, race relations are defined unequivocally in power terms. Sentimentality and circumlocution are brushed aside. The power dimension is brought into central position in the structure of interaction. The differential between conflict partners along this dimension is thus reduced. The power advantage of the dominant group is significantly limited. In this connection and perhaps only in this connection, it may be correct to liken embattled Negroes and resisting whites to "armed camps."

Second, alteration of the power dimension of interracial structure tends to modify status arrangements. In the traditional racial structure, discrimination and segregation cast whites and Negroes in rigid and separate orders of superiority and inferiority. The limited and stylized intergroup contacts are confined to a rigid and sterile etiquette. However, in realistic conflict initiating actors assume, for they must, a status coordinate with that of the opposition.[14]

Status coordination is one evident consequence of power equalization. Moreover, it is patently impossible to make demands and to sanction them while acting from the position of a suppliant. That is, the very process of realistic conflict functions to define adversaries in terms of self-conception as status equals. Martin Luther King perceives this function of realistic conflict in the following comment on the use of non-violent action and deliberately induced tension. "Non-violent direct action seeks to create such a crisis and foster such a tension that a com-

---

[13] Robert Bierstedt, "An Analysis of Social Power," *American Sociological Review*, 15 (December 1950), pp. 730–738. Bierstedt argues that numbers and organization as sources of social power are ineffectual without access to resources.

[14] Thomas F. Pettigrew, *A Profile of the Negro American* (Princeton: D. Van Nostrand Co., 1964), p. 167.

munity which has constantly refused to negotiate is forced to confront the issue. It seeks so to dramatize the issue that it can no longer be ignored."[15]

That is, social power is used to bring interactors into status relations where issues can be discussed, examined and compromised. There are no suppliants or petitioners and no condescending controllers in a negotiation relationship. By the very nature of the case, interactors occupy equal or approximately equal positions of both status and strength.

Third, power equalization and status coordination affect the interactional dimension of social structure. The up and down flow of interaction between super- and subordinates tends to level out in relations between positional equals. That is, rational demands enforced by calculated sanctions cannot be forced into the molds of supplication and condescension.

The leveling out of social interaction is inherent in such realistic conflict mechanisms as sit-ins, freedom rides, bloc voting, voter registration campaigns and boycotts. Thus, for example, the interruption of social interaction in a boycott implies an assumption of status equality and the leveling of interaction. The relationship that is interrupted is the up and down pattern inherent in the status structure of inequality. No relationship is revealed as preferable to the pattern of supplication and condescension. Whether such structural functions of realistic conflict become institutionalized in the larger social system will depend on the extent of goal achievement of the total Negro revolution. That is, structural consequences of conflict may be institutionalized through the desegregation and nondiscrimination of education, employment, housing, recreation and the like. Changes in these directions will provide system-relevant roles under terms of relatively coordinate status and power not only for the conflict participants, but also for many other individuals. Developments in these directions will also be influenced by many factors and trends apart from the process of realistic racial conflict.

We may now summarize the argument regarding the structural functions of realistic racial conflict in a series of propositions. Realistic conflict postulates race relations as power relations and undertakes to mobilize and apply the social power that is accessible to Negroes as a minority group.

In conflict, the traditional interracial structure is modified along three dimensions. The power differential between interactors is reduced; status differentials are restricted; and social interaction tends to level

---

[15] Martin Luther King, *Why We Can't Wait* (New York: Harper & Row, 1963), p. 81.

out in directionality. Whether these structural consequences of realistic conflict become institutionalized in the general social system will depend on the extent and duration of goal achievement in the larger social structure.

COMMUNICATIONAL FUNCTIONS

It is widely claimed that Negro aggression interrupts or reduces interracial communication. Whites and Negroes are thought to withdraw in suspicion and hostility from established practices of communication. The so-called "normal" agencies and bridges of intergroup contact and communication are believed to become inoperative. Such a view of conflict envisages Negroes and whites as hostile camps eyeing each other across a "no man's land" of antagonism and separation.

It is true that racial conflict tends to interrupt and reduce traditional communication between whites and Negroes. But traditional interracial communication assumes that communicators occupy fixed positions of superiority and inferiority, precludes the consideration of certain significant issues, and confines permitted interchanges to a rigid and sterile etiquette. "The Negro," write Killian and Grigg, "has always been able to stay in communication with the white man and gain many favors from him, so long as he approached him as a suppliant and as an inferior, and not as a conflict partner."[16]

It will be evident that intergroup communication under such structural conditions is both restricted in content and asymmetrical in form. However, our analysis indicates that realistic conflict functions to correct these distortions of content and form and to extend the communication process at the secondary mass media level.

First, realistic racial conflict heightens the individual level and extends the social range of attention to racial matters. Individuals who have by long custom learned to see Negroes only incidentally as part of the standard social landscape, are brought up sharply and forced to look at them in a new light. Persons who have been oblivious to Negroes are abruptly and insistently confronted by people and issues which they can neither avoid nor brush aside. Many individuals for the first time perceive Negroes as having problems, characteristics and aspirations that were never before recognized, nor at least so clearly recognized. Racial conflict thus rudely destroys what Gunnar Myrdal aptly called the "convenience of ignorance."[17]

---

[16] Killian and Grigg, op. cit., p. 7.
[17] Gunnar Myrdal, *An American Dilemma* (New York: Harper & Bros., 1944), pp. 40–42.

In *Freedom Summer,* Sally Belfrage gives a graphic personal illustration of the attention-arresting function of realistic racial conflict.[18] In the most crowded and hottest part of an afternoon the daughter of one of Greenwood's (Mississippi) leading families walked into the civil rights headquarters. In a lilting southern voice she asked to everybody in general: "I jus' wanted to know what y'all are up to over here."

At the same time the "race problem" is brought into the focus of collective attention by realistic conflict. Negroes as well as their problems and claims insist upon having both intensive and extensive consideration. To support this contention one has only to consider the volume of scientific, quasi-scientific and popular literature, the heavy racial loading of the mass media, and the vast number of organizations and meetings that are devoted to the racial issue.

Further, realistic racial conflict tends to modify both the cognitive and affective content of interracial communication. Under terms of conflict whites and Negroes can no longer engage in the exchange of standardized social amenities regarding safe topics within the protection of the status structure and the social etiquette. Communication is made to flow around substantive issues and the calculated demands of Negroes. Communication is about something that has real meaning for the communicators. It makes a difference that they communicate. In fact, under terms of realistic conflict it is no longer possible to avoid communicating. Thus Martin Luther King argued that non-violent mass action is employed to create such crisis and tension that a community which has refused to negotiate is forced to confront the issue.[19]

In conflict the affective character of communication becomes realistic. The communicators infuse their exchanges of cognitive meanings with the feelings that, within the traditional structure, were required to be suppressed and avoided. Negroes are permitted, indeed often expected, to reveal the hurt and humiliation and anger that they formerly were required to bottle up inside. Many white people thus were shocked to discover that the "happy" Negroes whom they "knew" so well were in fact discontented and angry people.

Thus the cognitive-affective distortion of traditional interracial communication is in some measure at least corrected. The flow of understanding and affection that was permitted and encouraged is balanced by normal loading of dissension and hostility. The relationship thus reveals a more symmetrical character of content and form.

Finally, attrition of primary contacts between unequals within the traditional structure and etiquette is succeeded, in part at least, by an

---

[18] Sally Belfrage, *Freedom Summer* (New York: The Viking Press, 1965), p. 48.

[19] King, op. cit., p. 81.

inclusive dialogue at the secondary communication level. The drama of conflict and the challenges of leaders tend to elevate the racial issue in the public opinion arena. The mass media respond by reporting and commenting on racial events in great detail. Thus millions of otherwise uninformed or indifferent individuals are drawn into the public opinion process which Ralph H. Turner and Lewis M. Killian have analyzed as defining and redefining the issue and specifying and solving the problem.[20]

Much obvious evidence reveals the secondary communication dialogue. Since 1954 a voluminous scientific, quasi-scientific and popular literature on the race issue has appeared. Further evidence is found in the heavy racial loading of newspapers, magazines, television and radio broadcasting and the motion pictures. The race problem has been the theme of numerous organizations and meetings at all levels of power and status. From such evidence it would seem reasonable to conclude that few if any Americans have escaped some degree of involvement in the dialogue over the race issue.

We may now summarize the argument briefly. Realistic racial conflict tends to reduce customary interracial communication between status unequals regarding trivial matters within the established communication etiquette. On the other hand, conflict tends to extend communication regarding significant issues with genuine feelings and within noncustomary structures and situations. At the secondary level both the volume of communication and the number of communicators are greatly increased by realistic conflict. These observations would seem to warrant the conclusion that communication within the general social system is extended by realistic racial conflict.

SOLIDARITY FUNCTIONS

A corollary of the claim that racial conflict interrupts communication is the assertion that conflict also is seriously, perhaps even radically disunifying. Struggles between Negroes and whites are thought to split the society and destroy social solidarity. It is at once evident that such a claim implies the prior existence of a unified or relatively unified biracial system. Notwithstanding difference of status and condition, the racial sectors are envisaged as joined in the consensus and structure of the society.

A judicious examination of the facts suggests that the claim that racial conflict is seriously, perhaps even radically disunifying is not altogether correct. On the one hand, the image of biracial solidarity tends

[20] Ralph H. Turner and Lewis M. Killian, *Collective Behavior* (Englewood Cliffs, N.J.: Prentice-Hall, 1957), chaps. 11 and 12.

to be exaggerated. On the other, realistic racial conflict serves some important unifying functions within the social system.

As Logan Wilson and William Kolb have observed, the consensus of the society is organized around a core of "ultimate values."[21] "In our own society," they assert, "we have developed such ultimate values as the dignity of the individual, equality of opportunity, the right to life, liberty, and the pursuit of happiness, and the growth of the free personality."

Far from rejecting or challenging these ultimate values, the ideological thrust of realistic racial conflict affirms them.[22] That is, the ultimate values of the society constitute starting points of ideology and action in racial conflict. As Wilson Record and others have observed, Negro protest and improvement movements are thoroughly American in assumption and objectives.[23]

This fact creates an interesting strategic dilemma for the White Citizens Councils, the resurgent Ku Klux Klan and similar manifestations of the so-called "white backlash." The ideology of racial conflict has preempted the traditional high ground of the core values and ultimate morality. The reactionary groups are thus left no defensible position within the national ethos from which to mount their attacks.

One consequence of realistic racial conflict, then, is to bring the core values of the society into sharp focus and national attention. People are exhorted, even forced to think about the basic societal tenets and to consider their meaning and applications. A dynamic force is thus joined to latent dedication in support of the unifying values of the society. Thus, as Coser has observed, far from being altogether disunifying, realistic conflict functions to reaffirm the core and unifying values of the society.[24] In other words the "two faces of society" are seen to be complementary and mutually supporting.

The primacy of core values in realistic racial conflict is revealed in many ways. Martin Luther King places the ultimate values of the society at the center of his theoretic system of non-violent mass action.[25] In his "Letter from Birmingham Jail" he refers to "justice," "freedom," "understanding," "brotherhood," "constitutional rights," "promise of democracy" and "truth." See how he identifies the goal of racial freedom with the basic societal value of freedom. "We will reach the goal

---

[21] Logan Wilson and William L. Kolb, *Sociological Analysis* (New York: Harcourt, Brace & Co., 1949), p. 513.

[22] Pettigrew, op. cit., p. 193.

[23] Record, op. cit.; Pettigrew, op. cit.; Broom and Glenn, op. cit.

[24] Coser, op. cit., pp. 127–128.

[25] King, op. cit., pp. 77–100.

of freedom in Birmingham and all over the nation, because the goal of America is freedom."[26]

One impact of realistic racial conflict is upon interpretation of core values and the means of their achievement. Thus, the issue is not whether or not men shall be free and equal, but whether these values are reserved to white men or are applicable to Negroes as well. Or again, the phrases "gradualism" and "direct action" depict an important point of disagreement over means to universally affirmed ends. But, it may be observed that when men agree on the ends of life, their quarrels are not in themselves disunifying.

Further, the very process of realistic racial conflict is intrinsically functional. Participants in the conflict are united by the process of struggle itself. The controversy is a unique and shared social possession. It fills an interactional vacuum maintained in the traditional structure by limited social contacts and alienation.

At the same time, as Coser has argued, a relationship established by conflict may lead in time to other forms of interaction.[27] It is conceivable that Negroes and whites who today struggle over freedom and justice and equality may tomorrow be joined in cooperation in the quest of these values.

Conflict is also unifying because the object of struggle is some social value that both parties to the conflict wish to possess or enjoy. The struggle tends to enhance the value and to reveal its importance to both actors. A new area of consensus is thus defined or a prior area of agreement is enlarged. For example, that Negroes and whites struggle through realistic conflict for justice or freedom or equality tends to clarify these values for both and join them in the consensus regarding their importance.

"Simultaneously," as Vander Zanden observes, "within the larger American society the Negro's tactic of non-violent resistance has gained a considerable degree of legitimacy."[28] That is, conflict itself has been defined as coming within the arena of morally justifiable social action. The means as well as the ends, then, are enveloped within the national ethos and serve to enhance societal solidarity. In this respect realistic racial conflict, like labor-management conflict, tends to enter the "American way of life" and constitutes another point of social integration.

Many years ago Edward Alsworth Ross pointed out that nonradical conflicts may function to "sew" the society together.

---

[26] Ibid., p. 97.
[27] Coser, op. cit., pp. 121–122.
[28] Vander Zanden, op. cit., p. 544.

Every species of conflicts interferes with every other species in society
. . . save only when lines of cleavage coincide; in which case they reinforce one another. . . . A society, therefore, which is ridden by a
dozen oppositions along lines running in every direction may actually be
in less danger of being torn with violence or falling to pieces than one
split just along one line. For each new cleavage contributes to narrow
the cross-clefts, so that one might say that society is sewn together by
its inner conflicts.[29]

In this sewing function, realistic racial conflict is interwoven with
political, religious, regional, rural-urban, labor-management, class and
the other persistent threads of struggle that characterize the American
social fabric. What is decisive is the fact that variously struggling factions are united in the consensus of the ultimate societal values. The
conflicts are therefore nonradical, crisscrossing and tend to mitigate
each other.

The proposition on the solidarity function of realistic racial conflict
can now be formulated briefly. The claims that racial conflict is disruptive of social solidarity, though partially true, tend to obscure other
important consequences. Conflict not only projects the combatants into
the social consensus; it also acts to reaffirm the ultimate values around
which the consensus is organized. Moreover, conflict joins opposing
actors in meaningful interaction for ends, whose importance is a matter
of further agreement. From this perspective and within a context of
multifarious crisscrossing threads of opposition, realistic racial conflict
is revealed as helping to "sew" the society together around its underlying societal consensus. We now turn to a consideration of certain
social-psychological consequences of realistic racial conflict.

IDENTITY FUNCTIONS

The fact is often overlooked that realistic racial conflict permits many
Negroes to achieve a substantial measure of identity within the American social system. This function of racial conflict is implied in the foregoing analyses of communication and solidarity. However, the analysis
of the identity function of racial conflict begins with a consideration of

---

[29] Ross, op. cit., pp. 164–165. Dahrendorf, op. cit., pp. 213–215, argues that
conflicts tend to become "superimposed," thus threatening intensification. "Empirical evidence shows," he writes, "that different conflicts may be, and often are,
superimposed in given historical societies, so that the multitude of possible conflict fronts is reduced to a few dominant conflicts. . . . If this is the case, (class)
conflicts of different associations appear superimposed; i.e., the opponents of one
association meet again—with different titles, perhaps, but in identical relations
—in another association." (Pp. 213–214.) Such an argument, however, fails to
recognize that conflicts may superimpose along religious, regional, ethnic or other
fronts and thus mitigate the strength of the class superimposition.

the alienation of the American Negro people. Huddled into urban and rural slums and concentrated in menial and marginal positions in the work force, Negroes are relegated to inferior and collateral statuses in the social structure. Within this structural situation discrimination prevents their sharing in the valued possessions of the society. Legal and customary norms of segregation exclude them from many meaningful contacts and interactions with members of the dominant group.

Isolated and inferior, Negro people searched for the keys to identity and belonging. The social forces that exclude them from significant participation in the general society also keep them disorganized. Thus identity, the feeling of belonging and the sense of social purpose, could be found neither in membership in the larger society nor in participation in a cohesive racial group. Generation after generation of Negroes live out their lives in fruitless detachment and personal emptiness. In another place the alienation of Negro teenagers has been described as follows.

> The quality of Negro teenage culture is conditioned by four decisive factors: race, inferiority, deprivation and youthfulness. Virtually every experience of the Negro teenager is filtered through this complex qualifying medium; every act is a response to a distorted perception of the world. His world is a kind of nightmare, the creation of a carnival reflection chamber. The Negro teenager's culture, his customary modes of behavior, constitute his response to the distorted, frightening, and cruel world that perceives with the guileless realism of youth.[30]

Yet the search for identity goes on. It takes many forms. In the Negro press and voluntary organizations it is reflected in campaigns for race pride and race loyalty. One sector of the Negro intelligentsia invented the "Negro history movement" as a device to create a significant past for a "historyless" people. For the unlettered and unwashed masses the church is the prime agent of group cohesion and identity. The National Association for the Advancement of Colored People and other militant organizations provide an ego-enhancing rallying point for the emancipated and the aggressive. The cult of Negro business, escapist movements like Father Divine's Heaven, and nationalist movements like Marcus Garvey's Universal Negro Improvement Association, and the Black Muslims provide still other arenas for the Negro's search for identity.

Despite this variegated panorama of effort and search, the overriding experience of Negroes remains isolation, inferiority and the ineluctable sense of alienation. Whether involved in the search or not, or perhaps

---

[30] Joseph S. Himes, "Negro Teen Age Culture," *Annals,* 338 (November 1961), pp. 92–93.

just because of such involvement, individuals see themselves as existing outside the basic American social system. Vander Zanden puts it this way: "By virtue of his membership in the Negro group, the Negro suffers considerably in terms of self-esteem and has every incentive for self-hatred."[31] Thus self-conception reflects and in turn supports social experience in a repetition of the familiar self-fulfilling prophecy.

In this situation, collective conflict had an almost magical although unanticipated effect upon group cohesion and sense of identity among Negroes. Group struggle, as Coser and others have pointed out, functions to enhance group solidarity and to clarify group boundaries.[32] The separations among collective units are sharpened and the identity of groups within a social system is established. In the course of conflict collective aims are specified, defined and communicated. Cadres of leaders emerge in a division of labor that grows clearer and more definite. Individuals tend to find niches and become polarized around the collective enterprise. All participants are drawn closer together, both for prosecution of the struggle and for common defense.

As the racial conflict groups become more cohesive and organized, the boundaries with other groups within the American social system become clearer. The distinction between member and nonmember is sharpened. Individuals who stood indecisively between groups or outside the fray are induced or forced to take sides. The zones of intergroup ambiguity diminish. Internally, the conflict groups become more tightly unified and the positions of members are clarified and defined more precisely.

Further, conflict facilitates linkage between the individual and his local reference group as the agent of conflict. The individual thus achieves both a "commitment"[33] and a "role" as a quasi-official group representative in the collective struggle. Pettigrew writes:

> Consider the Student Non-Violent Coordinating Committee (SNICK), . . . The group is cohesive, highly regarded by Negro youth, and dedicated entirely to achieving both personal and societal racial change. Recruits willingly and eagerly devote themselves to the group's goals. And they find themselves systematically rewarded by SNICK for violating the 'Negro' role in every particular. They are expected to evince strong racial pride, to assert their full rights as citizens, to face jail and police brutality unhesitatingly for the cause. . . . Note, . . . that these expected and

---

[31] Vander Zanden, op. cit., p. 546.

[32] Coser, op. cit., p. 34.

[33] Amitai Etzioni employs the concept "commitment" to designate one dimension of cohesiveness and operational effectiveness in complex organizations. See his *Complex Organizations: A Sociological Reader* (New York: Henry Holt Co., 1961), p. 187; and *A Comparative Study of Complex Organization* (Glencoe, Ill.: The Free Press, 1961), pp. 8–22.

rewarded actions all publicly commit the member to the group and its aims.[34]

In the general racial conflict system individuals may act as leaders, organizers and specialists. Some others function as sit-inners, picketers, boycotters, demonstrators, voter registration solicitors, etc. Many others, removed from the areas of overt conflict, participate secondarily or vicariously as financial contributors, audience members, mass media respondents, verbal applauders, etc.

In the interactive process of organized group conflict, self-involvement is the opposite side of the coin of overt action. Actors become absorbed by ego and emotion into the group and the group is projected through their actions. This linkage of individual and group in ego and action is the substance of identity.

Paradoxically, the personal rewards of participation in conflict groups tend to support and facilitate the larger conflict organization and process. Edward Shils and Morris Janowitz have noted this fact in the functions of primary groups in the German Army in World War II.[35] That is, for the individual actor the sense of identity is grounded and sustained by gratification of important personal needs.

In the case of realistic racial conflict, group-based identity functions to facilitate sociopsychic linkage between the individual and the inclusive social system. It was shown above that racial conflict is socially unifying in at least two ways. First, the conflict ideology identifies parties to the conflict with the core values of the social heritage. Thus sit-inners and demonstrators and boycotters and all the others in the drama of racial conflict conceive themselves as the latter-day warriors for the freedom, justice and equality and the other moral values that are historically and essentially American. For many Negroes the sense of alienation is dispelled by a new sense of significance and purpose. The self-image of these embattled Negroes is consequently significantly enhanced.

Second, the conflict process draws organized Negroes into significant social interaction within the inclusive social system. Some of the crucial issues and part of the principal business of the society engage Negroes of all localities and stations in life. Though often only vicariously and by projection, life acquires a new meaning and quality for even the poorest ghetto dweller and meanest sharecropper. The sense of alienation is diminished and the feeling of membership in the inclusive society is enhanced.

---

[34] Pettigrew, op. cit., pp. 165–166.
[35] Edward A. Shils and Morris Janowitz, "Cohesion and Disintegration in the Wehrmacht in World War II," *Public Opinion Quarterly,* 12 (Summer 1948), p. 281.

We may now formulate the argument as follows. Intense alienation kept alive the Negro's quest for identity and meaning. Miraculously almost, realistic racial conflict with its ideological apparatus and action system functions to alleviate alienation and to facilitate identity. Conflict enhances group solidarity, clarifies group boundaries and strengthens the individual-group linkage through ego-emotion commitment and overt action. In-group identity is extended to the larger social system through the extension of communication, the enlargement of the network of social interactions and ideological devotion to national core values. It may be said, then, that through realistic racial conflict America gains some new Americans.

MELVIN M. TUMIN

Violence and democracy

If this were five or seven years ago, some intellectual profit might be derived by speaking about "Some Positive Functions of Violence." But that lode has already been mined to utter exhaustion, so that not even strip-mining will yield enough ore to justify any serious investment.

Moreover, it is apparent that violence per se, like conflict, or peace, or war per se, cannot be judged as valuable or worthless. Further specifications are, obviously, always required—ends sought, values in balance, moral systems to be preserved. Even then, we are so lacking in the arithmetic required for moral or social balance that judgments of the net outcome are likely to be persuasive only to those who share common systems of weighting and preference. How much, for example, does the value of a smashed computer weigh against the value of 180 students momentarily "radicalized" by the sight of police dragging off the peer-group computer-smashers? And that is a relatively simple case; at least sufficiently simple so that we can predict how the polarization of opinion will line up. Maybe.

We are unavoidably led by these considerations to some matters of definition. Else we shall be debating things that are quite different, all under the name of violence. Let us start with the fact that legitimized wars are violent, and that police often use violence. If, then, we ask what we mean by applying the same term to those cases and to many others, such as street fights, riots, and the like, we see that the term violence is used to refer to the *application of force, actual or threatened, that results or promises to result in the harm or destruction of the person or property of others, or in the deprivation of their freedom.* This definition will cover the cases of war, police and street riots, and fist fights. It will also cover genocidal concentration camps and guerrilla wars and, unhappily, most of the practices followed in the rearing of children, in the conduct of classrooms, and in the establishment of durable patterns of dominance and subordination between spouses.

Now it doesn't make very good sense to have a term defined in such a way as to be equally applicable to wars, riots, genocide, and to child-rearing practices and marital relations. Those are not the same things. They differ in the intentions of the violent actors, in the degree of concern for the victim of violence, in the legitimacy of the action, and

Note: With a few minor changes, the text was delivered as an address to the 1970 annual meeting of the Eastern Sociological Society in New York City.
Source: *Dissent,* vol. 17 (July–August 1970), pp. 321–28.

in the degree of harm done or threatened. They also differ in the balance between short- and long-term loss and gain. Note here the presumed long-term gain of violence in child-rearing, as against the short- and long-term *loss* implied by murder and genocide.

Yet, however embarrassing it is to speak of the use of force in these diverse contexts, it is not easy to get away from the fact that the use of force, actual or threatened, to get one's own way over the will of others is a basic modality of human interaction, and nothing seems finally to be able to substitute for it, if we assume that conflict of wills is a persisting feature of human interaction. Of course, there may be those who insist that they have never interposed their wills by force against the wills of others, not even their children's. They would prefer to say they have reasoned, persuaded, cajoled, urged, bargained, compromised, and discussed. I am unwilling to dismiss such claims as *total* nonsense; there are obvious differences in the speed and frequency of resort to force. Yet, however infrequently one resorts to force (and I include the invocation of the legitimate authority of positions here, with its implied threats against the well-being of those who might defy that authority), forceful coercion *is* part of the human game.

Having said this, it is crucial to realize that there are vast differences among societies in the situations they legitimate as justifying the use of violence; in the honors they accord for violent behavior; in the violence of their public entertainment and spectacles; in the glory they impute to violent behavior; and, by contrast, in the extent to which they strive to produce citizens who are sufficiently compassionate and capable of identifying with others, so that they use force, if at all, only with the greatest of reluctance, the greatest of possible gentility, and the quickest possible removal of the forceful pressures.

All this is important, as I see it, so that we shall not be beguiled into accepting as legitimate the question as to why some people are violent and others are not, with its implication that we are dealing with utterly different brands and breeds of human beings.

The fact of the matter is that there *is* violence *in all of us,* and one doesn't need any instinctual theory to account for it. So, too, there is violence in all societies, for societies are the scenes in which the interaction among conflicting wills and purposes takes place. Knowing that may help us become a bit more compassionate in our public responses, even to the kinds of violent behavior that seem most frightening, namely, those that involve one-to-one violence, in situations in which we ourselves are often involved, such as walking in the park, coming home from the theater, and the like. In those cases, maximum identification with the victim is possible, and hence maximum fear is generated for our own safety. Under those circumstances, we are likely to react

with maximum punitiveness, being unable to keep our fears and righteous indignation from shaping our public responses. The implication
here is that those responses should be shaped not by fear and indignation but by a realization of the circumstances that led the offender to his
violent acts and what is required to reduce the likelihood that he and
others will repeat those acts.

The awareness of the extent to which all of us, as individuals and as
members of organized societies, are involved in the capacity for violence
is important, too, as a caution against overlooking our own frequent
use of violence in legitimate and approved contexts, and hence of how
much we officially sponsor violence. These are uses into which we are
socialized from earliest days on, by the model of child-rearing, by the
training in masculinity and standing up for one's rights, by the approval
of the maleness of the contact sports, by the concepts of family, tribal,
and national honor that call us to arms, with high, moral-sounding
phrases and much applause for violent acts committed in good names.

It is not, I *insist,* that violence *per se* in these contexts is less morally
worthy than nonviolence. It is, after all, simply sentimental to deplore
the use of force in human relations simply because it is force or because,
by definition, it involves harm or injury or destruction of property or
person or deprivation of freedom. There is nothing *intrinsically* wrong
with those either. For, there obviously are occasions when the use of
force is eminently justified, as when evil is sure to prevail unless superior counterforce is brought to bear against it, and the evil people and
conditions are forcefully repressed. The loftiness of the pacifist ideal is
matched only by its utter bankruptcy as a doctrine of social or political
action under most conceivable human circumstances.

No—the danger of violence lies first in its *self-commending* character. For it is beguiling; it produces results; it is often emotionally gratify-
ing far beyond compromise and discussion and yielding. For those very
same reasons, once under way, it is far less subject to rational control
and limitation than nonviolence. A primary reason here is the further
incitement to violence that the apparent suffering of the victim seems
to induce in those caught up in violent behavior. The dehumanization
of the victim that is required to permit the initial act of cruelty or
violence seems to be furthered by the triumph of violence and the apparent suffering of the victim. Perhaps this is because the victim's suffering is vivid testimony to his humanity; and until that evidence can
be violently expunged, the man committing violence cannot continue
his violence with an easy mind.

Saying these things causes me to wonder whether in fact I am so
much a product of my own culture and time that I cannot really en-

vision a world in which the resort to violence is absolutely minimal, and in which the training in childhood is such that cruelty and forceful harm to others is seen in just those terms, with all their implied condemnation. I may be making the mistake in characterizing as a pan-human modality something that is indeed parochial and culturally limited, but so deeply ingrained as not to be transcendable into a new way of thinking about men. I beg you, however, not to tax me with a lack of imagination. I have had my utopian dreams along with the best or worst of you. Rather, let us seek to discover the conditions of social organization that might minimize the use of violence.

I give you as a starter a dilemma to the effect that the condition necessary for making human beings out of prehuman babies is organized social life, and that organized social life always has boundaries that can be maintained only by some sense of loyalty and commitment to one's ingroups. In turn, this implies outgroups that are alien, strangers and desecrators of the secular and sacred norms, whether these are kin, clan, tribes, ethnic groups, or nation-states. The existence of these aggregates is therefore highly conducive to the use of force. Moreover, as they grow larger, from clan to state to nation, they almost always involve the accumulation of superior technologies of destruction as instruments of the collectivity, and hence make possible larger-scale human killing. A state may someday be created that does not reflect the special interests of one class over another. But that won't have anything to do with its need to resort to force to manage the diverse claims upon the common goods and services and to restrain the general range of deviation that is generic to all societies, but especially so in societies made up of diverse and numerous peoples. Above all, unless there exists some unenvisionable form of world society, those national aggregates seem unavoidably led to mutual destruction by actions they perceive as necessary for national survival.

Our own society is surely a curious mixture of peace and force. Perhaps more than any other large-scale society in the world we are nominally committed to the peaceful resolution of internal conflicts and have probably done no worse than most others in seeking peaceful means of reconciling international conflicts. I suppose I ought immediately to say that we have done no better than others either, lest someone see evil intentions in my phrases. In any event, given this commitment in our *ideals,* we are surely a sad sight in our *actualities.* Any analysis of the causes of violence in the United States, and especially of criminal violence, has to take into account the role of social and economic inequalities (in the face of claims to equal opportunity, and the pressure to live well and ostentatiously) in the production of criminal violence, especially of such acts as robbery.

I am not yet including political violence—in the ghettos and on the college campuses. For the moment I deliberately confine myself to the more common forms of criminal violence, as defined for instance by the FBI Index. Violent seizure of what one wants when one cannot get it without violence seems to be now, as always in our history, a fairly normal procedure for two segments of our population. First, the wealthy and the powerful who, when blocked by existing laws or rules from having their way, are capable, by stealth or force or both, of altering the rules or avoiding them, without much fear of reprisal. Second, the group that, because of its deprived and degraded condition of life, acts as though it had little or nothing to lose and hence is "free" to engage in violent behavior without serious concern for the possible negative consequences if caught.

Predictably, the focus of concern and indignation regarding violence is upon the second group, since the depredations of the first group, however much more injurious to the public well-being, are either concealed from the public view or are converted by semantic legerdemain into contributions to the public welfare. It is quite evident, however, that the normally punitive and indignant responses of the public to the violence of the deprived have done little or nothing to reduce the likelihood of more violence in the future. It seems equally clear that if we wish people to seek their ends with the same steady refrain from violence which we practice, we have to make it as possible for them as it is for us to achieve their life's ambitions through peaceful, noncriminal means.

If one says petulantly, in response, that after all one has worked *his* way through life arduously, nonviolently, and without resort to crime, then the answer clearly is that we shall have to provide the same kinds of life histories for those whom we wish to convert to nonviolent behavior. Similarly, if we wish others to be as restrained by concern for consequences as we are by our consideration of what there is to lose for us, then we shall have to see to it that they have as much to lose and that they can perceive things this way. Or we shall have to see to it that the same preponderance of noncriminal, nonviolent stimuli, associations, and rewards are present in their lives as in ours. Or, if you prefer a criminal or violent subculture theory, then we shall have to create the same kinds of noncriminal subcultures for *their* exposure. Or, if you prefer a "drift" theory of delinquency and violence, then we shall have to provide the same kinds of blockages to drift into delinquency and violence as are present in our lives.

I take it, moreover, that I don't have to spend even a moment here discussing the contribution of our prisons and our usual treatment of criminals to the furtherance of their criminal and violent careers. That, of course, is so painfully evident that we are restrained from tearing down prison walls with our own hands only because we wouldn't know what to substitute and because there would be many, many more opposed to us who believe in prisons and all they imply.

The issues of criminal violence are not exhausted, however, by dealing only with robbery, mugging, and the like. We are confronted with the fact that two violent crimes, murder and rape, are often best understood as violence among intimates.

More than half, and sometimes as many as two-thirds or three-quarters, of these two acts are committed by people against others with whom they have had some degree of previous intimacy, including husband-wife, parent-child, and brother-sister relationships. The same emotions that permit people in these relationships to be benignly concerned with each other provide the psychic triggers to violence when the conditions of peaceful intimacy are betrayed or violated. Because these are mostly thoughtless, mindless, spontaneous acts, they are probably outside the reach of normal deterrence, except among those who have so very much to lose if caught that they are bereft even of the power to act out their most intense passion.

So, wounded as many of us are by that impotence induced by future-mindedness, we suffer, instead, ulcerated colons or deeply-gnashed and ground-down teeth, or other psychosomatic ailments, plus endless wounded pride, as our price for keeping the peace. And even if we were to let ourselves go and indulge our rage, most of us would probably find ourselves so horrified by our first acts of "self-liberation" as from then on to be permanently imprisoned by contrition and shame. Or, worse still, we might develop a real taste for violent indulgence, and discover ourselves in endless conflict between our former and new selves.

In any event, it is important to make distinctions among the various acts all of which are classified as criminal violence, and to see how utterly different in onset, actors, consequences, motives, and the like they often are. After all, rape, especially when it is postcoital regret, as it often is, is hardly the same action system as assaulting a strange woman in whose purse *alone* you are interested, but whom you must hurt enough to be sure she cannot identify you. Such diversity of motives and other parts of the action systems in various violent crimes is an elementary consideration for sophisticated sociologist. But how little this notion seems to have penetrated the minds of the lay public and of our government officials!

Fritz Redl has recently written a gorgeous paper on violence in the schools, in which he delineates 12 different sets of motives and reasons behind violent actions by school children. These actions are so diverse in their motivation and so utterly different in what they call for by way of appropriate response, that to treat them homogeneously as violence is to be absurd. If this is true.for school children, it cannot be less true for adults.

Turning to political violence brings us to quite a different set of issues. Let it be acknowledged at the outset that this society is now engaged in what many, including myself, consider to be an utterly unwarranted and murderous war. I do not think the other side is any better, morally or politically, and in peacetime they are politically far worse than we are as a system. But that is not the issue, because I do not think we are doing anything effective to see to it that in peacetime they may have the same system of peaceful resolution of internal conflicts that we do. I do not for a moment deny that our so-called national leaders believe their own slogans. That is a cause for despair. I am sure they believe their slogans about preserving democracy and the free world. But the fact of the matter is that they are not accomplishing this at all; and, of course, there is no solution at this moment, and given these costs, except to stop the war immediately. So any discussion of internal violence committed by radical or other students in the name of stopping the war has to take account of the war and all it implies.

There is today in our society a very tenuous balance of diverse political forces, with the majority seeming inclined to advocate and applaud forceful repression of all kinds of liberties and freedoms in the name of peace and order. Given this condition, one has to hope and pray that our antiwar protesters will be more rational, circumspect, restrained, calculating, and knowledgeable than we or anybody has any right to expect them to be under the circumstances.

On the one hand, we cannot urge them to withhold their demonstrations and their protests simply because they may evoke the bitter antilibertarian sentiments and approval of authoritarian power that seem to characterize many of our fellow citizens. Yet we dare not neglect these possibilities. For after all, as a *collective* society, we are, in our *formal* operations, probably much more democratic than one would expect, given the sentiment-structure and proclivities for authoritarianism that seem to characterize so many of the increasingly less silent majority. Hence, while one cannot argue against demonstrations on the grounds that they may enrage others, one can urge that the demonstrators exercise a modicum of rational calculation in behalf of preserving the fabric of democratic processes, for them and for us.

For there is a great current threat to that unbelievable and marvelous social invention called democratic polity. It is a very tender and easily bruised plant. Its roots are always shallow. It needs extraordinary care and cultivation. It is all too easily overcome by noxious airs and weeds. Enough of this horticultural metaphor. The fact of the matter is that there is no conceivable decent life possible by any of the values that most of us have come to appreciate if we do not have a democratic society. And so we must ask our young people and our other protesters (and ourselves) not to let their despair and impatience lead them to deal lightly with democracy. We have barely begun to establish democracy in this country. We shall ruin it for sure if we start matching violence with violence.

Nor can we afford to overlook distinctions between more and less democratic societies or mechanisms. We cannot afford to clamor for taking the whole society down because it is so rotten in so many of the things it does. For, on the balance, there is still much to cherish and cultivate and harbor and protect.

I do not believe that President Nixon or Vice-President Agnew are capable of appreciating these distinctions, however unsubtle they are. We are in that ironic situation where we have to ask ourselves, and others like us, including our children and our students, to be more sensible, more wise, more restrained, more concerned for the welfare of our society and the preservation of our barely flourishing democratic processes than the elected officials who are selected and paid to do just that for us.

Free speech in this country is so very limited and yet so far more ample and broad-reaching than any conceivable alternative system might provide today or tomorrow, that those who need free speech to live, as all of us do, cannot sanction a policy, however righteously motivated, of meeting the denial of free speech by some with a denial of free speech to others. I am not sure at all that virtue will triumph. It almost never does. But then there is no alternative, because the other possible courses of action involve us in choosing whose *dictatorial* authority we prefer. And I prefer none.

The same considerations, of course, apply to the fight against inequality, whether between black and white, and whether economic, social, or political. The dramatic and symbolic value of violent acts of protest and demonstration cannot be denied. But that value has to be weighed against the overall consequences, now and in the future. At least *I* have to weigh them in judging them. If I were black and poor, I cannot guarantee that I would not be more persuaded by my despair and rage at the slow pace of change than I would be by rational calculations about possible futures, slowly eked out over a lifetime of pain and denial.

But that does not make correct the policies advocated out of despair. It only makes them understandable. There is still a visible enough chance of slow improvement toward greater equality in this country for me, in my judgment, to insist on preserving those mechanisms over other political programs, simply because all other alternatives that I have heard are sure to take us all beyond recovery of anything decent. It is surely one of the gifts of life and of an advantaged position, and one of its attendant obligations, to advocate programs that one can see as more correct and promising than others, however unappealing they are to the victims of the situations one is trying to correct. Victims may speak with true, righteous indignation from their hearts. But that isn't necessarily the same as sound politics.

I was saved during my youthful Bolshevism by professors who understood what was agitating me and others like me, and who were unwilling to discard me on the academic junk heap simply because I was wild and irrational in my politics. In retrospect I am aware how important it was that I made it possible, by not being myself totally impossible, for them to protect me from others who did not understand. I was also saved by the fact that I did not have a subculture of campus violence to reinforce my own very hesitant tendencies in that direction. It was, I confess, rather easy to prate Bolshevik doctrines about the "transitional dictatorship of the proletariat" so long as I did not have to face the consequences of that system in action or of the actual violent revolutionary actions that other circumstances might have called forth.

I do not expect my students to be any wiser than I was. And I am aware of the supportive subcultures of violence that have sprung up on campuses and of how exhilarating they can be. But I know, too, that the most irresponsible among the students threaten that incredibly beautiful thing called the free university as much as do those many mindless educators who resist all change. One cannot prefer the embittered clamor by the aged for stability to the exuberance of the youth for destructiveness, or vice versa. They are both antagonistic to decent civility and society.

There are at least two rules here that must be followed if any of us is to have a chance to survive these challenges. The first is that one must be prepared to lose once in a while, and to search for ways to win again within the framework of organized social life, assuming the processes of change are available. Those who are not prepared to lose cannot live in a democracy, and they are enemies of democracy.

The other rule, just as basic, is that a democracy means participation in decision-making at all relevant points by all persons affected by the decisions. The ancient and traditional model of the wise captor and the humble captive that has dominated campuses heretofore no longer will work. Fortunately, some exemplary campuses are beginning to develop mechanisms to enforce both those rules—the rules of alternating winning and losing, without destroying the fabric of the organized life; and the rule of maximizing relevant participation. Therein lies our only hope.

Those rules also tell us what is wrong with violence and what is right about nonviolence. Violence, it is clear, means the suspension or the destruction of democracy. For, however much it may be true that democratic societies have come into being only after violent overthrow of the previous societies, it is equally true that democracies could not begin to survive until they had purged their systems of the revolutionary cast of mind and of those cultivated inclinations to resort to violence. By inference this tells us what is right about democracy. Among other things, it minimizes the resort to violence.

I am obviously giving top priority to the maintenance and strengthening of democracy and equality in any set of solutions offered for present-day problems. In these regards, this is a position that is substantially different from those being offered from the Right and the so-called Left. The Right is saying, in effect, that we must have order and stability at virtually any cost. The so-called Left is saying that we must have change at virtually any cost. What we will surely get if either side prevails is the range of any and all, and mostly negative, costs, and that means costs to the values of democracy and equality. If the "Right" is wrong in urging forceful repression of general freedoms and the suspension of democratic governance in order to yield order and stability, the "Left" is no less wrong in urging the same things in the name of their slogans.

It will no longer do to endorse the destruction by either side because we understand and commiserate with what led people to engage in the destruction. Those who believe that this society is so totally bad that it must be torn down come what may and, along with it, the universities, are as cruel and vicious enemies of democracy, fair play, and equality as those who believe and act as if this society was totally good and must be preserved intact at any cost.

I am aware, as the prophet has warned, that those who stand in the middle during historical moments when everything is polarized are likely to get symmetrical bumps on both sides of their heads. But where else is there to stand?

C. Factual and research considerations

DONALD VON ESCHEN, JEROME KIRK, and MAURICE PINARD

The organizational substructure of disorderly politics

According to the theory of mass society, organizational membership drags people into routine politics, while discouraging participation in direct action movements. The thesis of this paper is that this theory needs severe modification. First, for an important class of organizations—organizations with goals unincorporated by the larger society or containing members with interests or values that are unincorporated—membership increases rather than inhibits participation. This is indicated both by a theoretical analysis of mass theory and by data gathered from participants in the Negro sit-in movement of the early 1960s. Second, this data indicates that the existence of many such organizations is necessary if a direct action movement is to be strong. Thus, not only routine, but disorderly politics too requires an organizational substructure to create and sustain it. Third, the data indicates that the substructures of these two types of politics are not totally distinct, but rather share certain organizations in common. Some organizations seem to generate participation in both types simultaneously, while others may, at one point in their history, inhibit participation, but at another, when a movement has gathered strength, generate it. In short, theory and data suggest the need for a major revision of mass theory which takes the variable of unincorporation into account.

Most formal democracies have experienced mass movements that go outside the routine channels of political action to obtain their aims. These movements often engage in illegal or semi-illegal acts and occasionally, intentionally or unintentionally, generate violence. Because they bypass normal channels, they are generally termed direct action movements. Because they frequently give rise to disorder, the kind of politics they involve might best be termed disorderly politics. The cause of such movements has not yet been resolved. One of the more common

Note: We would like to thank Charles Perrow for comments on an earlier draft of this paper. As he disagreed with parts of our analysis, however, he should not be held responsible for any errors it may contain.

Source: *Social Forces*, vol. 49 (June 1971), pp. 529–44.

explanations for their rise argues in terms of "hard" deprivations—deprivations of income, status, power—and facilitating conditions. Thus, for example, the trade union movement, which involved considerable disorder in its early phases, has been explained in terms of such deprivations as long hours, low prestige, and the like, and in terms of such facilitating conditions as the growth of large plants, plants which broke the personal ties between worker and manager, permitted the concentration of activists, etc. This perspective can be termed the class theory of direct action movements. Recently, however, sociologists and other writers have stressed an alternative theory, the theory of massification.[1] This theory points to organizational membership as its central explanatory variable. A rich organizational life, it is argued, drags people into routine politics while simultaneously reducing their alienation from the system, leading in this way to restrained "rational" politics. An impoverished organizational life, on the other hand, leads to alienation and a consequent susceptibility to mass, direct political action. It constitutes the basis for disorderly politics.

The theories are not entirely distinct conceptually. Both, for instance, stress lack of power as a major cause of participation in direct action movements. But, in general, the thrust of the two theories is in quite different directions. Mass theorists stress a "soft" deprivation—personality disorder—and they see people joining direct action movements less because they are deprived than because, without organizational membership, they are not sufficiently subject to social control, are not socialized to support routine and abhor disorderly politics, are not provided with accurate information about the latent functions of the system and the limited possibilities of change, etc. Mass theory thus adds a distinct perspective to our understanding of direct action movements. In particular, when it stresses personality disorders and inaccurate information, it tends to stand Marx, one of the major class theorists, on his head, suggesting that it is not, as he argued, false consciousness that prevents such movements, but that rather causes them.

Which theory is true? On the basis of both a theoretical analysis and an analysis of data collected from participants in a recent direct action movement involving considerable disorder—the Negro sit-in movement

---

[1] The writers and works generally cited as being in this tradition are Arendt (1958), Kornhauser (1959), Nisbet (1953), and Selznick (1960). It is not clear to us that all these writers are saying precisely the same things. We have had to choose among them, therefore, in our exposition of the theory. As Kornhauser's statement is the fullest and as it consists of a synthesis of the writings of the others (insofar as this is possible), our treatment shall rely primarily on his analysis.

of the early 1960s[2]—we shall argue that mass theory contains serious defects.[3]

1. We shall argue that organizational involvement does not necessarily decrease participation in direct action movements and that the participants cannot therefore be regarded as unusually massified.

2. On the contrary, some organizations, in fact, increase participation. Thus, disorderly politics has an organizational substructure dragging people into activity just as does routine politics.

3. Furthermore, we shall argue that this substructure is of major importance, that without it strong movements would be much less likely to arise.

4. And this thesis is not simply trivially true. Mass theorists would grant that organizations directing movements increase the participation of their members. But we shall argue that the organizational substructure is much wider than this; that potentially, in fact, it consists of all organizations with members whose values or interests are unincorporated in the larger society, incorporation being defined here as the ability to effectively influence public policy to resolve one's grievances.

5. This means that even organizations that normally inhibit such participation may at times generate it.

6. Because of the breadth of this substructure, many of these organizations generate participation in both disorderly and routine politics. Thus, we shall argue that no absolute distinction between these types of political action should be made; that which a person chooses depends heavily on which he sees as being more effective, and this is strongly conditioned by his previous experiences.

7. Finally, we shall argue that organizational involvement does not always reduce alienation. Whether this occurs depends on whether the organization is able to generate power.

---

[2] That the sit-in movement was a direct action movement is probably clear to most readers; that it was disorderly, may not be. Nevertheless, disorderly it frequently was. Demonstrators broke trespass laws and were arrested for doing so. Demonstrations triggered mob violence by white opponents of the movement, attacks which occasionally led to counter-violence by Negro bystanders. For an argument that this disorder was an essential feature of the political process by which the sit-in movement attained some of its ends, see Von Eschen et al. (1969a; 1969b).

[3] In this paper we concentrate on the role of *alienating* organizations and their crucial importance as a substructure for the emergence of direct action movements. A theoretical critique of mass theory, taking into account other types of organizations and, in addition, informal networks, can be found in Pinard (1968). Empirical evidence supporting this critique can be found in Pinard (1971: chap. 11).

8. Furthermore, at times, power may be generated by disorderly politics (often can only be so generated) rather than through the use of routine methods.[4] Organizations may thus reduce alienation not by inhibiting direct action, but by generating it.

THE POLITICS OF MASS SOCIETY: A STATEMENT OF THE THEORY

Our counter-propositions flow not simply from the sit-in data; they are implied by mass theory itself once that theory is subjected to a logical analysis. In fact, the first two propositions were arrived at through such analysis *before* the data were collected, the research being designed to test them. To show that a logical analysis of mass theory implies the counter-propositions, we need a statement of the theory.

The theory has two parts.

First, it argues that organizations drag people into routine politics. They do this by throwing them into contact with politically involved people, integrating them into communication channels where they learn of pending political decisions likely to affect their fate, etc. Furthermore, it is argued that without this organizational life most men would be politically apathetic, so that such involvement does not simply aid participation, it is of major importance for it. We think the evidence for this part of the theory is relatively adequate.[5]

Second, it argues that organizations inhibit participation in disorderly politics. They do this by reducing alienation from the political system and this is done in at least the following ways:

A. The increased activity in routine politics generated by organizational involvement itself inhibits participation by giving the individual political control. At the same time, trade unions, professional associations, etc., give him direct control over his work. In short, integration into organizations reduces the need to engage in disorderly politics by preventing deprivations of power, income and status.

B. Associations provide their members with fellowship, giving them more satisfactory lives and consequently greater satisfaction with the system.[6]

---

[4] For an analysis of how direct action movements can generate power and the conditions under which they will be successful, see Von Eschen et al. (1969a; 1969b).

[5] The role secondary organizations play in dragging people into *routine* politics has been particularly well demonstrated by Lipset et al. (1956; esp. 69–105). See also Erbe (1964).

[6] Nisbet (1953), for instance, writes about modern man "seeking fellowship in some kind of moral community," about his "isolation," about the "misery of estrangement, the horror of aloneness," etc.

C. Organizations provide their members with accurate information about the functioning of the society, economy, polity, and international system, thus inhibiting participation in direct action movements by providing people with an understanding of the latent functions of apparently dysfunctional arrangements and by preventing unrealistic hopes.

D. Organizations provide their members with interests that distract them from politics by capturing their emotions, time, and energy.

E. Organizations socialize their members to accept society and its rules of the game. The procedural life of these groups trains their members in the habits of democratic action—debate, negotiation, compromise, etc.—while they simultaneously propagandize their members to accept disagreeable features of their society (e.g., the American Farm Bureau Federation asks its members to take responsibility for their deteriorating economic position rather than blaming the government or "the system").

In addition, although this has not been stressed by mass theorists, it seems likely that:

F. Organizations sanction deviant members. As non-routine action is generally disapproved, we can expect groups to bring sanctions to bear on any of their members who should attempt to engage in it.

Now, it is our contention that a logical analysis of this theory implies our counter-propositions. Empirical data from the sit-in movement confirms this analysis.

THE POLITICS OF MASS SOCIETY: A THEORETICAL AND EMPIRICAL CRITIQUE

The first thing to note about this theory is the subordinate role assigned to "hard" deprivations. They are mentioned only in point A. The rest of the points stress factors with a totally different thrust. In particular, insofar as the mass theorist stresses fellowship and information, the analysis gives the impression that people revolt only through error; that is, through displacement of frustration and through lack of information (as if accurate information would always reveal that no radical changes in the system are needed and that what changes are necessary can always be brought about through routine means). Insofar as socialization is stressed, the analysis gives the impression that revolts occur only through a failure of social control. Similarly, the other points minimize the role of real grievances.

But it is a mistake to ignore the role of "hard" deprivations. Such deprivations clearly underlay most of the movements that have so concerned mass theorists. For instance, economic grievances clearly were a major factor in the rise of Nazism and Communism in pre-war Germany. As Pratt (1948) has shown, the strength of the vote for these two parties varied with the depths of the economic crisis, both parties losing votes with the momentary upturn in the economy of 1924.[7] Similarly, deprivations underlay the Communist movement in France and Italy as has been shown by Cantril (1958). The same was true for Poujadism (Lipset, 1960:159–160), and Trow (1958) has argued this for McCarthyism in the United States.[8] We have shown in another paper (Pinard et al., 1969) the importance of deprivations for participation in the direct action movement studied empirically in this paper—the Negro sit-in movement.

The second thing to note about the theory is that insofar as mass theorists do assign importance to deprivations, they assume that they can be prevented by organizational membership.

But clearly this too is not always true. There are many conditions in any society that are only marginally susceptible to organizational control. Individuals with values fundamentally opposed to the current organization of society—individuals, say, committed to disarmament, or to a substantial redistribution of income, and the like—are not likely to be able to fundamentally alter the society through organizational membership. This inability of organizations to prevent deprivations is particularly clear when a racial or ethnic subgroup is subjected to a subordinate position by an adamant majority, as are Negroes in the U.S. It is clear, also, during severe economic crises of the sort underlying those movements over which mass theorists have been most concerned. For instance, in pre-war Germany, the Nazi and Communist movements were due largely to the depression, but depressions hurt the organized as well as the unorganized. Similarly, organizations offer little protection for doomed classes, such as the small businessmen supporting Poujade, a class being crushed by the long-term trend toward economic rationalization.[9]

These two criticisms, when combined with the propositions of mass theory itself, imply our counter-propositions.

Proposition 1. Not all organizations inhibit participation in disorderly politics. Thus one should not expect participants to be unusually massified.

---

[7] We no longer have access to Pratt's thesis and thus cannot cite the exact page references.

[8] Trow (1958) demonstrates that support for McCarthy came most heavily from small businessmen, a "doomed" class in a rationalizing society.

[9] For an elaboration of this argument about doomed classes, see Gusfield (1962).

Mass theory argues that organizations inhibit participation in disorderly politics by preventing deprivation and socializing individuals to accept whatever society provides them. But we now have reason to believe that organizations containing deprived individuals are, at times, not likely to have the power to reduce deprivations. Furthermore, insofar as they represent the interests of deprived people, they will have goals in opposition to the larger society, thus failing to socialize their members to accept the society. Such groups with oppositional goals and little power we will call alienating organizations. For these organizations, points A and D of mass theory are inapplicable. Thus, without distinguishing types of organizations, we should not expect the theory to hold.

This is what our data show.

Late in 1961, several African diplomats traveling between New York and Washington, D.C., were refused service in restaurants on Route 40 in Maryland. CORE (the Congress of Racial Equality) responded by organizing a demonstration in cooperation with local civil rights organizations. On December 16, an estimated 500 to 600 demonstrators from the Eastern seaboard converged on the Maryland section of Route 40, testing to see if restaurants had desegregated, and, if they hadn't, "sitting in," establishing picket lines, and occasionally submitting to arrest. Of these, 386 filled out self-administered questionnaires.[10]

We asked the participants to mention the two organizations most important to them, excluding churches and those organizations sponsoring the demonstrations. They were then asked to place a check in one of a series of concentric circles according to how far they felt from the center of things in each organization. This was taken as a measure of how

---

[10] Although only two-thirds of the demonstrators filled out questionnaires, and some of these only filled them out in part, we believe that the sample is, by and large, representative of the total group of demonstrators. The reason is that noncompletion was largely a random process. Of greatest importance, it was not due to refusal. We had been given the explicit and public approval of the CORE leadership to hand out questionnaires. Given this approval, virtually none of the demonstrators objected to filling them out. Instead, non-completion resulted largely from the following process: Before demonstrating, the participants were formed into "demonstrating groups" of from 8 to 10 persons. These groups were then dispatched, one by one, to targets from an assemblage point as the need arose. All groups either formed at or were supposed to pass through the assemblage point in Baltimore. It was at this point that we handed out questionnaires. The respondents worked at answering the questions until their group was dispatched to a target. For some groups, dispatching occurred before they could finish, with the result that their questionnaires were either not returned or were returned only partially completed. This should not, however, bias the sample, for both assignment to a group and the selection of a group to hit a particular target was essentially random. Thus, we have no reason to believe our sample is biased in any way.

TABLE 1

Neither length of participation nor amount of participation is inversely related to sheer organizational involvement

	Number of organizations into which respondent reports himself integrated		
	≥2	1	None
Percent who joined a year or more ago...............	67% (24)	30% (70)	30% (175)
Percent on ≥ three previous demonstrations...........	80% (25)	58% (72)	48% (182)

Note: In all tables, numbers in parentheses are the case bases of the corresponding percentages.

involved or integrated they were in the group. That it was a valid measure is suggested by its high correlation with office-holding: In nearly half the cases where a respondent was classified as being highly integrated, he either had held or was holding an office in the organization. This was true in only 8 percent of those cases where respondents were not so classified. In Table 1 we have divided our respondents according to the number of groups in which they reported being near the center of things; none, one, or two or more. Their degree of participation in the sit-in movement was measured by how long they had been in the movement and how many times they had been out on demonstrations. As the table shows, among the sit-inners, increased organizational involvement did *not* decrease participation.

If organizational involvement does not uniformly inhibit participation, we should not expect participants in mass movements to be unusually massified. This too is what our data show. Approximately 62 percent of the demonstrators mentioned at least one organization. (Note that this is greater than is indicated by the marginals in Table 1, because there we counted only those *highly* involved.) In addition, of those mentioning organizations, 42 percent had held or were holding an office in at least one of their organizations. This rate of membership compares well with the rates found in national surveys.[11]

Proposition 2. Alienating organizations increase rather than inhibit participation in disorderly politics.

The causal mechanisms set forth by mass theorists suggest that alienating organizations should generate rather than inhibit participation in disorderly politics. The socialization mechanism should increase dissatisfaction with society rather than its acceptance and this dissatisfaction should push individuals toward direct action given the lack of routine power possessed by the group. The information mechanism should provide information about the dysfunctions of society, and

---

[11] See Rose (1967:218–221) for a summary of these surveys.

about the availability of non-routine means. The focusing mechanism should make politics the center of the members' concern (rather than distracting them from it). The sanction mechanism should pressure members of groups sympathetic to direct action to participate. Finally, if fellowship is in fact provided by organizations, the possibility of withdrawing it provides the group with a particularly powerful sanction to be used in mobilization. Thus, through the *same* causal processes at work in normal groups, alienating organizations should sustain rather than inhibit participation.

This again is what our data show. Prior to running any tables, we coded the groups in which our respondents were involved into two classes—alienating and conformist—the former being those organizations with oppositional goals and little power. Thus, among groups specifically concerned with integration, the National Association for the Advancement of Colored People, the Southern Christian Leadership Conference, etc., were classified as alienating, while such groups as the Urban League were classified as conforming. Among political groups, the Americans for Democratic Action, the Young People's Socialist League, etc., were classified as alienating, while such groups as the Democratic and Republican parties were classified as conforming. Finally, such nonpolitical groups as sororities, the Y.M.C.A., and Newman Club were classified as conforming.

Some illustrations should make the criteria and process of classification clear. Let us begin by taking an easy case, the contrasting classification of the Republican party and the Young People's Socialist League. Two criteria had to be met before a group could be classified as alienating: it had to have goals in fundamental opposition to the larger society, *and* it had to be relatively powerless to implement these goals. Clearly, the YPSL had such goals and the Republican party not; and clearly, too, YPSL had little power, while the Republican party has substantial influence. The placement of most organizations was clearcut in this manner. The problem arises with organizations close to the borderline. To illustrate the care taken to make accurate classifications of these organizations, let us indicate how we arrived at the contrasting classification of the NAACP and the Urban League. On first sight it might be thought that, in terms of goals, both organizations should be classified as alienating; while in terms of power, conforming. However, applying our two criteria carefully, on the basis of our information about the nature of these two organizations in 1960–61, this did not seem to us to be the case. The NAACP in 1960–61, the time of our study, articulated a major critique of U.S. society. It was not clear to us that the Urban League did. First, the senior author of this paper had interviewed a large number of Negroes in Gary, Indiana, in 1957–59, and had been struck by the degree to which members of the Urban League stressed self-improvement as the means of advancement for Negroes, as opposed to the active struggle against whites emphasized by the NAACP. Second, a striking difference between these organizations showed up in a study James Wilson (1960) carried out at about the same time in Chicago. His data indicated that the organizations differed greatly in the degree of white participation at the leadership levels, the NAACP having very little, while the Urban League had considerable, and that the organizations were perceived quite differently by whites, the NAACP being perceived by many whites as "too radical." Finally, the Baltimore Urban League, the major source of Urban League participation in the Maryland demonstrations we studied, did not, in 1961, appear to be in fundamental opposition to whites, in sharp contrast to the Baltimore NAACP, which was highly militant. In short, in terms of goals, the NAACP was clearly alienating, while this was not clear for the Urban League. Turning now to power, it might be argued that the NAACP had substantial power, as indicated by its success in getting legal action against school desegregation. However, this fails to take into account the multiplicity of the goals of the NAACP, which included not just school desegregation, but equal employment, open housing, an end to police brutality, etc. Although the NAACP might obtain some of these goals, it was unlikely to obtain most without a prolonged struggle. In terms of this range of goals, the NAACP had relatively little power, and thus was classified as alienating.[12] Similar lines of reasoning were used to classify the ADA as alienating, and the Democratic party as conforming, etc. No doubt some organizations near the borderline were misclassified, as it was impossible to have complete information on each organization, but given that most organizations were not near the borderline and that as much care was taken as possible with those that were, errors should be minimal. And insofar as a few errors were made, *this would, at worst, weaken our results, not bias them in favor of our theory.*

With the classification made, we are able to present evidence for *Proposition 2.* Table 2 shows that only conforming groups inhibit participation; alienating groups increase it. This was true not only for the sample as a whole, but for whites and Negroes considered separately (table not shown).

Of course, it might be argued that we have the causal direction confused; that a common factor, such as ethical concern, a propensity to activity, or whatever, causes people to simultaneously join both alien-

---

[12] Since we concluded that the Urban League in 1960–61 did not have goals in *clear* opposition to the larger society, a consideration of its power is unnecessary. A lack of oppositional goals is sufficient to classify an organization as conformist.

TABLE 2

Conforming organizations reduce and postpone the participation of their members in the sit-ins, while alienating organizations increase it

	Number and kinds of organizations into which respondent reports himself integrated			
	≥2 Alienating	1 Alienating	None	1-2 Conforming
Percent who joined a year or more ago..................	59% (17)	34% (56)	30% (175)	14% (16)
Percent on ≥ three previous demonstrations.............	94% (17)	65% (57)	49% (181)	35% (17)

Note: X^2 for length of participation is 8.70, 3 df., $p < .05$. X^2 for number of demonstrations is 17.85, 3 df., $p < .001$.

ating organizations and direct action movements, and that, therefore, the association in the table is spurious. We feel strongly, however, that it is not spurious—that although people do join alienating organizations out of ethical concerns and the like, these organizations add strong *additional* impetus to the initial motivations. This feeling is based on close observation of the operation of these groups. Through a whole host of psychological mechanisms (cognitive dissonance, selective information, etc.) they create additional commitment to the concerns members initially bring to the group. In addition, they create communication ties which make withdrawal from activity extremely difficult. The member who would like to withdraw is constantly appealed to for help in "emergency" situations (in fact, there seem to be no other kind) and they are appealed to on ethical grounds they cannot easily, that is, in good conscience, avoid.

Proposition 3. Alienating organizations are of great importance in generating direct action movements; without them strong movements would be much less likely to arise. Thus, disorderly politics requires and has an organizational substructure just as does routine politics.

If the causal direction is as we have argued, then we have here a parallel to routine politics; that is, disorderly politics, too, has an organizational substructure which drags people into political activity. Furthermore, there is no *a priori* reason why this substructure should not be as important for disorderly politics as it is alleged to be for routine politics. The arguments about contacts with the politically active, and the like, should apply equally well to both. In addition, our data provide evidence of the substructure's importance.

First, even allowing for some spuriousness, the strength of the association in Table 2 is impressive, indicating that organizational involvement is a major cause of participation. Second, the association between

organizational involvement and time of entrance indicates that the
initial core of the movement was probably heavily drawn from those in
organizations. This core is necessary to create a movement in which
less organizationally involved individuals might later participate. Third,
organizational involvement pulled in people who would not otherwise
have been involved, but whose participation was crucial to the development of the movement.

One such group consisted of high-status individuals. We have shown
elsewhere (Pinard et al., 1969) that lower-status people are hard to
draw into a movement initially because they feel so powerless that they
are not able to perceive the potentiality of a small movement. If a
movement had to rely on them alone, it would never grow large enough
to attract them. In its initial stage, therefore, a movement must rely on
individuals of higher status. But these individuals, our data indicated,
are held out because their deprivations are less. How, then, are they
to be recruited? The answer lies in their higher level of organizational
involvement. Table 3 shows that organizations succeed in drawing
them in.

Another group were non-ideologues. Again, we have shown elsewhere (Pinard et al., 1969; Von Eschen et al., 1969a) that a major
factor leading to participation was possession of a well-worked out
critique of a number of aspects of U.S. society from a leftwing position;
that is, possession of a leftist ideology. Such an ideology generated participation both because it meant a broad discontent with U.S. society,
thus laying the affect base necessary for recruitment to a change-

TABLE 3

Integration into alienating organizations brings out the otherwise inactive
high-status participant

	Kind of organizations into which respondent reports himself integrated	
Occupational status of respondent[1]	Alienating	None
Percent on three or more previous demonstrations		
High	71% (24)	39% (44)
Upper middle	72% (22)	54% (88)
Lower middle and low	— (1)	72% (21)

Note: Considering high-status participants only, the difference in participation between those in
alienating organizations and those in none yields $t = 2.53$, $p < .006$, one-tailed test. Considering only
those in no organizations, the differences in participation between those of high status and those of lower-
middle or low status yields $t = -2.47$, $p < .007$, one-tailed test.
[1] "North-Hatt" scores for occupations given in response to the question:
Students: "What job are you training for in school?"
Non-students: "What is your job?"
The lower-middle and low category includes all occupations assigned scores of 71 or below (i.e., below,
approximately, the prestige of an undertaker, a grade school teacher, or a reporter). The high category
includes occupations with scores of 85 or above (i.e., approximately the prestige level of a lawyer, a
psychologist, a pilot, or a civil engineer).

oriented movement, and because, for many leftist ideologues, their ideology contained a set of beliefs about the "forces of history" in which these forces were seen as being on their side, thus making participation appear worthwhile. However, an important finding of political sociology is that the number of ideologues, left or right, in most societies is very limited.[13] If a movement is to attain any size, it must, therefore, attract non-ideologues. Table 4[14] shows that organizational involvement draws in this otherwise hard to recruit group.[15]

---

[13] See Campbell et al. (1960:188–265) and Converse (1964) for data on the rarity of ideologues, left or right, in U.S. society. See Converse and Dupeux (1962) for their rarity even in France.

[14] The measure of ideologues used in this table was constructed as follows: because the field work conditions prevented the use of a long questionnaire, we had to measure ideology indirectly. From participant observation, we knew that most leftist ideologues labeled themselves politically. Those furthest to the left considered themselves socialists. The rest either regarded themselves as independents to the left of the Democratic party or as Democrats, but in the left, i.e., ADA, wing of the party. A first approximation was thus to use party identification as a measure; and such a measure does, in fact, correlate with participation, socialists showing the most, and Republicans, the least, participation (see Table 9 in Von Eschen et al., 1969a). However, such a measure in itself was not fully adequate, for many people acquire a party identification not by thought and conviction, but by inheritance, so that possession of a left party identification does not necessarily indicate an understanding of and commitment to a leftist ideology. It was thus necessary to purify the measure by separating those who possibly had inherited their political preferences from those who had not. This was done by determining whether respondents with a left party identification had moved to the left of their mother's preference. The preference of their mother was used rather than that of their father for several reasons. First, many more respondents reported their mother's than their father's preference. Second, studies (see for instance, Lane and Sears, 1964:20–21) have indicated that it makes little difference whether mother or father is used, as in most U.S. families spouses share the same preferences. And finally, evidence indicates that, in those cases where parents do disagree, children are slightly more likely to inherit their mother's than their father's identification (Maccoby et al., 1956:301). The importance of purifying the measure in this way was indicated empirically by the fact that the relation between party identification and participation just mentioned was almost entirely accounted for by those who clearly had adopted their own party identification (table not shown). The final step was to dichotomize the data in such a way that they could be used, with our small case base, as a control variable in our tables. This was done by putting in the ideologue category all socialists plus those independents and Democrats who had moved to the left of their mothers, and putting in the non-ideologue category all others. "Democrats left of mother" were included in the ideologue category not only in order to have sufficient cases to make controls, but because participant observation and informal interviews indicated that *most* such persons were *left-wing* Democrats. This should not, therefore, distort the results, particularly when it is noted that "Democrats left of mother" account for only 21 percent of the cases in the ideologue category, while independents left of the Democratic party and socialists account for 31 percent and 48 percent respectively, or 79 percent together.

[15] Note that Lipset et al. (1956) also found this phenomenon in their study of the I.T.U. Club membership was considerably more important for non-ideologues than for ideologues. As this was a study of routine politics, we have here a par-

TABLE 4

Integration into alienating organizations is more important for non-ideologues than for ideologues

	Number and kind of organizations into which respondent reports himself integrated			
	≥2 Alienating	1 Alienating	None	1–2 Conforming
Percent who joined movement a year or more ago[1]				
Ideologues[2]................	44% (9)	30% (27)	44% (57)	40% (5)
Non-ideologues............	75% (4)	40% (25)	23% (94)	16% (8)
Percent on three or more previous demonstrations[3]				
Ideologues................	89% (9)	82% (27)	68% (57)	60% (5)
Non-ideologues............	100% (4)	52% (25)	41% (99)	25% (8)

Note: Percentages with bases as small as 4 or 5 are presented in this and following tables because of the striking character of the results. These cells are combined, however, with adjacent ones when computing tests of significance. It must be stressed that the tests of significance used in this paper, t and X^2, frequently yield underestimates, for they often throw away an important property of the data, its uniform order. This happens, for instance, when four cells in which the percentages increase uniformly are collapsed into two in order to compute t. The same is the case when X^2 is applied, for a X^2 of equal value would result if the order of the cells were scrambled.

[1] For ideologues, $t = -.99$, $p < .32$. For non-ideologues, $t = 1.79$, $p < .04$, one-tailed test.
[2] See footnote 14 in the text for a description of the way the index of this variable was constructed.
[3] For ideologues, $t = 2.67$, $p < .004$, one-tailed test. For non-ideologues, $t = 1.86$, $p < .04$, one-tailed test.

Thus, in a number of ways, organizational involvement turns out to be important. In a sense, then, organizations, not massification, are responsible for the rise of direct action movements. Only organizations are able to sustain the high level of activity necessary to generate the core of a movement.

Proposition 4. The organizational substructure of disorderly politics consists of more than simply movement organizations. It consists, in addition, of those organizations committed to the ends of the movement, but opposed to or uncertain about its means. It may even include organizations with more general, or even different, ends if these are in opposition to the larger society.

To assert that organizational involvement is of great importance for participation would be meaningless if only movement organizations were meant, that is, the organizations directing or "constituting" the movement. But theoretical considerations suggest that the organizational substructure should be wider than this. Groups sharing the ends of the movement but opposed to or ambivalent about its means should also generate participation. Such groups will socialize their members to be dissatisfied with the society, and for many of their members this

_____
ticularly good example of a point to be made later, that routine and disorderly politics are both *politics,* and that their explanations share many features in common.

dissatisfaction will override commitment to routine means. They also will provide information, both formally and informally, about current direct actions, thus widening the action alternatives available to their members, etc. But this is not the only type of additional group that should generate participation. It should be noted that even groups with more general or even different ends may do this if they have oppositional goals, for dissatisfaction tends to generalize, and thus any direct action movement whose ends are not incompatible with those of such groups may receive support from some of their members as a general attack on the system. Again, and for the same reasons listed above, this will be true even if the group does not fully approve of direct action.

That such nonmovement organizations do generate participation is indicated by our data. Table 5 classifies the alienating organizations mentioned by our respondents along the dimensions just delineated; whether their goals were explicitly the same as the movement's, namely integrationist, and whether they approved of direct action as a means. An example of an integrationist organization ambivalent about direct action as a means is the NAACP; an example of one not ambivalent would be SCLC. An example of an organization with different formal goals and ambivalent about direct action would be the Committee for a Sane Nuclear Policy; of one not ambivalent, the Committee for Non-Violent Action. Finally, examples of organizations with diffuse goals, one of which may be integration, but which are opposed to non-routine methods would be the ADA or the American Civil Liberties Union. An example of one ambivalent would be the Socialist party; and of one not ambivalent, The Young Socialist Alliance. The percentages in the table are the frequency with which each type was mentioned by our respondents.

The first thing to note is that these organizations are primarily *not* movement organizations, for we largely excluded such organizations by asking our respondents not to mention organizations sponsoring the

TABLE 5

Types and frequency of alienating organizations mentioned by respondents (in percent)

		Goals of the organization			
		Specific		Diffuse	
		Integration	Other		Total
	Routine	0.0	0.0	13.8	13.8
Methods	Ambivalent	36.9	18.7	15.3	70.9
Advocated	Direct	6.4	5.4	3.4	15.2
	Total	43.3	24.1	32.5	99.9

demonstrations. Only the 6.2 percent which both seek integration and advocate direct action can be considered movement organizations. Second, note that many organizations seek integration but are ambivalent about means. A major such organization of this type was the NAACP. Lomax (1963:112–116) has argued that the NAACP was basically oriented toward legal (i.e., routine) action, and at the time of our study had not nationally sponsored direct action, thus being at best ambivalent on the question. Yet there can be little doubt that it has increased Negro dissatisfaction with the subordinate position of blacks in U.S. society. The frequency with which our respondents mentioned this organization indicates that it pushed its members toward direct action in spite of its bias toward routine means. A mass theorist, of course, might argue that he meant to exclude such groups—groups in favor of the end but not the means of the movement—from his theory, but it seems clear that this is not the general thrust of the theory: that the NAACP should have inhibited participation by generating, as it did, a measure of routine power. But even if one granted this exemption, the third thing to note about the table is that a large proportion of the organizations did not have integration as their primary end. Yet these groups, too, generated participation, as is indicated in Table 6. Note, too, that many of these groups also were ambivalent at best about direct action. Clearly, then, the organizational substructure of disorderly politics is considerably wider than simply movement organizations.

TABLE 6

Integration into alienating organizations increases activity in the sit-in movement even when they are not civil rights organizations

	Number and kinds of organizations into which respondent reports himself integrated			
	2 Alienating	1 Alienating	None	1–2 Conforming
Civil rights organizations only[1]				
Percent who joined a year or more ago	75% (4)	36% (28)	32% (165)	—(0)
Percent on ≥ three previous demonstrations	100% (4)	68% (28)	49% (181)	—(0)
Non–civil rights organizations only[2]				
Percent who joined a year or more ago	71% (7)	40% (20)	32% (165)	21% (14)
Percent on ≥ three previous demonstrations	86% (7)	65% (20)	49% (181)	28% (15)

[1] Comparing those in alienating organizations with those not, t for length of participation is 1.27, $p < .10$, one-tailed test; and for number of demonstrations, $t = 2.37$, $p < .008$, one-tailed test.
[2] Comparing those in alienating organizations with those not, t for length of participation is 1.73, $p < .05$, one-tailed test; and for number of demonstrations, $t = 2.23$, $p < .02$, one-tailed test.

Proposition 5. The organizational substructure may even contain some conformist organizations. In short, it contains potentially all groups with members whose interests or values are unincorporated in the larger society.

The organizational substructure is wider even than that suggested by Table 5. There is no reason why even organizations with conformist goals may not generate participation if they contain members whose interests or values are unincorporated. These members can *informally* socialize one another, can provide *informal* means of communication, etc. Furthermore, once a movement has started and the hopes of un-incorporated individuals have been aroused, they can use the con-forming groups of which they may be members as a base for organizing; converting, in a sense, these organizations from conforming to alienating ones.

Two striking examples of this occurred during the sit-in movement in Baltimore.

One was a remarkable set of demonstrations carried out by students from a Negro college in Baltimore against a nearby segregated theater. The unusual feature of these demonstrations was their size, particu-larly in light of the previously low level of activity of students from this college. Only a small proportion of them had come out on any of the demonstrations held in Baltimore the previous year, even though there was a civil rights organization on campus. This was true even when these demonstrations were at their height. Our Route 40 sample, for instance, included only 31 of these students, and this was out of a student body of over 2,500. This low participation had been a source of puzzlement to us. We were quite surprised, then, when the number demonstrating against the theater swelled from an initial 50 to 100, 200, and then to over 800. Furthermore, over 400 students were willing to go to jail (raising the total bail to more than $180,000). What was the cause of this extraordinary increase in participation?

The answer to this, as we pieced it together from informal inter-views, sheds considerable light on the role of organizations. A crucial factor seems to have been the composition of the leadership of the demonstrations. They were led not by the usual alienating organizations containing but a small part of the student body, but by conforming organizations into which most of the school was integrated. The chief instigator of the demonstrations was the leader of the student council, and the fraternities and sororities played leading parts, contrary to their previous activity. In our Route 40 sample we had practically no mem-bers of these organizations, and those we did have were among the least active of the participants. In the case of the theater demonstrations, however, we were told that fraternal groups actually competed with one another, *as groups,* to see which could get the most arrested.

A second striking example occurred somewhat later, during demonstrations at a segregated amusement park. Again the demonstrations were of unusual size. And again this seems to have resulted from the commitment of previously conforming organizations, in this case churches. The normal impact of white church organizations in Maryland had been to inhibit participation, as can be seen in Table 7. Yet in the case of the amusement park, both Protestant and Catholic churches had decided to lend support. The result was a set of particularly large demonstrations. The picket lines were filled with white priests, nuns, and parishioners, most of whom had been brought to the scene of the demonstrations in buses chartered by the churches, and who had come as members of parish *organizations* in *collective* protest against discrimination. (Note, too, that Table 7 shows that, for Negroes, *intense* integration into the churches increased rather than inhibited participation. Consider also that much of the civil rights movement during this period was led by black ministers and staffed by their younger parishioners. Thus, although churches are generally regarded as conforming organizations, for blacks, their churches from the very first were involved in direct action.)

In short, conforming groups, too, generate participation. The crucial factor seems to be whether they contain members with values and interests unincorporated in the larger society; blacks in the case of the Negro fraternities and sororities, and ministers and priests in the case of the white churches. In fact, it seems that the following process may frequently occur: at first, only those in alienating organizations participate. Then, as the movement begins to grow, the unorganized are drawn in. Finally, either because of a crisis, or because the movement has demonstrated its effectiveness, or because people have gotten used

TABLE 7

Church attendance decreases early joining for whites, but not for devout Negroes

		Respondent attends church		
	Never	Less than once a month	1–3 times a month	Every week
Percent who joined a year or more ago				
Whites[1]	43% (109)	25% (40)	21% (19)	7% (15)
Negroes[2]	52% (21)	37% (16)	17% (29)	40% (35)

[1] $X^2 = 11.92, 3\ df., p < .02.$
[2] The difference between those never attending church and those attending every week yields a $t = -0.90$, $p < .47$, two-tailed test, while the difference between those attending church every week and those attending but 1–3 times a month yields a student's $t = -2.02, p < .05$, two-tailed test.

to direct action and no longer regard it as illegitimate, some previously conforming organizations, too, start to give the movement support. These organizations become, in a sense, alienating organizations. Note that they then generate greater participation than is characteristic of the unorganized, again indicating the importance of organizations for participation.

Proposition 6. The organizational substructure of disorderly politics is not entirely distinct from that for routine politics. Some organizations generate participation in both. Which is chosen by an individual depends partly on which type is seen as most effective, and this is strongly influenced by experience.

We have just seen that the organizational substructure is broader than simply movement organizations, consisting as well of organizations with the same end, but biased toward other means; of organizations with different, although still oppositional ends, many of which also prefer other means; and even of organizations with conforming ends which thus prefer routine methods. Note that in Table 5, the overwhelming majority of organizations fall either in the routine or ambivalent category. Thus, many of the organizations that generate disorderly politics clearly also generate participation in routine politics. What this indicates is that the crucial factor determining the means used is, *in the long run,* not an abstract commitment to one means over another, but the degree to which an end can be obtained through a particular means. If an end can be obtained through routine means, these will be the means used. If not, or if it can be only very partially obtained in this way, people in time will turn to other means. What counts, in short, is the degree of incorporation.

Proposition 7. Organizational involvement does not always reduce alienation.

The argument that organizations reduce alienation rests on the thesis that they reduce deprivation by giving power and that they socialize their members to accept the system and its rules of the game. But we have shown that all organizations do not do these things. Thus, we should not expect all organizations to reduce alienation. This is what our data show.

Alienation can be conceived of as having at least two components; an intense dissatisfaction with the present state of society, and an absence of faith in normal political action as an effective way to remedy things. We do not have a measure of the first component, but we do have a measure of the second. We asked our respondents to agree or disagree on a Likert-type scale with the following statements: "All politicians are corrupt," "There is really little difference between the Republican and Democratic parties," and "Letters provide a good way for a citizen to make his voice count in public policy." A respondent was counted as highly alienated if he gave two of the following three responses: strongly agree with the first statement, strongly agree with the second, disagree with the third.

As mass theorists would predict, alienation is strongly related to participation; 74 percent of the highly alienated respondents ($N = 53$) had been out on three or more demonstrations, whereas this was true of only 47 percent of the less alienated ones ($N = 223$). However, organizational involvement does not uniformly decrease alienation. Alienating organizations, if anything, increase it. Of those integrated in alienating organizations, 27 percent gave highly alienated responses ($N = 66$). This was true of only 22 percent of those integrated into no organizations ($N = 170$).

Proposition 8. Whether an organization reduces alienation depends on whether it gives power. Power may be given by disorderly politics as well as by routine politics. Alienating organizations may at times reduce alienation precisely by generating direct action rather than inhibiting it.

It is important to note, however, that alienating organizations do not increase alienation under all circumstances. Table 8 shows that, for non-ideologues, involvement in an alienating organization reduced alienation. The impact was not great, but given that alienating organizations increase dissatisfaction with one's position in society, the net reduction observed may represent a considerable gross reduction.

What explains this? We suggest that the explanation lies in the power over the routine system given by these organizations, power generated by them through non-routine action. These organizations either directed

TABLE 8

For non-ideologues, integration into an alienated organization reduces extreme political alienation

	Respondent reports himself integrated into	
	Alienating organizations only	No organizations
Percent highly alienated on the alienation index		
Ideologues[1]	44% (34)	22% (54)
Non-ideologues[2]	4% (28)	16% (103)

[1] A comparison of those in alienating organizations with those in none yields a $t = 2.17$, $p < .02$, one-tailed test.

[2] Comparing those in alienating organizations with those in none yields a Fisher's exact of $p < .156$.

TABLE 9

Participants in the sit-ins have become more hopeful about the chances for desegregation, and this is more true for Negroes than whites

	Since joining movement, expectations of desegregation have		
	Increased	Remained about the same	Decreased
Whites..............................57%		40%	4% N = 239
Negroes............................79%		19%	1% N = 139

Note: Comparing whites with Negroes in terms of the degree to which their expectations of desegregation have increased yields $t = -4.37$, $p < .0005$.

the sit-ins, constituted an informal base for organizing them, or engaged in concurrent lobbying; that is, they were heavily responsible for the demonstrations. The demonstrations in turn had a powerful effect on the routine system. Politicians were forced to take a stand, and many of them responded favorably; liberals were mobilized to work inside the system for desegregation; and so forth. This generation of power considerably reduced the pessimism of demonstrators about the possibilities of gaining concessions from the routine system. This is indicated in Table 9. That this reduction in pessimism was particularly strong for those in alienating organizations, the organizations heavily responsible for the demonstrations, is seen in Table 10. It seems highly plausible that this reduction in pessimism about getting concessions from the routine system would lead to a reduction in alienation from that system, and that, therefore, it was the power generated by the alienating organizations that accounts for the reduction.

This interpretation is lent plausibility by noting that this reduction in alienation was selective. It occurred only for non-ideologues. The

TABLE 10

Integration into alienating organizations reduces pessimism

	Respondent reports himself integrated into		
	Alienating organizations only	No organizations	Conforming organizations only
Percent disagreeing that Baltimore restaurants will be desegregated by the middle of 1962			
Whites........................31% (55)		37% (103)	44% (9)
Negroes....................... 8% (13)		25% (63)	29% (7)
Total..........................26% (68)		33% (166)	38% (16)

[1] Comparing those in alienating organizations with those not yields a $t = -1.51$, $p < .066$, one-tailed test.

major difference between ideologues and non-ideologues is in the nature of their goals. For the latter they are specific, for the former diffuse (multitudinous). For those with many goals, the achievement of only one can have little impact on their degree of alienation, and this is true even if their pessimism about attaining a single goal is reduced. This interpretation is lent further plausibility by noting that the reduction in pessimism was greater for Negroes than whites (see Table 9). Negroes were much more likely to have a single goal, desegregation, than were whites, many of whom were ideologues, and all of whom had a less direct stake in desegregation and, thus, held other important goals as well. Therefore, the impact of actually exercising power over the routine system should have been greater for Negroes, as the data indicate.

If our argument is correct, then we have here a situation in which alienating organizations reduced alienation over the routine system not by inhibiting direct action, but by generating it. We also have a situation in which the crucial factor is not organizational involvement, but power. If alienating organizations cannot generate power even through direct action, as surely will frequently be the case, then they will not decrease alienation, but increase it. This probably is what has happened to the black movement since 1965, the year it was last able to wrest substantial concessions from the routine system.

CONCLUSIONS

In sum, the crucial difference between our argument and mass theory is that we root the major causes of direct action movements not in lack of organizational involvement, but in lack of incorporation. Thus, if the values or interests of a population subgroup are not incorporated by the larger society, then insofar as individuals from this subgroup are in organizations, these organizations will ultimately generate rather than inhibit participation. From these propositions follow all the rest: that some organizations increase participation, that disorderly politics has an organizational substructure just as does routine politics, that it consists of all organizations with members whose values and interests are unincorporated; that therefore all organizations do not reduce alienation; that some may do so by achieving incorporation not through routine but through direct action; that if they cannot, they may generate revolutionary activity, etc.

Essentially, we regard direct action not as something totally unique and extraordinary, but as a form of politics similar in many ways to routine politics, and thus not requiring a new complicated theory to explain [it. The] same factors explain it that we use to explain routine politics—a conflict of interests, [and] the choice of effective means to achieve these interests. That direct action is a form of politics we feel is indicated by the fact that some organizations generate participation in both. Thus, throughout the paper, we have used the terms direct action movement and disorderly *politics* interchangeably. The role organizations play in disorderly politics is essentially the same as it is in routine politics—to drag people into activity, even, if the circumstances warrant it, into revolutionary activity. This view directly contradicts the main proposition of mass theory, for it implies that, under conditions of deprivations, the more organizationally dense a society is, all other things being equal, the more direct action movements it should experience.[16]

REFERENCES

Arendt, H. *The Origins of Totalitarianism.* New York: Meridian Books, 1958.

Campbell, A., P. Converse, W. Miller, and D. Stokes. *The American Voter.* New York: Wiley, 1960.

Cantril, H. *The Politics of Despair.* New York: Basic Books, 1958.

Converse, P. "The Nature of Belief Systems in Mass Publics." In D. Apter (ed.), *Ideology and Its Discontents.* New York: Free Press, 1964.

Converse, P., and G. Dupeux. "Politicization of the Electorate in France and the United States." *Public Opinion Quarterly* 26 (Spring 1962): 1–23.

Erbe, W. "Social Involvement and Political Activity: A Replication and Elaboration." *American Sociological Review* 29 (April 1964): 198–215.

Gusfield, J. "Mass Politics and Extremist Politics." *American Sociological Review* 27 (February 1962): 19–30.

Kornhauser, W. *The Politics of Mass Society.* Glencoe, Ill.: Free Press, 1959.

Lane, R., and D. Sears. *Public Opinion.* Englewood Cliffs, N.J.: Prentice-Hall, 1964.

Lipset, S. *Political Man.* New York: Doubleday, 1960.

Lipset, S., M. Trow, and J. Coleman. *Union Democracy.* Glencoe, Ill.: Free Press, 1956.

Lomax, L. *The Negro Revolt.* New York: American Book, 1963.

Maccoby, E., R. Matthews, and A. Morton. "Youth and Political Change." Pp. 299–307 in H. Eulau, S. Eldersveld, and M. Janowitz (eds.), *Political Behavior.* Glencoe, Ill.: Free Press, 1956.

Nisbet, R. *The Quest for Community.* New York: Oxford University Press, 1953.

Pinard, M. "Mass Society and Political Movements: A New Formulation." *American Journal of Sociology* 73 (May 1968): 682–690.

———. *The Rise of a Third Party: A Study in Crisis Politics.* Englewood Cliffs, N.J.: Prentice-Hall, 1971.

---

[16] For a similar argument, see Gusfield (1962).

Pinard, M., J. Kirk, and D. Von Eschen. "Processes of Recruitment to the Sit-In Movement." *Public Opinion Quarterly* 33 (Fall 1969): 355–369.

Pratt, S. "The Social Basis of Nazism and Communism in Urban Germany." Unpublished M.A. thesis, Michigan State College, 1948.

Rose, A. *The Power Structure: Political Processes in American Society.* New York: Oxford University Press, 1967.

Selznick, P. *The Organizational Weapon.* Glencoe, Ill.: Free Press, 1960.

Trow, M. "Small Business and Support for McCarthy." *American Journal of Sociology* 64 (November 1958): 270–281.

Von Eschen, D., J. Kirk, and M. Pinard. "The Conditions of Direct Action in a Democratic Society." *Western Political Quarterly* 22 (June 1969): 309–325. (a)

———. "The Disintegration of the Negro Non-Violent Movement." *Journal of Peace Research* 3 (1969): 216–234. (b)

Wilson, J. *Negro Politics.* Glencoe, Ill.: Free Press, 1960.

D. Policy and practice considerations

HARRY SPECHT

Disruptive tactics

There is both confusion and uncertainty about the use of disruptive tactics to bring about planned change in American communities. The confusion, in part, grows out of a major problem the United States faces today—violence, its causes and resolution. Indeed, it is the major problem throughout the world, which we have succeeded so little in dealing with. In addition, in the social sciences as in social work there is neither extensive knowledge about the dynamics of either disruption or violence nor systematic processes the practitioner can use to deal with them.[1]

The idea of government by and through elected officials is being seriously questioned on all sides. Many have lost confidence in the viability of established democratic political structures—students and other young people, minority groups, and the political left. But today, the ubiquity of violence and illegal behavior in American communities is only a reflection of the violence and lawless behavior supported by many of the country's leaders. Thus, the mayor of a large city castigated his police force for not "shooting to kill or to maim" young arsonists and looters; the governor of a large state called rioters "mad dogs"; and the former President lost his credibility when the deception, corruption, and violence of the country's foreign policy became evident.

It seems that Fanon's belief in the cleansing force of violence and the need to use violence as an agent of change is gaining wide support as many white families buy guns to defend themselves against blacks, black action groups arm to protect themselves against the police, and the police increase their arsenals to defend the cities against black insurgents. It is as though the whole country is caught by Fanon's ideas:

> For if the last shall be first, . . . this will only come to pass after a murderous and decisive struggle between the two protagonists. That

Note: An earlier version of this paper was presented at the National Conference on Social Welfare, May 29, 1968, in San Francisco, California.

Source: Reprinted with permission of the National Association of Social Workers, from *Social Work,* Vol. 14, No. 2 (April 1969), pp. 5–15.

[1] Raymond C. Mack, "Components of Social Conflict," *Social Problems,* Vol. 12, No. 4 (Spring 1965), pp. 388–397.

affirmed intention . . . can only triumph if we use all means to turn the scales, including, of course, that of violence.[2]

It is only in a climate of unreason that this mixture of "blood and anger," which can lead to insurrection, becomes thoroughly confused with legitimate dissent and political radicalism. We should not talk of crime in the streets or violence on the campus in shocked dismay when the larger part of the nation's resources are being used to fashion this country into the world's greatest instrument of violence.

A discussion of the moral and ethical, as well as the programmatic, consequences of disruptive tactics used in efforts at planned change presupposes the existence of some organized system of available tactical choices. This paper will first distinguish different kinds of tactics that constitute the spectrum of choices and then discuss disruptive tactics in detail. This order is necessary if the use of disruptive tactics is to be understood as a consciously planned choice made on the basis of moral and ethical considerations as well as strategic objectives. The author uses "strategy" to refer to an over-all plan of action and "tactics" to indicate the more specific actions of moving and directing resources to attain goals. Strategy requires a long-term plan of action based on some theory of cause and effect, while tactics are the somewhat more constant methods of action.

WHY DISRUPTION?

What is it about issues that makes them subject to one or another set of tactics? Warren describes the association between different modes of intervention and different responses to issues.[3] (Modes of intervention are categories of tactics.) The range of responses to issues he describes are the following: (1) *issue consensus,* when there is a high possibility of agreement between the action and target system; (2) *issue difference,* when for one reason or another the parties are not in complete agreement but there is a possibility of agreement; and (3) *issue dissensus,* when there is no agreement between the parties. Consensus is associated with collaborative modes of intervention; difference with campaigns of a competitive, persuasive, or bargaining nature; and dissensus with contests in which there is a high degree of conflict between the parties. (Conflict may be considered as an element in all modes of intervention

---

[2] Frantz Fanon, *The Wretched of the Earth* (New York: Grove Press, 1963), p. 37.

[3] Roland L. Warren, *Types of Purposive Social Change at the Community Level,* University Papers in Social Welfare, No. 11 (Waltham, Mass.: Florence Heller Graduate School for Advanced Studies in Social Welfare, Brandeis University, 1965).

TABLE 1

Change: Perceptions, responses, and modes of intervention

Perception of change	Response	Mode of intervention
Rearrangement of resources	Consensus	Collaboration
Redistribution of resources	Difference	Campaign
Change in status relationships	Dissensus	Contest or disruption
Reconstruction of the entire system	Insurrection[1]	Violence

[1] Insurrection is used here because the word "revolution" can only be applied to a successful insurrection.

to some degree.) In this paper, disruptive and contest tactics will be associated with dissensus.

The question still remains: Why these responses? The response to an issue, whether rational or not, indicates how the issue is *perceived* by the different parties; perception determines response. By extending Warren's typology, the associations among different perceptions of change, responses to the change, and the kinds of intervention these responses command may be suggested. Table 1 combines these elements but adds violence as a fourth mode of intervention based on a perception of change that aims at "reconstruction of the entire system" to which the response is "insurrection."

PERCEPTIONS, RESPONSES, INTERVENTIONS

Collaboration is based on consensual responses to planned changes that are perceived as a rearrangement of resources. For example, the parties to the change are in essential agreement about the co-ordination or reorganization of services. No one thinks they will lose a great deal in the change. Until only recently, there had been a rather narrow concentration on this kind of intervention in social work, based on work with homogeneous and elitist types of community action systems. For the most part, the action system (that undertaking change) and the target system (that being changed) are identical, and the client system (on whose behalf change is sought) is probably not involved at all. The role of the worker is most frequently that of enabler and educator.

Redistribution of resources is a qualitatively different perception of a change. One of the parties expects he will end up with more or less of something (money, facilities, authority) but, because they perceive the need to remain within the rules of the game—the institutionalized system of competition—the contending parties utilize campaign tactics to persuade, negotiate, bargain, and, eventually, compromise and agree. The action, target, and client systems might be expected to appear as separate entities, with the action system serving as mediator or arbitrator between the other two. The role of the professional change agent is most likely to be that of advocate.

Contest or disruption is generated by a challenge to existing status relationships and this view of change creates an entirely different type of discourse than any of the others mentioned. Contest or disruption is rooted in the competition for power in human relations. Status relationships refer to the social arrangements (the institutionalized system) by which promises, expectations, rights, and responsibilities are awarded, and the social arrangements always give more to some than to others. A threat to the system of relationships in which some people have power over others is the basis for this kind of response whether it involves parents and children, welfare workers and clients, students and teachers, or blacks and whites. None surrenders power voluntarily. The ability to perpetuate these patterns of varied and complex relationships long after the historical conditions that gave rise to them cease to exist is a human quality but also creates conflict.

When community issues are perceived by one group as eliminating or diminishing its power over others, the response will be dissensus; contest and disruption, the result. "To carve out a place for itself in the politico-social order, a new group may have to fight for a reorientation of many of the values of the old order" is the way Key states this proposition.[4] In these kinds of change efforts, the action and target systems are distinctly separate and the client system is closely aligned or identical with the action system. The role of the community worker is that of partisan or organizer.

A change perceived as intended to overthrow the sovereign power of the state is responded to as insurrection. The mode of intervention associated with it—violence—is not part of the arsenal of tactics available to professional social workers and, therefore, the author will not comment on the relative positions of the action, target, and client systems or the worker's professional role. However, these tactics do pose serious dilemmas for community change agents, which will be discussed in the final section of the paper.

However, it should be said here that the major overriding objective of community organization is to enable communities to create a strategy of reconciliation, to move from insurrection to contest, to campaign, to collaboration. It is necessary for the professional change agent who utilizes the tactics described in this paper to operate with goals that will, as Cloward puts it "eventually heal, not further disrupt."[5]

---

[4] V. O. Key, Jr., *Politics, Parties and Pressure Groups* (5th ed.; New York: Thomas Y. Crowell, 1964), p. 48.

[5] Richard A. Cloward, "A Strategy of Disruption," *Center Diary: 16* (January–February 1967), p. 34.

EXAMPLES

The following examples will illustrate the interplay of the three elements that comprise Table 1: perceptions, responses, and modes of
intervention.

Objectively, fluoridation should present a good case for collaborative
modes of intervention. It is said to be sensible, scientific, and not only
inexpensive, but money-saving. Many health officials and community
organizers have approached it with exactly that logical frame of mind
because superficially fluoridation would appear to be a rather simple
rearrangement of resources that calls for an educational mode of intervention. Yet the issue of fluoridation has been the basis for harsh,
vindictive social conflicts in hundreds of communities in the United
States.[6]

There appear to be two major sets of reasons for the resistance. First,
there are those people who question the effectiveness of the proposed
change or who fear that fluoride may be poisonous. This type of resistance does yield to collaborative modes of intervention.[7] But the
second basis for resistance does not respond to such methods at all.
This is resistance based on the belief that fluoridation infringes on the
rights of individuals, that "compulsory medication" usurps the rights
of free men. Green supports this contention with concrete findings. His
research indicates that indignation over the *presumed* violation of personal freedom is more fundamental than the danger of poisoning. The
fear of poisoning symbolizes a disposition to see fluoridation as an
insidious attack by a vague constellation of impersonal social forces
bent on usurping the powers and prerogatives of the common citizen,
and the root cause of this feeling of being victimized experienced by
active opponents of fluoridation is the increasing remoteness and im-
personality of the sources of power and influence affecting the daily life
of the individual.[8] In short, the issue of fluoridation becomes a contest
when it is perceived to be a threat to status.

Another example of the delicate balance between perceptions of
change as a redistribution of resources and an alteration in status is
provided by Marris and Rein in their analysis of community action
programs. They pose this question: If community planners had larger
grants of money available to them, would it have been easier for them

---

[6] "Trigger for Community Conflict," entire issue of the *Journal of Social Issues,* Vol. 17, No. 4 (October 1961).
[7] Benjamin D. Paul, "Fluoridation and the Social Scientist: A Review," in ibid.,
p. 5.
[8] Ibid., p. 7.

to move the bureaucracies along the lines of the change they desired? This is their answer:

> If the funding agencies had offered more money, they would . . . have given communities a greater incentive to meet the criteria of concerted action. But they would also have raised the stakes in the competition for control of the project's resources. . . . A marginal addition to the city's resources stood at least a chance of insinuating an influence for change, without intruding a challenge to bureaucratic authority too obvious to overlook.[9]

This suggests that an increase in the amount of resources may convert a perception of change from one of a rearrangement or a redistribution to a change in status.

The civil rights movement seems to have shifted in the last five years from a major focus on the rearrangement and redistribution of resources to a greater concern with change in status. Of course, all along, the demands being made by the movement may have *required* change in status for success, but the movement has increasingly recognized that the power of whites over blacks is the issue, as is pointed out in the following statement by Hamilton: "While there are masses of poor, powerless whites, they do not *perceive* [italics added] their condition as a result of deliberate policy. . . . Many blacks do have such a view."[10]

Memphis, Tennessee, in the events preceding the assassination of Martin Luther King, was not confronting a simple question of the redistribution of resources as in an ordinary labor dispute. That the striking workers recognized the question of status was quite evident in their signs that read: "I Am a Man!" for indeed it was their manhood they perceived to be at stake. That the mayor of Memphis saw it the same way is clear from his statement that he would be damned if he would be the first southern mayor to bargain collectively with a black union.

TACTICS

Modes of intervention comprise sets of tactics. While the purpose of this paper is to discuss disruptive tactics, the idea that there is a dynamic relationship between tactics used for different modes of intervention is helpful in understanding their use. Table 2 suggests what this relationship may be.

---

[9] Peter Marris and Martin Rein, *Dilemmas of Social Reform* (New York: Atherton Press, 1967), p. 158.

[10] Charles Hamilton, "The Meaning of Black Power," reprinted from the *New York Times* in the *San Francisco Chronicle*, "This World," April 21, 1968, p. 25.

TABLE 2

The relationship between tactics and modes of intervention

Mode of intervention	Tactics
Collaboration	Joint action
	Cooperation
	Education
Campaign	Compromise
	Arbitration
	Negotiation
	Bargaining
	Mild coercion
Contest or disruption	Clash of position within accepted social norms
	Violation of normative behavior (manners)
	Violation of legal norms
Violence	Deliberate attempts to harm
	Guerrilla warfare
	Deliberate attempts to take over government by force

These behaviors constitute a continuum of interventive modes rather than discrete actions. A strategy for change might utilize tactics from one or more modes of intervention simultaneously, depending on the goals of the action system and the organizational context within which it operates.[11] For example, in *A Manual for Direct Action,* a handbook of action for civil rights and other nonviolent protests, the authors instruct organizers in the use of bargaining and educational tactics along with disruptive tactics, and sometimes all three are directed at the same system.

> Poor negotiation . . . can bring a return to open conflict. . . . [In work with the target system] describe the results of change as *less* threatening than the opponents suppose, and . . . describe the results of not changing . . . as *more* threatening than . . . change. . . . Bring illustrations of successes in other places.[12]

[11] For an interesting discussion of the relationship between these variables see Martin Rein and Robert Morris, "Goals, Structures, and Strategies for Community Change," in Mayer N. Zald, ed., *Social Welfare Institutions* (New York: John Wiley & Sons, 1965), pp. 367–382.

[12] Martin Oppenheimer and George Lakey, *A Manual for Direct Action* (Chicago: Quadrangle Books, 1964), p. 24. An interesting related question that cannot be considered in this paper is how the structure of an action system is related to these modes of intervention. All action systems expand and contract throughout their history and one might predict the relationship between organizational structure and tactical choices. For example, movement to insurrection would be accompanied by narrowing the action system and movement from campaign to collaboration by its expansion.

What is meant by disruptive tactics? They are used by one or both parties to a contest. Their purpose has been described as preventing an opponent from continuing to operate, to neutralize, injure, or eliminate him.[13] Warren describes tactics as "processes where deliberate harmful activity is directed toward an opposing party."[14] However, in the strategic viewpoint outlined in this paper, disruptive tactics are considered those that aim in different ways to move the other party toward some acceptable reconciliation. The term "disruptive" seems most appropriate for these tactics because their major objective is to *prevent* the target system from continuing to operate as usual, i.e., to disrupt, but *not* to injure, harm, or destroy. The latter are the goals of the tactics of violence.

DISRUPTIVE TACTICS

Clash of position

This tactic is used within accepted social norms and essentially involves such actions as debate, legal disputes, written statements of intent, or public speeches. The objective of this tactic is to bring the issue to the attention of the public, usually in such a way as to mobilize sympathy from the larger community as well as to stir discontent among the "oppressed."

The way in which Gandhi's philosophy of nonviolence has been popularized in the United States often causes Americans to overlook many of the subtle meanings of the elaborate system Gandhi developed, which he called *satyagraha* (search for truth). *Satyagraha* is a complicated and difficult term to define because it embraces both a philosophy of life as well as a methodology of social action and, therefore, is certainly a more developed system than the one described in this paper. It is a refined technique for social and political change that transcends the simple concepts of civil disobedience, nonviolence, or disruptive behavior.

In the Gandhian view, clash of position comes at quite an advanced stage in dealing with an issue, and a number of other steps are required before a *satyagrahi* makes use of this tactic, such as negotiation, arbitration, reasoning, and other methods designed to win over the opponent. Civil disobedience is, of course, one of the final stages of this action system.[15]

---

[13] Lewis Coser, *The Functions of Social Conflict* (Glencoe, Ill.: Free Press, 1956), p. 8.

[14] Warren, op. cit., p. 29.

[15] Joan V. Bondurant, *Conquest of Violence* (Berkeley: University of California Press, 1965), pp. 40–41.

Oglesby and Shaull, in analyzing the process by which the oppressed become revolutionaries, describe a clash of position as the tactic of "mass-based secular prayer." This appeal to a higher power, they say, sometimes results in change. More often, it shows the victim-petitioner that change is more difficult to achieve than he imagined, and this may become "the spiritual low point of the emergent revolutionary's education," for he learns that "the enemy is not a few men, but a whole system."[16]

Violation of normative behavior

This tactic refers to actions that might be viewed as a moving away from what may be deemed good manners and involves activities like marches, demonstrations, boycotts, protests, vigils (extended demonstrations), rent strikes, dropping out, haunting (following one's opponent for long periods), renouncing honors, *hartals* (having large masses of people stay at home, a sort of spiritual variation of a general strike), fasts, and interjection (having large masses of people congregate in an area, as, for example, 10,000 Japanese did in 1956 to prevent successfully the use of the site for a U.S. Air Force base). The objectives of these actions are the same as those listed under the heading "clash of position" as well as to generate conscience, discomfort, and guilt in the oppressors and an *esprit de corps* among the oppressed.

This tactic, more than any others, demonstrates the effects of changing social and legal definitions of behavior. Rent strikes and boycotts, for example, lie in a gray area between violation of normative behavior and violation of law. The increased number of protests by citizens over the last decade has elevated demonstrations and marches to a tactic that is more like a clash of position than anything else. One can hardly announce a grievance today without a public demonstration of some sort. Furthermore, the tactic of choice is, to some degree, specific to the group. For example, only those who have been included in society can drop out; that tactic is available to middle-class college students, not to the hard-core unemployed of the ghetto. Fasting, a technique used with enormous success by Gandhi, is reserved for situations in which there is a rather special relationship of mutual respect between the opposing parties.

Moreover, tactics are *patterned* group behaviors. Whether used consciously or not, the styles of action in different action systems are based on numerous group and organizational variables, such as social class, ideology, resources, and values.

[16] Carl Oglesby and Richard Shaull, *Containment and Change* (New York: Macmillan Co., 1967), p. 145.

Violation of legal norms

This tactic includes techniques like civil disobedience and non-cooperation, tax refusal, sit-ins, draft resistance, and other violations of law. Carried to its final stages in *satyagraha,* this tactic includes usurping the functions of government and setting up a parallel government. The objectives of this tactic include all those listed for the other types of disruptive tactics and, in addition, they aim to demonstrate that people feel strongly enough about an issue to expose themselves to the danger of punishment by legal authorities for violating the law.

Civil disobedience presupposes an absence of, or inadequacy in, established law that morally justifies violation of it. The difficult moral question with which action systems must deal is whether they can find it morally correct to disobey an unjust law to protest its injustice or a morally just law to protest another injustice. Based on a philosophical anarchism and the concept of "natural rights," these acts have quite an honorable tradition in American life—a tradition that recognizes that the legal system is and always will be imperfect; the majority, whose wishes the laws (at least theoretically) are supposed to reflect, is itself imperfect; and all moral values have not been and never will be enacted into law.[17]

There are specific requirements of actions classified as nonviolent civil disobedience. They are only utilized after all other remedies have been exhausted and are used openly and selflessly. (That is, the actions have a public character and are carried out with public explanations of the reasons for the action in the name of some higher morality.) Furthermore, they are utilized with an awareness of the consequences for the participants.[18] These tactics are exemplified by the nonviolent resistance to police enforcement of laws. Indeed, the major tenet of those who have committed themselves to these actions expresses a profound faith in the value of the existing legal-political system and it is the absence of this faith that characterizes changes perceived as insurrection. While rebellion may claim moral justification, unlike civil disobedience its aim is to overthrow the social order, not to change and reconcile. This separation between the legality and the morality of the social order was precisely the distinction Socrates made in recognizing the right of his judges to condemn him to death.

---

[17] Vernon Louis Parrington, *Romantic Revolution in America, 1800–1860,* "Main Currents in American Thought" (New York: Harcourt, Brace & Co., 1930), pp. 271–460.

[18] John de J. Pemberton, Jr., "Is There a Moral Right to Violate the Law?" *Social Welfare Forum, 1965* (New York: Columbia University Press, 1965), pp. 194–195.

OBJECTIVES AND EFFECTIVENESS

It should be noted that the direction of issues can be from consensus to violence or the reverse, but, as Simmel pointed out in his still relevant seminal work on conflict written in the early 1900's, "the transitions from war to peace constitute a more serious problem than does the reverse."[19] Certainly, the use of disruptive tactics has the potential for great harm to the group in whose interests they are used. It allows the oppressor to put increasingly fewer limits on himself, freeing him to act disruptively or violently when he might otherwise have been constrained to avoid such behavior. For example, the police in many cities have attacked demonstrators with obvious relish when they used what the police perceived to be tactics of violence, as was the case in the anti-draft demonstrations of October 1967 when some student groups attempted to shut down draft centers by violent means. In just this way, Mayor Daley attempted to justify the attacks on demonstrators by the Chicago police during the 1968 Democratic Convention.

Violent tactics can provide the other party with the opportunity to "change the subject," so that the public's concern switches from the issue to the illegal behavior of the demonstrators. Both King and Gandhi always consciously sought to use nonviolent techniques as a rein on the violence of the established ruling class—"to keep the conversation open and the switchblade closed"[20]—and the correctness of their views is borne out by the fact that there were fewer deaths in ten years of nonviolent direct action in the South than in ten days of northern riots.

Stinchcombe asserts that the resort to violent tactics is related to the strengths of social norms governing the use of violence in society. In particular, his comments point up that nonviolent methods are viable only as long as civil authorities continue to accept the responsibility for carefully controlling their own use of violence in dealing with civil disputes. He says:

> The crucial question . . . about the violent organizations of a society [i.e., the police and the army] is how far their entry into politics is governed by an understood set of limiting norms. For if the army and police enter the conflict unconditionally on one or another side of the conflict, supplying a ruling group or a revolutionary group with unlimited power to dispose of its enemies, then competition for place among organizations tends to become unlimited. Because the opposition to currently ruling powers is equally punished, whether it uses speech

---

[19] Georg Simmel, "On Conflict," in Talcott Parsons, ed., *Theories of Society* (New York: Free Press of Glencoe, 1961), p. 1325.

[20] Oglesby and Shaull, op. cit., p. 149.

or riot, opponents are likely to choose the most effective means . . . of combatting government terror [which] are not always peaceful. And a government or revolutionary group supported by the army and police in an unlimited fashion is likely to undertake to root out its opposition, rather than to limit the opposition to approved means of conflict.[21]

To use disruptive tactics, several questions must be considered by the action system: Is the stress that stimulated the use of these tactics recognizable to the opponent? Is there support and reassurance to the opponent whose change is desired that the extent of change is not unlimited? Have encounters opened or closed communication between contending parties? Has there been an adequate process of inquiry and exploration prior to the disruption? In the Gandhian use of disruptive techniques, the major question asked of the *satyagrahi* is whether he has engaged the opponent in a manner designed to transform the complexity of relationships so that new patterns may emerge.[22] When all these attempts fail, violent tactics become a likely alternative.

TACTICS OF VIOLENCE

Insurrection differs from disruption both in the tactics used and the ends sought. It is not a call to resist the immoral acts of legitimate authority, but the withdrawal of legitimacy from the sovereign authority. It ties up the conflict over status relationships with something much larger, whereby the entire system is viewed as impossible to reform.

> The leap into revolution leaves "solutions" behind because it has collapsed and wholly redefined the "problems" to which they referred. The rebel is an incorrigible absolutist who makes the one grand claim that the entire system is in error.[23]

The tactics of violence are not available for use by the professional social reformer for several reasons. Quite practically, he cannot practice social work if he is a fugitive from justice, in jail, or dead. But, more important, a professional receives his sanction for practice from the larger society he serves and its legal and political systems. Morally, he may reach the conclusion that the framework is no longer worthy of legitimacy, and it is certainly difficult to argue that the moral basis for that choice does not exist in today's society. But it should be clear that this is the choice that must be made, and the professional should

[21] Arthur L. Stinchcombe, "Social Structures and Organizations," in James G. March, ed., *Handbook of Organizations* (Chicago: Rand McNally, Co., 1965), p. 97.
[22] Bondurant, op. cit., p. viii.
[23] Oglesby and Shaull, op. cit., p. 146.

not be confused about what he is undertaking when he commits himself to violence.

This confusion is often encountered among students who think their protest actions should lead to a reversal of policy even if their behavior is violent. But to be a revolutionary requires that one believe that policy *cannot* be changed without replacing the government by force.

The social worker's authority stems from his knowledge, values, skills, and sanction to deal with social welfare institutions and to use social work methods. Although he may give his personal commitment to rebellion, it is improper to use his authority to give legitimacy to the destruction of institutions. This is when the larger strategy that directs a professional's work is especially important because it forces him to test his choice of a specific tactic in relation to its historical perspective. Is the choice of tactics dictated by his view of the long-range struggle and within a professed area of competence? Disruption used without some strategy for change is unlikely to achieve anything but escalation to violence; it certainly will not provide a means for changing the structure of American society.

The task of the intellectual leaders of any community undertaking is to help community action systems maintain freshness and vigor in moving toward goals by elucidating the legal, political, and historical relationships that underlie their efforts.[24] Invariably, revolutionary movements develop with strong, narrow ideologies that monopolize the conduct of the struggle over issues and bind the rebels in a united contempt for all other solutions. Social workers should expect neither support nor quarter from revolutionary groups because, as a rule, they consider others who are struggling on the same side to be more dangerous than the oppressor since they must disallow any who would offer an appealing alternative. They represent the other side of oppression, "killing their way to power."[25] They believe, with Fanon, that "no gentleness can efface the marks of violence; only violence itself can destroy them."[26]

The question for the professional is whether his objective is to enable people to make choices or to assert *his* choice and cast his lot with those who have arrived at *the* solution. Social work operates in a framework of democratic decision-making, and if one decides that the framework is no longer viable, then there is no profession of social work to be practiced.

---

[24] Harry Specht, *Urban Community Development,* Publication No. 111 (Walnut Creek, Calif.: Council of Community Services, 1966), p. 44.

[25] Robert Pickus, "Civil Disobedience But Not Violence," *Dissent,* Vol. 15, No. 1 (January–February 1968), p. 21.

[26] Fanon, op. cit., p. 21.

DILEMMA

As long as this country participates in unjust wars of conquest and does not provide the resources needed to deal with domestic crises of racism, poverty, and other social injustices, all professionals will face the dilemma of either working through institutions they believe may be unable to overcome social rot or participating in their destruction. But that awful choice should be made with clarity about the consequences for professional status as well as the objectives to be served.

Guevara was extremely clear about the preconditions for choosing revolutionary tactics:

> It must always be kept in mind that there is a necessary minimum without which the establishment and consolidation of the first center . . . [of guerrilla warfare] is not practicable. People must see clearly the futility of maintaining the fight for social goals within the framework of civil debate. . . . Where a government has come into power through some form of popular vote, fraudulent or not, and maintains at least an appearance of constitutional legality, the guerrilla outbreak cannot be promoted, since the possibilities of peaceful struggle have not yet been exhausted.[27]

These clear guides notwithstanding, many young people attempt to impose the strategies of Fanon, Debray, and Guevara on the American society. Given Guevara's preconditions for revolution, these philosophies of social change in the "Third World" can provide vicarious pleasures for American radicals but not realistic action strategies. Moreover, as Lasch warns: "While violence as a meaningful strategy is tactically premature in the United States, without other strategic perspectives militancy will carry the day by default and is dangerous because it may support the development of an American fascism."[28]

The New Left and student politics should not be dismissed out of hand. Surely they have created a valuable training ground in which a new generation can test its solutions to social and political problems. However, other persons who are committed to radical social change are often caught between two worlds. They have spent much of their lives working to reform the established order and find their perspective inadequate and their strategy ineffective—or at least they are viewed that way by young people. It is like the dialogue between mother and son in a poem by Aimé Césaire:

---

[27] Ernesto Che Guevara, *Guerrilla Warfare* (New York: Monthly Review Press, 1961), pp. 15–16.

[28] Christopher Lasch, "The Trouble with Black Power," *New York Review of Books,* Vol. 10, No. 4 (February 29, 1968).

THE MOTHER:

My race—the human race. My religion—brotherhood.

THE REBEL:

My race: that of the fallen. My religion . . . but it's not you that will show it to me with your disarmament. . . . 'tis I myself, with my rebellion and my poor fists clenched and my wooly head. . . .[29]

CONCLUSION

Perhaps, though, new ways may be found to define the roles of reformer and revolutionary despite their seemingly irreconcilable divergence. For example, Shaull, in coming to grips with this dilemma, suggests that it may be oversimplified. He proposes a "political equivalent" of guerrilla warfare and suggests that greater attention be given to the question of the relationship of those working for radical change and the institutions of the established order. He says: "Service in the framework of a particular institution does not necessarily demand complete subservience to it."[30] In Shaull's view, revolutionaries can contribute to the renewal of institutions by being in but not of these structures, by living as exiles within their own society. Whether this alternative is a viable one or simply Utopian cannot be decided without some exploration but, given the size of this society's institutions and the enormous concentration of power within them, it is certainly an important alternative to consider.

Ultimately, choice of tactics must rest on our beliefs about this society. If we believe it is possible to move the community, we can continue to work for change through its institutions. If it is not possible, then God help us all, for then we must either continue to act in a drama that has lost its purpose or join in the destruction of society. Disruption and violence can contribute to change, but more than that will be required for reconciliation—more than that is required to transform America.

---

[29] Quoted in Fanon, op. cit., p. 86.
[30] Oglesby and Shaull, op. cit., pp. 196–197.

NAME INDEX

SUBJECT INDEX

THE BOOK MANUFACTURE

Issues in Race & Ethnic Relations: Theory, Research and Action was set in linotype, and printed and bound at Kingsport Press. Cover design was by Charles Kling & Associates. The type is Times Roman with Spartan display.